SCOTTISH REPOSSESSIONS
THE MORTGAGE RIGHTS
(SCOTLAND) ACT 2001

AUSTRALIA
Law Book Co.
Sydney

CANADA and USA
Carswell
Toronto

HONG KONG
Sweet & Maxwell Asia

NEW ZEALAND
Brookers
Wellington

SINGAPORE and MALAYSIA
Sweet & Maxwell Asia
Singapore and Kuala Lumpur

SCOTTISH REPOSSESSIONS THE MORTGAGE RIGHTS (SCOTLAND) ACT 2001

Mark Higgins, LLB (Hons), Dip. LP., N.P.

Head of Litigation at Golds Solicitors
Member of Diligence Committee of Law Society of Scotland

W. GREEN/Sweet & Maxwell Ltd
EDINBURGH
2002

Published in 2002 by W. Green & Son Ltd
21 Alva Street
Edinburgh EH2 4PS

*Typeset by LBJ Typesetting Ltd of Kingsclere
Printed and bound in Great Britain by
Athenaeum Press Ltd, Gateshead, Tyne and Wear*

No natural forests were destroyed to make this product;
only farmed timber was used and replanted

A CIP catalogue record for this book is available from the
British Library

ISBN 0414 014 650

© W. Green 2002

All rights reserved. UK statutory material in this publication is acknowledged as Crown copyright. No part of this publication may be reproduced or transmitted in any form or by any means, or stored in any retrieval system of any nature, without prior written permission of the copyright holder and publisher, except for permitted fair dealing under the Copyright, Designs and Patents Act 1988, or in accordance with the terms of a licence issued by the Copyright Licensing Agency in respect of photocopying and/or reprographic reproduction. Full acknowledgment of publisher and source must be given. Material is contained in this publication for which publishing permission has been sought, and for which copyright is acknowledged. Permission to reproduce such material cannot be granted by the publishers and application must be made to the copyright holders.

Extract from *Royal Bank of Scotland v. Etridge (No. 2)*
[2001] 3 W.L.R. 1021 is reproduced with the kind permission of The Incorporated Council of Law Reporting
Extract © The Incorporated Council of Law Reporting
2001

CONTENTS

Foreword vii
Table of Cases ix
Table of Statutes xiii
Table of Statutory Instruments xix

1. The Repossession Framework 1
2. The Initial Stages—Standard Securities 7
3. The Initial Stages—Pre-Existing Forms of Security 32
4. Determination of Court Proceedings—Part I 37
5. Determination of Court Proceedings—Part II 77
6. Special Cases 104
7. Recovering the Subjects 117
8. Repossession Sales 146
9. Future Developments in Repossession Law 164

Appendix 1
The Mortgage Rights (Scotland) Act 2001 173

Appendix 2
Scottish Statutory Instruments Made Under or in Relation to
    The Mortgage Rights (Scotland) Act 2001 185

Appendix 3
Style Minute Under Rule 34.12(1) of the OCR 194

Appendix 4
The Conveyancing and Feudal Reform (Scotland) Act 1970
    Part II 196

Appendix 5
Schedules 3, 6 and 7 to the Conveyancing and Feudal Reform
    (Scotland) Act 1970 211

Appendix 6
Guidelines Identified by Lord Nicholls in *Royal Bank of Scotland
    plc v. Etridge (No. 2)* 219

Index 223

For Rachel

FOREWORD

The timing of this book coincides with the introduction of the most significant change to Scottish repossession law for many years, the Mortgage Rights (Scotland) Act 2001. There have also been recent, significant developments in the interpretation of the existing law in areas ranging from calling-up notices to creditors' expenses. The decision of the Scottish Executive to introduce a nationwide Mortgage to Rent scheme seems set to change the repossession landscape still further. I hope to have given some insight into each of these changing areas over the course of this book.

This is intended primarily to be a work of practical use. I hope the book will particularly assist those involved in repossession litigation as it is here that the most substantial changes are taking effect. Repossession law is now comprised in several major statutes with substantial common law and, in a good many areas, conflicting views as to the correct legal position. If the text allows those acting for creditors or debtors to ascertain the legal position more easily than has been possible to date, as I hope, that will be a worthwhile result indeed.

I want to thank all the people who have helped me with this book including Myra Scott, Ellis Simpson, Jonathan Edwards, Stephen Gold, Gary Clark, Stephanie McPhail, Patricia Kaye, Linda Sinclair, Kate Marshall, Jim Bauld, Ian Gillies, Cathie Craigie, Garry Gibson and my publisher Jill Barrington. Any errors are my own. Special thanks are due to the women in my life; my mother Kathleen, my daughter Leah and above all my wife Rachel.

I have attempted to state the law as correct to May 1, 2002.

TABLE OF CASES

A (A Mental Patient) v. The Scottish Ministers, 2001 S.C. 1; 2000 S.L.T. 873. . . . . . . 5.14
Abbey National Building Society v. Barclays Bank, 1990 S.C.L.R. 639. . . . . 8.16
Abbey National plc v. Arthur and Sutherland, 2000 S.L.T. 103; 1999 G.W.D. 34–1640. . . . . 6.3, 7.2
Aberdeen Trades Council v. Shipconstructors and Shipwrights Association, 1949 S.C. (HL) 45. . . . . 8.1, 8.13
Advocate (Lord) v. Aero Technologies Ltd (in receivership), 1991 S.L.T. 134. . . . . . 7.7.3
—— v. Bank of India, 1991 G.W.D. 13–823. . . . . 8.16, 8.18
Ahmed v. Clydesdale Bank plc, 2001 S.L.T. 423; 2000 G.W.D. 27–1037. . . . . 5.2, 5.6
Albany Homes Loans Ltd v. Massey; *sub nom.* Massey v. Albany Life Assurance Co Ltd [1997] 2 All E.R. 609; [1997] 2 F.L.R. 305. . . . . 5.14
Albatown Ltd v. Credential Group Ltd, 2001 G.W.D. 27–1102. . . . . 1.2
Alliance & Leicester Building Society v. Hecht, 1991 S.C.L.R. 562. . . . . 6.3, 8.17
Armstrong, Petr, 1988 S.L.T. 255. . . . . 7.6.1, 8.11
Ascot Inns Ltd (in receivership) v. Braidwood Estates Ltd, 1995 S.C.L.R. 390. . 7.4, 7.5.1, 7.8
Associated Displays Ltd (in liquidation) v. Turnbeam Ltd, 1988 S.C.L.R. 220. . . . . . . 8.11

Baillie v. Shearer's Judicial Factor (1894) 21R. 498. . . . . 7.5.3
Bank of Credit v. Thompson, 1987 G.W.D. 10–341. . . . . 8.9
Bank of Credit and Commerce International SA v. Aboody [1990] 1 Q.B. 923; [1989] 2 W.L.R. 759. . . . . 5.7
Bank of Scotland v. Cameron, 1989 S.L.T. (Land Ct.) 38; 1988 S.L.C.R. 47. . . . . 6.2
—— v. Community Charges Registration Officer for Central Region, 1991 S.C.L.R. 394. . . . . 7.4, 7.7.2
—— v. Fernand, 1997 S.L.T. (Sh.Ct) 78; 1997 Hous. L.R. 65. . . . . 2.3.5, 2.4.2, 2.7.1
—— v. Flett, 1995 S.C.L.R. 591. . . . . 2.2.6
—— v. Grimes [1985] Q.B. 1179; [1985] 3 W.L.R. 294. . . . . 4.3.3
—— v. Millward, 1999 S.L.T. 901; 1998 S.C.L.R. 577. . . . . 2.3, 2.7, 4.2.26
Barclays Bank plc v. O'Brien [1994] 1 A.C. 180; [1993] 3 W.L.R. 786. . . 5.3, 5.4, 5.7, 5.10
Barret v. Halifax Building Society (1995) 28 H.L.R. 634. . . . . 4.3.3
Bass Brewers Ltd v. Humberclyde Finance Group Ltd, 1996 G.W.D. 19–1076. . . . . . 8.16
Begbie v. Boyd (1837) 16S. 232. . . . . 7.5.4
Bisset v. Standard Property Investment plc, 1999 G.W.D. 26–1253. . . . . 8.8, 8.11, 8.12
Bradford & Bingley Building Society v. Walker, 1988 S.L.T. (Sh.Ct) 33. . . . . 3.5
Braithwaite v. Bank of Scotland, 1999 S.L.T. 25; 1997 G.W.D. 40–2037. . . . . 5.5
Bristol & West Building Society v. Ellis (1997) 29 H.L.R. 282; (1997) 73 P. & C.R. 158. . . . . 4.3.1
Broadway v. Clydesdale Bank plc, 2000 G.W.D. 19–763. . . . . 5.8, 5.11
—— v. —— (No.2) 2001 G.W.D. 14–552. . . . . 5.4, 5.6, 5.7, 5.8

CIBC Mortgages v. Pitt [1994] 1 A.C. 200; [1993] 3 W.L.R. 802. . . . . 5.2
Cameron v. Abbey National plc, 1999 Hous. L.R. 19. . . . . 6.2
Cairney v. Bulloch, 1994 S.L.T. (Sh.Ct) 37; 1993 S.C.L.R. 901. . . . . 4.2.27
Cedar Holdings Ltd v. Iyyaz, 1989 S.L.T. (Sh.Ct.) 71; 1989 S.C.L.R. 236. . . . . 2.2.10
Chapman v. U.K., Appl. No. 27238/95. . . . . 5.14
Cheltenham and Gloucester BS v. Grant (1994) 26 H.L.R. 703. . . . . 4.3.2
Cheltenham and Gloucester Building Society v. Norgan [1996] 1 W.L.R. 343; [1996] 1 All E.R. 449. . . . . 4.2.14, 4.3.1, 9.4.2
Cheltenham and Gloucester Plc v. Krausz [1997] 1 W.L.R. 1558; [1997] 1 All E.R. 21. . . . . 4.3.3
Christie's Executrix v. Armstrong, 1996 S.C. 295; 1996 S.L.T. 948. . . . . 8.17
Clancy v. Caird, 2000 S.C. 441; 2000 S.L.T. 546. . . . . 5.14
Clydesdale Bank v. Adamson, 2001 G.W.D. 27–1082. 2.2.5, 2.4.1, 5.7

Clydesdale Bank plc v. Black, February 26 and 27, 2002. . . . . 5.12
—— v. Davidson, 1993 S.C.L.R. 984. . . . . 2.6
—— v. ——, 1998 S.C. (H.L.) 51; 1998 S.L.T. 522. . . . . 6.2
—— v. Mowbray, 1988 G.W.D. 23–987. . . . . 2.2.5, 2.2.6, 2.2.11, 2.4.5
—— v. ——, 1989 G.W.D. 27–1212. . . . . 2.4.5
—— v. ——, 2000 S.C. 151; 1999 G.W.D. 40–1951. . . . . 5.18, 5.20
Commercial and General Acceptance v. Nixon (1983) 152 C.L.R. 491. . . . . 8.12
County Properties Ltd v. The Scottish Ministers, 2002 S.C. 79; 2001 S.L.T. 1125. . . . 5.13

Daniels v. Walker [2000] 1 W.L.R. 1382. . . . . 5.16
David Watson Property Management v. Woolwich Equitable Building Society, 1989
    S.L.T. (Sh.Ct) 74; 1989 S.C.L.R. 276. . . . . 7.7.1
—— v. ——, 1990 S.L.T. 764; 1990 S.C.L.R. 517. . . . . 7.1, 7.5.1, 7.5.2, 7.7.1, 7.8, 8.6
—— v. ——, 1992 S.L.T. 430; 1992 S.C. (H.L.) 21; 1992 S.C.L.R. 357. . . . . 7.7.1
Dawson v. R. Gordon Marshall & Co., 1996 G.W.D. 21–1243. . . . . 8.17
Dick v. Clydesdale Bank plc, 1991 S.L.T. 678. . . . . 8.10, 8.12, 8.13
Disblair Estates Ltd v. Jackson, unreported, Aberdeen Sheriff Court, November 24,
    1982. . . . . 3.5
Donald v. Donald, 1913 S.C. 274; (1912) 2 S.L.T.436. . . . . 5.1
Donoghue v. Poplar Housing & Regeneration Community Association Ltd; Poplar
    Housing & Regeneration Community Association Ltd v. Donaghue. *See* Poplar
    Housing and Regeneration Community Association Ltd v. Donoghue
Duncan v. Mitchell & Co. (1893) 21R. 37. . . . . 8.1

Edinburgh D.C. v. Davies, 1987 S.L.T. (Sh.Ct) 33. . . . . 4.2.23
Elswick Bay Shipping Co Ltd v. Royal Bank of Scotland plc, 1982 S.L.T. 62. . . . . . . 2.2.5

First National Bank plc v. Syed [1991] 2 All E.R. 250; (1991) 10 Tr. L.R. 154. . 2.5, 4.3.3
Forbes v. Armstrong. *See* G Dunlop & Son's Judicial Factor v. Armstrong
Forsyth v. The Royal Bank of Scotland plc, 2000 S.L.T. 1295. . . . . 5.7, 5.9, 5.11
Fredin v. Sweden (1991) 13 E.H.R.R. 784. . . . . 5.14

G Dunlop & Son's Judicial Factor v. Armstrong; *sub nom.* Forbes v. Armstrong,
    1994 S.L.T. 199; 1993 S.C.L.R. 204 and 1995 S.L.T. 645. . . . . 6.3, 6.4, 7.6.1
Gallagher v. Ferns, 1998 S.L.T. (Sh.Ct) 79; 1998 G.W.D. 4–186. . . . . 4.2.29, 4.2.30
Gardiner, Petr, 2001 G.W.D. 38–1433. . . . . 2.2.5, 2.2.7, 2.3.8
Gasus Dosier-und Fodertechnik v. Netherlands, 1995 A 306–B. 5.14
Gemmel v. Bank of Scotland, 1998 S.C.L.R. 144. . . . . 7.3
Gordaviran Ltd v. Clydesdale Bank plc, 1994 S.C.L.R. 248. . . . . 8.8, 8.9, 8.11
Govan Housing Society v. Kane, July 6, 2001, unreported. 4.2.26, 4.2.29
Grantly Developments v. Clydesdale Bank plc, 2000 G.W.D. 6–213. . . . . 2.2.7
Gray v. Binny (1879) 7R. 332. . . . . 5.6

Halifax Building Society v. Gupta, 1994 S.L.T. 339. . . . . 2.4.5, 4.2.2, 4.2.12, 7.6.1
—— v. Smith, 1985 S.L.T. (Sh.Ct) 25. . . . . 8.15, 8.16
Hambros Bank Ltd v. Lloyds Bank plc, 1999 S.L.T. 49; 1997 S.C.L.R. 1104. . . 1.2, 7.6.2.3
Harris v. Abbey National plc, 1997 S.C.L.R. 359; 1996 Hous. L.R. 100. . . . . 7.3
Hewit v. Williamson, 1999 S.L.T. 313; 1998 S.C.L.R. 601. . . . . 2.2.6, 5.4, 6.4
Hill Samuel v. Haas, 1989 S.L.T. (Sh.Ct.) 68; 1989 S.C.L.R. 210. . . . . 2.2.10, 4.2.29, 4.2.30
Holt Leisure Parks Ltd v. Scottish & Newcastle Breweries plc, 1996 G.W.D.
    22–1284. . . . . 7.5.2
Household Mortgage Corporation plc v. Diggory. 4.2.25

Inglis' Trs v. Macpherson (1911) 2 S.L.T. 176. . . . . 3.4

Karl Construction Ltd v. Palisade Properties plc, 2002 S.L.T. 312; 2002 G.W.D.
    7–212. . . . . 5.13, 5.14
Kaur v. Singh, 1999 S.C. 180; 1999 S.L.T. 412; 1998 S.C.L.R. 849. . . . . 7.4
Kerr v. McArthur's Trs (1848) 11D. 301. . . . . 7.6.1, 8.10

Leslie v. Leslie, 1987 S.L.T. 232. . . . . 5.1

Table of Cases

McCabe v. Skipton Building Society, 1994 S.L.T. 1272; 1994 S.C.L.R. 501. . . . . 5.4
McLeod v. Cedar Holdings Ltd, 1989 S.L.T. 620. . . . . 5.2
McNab v. Clark (1889) 16R. 610. . . . . 7.6.1
Macrae v. Leitj, 1913 S.C. 901. . . . . 7.5.2
McWhirter v. McCulloch's Trs (1887) 14R. 918. . . . . 7.6.1
Marshall's Trs v. Banks, 1934 S.C. 405. . . . . 7.5.2
Massey v. Albany Life Assurance Co Ltd. *See* Albany Homes Loans Ltd v. Massey. . . . .
Mellacher v. Austria (1990) 12 E.H.R.R. 391. . . . . 5.14
Milmor Properties Ltd v. W & T Investment Co Ltd, 1999 S.C.L.R. 910. . . . . 3.5
Murie McDougall Ltd v. Sinclair, 1994 S.L.T. (Sh.Ct) 74; 1994 S.C.L.R. 805. . . . . 2.5
Mountstar Metal Corporation Ltd v. Cameron, 1987 S.L.T. (Sh.Ct) 106. . . . . . 2.2.10, 3.5

National and Provincial Building Society v. Lloyd [1996] 1 All E.R. 630; (1996) 28
  H.L.R. 459. . . . . 4.3.1
—— v. Riddell, 1986 S.L.T. (Sh.Ct) 6. . . . . 2.2.10
Newcastle Building Society v. White, 1987 S.L.T. (Sh.Ct) 81. 8.15
Niemitz v. Germany, 1992 A. 251–B. 5.14
Northern Rock Building Society v. Barclays Bank plc. 7.4.1
—— v. J.W. Wood, Community Charges Registration Officer, 1990 S.L.T. (Sh.Ct)
  109. . . . . 7.4, 7.7.2

Parker v. British Airways Board [1982] Q.B. 1004; [1982] 2 W.L.R. 503. . . . . 7.3
Poplar Housing and Regeneration Community Association Ltd v. Donoghue; *sub
  nom.* Donoghue v. Poplar Housing & Regeneration Community Association
  Ltd; Poplar Housing & Regeneration Community Association Ltd v.
  Donaghue [2002] Q.B. 48; [2001] 3 W.L.R. 183. . . . . 5.14
Prestwick Investment Trust v. Jones, 1981 S.L.T. (Sh.Ct) 55. . . . . 3.5
Provincial Building Society v. Menzies, 1984 S.L.T. (Sh.Ct) 81. . . . . 2.2.10, 3.5

Rankin v. Russell (1868) 7M. 126. . . . . 3.4
Rimmer v. Thomas Usher & Son Ltd, 1967 S.L.T. 7; 1966 S.L.T. (Notes) 76. . . . . . . 8.13
Ross and Bonnyman Ltd v. Hawson Garner Ltd, 2001 S.L.T. (Sh.Ct) 134; 2001
  G.W.D. 25–921. . . . . 4.2.25
Royal Bank of Scotland v. Clark, 2000 S.L.T. (Sh.Ct) 101; 2000 S.C.L.R. 193. . 2.2.4, 5.1,
  5.4, 5.7, 5.9
—— v. Etridge (No.2) [2001] 3 W.L.R. 1021; [2001] 4 All E.R. 449 affirming [1998]
  4 All E.R. 705; [1998] 2 F.L.R. 843. . . . . . . 5.2, 5.5, 5.7, 5.9, 5.10, 5.11, 5.12, 14.1, 14.2
—— v. Johnston, 1987 G.W.D. 1–5. . . . . 8.10, 8.11
—— v. Kinnear, 2001 G.W.D. 3–124. . . . . 5.19, 5.20
—— v. Marshall. 2.2.5
—— v. Shanks, 1998 S.L.T. 355. . . . . 2.2.5, 2.2.11, 5.4
—— v. Wilson, 2001 S.L.T. (Sh.Ct) 2; 2000 G.W.D. 17–689. . . . . 5.1, 5.5, 5.7, 5.10
Royal Trust Co. of Canada v. Markham [1975] 1 W.L.R. 1416; [1975] 3 All E.R. 433   4.3.2

St Brice v. Southwark LBC [2001] EWCA Civ 1138; [2002] L. & T.R. 11. . . . . 5.14
Scottish Heritable Security Co Ltd v. Allan, Campbell & Co (1876) 3R. 333. . . . . 1.3
Scottish Property Investment Company Building Society v. Horne (1881) 8R. 737. . . . 3.4
Security Pacific Finance Ltd v. Graham, 1995 G.W.D. 29–1545. . . . . 5.2
Selby's Heirs v. Jollie [1795] Mor. 13438. . . . . 7.5.3
Sheriff Clerk of North Strathclyde v. Paterson, unreported, June 11, 1984. . . . . 8.15
Skipton Building Society v. Wain, 1986 S.L.T. 96. . . . . 7.4, 7.4.1, 7.7.2, 8.10
Smith v. Bank of Scotland, 1997 S.L.T. 1061; 1997 S.C. (HL) 111   5.1, 5.4, 5.8, 5.10, 5.12
Sowman v. City of Glasgow D.C., 1983 S.L.T. 132. . . . . 8.16
Speirs and Knox v. Marshall's Trs (1904) 11 S.L.T. 599. . . . . 7.7.2
Stewart v. Brown (1882) 10R. 192. . . . . 8.10
Sutherland v. Sutherland (1843) 5D. 544. . . . . 2.2.7
Sykes (J) & Sons (Fish Merchants) Ltd v. Grieve, 2002 S.L.T. (Sh.Ct) 15; 2001
  G.W.D. 23–866. . . . . 1.2, 2.2.11, 2.2.12, 2.4.5

Tamroui v. Clydesdale Bank plc, 1997 S.L.T. (Sh.Ct) 20; 1996 S.C.L.R. 732. . . . . 6.2
Telfer v. Glasgow Corp., 1974 S.L.T. (Notes) 51. . . . . 7.7.3

The County Council of the County of Renfrew v. Binnie (1898) 1F. 186. . . . . 4.2.6
Thomson v. Yorkshire Building Society, 1994 S.C.L.R 1014.. . . . . 2.2.4, 5.21, 8.11
Trade Development Bank v. Crittal Windows Ltd, 1983 S.L.T. 510. . . . . 7.5.2
—— v. David W. Haig (Bellshill) Ltd, 1983 S.L.T. 510. . . . . 6.2
Trade Development Bank v.Warriner and Mason (Scotland) Ltd, 1980 S.L.T. 223. . . 6.2,
7.5.2
Trustee Savings Bank v. Balloch, 1983 S.L.T. 240. . . . . 5.4

UCB Bank plc v. Hire Foulis Ltd (in liquidation), 1999 S.L.T. 950. . . . . 7.5.1
United Dominions Trust Ltd, Noters, 1977 S.L.T. (Notes) 56. 8.19
—— v. Site Preparations Ltd (No.1), 1978 S.L.T. (Sh.Ct) 14. . . . . 2.7.2, 4.2.2, 7.6.1
—— v. —— (No.2), 1978 S.L.T. (Sh.Ct) 21. . . . . 2.3.1, 2.7.2

Wilson v. First County Trust Ltd: *sub nom.* Wilson v. First National Trust Ltd
  (No.1) [2001] Q.B. 407; [2001] 2 W.L.R. 302. . . . . 5.14
—— v. First National Trust Ltd (No.1). *See* Wilson v. First County Trust Ltd. . . . .
—— v. Skipton Building Society, 1995 G.W.D. 37–1895. . . . . 2.2.4, 2.2.7
—— v. Target Holdings, 1995 G.W.D. 31–1599. . . . . 7.6.2.3
—— v. Cotias Investments Inc., 2001 S.L.T. 353; 2000 S.C.L.R. 324. . . . 5.4, 5.5, 5.7, 5.11

TABLE OF STATUTES

1857	Registration of Leases (Scotland) Act (19 & 20 Vict. c. 26)—	
	s. 1	7.5.2
	s. 4	7.5.2
1875	Explosives Act (38 & 39 Vict. c. 17)—	
	s. 23	7.7.3
1891	Stamp Act (54 & 55 Vict. c. 39)—	
	s. 54	7.5.4
1894	Heritable Securities (Scotland) Act (57 & 58 Vict. c. 44)	2.2.10, 4.2.22, 4.2.25, 4.2.26, 7.5.1, 8.14
	s. 3	7.5.1
	s. 5	2.2.10, 4.2.2, 3.3, 3.4, 3.5, 4.2.6, 4.2.8, 4.2.9, 4.2.11, 4.2.21, 4.2.22
	s. 7	7.5.2, 7.5.4
	s. 11	8.14
	s. 15	7.5.1
1907	Sheriff Courts (Scotland) Act (7 Edw. 7, c. 51)—	
	s. 5(4)	5.1
	Sched. 1	2.2.11, 4.2.22
	Form O6	4.2.26
	r. 34.8	4.2.26
1924	Conveyancing (Scotland) Act (14 & 15 Geo. 5, c. 27)	3.3
	s. 25(1)(a)	7.1, 7.5.1, 7.5.3
	s. 32	6.4
	s. 33	3.3
	s. 34	3.3
	s. 35	3.3
	s. 35(3)	8.1
	s. 36	3.3, 8.1
	s. 38	8.8
	s. 40	8.1
	s. 40(1)	8.8
	s. 41	8.19
	Sched. M, Form 1	3.3
1948	Companies Act (11 & 12 Geo. 6, c. 38)—	
	s. 227	8.19
1955	Crofters (Scotland) Act (3 & 4 Eliz. 2, c. 21)—	
	s. 3(3)	6.2
1956	Valuation and Rating (Scotland) Act (4 & 5 Eliz. 2, c. 60)—	
	s. 16	7.7.2

1959	Building (Scotland) Act (7 & 8 Eliz. 2, c. 24)—	
	s. 10	7.7.2
1960	Occupiers Liability (Scotland) Act (8 & 9 Eliz. 2, c. 30)	7.7.3
1970	Administration of Justice Act (c. 31)—	
	s. 36	4.3, 4.3.3
	s. 38A	2.5
	Conveyancing and Feudal Reform (Scotland) Act (c. 35)	2.1, 2.2.10, 2.3.7, 2.4, 2.4.6, 3.1, 3.3, 4.2.3, 4.2.22, 4.2.23, 4.2.25, 4.2.29, 7.1, 7.4, 7.5.3, 7.6, 7.6.2.2, 7.7.4, 9.1
	Pt II	1.5, 2.2.11, 4.2.8, 4.2.33
	s. 9	**12.1**
	(3)	1.2
	(4)	1.2
	(8)(b)	1.2
	(c)	1.2
	s. 10	5.18, **12.2**
	(1)(a)	1.3
	s. 11	**12.3**
	(1)	1.4
	(2)	1.4
	(3)	1.5, 2.7.1
	(4)(b)	1.5
	s. 12	**12.4**
	s. 13	5.18, **12.5**
	s. 14	5.18, **12.6**
	s. 15	**12.7**
	s. 16	**12.8**
	s. 17	6.4, **12.8**
	s. 18	6.4, **12.9**
	(1)	6.4
	(2)	2.2.11
	(3)	6.4
	(4)	6.4
	s. 19	2.1, 2.2.8, 2.7, 4.2.6, 4.2.26, **12.10**
	(2)	4.2.30
	(3)	4.2.30
	(4)	4.2.29, 4.2.30
	(5)	4.2.30
	(6)	4.2.25, 4.2.30, 4.2.31, 4.2.31
	(7)	4.2.32
	(8)	4.2.25
	(9)	2.2.5, 2.2.6, 2.2.12, 2.2.14
	(10)	4.2.9

1970 Conveyancing and Feudal Reform (Scotland) Act —*cont.*

s. 19(10A) 4.2.9
   (10B) 4.2.9
   (11) 2.2.4, 4.2.18
s. 19A 4.2.26, 4.2.30
   (1) 4.2.26
   (2) 4.2.26
   (3) .. 4.2.22, 4.2.26, 4.2.29, 4.2.30
s. 20 ... 2.2.4, 2.2.10, 2.2.12, 7.1, 7.7.2, **12.11**
   (1) ... 2.24, 2.2.12, 3.5, 7.5.2
   (2) 2.7.1, 8.1
   (3) 2.2.11, 7.1, 7.4, 7.5.2
   (4) 7.1, 7.5.2
   (5) 6.2, 7.1, 7.4, 7.5.1, 7.5.2, 7.7.1
     (a) 7.5.2
     (b) 7.5.3, 7.7.1, 7.7.2
s. 21 .. 2.3.9, 2.5, 2.7, 4.2.6, **12.12**
   (1) 2.3, 2.3.1, 4.2.30
   (2) 4.2.25, 4.2.31, 4.2.32
   (2A) ... 4.2.22, 4.2.26, 4.2.30
   (4) 2.3.5
s. 22 .... 2.3.5, 2.3.7, 2.3.13, 2.5, **12.13**
   (1) 2.2.11, 2.3.7
   (2) 2.3.7
   (3) 2.2.11, 2.3.7
   (4) 2.3.7
s. 23 .... **12.14**
   (1) 2.3.5
   (2) 2.3.5, 2.7.1, 8.1
   (3) 2.3.12, 6.4
   (4) 4.2.25
s. 24 ... 2.1, 2.2.10, 2.2.11, 2.3.7, 2.3.11, 2.3.12, 2.3.13, 2.4, 2.4.1, 2.4.2, 2.4.5, 2.7.1, 4.2.2, 4.2.6, 4.2.8, 4.2.9, 4.2.11, 4.2.18, 4.2.21, 4.2.22, 4.2.26, 4.2.27, 5.14, 5.21, 7.1, 7.4, 7.5.1, 7.5.4, 7.6.1, 8.1, 8.5, 8.19, **12.15**
   (1) 2.2.11, 2.7.2, 4.2.2
   (2) 2.4.1
   (3) 4.2.23, 4.2.26
   (4) 4.2.26
     (a) 4.2.31
s. 25 ..... 6.5.2, 7.2, 7.5.4, 7.6.1, 7.7.2, 8.1, 8.8, 8.9, 8.10, 8.11, 8.12, **12.16**
s. 26 .... 8.15, **12.17**
   (1) 8.4, 8.15
   (2) 6.4, 8.14
s. 27 .. 5.18, 7.7.2, 8.8, 8.13, 8.16, 8.17, **12.118**
   (1) 8.16
     (a) 8.16
     (b) 8.14, 8.16
     (c) 8.16

1970 Conveyancing and Feudal Reform (Scotland) Act —*cont.*

s. 27(1)(d) 8.16
   (2) 8.14, 8.17
s. 28 .... 7.7.2, **12.19**
   (1) 2.2.11, 7.5.4
   (2) 7.5.4
   (3) 7.5.4
   (4) 7.5.4
   (5) 7.5.4
   (6) 7.5.4
     (c) 8.14
   (7) 7.5.4
   (8) 7.5.4
s. 29 .... 2.2.11, 4.2.10, **12.20**
   (1) 8.14
s. 30 .... **12.21**
s. 31 .... 1.2, **12.22**
s. 32 .... 8.19, **12.23**
s. 35(1) 8.1
s. 53(1) 2.2.5, 2.3.6
Sched. 3 .... 1.4, 1.5, 2.4.2
Standard Conditions—
1 .... 1.5, 2.3.7, **13.1**
   (a) 7.5.3
   (b) 7.5.3
   (c) 7.5.3
2 .... 1.5, 7.5.3, **13.2**
   (a) 7.5.3
   (b) 7.5.3
3 .... 1.5, **13.3**
   (b) 7.7.1, 7.7.2
4 .... 1.5, **13.4**
5 .... 1.5, **13.5**
6 .... 1.5, 6.2, **13.6**
7 .... 1.5, 7.5.3, 7.7.1, 7.7.2, **13.7**
   (1) 7.5.3
   (2) 7.5.3
   (3) 1.5, 5.18, 7.5.3
8 .... 1.5, 2.1, 2.2, **13.8**
9 .... 2.1, 2.7, 7.4, 7.7.2, **13.9**
   (1)(a) 1.5, 2.2.4, 2.2.10, 2.4, 7.1
   (b) 1.5, 2.2.4, 2.3.1, 2.4, 2.4.1, 2.4.2, 2.4.5, 4.2.2
   (c) 1.5, 2.4, 2.4.2, 2.7.2
   (2) 2.7.2
     (a) 2.7.2
     (c) 2.7.2
10 .... 1.5, 2.3.5, 7.1, 7.6.1, 7.7.2, **13.10**
   (1) 1.5, 2.2.10
   (2) 1.5, 2.3.5, 7.4, 8.1
   (3)–(5) 7.4
   (3) 1.5, 7.4, 7.5.1
   (4) 1.5, 7.4, 7.5.2
   (5) 1.5, 7.4, 7.5.2, 7.7.1
   (6) 1.5, 2.3.5, 7.2, 7.5.3
   (7) 1.5, 2.3.5, 7.5.4
11 .... 1.5, 6.4, **13.10**
   (1) 6.4

Table of Statutes

1970 Conveyancing and Feudal Reform (Scotland) Act —*cont.*
- 11(2) 6.4
- (3) 6.4
- (4) 6.4
- (5) 6.4
- (3)–(5) 1.5
- 12 .... 2.2.8, 2.3.9, 5.18, 6.2
- Sched. 5,
  - Form A 6.4
  - Form B 6.4
  - Form C 6.4
- Sched. 6,
  - Form A 2.2, 2.2.1, **13.11**
  - Form B 2.3.2, **13.12**
  - Form BB 4.2.26, 4.2.30
  - Form C ... 4.2.9, 4.2.32, **13.13**
  - Form D 4.2.32, **13.14**
  - Form E 4.2.26, 4.2.27
  - Form F 4.2.26
- Sched. 7 .... 2.25, 2.4.1
  - para. 1 .... **13.15**
  - para. 2 .... **13.16**
  - para. 3 .... **13.17**

1971 Redemption of Standard Securities (Scotland) Act (c. 45) 6.4
- s. 1 ..... 12.3, 12.9, 12.14, 12.19, 12.23

Sheriff Courts (Scotland) Act (c. 51) 3.4, 3.5
- s. 35(1)(c) 3.5
- Sched. 1 .... 4.2.6

1973 Administration of Justice Act (c. 15)—
- s. 8 .... 4.3
- s. 8(2) 4.3.3

1974 Land Tenure Reform (Scotland) Act (c. 38)—
- s. 8 .... 7.5.2
- s. 11 .... 6.4
- s. 11(4) 6.4
- s. 11(6) 12.9
- s. 12 .... 6.4

Consumer Credit Act (c. 39) .. 2.1, 2.5, 2.6, 6.4, 8.11
- s. 16 .... 2.5
- s. 21 .... 2.5
- s. 87 .... 2.5
- s. 88 .... 2.5
- s. 126 .... 2.5
- s. 127(3) 5.14
- s. 129 .... 2.5
- s. 135 .... 2.5
- s. 170(3) 2.5
- s. 173 .... 2.5
- s. 177(2) 8.19

1975 Sex Discrimination Act (c. 65)—
- Sched. 3, para. 3(5)(b) 13.9

1976 Divorce (Scotland) Act (c. 39)—
- s. 6 .... 5.2

Race Relations Act (c. 74)—
- Sched. 1, para. 3(5)(b) 13.9

1979 Land Registration (Scotland) Act (c. 33)—
- s. 15(3) 12.4
- Sched. 2,
  - para. 4 .... 12.19

1980 National Heritage Act (c. 17)—
- Sched. 1,
  - para. 3(4)(b) 13.9

Tenants' Rights etc. (Scotland) Act (c. 52) .. 4.2.23

1981 Matrimonial Homes (Family Protection) (Scotland) Act (c. 59) ... 4.2.7, 6.5. 6.5.1, 6.5.2, 8.6
- s. 1(1) 6.5
- s. 6 .... 6.5.2
- s. 6(3) 6.5.1
- s. 8 .... 6.5.1
- s. 8(1) 6.5.1, 6.5.2
- s. 8(2) 6.5.1
- s. 8(2A) 6.5.1
- s. 20 .... 12.10
- s. 22 .... 8.6

1982 Civil Jurisdiction and Judgements Act (c. 27) 2.2.11
- Sched. 1,
  - Title II,
    - Art. 16 .... 2.2.11

Aviation Security Act (c. 36)—
- Sched. 1,
  - para. 11 .... 12.1

Civic Government (Scotland) Act (c. 45) 7.7.2
- s. 87 .... 7.7.2

1984 Roads (Scotland) Act (c. 54)—
- s. 13 .... 7.7.2
- s. 151 .... 7.7.2

Rent (Scotland) Act (c. 58) 6.2

1985 Companies Act (c. 6)—
- s. 653 .... 7.7.4

Insolvency Act (c. 65)—
- Sched. 8, para. 18 .... 13.9

Bankruptcy (Scotland) Act (c. 66) 6.3
- s. 31 .... 4.2.7, 6.3
- s. 32 .... 6.3
- s. 33(3) 6.3
- s. 39 .... 6.3
- s. 39(4) 6.3
- s. 41(1)(b) 6.5.2
- s. 55(3) 6.3
- s. 75(9) 2.7.2
- Sched. 4,
  - para. 16 .... 6.3

1985	Bankruptcy (Scotland) Act—cont.		1992	Local Government Finance Act—cont.
	Sched. 7,			Sched. 11,
	para. 8	13.9		Pt II,
	Law Reform (Miscellaneous Provisions) (Scotland) Act (c. 73)—			paras 7–8 .... 7.7.3
				para. 22 .... 7.7.2
			1993	Bankruptcy (Scotland) Act (c. 6) 6.3
	s. 4 .... 7.5.2			
	s. 5 .... 7.5.2		1994	Value Added Tax Act (c. 23) 7.5.1
	s. 9(3) 7.4			
	s. 13 .... 6.5.1			Sched. 4,
1986	Insolvency Act (c. 45)—			para. 7 .... 8.7
	s. 127 .... 8.19		1995	Requirements of Writing (Scotland) Act (c. 7) 7.5.2
	s. 145(1) 6.3			
	s. 185(1)(b) 6.3		1997	Building Societies Act (c. 32)—
	Sched. 14 .... 13.9			
	Building Societies Act (c. 53)—			s. 12(2) 8.10
				Contract (Scotland) Act (c. 34)—
	s. 11(10) 12.19			
	s. 11(15) 12.19			s. 2 .... 7.6.2.3
	s. 119(2) 8.10		1998	Data Protection Act (c. 29) .. 2.2.6, 4.2.27
	Sched. 4, para. 1(1)(a) 8.10			
1987	Debtors (Scotland) Act (c. 18)—			Sched. 1,
				Pt I,
	s. 1 .... 4.2.14			para. 1 .... 4.2.27
	Housing (Scotland) Act (c. 26) 7.7.5			Pt II,
				para. 1(2) 4.2.27
	s. 32 .... 4.2.16			Sched. 2 .... 4.2.27
	s. 108(1) 7.7.5			Sched. 2,
	s. 108(2) 7.7.5			para. 3 .... 4.2.27
	s. 108(3) 7.7.5			Sched. 3 .... 4.2.27
	s. 109(1) 7.7.5			para. 7(1)(b) 4.2.27
	Abolition of Domestic Rates (Scotland) Act (c. 47)—			Human Rights Act (c. 42) ... 4.3.1, 5.13, 5.14, 5.15, 5.16
	s. 7 .... 7.7.2			s. 3 .... 5.13
	s. 16(1) 7.7.2			s. 4 .... 5.15
1988	Court of Session Act (c. 36)—			s. 6 .... 5.13
				s. 6(3)(a) 5.13
	s. 47 .... 2.2.7			s. 8(3) 5.15
	Housing (Scotland) Act (c. 43) 5.14, 6.2			Scotland Act (c. 46)—
				s. 29 .... 5.15
	s. 18 .... 4.2.11, 6.2			s. 57 .... 5.15
	s. 18(3) 6.2		2000	Abolition of Feudal Tenure etc (Scotland) Act (asp 5)—
	s. 21(4) 5.14			
	Sched. 5, Pt I 6.2			
	ground 2 .... 6.2			s. 13(2) 7.7.1
1990	Environmental Protection Act (c. 43)—			s. 17 .... 8.4
				s. 50 .... 1.2
	Pt IIA 7.7.4			s. 76(1) 1.2
	s. 78A(9) 7.7.4			Sched. 12,
	s. 78E 7.7.4			Pt I 12.1, 12.2, 12.3, 12.4, 12.5, 12.7, 12.8, 12.9, 12.10, 12.21
	s. 78F 7.7.4			
	s. 78F(2) 7.7.4			
	s. 78F(4) 7.7.4			para. 30(6) 1.2
1992	Local Government Finance Act (c. 14) 7.7.3		2001	Housing (Scotland) Act (asp 10) .. 4.2.13, 4.2.15, 4.2.16, 6.2
	s. 75 .... 7.7.2			s. 3 .... 4.2.16
	s. 75(2)(a) 7.2			s. 11(1) 6.2
	s. 75(2)(f)(iii) 7.7.2			(4) 6.2
	s. 76 .... 7.7.2			s. 16 .... 4.2.11
	s. 99(1) 7.7.2			(3)(a) 4.2.13
	s. 100 .... 7.7.2			(d) 4.2.15

Table of Statutes

2001 Housing (Scotland) Act—*cont.*
s. 57 .... 6.2
s. 83(3) 6.2
s. 111 .... 6.2
Sched. 1,
  para. 7 .... 6.2
Sched. 3,
  para. 2(1)(a)(ii) 4.2.7
Mortgage Rights (Scotland)
  Act (asp 11) 2.2.1, 2.2.6,
    2.2.9, 2.2.10, 2.2.13,
    2.2.14, 2.3.2, 2.3.3, 2.3.4,
    2.3.7, 2.3.10, 2.3.12,
    2.3.13, 2.4.2, 2.4.5, 2.4.6,
    2.7, 3.5, 4.1, 4.2.1, 4.2.3,
    4.2.4, 4.2.6, 4.2.7, 4.2.8,
    4.2.22, 4.2.25, 4.2.33,
    4.2.36, 4.3, 4.3.1, 5.17,
    6.2, 6.5, 6.5.2, 6.6.1,
    6.6.2, 6.6.3, 7.2, 8.5, 9.1
s. 1 ... 4.2.5, 4.2.7, 4.2.10, 4.2.18,
    10.1
s. 1(1) 4.2.4, 4.2.6
  (c) 3.5, 4.2.8
  (2) 4.2.4, 4.2.7, 4.2.12
    (b) 6.5
    (c) 4.2.7
  (3) 4.2.7
  (4) 4.2.9
    (a) 4.2.9
    (b) 4.2.9
    (c) 4.2.8, 4.2.9
  (5) 4.2.9
  (6) 4.2.8
  (7) 4.2.9, 4.2.37
  (8)(a) 4.2.9
    (ii) 4.2.9
    (b) 4.2.9
s. 2 .. 4.2.4, 4.2.10, 4.2.11, 4.2.18,
    4.2.20, 4.3, 5.14, 5.20, **10.2**

2001 Housing (Scotland) Act—*cont.*
s. 2(1)(a) 4.2.11
  (ii) 4.3, 8.5
  (iii) 4.3
  (b) 4.2.11
(2) 4.2.11, 4.2.12
  (b) .. 4.3, 4.3.3, 6.6.1, 9.2.5
  (c) 6.6.3, 9.2.5
  (d) 4.2.7, 6.2
(3) 4.2.18
(4) 4.2.18, 4.2.36, 4.3
(5) 4.2.18
  (b) 4.2.36
(6) 4.2.18
(7) 4.2.7, 4.2.10, 4.2.12
s. 3 .... 8.5, **10.3**
(1)(a) 4.2.20
  (b) 4.2.20
(2) 4.2.20
s. 4 .... 4.2.26, **10.4**
(1) 4.2.22, 4.2.26, 4.2.30
(2) 4.2.22, 4.2.26, 4.2.30
(3) 4.2.23, 4.2.26
(4) 4.2.26
(5) 4.2.25, 4.2.26
s. 5 .... 4.2.33, **10.5**
s. 6 .... 4.2.33, **10.6**
s. 7 .... **10.7**
(3) 4.2.1
Sched. **10.8**
Pt I 4.2.21, **10.9**
  para. 1 .... **10.10**
  para. 2 .... **10.11**
  para. 3 .... **10.12**
  para. 4 .... **10.13**
  para. 5 .... **10.15**
Pt II **10.16**
  Form 1 ...... 4.2.26, 4.2.27,
    10.17
  Form 2 .... 4.2.26, **10.18**

TABLE OF STATUTORY INSTRUMENTS

1976 Summary Cause Rules, Sheriff Court (S.I. 1976 No. 476) 4.2.25
1983 Consumer Credit (Increase of Monetary Limits) Order (S.I. 1983 No. 1878) 2.5
1986 Housing Defects (Application to Lenders) (Scotland) Regulations(S.I. 1986 No. 843) 12.16, 12.18
Insolvency (Scotland) Rules (S.I. 1986 No. 1915) 6.3
r. 4.66(6) 6.3
1987 Income Support (General) Regulations (S.I. 1987 No. 1967) 6.6.1
1989 Consumer Credit (Exempt Agreements) Order (S.I. 1989 No. 869) 2.5
1990 Act of Sederunt (Amendment of Sheriff Court Ordinary Cause, Summary Cause and Small Claim Rules) (S.I. 1990 No. 661) 2.2.11
1992 Council Tax (Exempt Dwellings) (Scotland) Order (S.I. 1992 No. 1333) 7.7.3
Sched. 7.7.2
1993 Act of Sederunt (Ordinary Cause Rules) Sheriff Court (S.I. 1993 No. 1956) 2.2.11, 4.2.6
r. 3.2(3) 4.2.6
Chap 5 .... 4.2.22, 4.2.25
r. 5.10 .... 4.2.27
r.34.10(1) 2.2.11, 4.2.27
r. 34.10(1)(b) 7.5.2
r. 34.10(1)(c) 2.3.7
r. 34.10(1)(d) 2.3.7
r. 34.10(1)(e) 7.5.4
r. 34.10(2) 2.2.11
r. 34.12(1) 4.2.8
r. 34.12(2) 4.2.8
r. 107A(1) 2.2.11
r. 107A(2) 4.2.18
Form O2A 4.2.8
Form O5A 4.2.8, 4.2.27
Form O6 .... 4.2.8

1995 Value Added Tax Regulations (S.I. 1995 No. 2518)—
reg. 27 .... 8.7
1998 Consumer Credit (Increase of Monetary Limits) (Amendment) Order (S.I. 1998 No. 996) 2.5
1999 Act of Sederunt (Summary Applications, Statutory Applications and Appeals etc. Rules) (S.I. 1999 No. 929) 4.2.8
r. 2.7(7A) 4.2.8
r. 2.22A(1) 4.2.8
r. 2.22A(3) 4.2.8
r. 3.4.1 .... 4.2.27
r. 3.4.2 .... 2.2.44
Form 6A 4.2.8
Form 6B 4.2.8, 4.2.27
Form 7 .... 4.2.8
2002 Income Support (General) (Standard Interest Rate Amendment) (No. 2) Regulations (S.I. 2002 No. 338) 6.6.1

Scottish
2001 Mortgage Rights (Scotland) Act 2001 (Commencement and Transitional Provision) Order (S.S.I. 2001 No. 418 (C.18)) ... 4.2.1, 4.2.9, **11.1**
Mortgage Rights (Scotland) Act 2001 (Prescribed Notice) Order (S.S.I. 2001 No. 419)4.2.20, **11.2**
2002 Act of Sederunt (Amendment of Ordinary Cause Rules and Summary Applications, Statutory Applications and Appeals etc. Rules) (Applications under the Mortgage Rights (Scotland) Act 2001) (S.S.I. 2002 No. 7) 4.2.6, 4.2.8, 4.2.26, **11.3**

CHAPTER 1

THE REPOSSESSION FRAMEWORK

Introduction

The rise in home ownership over the last three decades has been 1.1 exponential. Current statistics suggest that two thirds of householders in Scotland own their own homes.[1] The vast majority of home owners have, or at least had, a mortgage[2] over their property.

Mortgage lending has clear benefits in modern society. It offers large sectors of society the ability to purchase their own homes, thereby spreading wealth and ensuring security of accommodation. However, an inevitable consequence is that failure to comply with mortgage conditions can lead to repossession[3] of the subject property. The ability of mortgage lenders to repossess is fundamental to the system.[3a] Without it no mortgage lending would be possible as there would be no effective security for the advances made. As security is only called upon in times of difficulty, the importance of repossession law is never more central than at times of recession or other relatively weak economic conditions.[4]

The Form of Security

Since the coming into effect of the Conveyancing & Feudal Reform 1.2 (Scotland) Act 1970,[5] the only manner in which it has been competent to secure a right over an interest in land, in security of a debt, is by the use

---

[1] Scottish figures have traditionally lagged behind the rest of the U.K. where, even by 1992, the figure was 70 per cent.

[2] The use of the word "mortgage" in this field has been criticised by legal purists (see for example para. 4.2.1). That said, it is by far the most commonly used word among the population as a whole to describe the security relationship following an advance made by a heritable creditor to a debtor. Nonetheless, I have tried to avoid using the word in discussion of the substantive law below.

[3] The use of the word "repossession" throughout this book is in its colloquial sense meaning recovery by a creditor of heritably secured property. This book does not cover evictions from tenanted property, except where those are effected at the instance of a heritable creditor.

[3a] In April 2002, the Scottish Executive said, in a consideration of the law including the area of repossessions, "ejection remains a necessary means of enforcement for the protection of the interests of heritable proprietors": *Enforcement of Civil Obligations in Scotland—A Consultation Paper*, para. 5.324.

[4] Though the economic difficulties in 2002 are nowhere near their level during the recession of the early 1990s. The number of secured loans more than 2.5 per cent in arrears was approximately five times higher then than at present, although even now there are estimated to be more than 150,000 mortgages in that category throughout the whole of the U.K. In the year 2000 (the most recent year for which statistics are available), 6,597 actions were initiated by creditors to recover possession of heritable property: *Civil Judicial Statistics*.

[5] On November 29, 1970. This Act (c.35) is referred to in this book as "the 1970 Act". References to statutory provisions in this Chapter are to the 1970 Act unless otherwise stated.

of a standard security.[6] As a result, all securities granted by debtors in favour of heritable creditors from November 1970 must be in the form of standard securities.[7] If the deed is not in that form, it is void and unenforceable.[8] The forms of security which existed prior to the coming into force of the 1970 Act,[9] while they may no longer be used to secure rights as before, remain valid for any security created before the use of the standard security was made mandatory.[10] It is obvious that a heritable creditor may only enforce his rights if the security under which he does so remains in place and has not been discharged.[11] It will also be apparent that there are very few continuing loans now in existence for which security was created prior to November 1970 and which have not since been discharged.[12]

These factors mean that the application of the law on such pre-existing forms of security is very rare. In fact, the majority of repossession cases where the loan is secured by a standard security is now so overwhelming that it includes perhaps all but one in 1,000 domestic repossession matters.[13] While the law on these pre-existing forms of security is considered in this book for the sake of completeness, these odds are reflected in the emphasis given throughout this text to the terms of the 1970 Act and its amendments and interpretation, and in the lack of emphasis on the law relating to pre-1970 Act securities.[14]

---

[6] s.9(3).
[7] The only exception, under s.9(8)(b), is where the land is an entailed estate, in which case a bond and disposition in security should be used, but entailed estates have long been obsolete and will soon be abolished when s.50 of the Abolition of Feudal Tenure etc (Scotland) Act 2000 (asp 5) comes into force (no date has yet been fixed). Section 76(1) and Sched. 12 para. 30(6) of that Act prospectively amend s.9(8)(b) of the 1970 Act accordingly.
[8] s.9(4)
[9] Referred to hereafter as the pre-existing forms of security or pre-1970 Act securities.
[10] s.31
[11] Similarly, the security may only be enforced if the obligation which it secures has not been extinguished: for an interesting recent discussion of this issue, see the decision of Lord Macfadyen in *Albatown Ltd v. Credential Group Ltd*, 2001 G.W.D. 27–1102. In *Sykes v. Grieve*, 2002 S.L.T. (Sh.Ct) 15, Sheriff Principal MacInnes Q.C. said (p17B) "[b]efore the procedures set out in the [1970] Act could be followed, there had to be a debt in existence at the time when the calling-up notice was served." In *Hambros Bank Ltd v. Lloyds Bank plc*, 1999 S.L.T. 49, Lord Hamilton held (p52F) "[n]otwithstanding that *ex facie* of the record a security remained in force, it could be extinguished by payment or discharge of the relative debt."
[12] The average house in 1970 could be acquired for around £6,000 (and flats for around £3,500), a sum which even in full would be well within the capability of many debtors to repay now by some or other means, but it must be remembered that interest and further advances may have been added to the sum originally advanced.
[13] It is not surprising that the ratio is so high as very few mortgages will have been in existence for more than 31 years. The proportion of cases on the pre-existing law is higher in commercial cases but they are still very rare. In April 2002, the Scottish Executive said "it is thought that there are now few holders of bonds and dispositions in security": *Enforcement of Civil Obligations in Scotland—A Consultation Paper*, para. 5.307. It must not be forgotten that the standard security may secure an obligation other than to pay money (under s.9(8)(c)) but that is very much the exception.
[14] For a detailed review of the law on such securities, see Gordon, *Scottish Land Law* (2nd ed., 1999), paras 20–04 *et seq*.

Other Remedies

The law also permits the exercise by a heritable creditor of remedies 1.3
other than those directly and exclusively related to recovery of the
security subjects[15] but these do not relate to the process of repossession
and indeed are not specific to creditors in heritable securities.[16] Such
remedies fall within the general law of debt enforcement, which is
beyond the scope of this work.[17]

The Standard Security

Having been recorded, the standard security operates to vest the interest 1.4
over which it is granted as a security for the performance of the contract
to which the security relates.[18] This makes clear that the basis of any
enforcement action in relation to the security subjects by the creditor,
such as an action for repossession, is based on the terms of the standard
security and the provisions in the 1970 Act relating thereto.

The precise terms of the standard security will vary from case to case
but the 1970 Act provides that the conditions in Schedule 3 to the Act,
referred to there and hereafter as "the standard conditions", shall
regulate every standard security.[19] These are of great significance to the
process of repossession and the powers available to the creditor both
before and after recovery of the security subjects.

The Standard Conditions[20]

The act sets out twelve standard conditions to which the parties to a 1.5
standard security are required to adhere. Extra or different conditions
may be narrated in the deed or in a separate deed of variations, although
the Act prohibits the variation of certain of the standard conditions.[21]

---

[15] Such as an ordinary action for payment (based on the personal obligation of the debtor to repay the creditor the sum secured: s.10(1)(a)); summary diligence based on the same obligation and a consent to execution (if one exists) within the standard security; poinding of the ground; and adjudication (at least until it is abolished, if the recommendation of the Scottish Law Commission is followed: see para. 9.3.1). None of these is remotely attractive when compared to the creditor's more straightforward and effective remedy of seeking to recover and/or sell the security subjects. As a result, their application in these circumstances, at least prior to repossession of the security subjects by the creditor, is so rare as to be capable of being discounted for all practical purposes.

[16] Although poinding of the ground was generally used only by the holders of heritable securities (the only others being entitled to exercise being creditors with a right in relation to a debt affecting the land, such as a creditor in a real burden). However, its use is in any event now more or less obsolete, not least because a creditor in the most common pre-existing form of security, the *ex facie* absolute disposition, was not entitled to use the remedy: *Scottish Heritable Security Co Ltd v. Allan, Campbell & Co* (1876) 3R. 333. It is also important not to overlook the importance of the floating charge to heritable creditors, particularly in commercial transactions. The exercise of remedies under a floating charge falls within the law of receivership and is not covered further in this book.

[17] For a full consideration of the law of debt, see Wilson, *The Scottish Law of Debt*, (2nd ed., 1991).

[18] s.11(1).

[19] s.11(2), unless varied (where possible).

[20] For further discussion, see Talman (ed.), *Halliday's Conveyancing Law & Practice* (2nd ed., 1997) Vol. II, Chap. 53.

[21] See *infra*, nos 53–55.

In practice, the majority of mortgage lenders have their own specific conditions which alter the standard conditions.[22] Generally, however, the varied conditions do not depart significantly from those set down in Schedule 3 to the Act[23] and, invariably, cover many of the same principles as those in the 1970 Act.

The full text of the standard conditions is set out in the Appendix.[24] The first six of these, any or all of which may be varied, concern the maintenance of the value of the secured property and place certain obligations upon the debtor which the creditor can carry out[25] if the debtor fails to do so.

The most important provisions of these conditions are as follows[26]; the debtor must maintain the security subjects in good and sufficient repair to the reasonable satisfaction of the creditor,[27] including carrying out all necessary repairs and making good all defects within such reasonable period as the creditor may require[28]; the debtor must complete, as soon as practicable, any unfinished buildings and works forming part of the security subjects to the reasonable satisfaction of the creditor and must not demolish, alter or add to any buildings or works forming part of the security subjects[29]; the debtor must observe any condition or perform any obligation lawfully binding on him in relation to the security subjects[30]; the debtor must take, as soon as practicable, all reasonable or necessary steps to comply with or object to any planning notice affecting or likely to affect the security subjects[31]; the debtor must insure the security subjects, intimate to the creditor any occurrence which may give rise to a claim under the policy and refrain from any act or omission which would invalidate the policy[32]; and the debtor must not let[33] the security subjects without the prior consent in writing of the creditor.[34]

The remaining standard conditions[35] deal with the creditor's rights to enforce the security and allow the creditor to recover from the debtor any expenses incurred in exercising those rights. First, the creditor is given the power under standard condition 7 to perform obligations on the failure of debtor to do so and to recover all reasonably incurred expenses of doing so from the debtor. The creditor's power to recover expenses is also set out in standard condition 12 which allows the creditor to recover all expenses reasonably incurred by him in calling-up

---

[22] On variation of standard conditions generally, see Cusine, *Standard Securities* (1991) paras 5–16 *et seq*.

[23] Although they may impose more onerous obligations on the debtor where the creditor is not prohibited from doing so.

[24] See paras 13.1 *et seq*.

[25] Under standard condition 7.

[26] This list is by definition not an exhaustive list of the terms of the standard conditions, for which terms see paras 13.1 *et seq*.

[27] And, as a necessary consequence, the debtor is obliged to allow the creditor to examine the condition of the subjects.

[28] Standard condition 1.

[29] Standard condition 2.

[30] Standard condition 3.

[31] Standard condition 4.

[32] Standard condition 5.

[33] Or sub-let.

[34] Standard condition 6; see para. 13.6.

[35] With the single exception of standard condition 11.

the security, realising it or exercising any powers under the security.[36] The creditor is also given power to enter the security subjects for the purpose of performing such obligations at all reasonable times after giving seven days written notice to the debtor.[37] The debtor is entitled to exercise his right (if any) to redeem the security on giving notice of his intention so to do and where the debtor has exercised a right to redeem, and has made payment of the whole amount due, the creditor is obliged to grant a discharge of the security.[38]

For the purposes of a discussion on repossessions, there is no doubt that the most important standard conditions of all are those dealing with calling-up, default and the rights of the creditor on default. Subject to the terms of the security, the creditor is entitled to call-up a standard security in the manner prescribed by section 19 of the 1970 Act.[39] The debtor is held to be in default in a variety of circumstances. First, he is in default where a calling-up notice in respect of the security has been served and has not been complied with.[40] Next there is default by the debtor in the case of a failure to comply with any other[41] requirement arising out of the security.[42] Finally, the debtor is held to be in default where the proprietor of the security subjects has become insolvent.[43]

The creditor is given very extensive rights where the debtor is in default by the operation of standard condition 10[44] including, *inter alia*, the following; the creditor may sell the security subjects or any part thereof[45]; he may enter into possession of the security subjects and receive or recover rents[46]; in the circumstances where he has entered into possession, he may let the security subjects[47] and there are transferred to him all the rights of the debtor in relation to the granting of leases[48]; the creditor may effect all necessary repairs to maintain the subjects in good repair and may reconstruct, alter and improve the subjects to maintain their value[49]; and the creditor may apply to the court for a decree of foreclosure.[50]

It is provided[51] that of these standard conditions dealing with the powers of the creditor and the default of the debtor, all may be varied[52]

---

[36] For further discussion of expenses, see paras 5.17 *et seq.*

[37] Standard condition 7(3).

[38] Standard condition 11; for further discussion of issues surrounding redemption, see para. 6.4.

[39] Standard condition 8; see para. 2.2.

[40] Standard condition 9(1)(a).

[41] That is, other than failure to comply with a calling-up notice.

[42] Standard condition 9(1)(b).

[43] Standard condition 9(1)(c); see para. 2.7.2.

[44] Though standard condition 10(1) makes clear that the exercise of these rights must always be "in accordance with the provisions of Part II of this Act and of any other enactment applying to standard securities".

[45] Standard condition 10(2).

[46] Standard condition 10(3).

[47] Standard condition 10(4).

[48] Standard condition 10(5).

[49] Standard condition 10(6).

[50] Standard condition 10(7).

[51] s.11(3).

[52] But not varied in such a way as to circumvent the restrictions on variation of other standard conditions: s.11(4)(b).

other than those dealing with the powers of sale[53] and foreclosure[54] and with procedure on redemption.[55]

The Pre-existing Forms of Security

1.6 Prior to the creation of the standard security and its mandatory use, as discussed above, heritable securities were generally in three forms; a bond and disposition in security; a bond of cash credit and disposition in security; and an *ex facie* absolute disposition. Securities created before November 29, 1970 will be in one of these formats and enforcement is regulated by the rules relating to these older forms of security.[56] While there are some similarities with the procedures required for enforcement of a standard security, there are important differences and, for ease of reference, it is more convenient to deal separately with the initial stages of the repossession process as it applies, on the one hand, to standard securities and, on the other, to the pre-existing forms of security.[57]

---

[53] Standard condition 10(2); though Professor Halliday took the view that even this could be varied in a manner favourable to the debtor: Talman (ed.), *op. cit.*, para. 53–06.
[54] Standard condition 10(7); Talman (ed.), *op. cit.*, para. 53–06.
[55] Standard condition 11(3)—(5).
[56] See Chap. 3.
[57] For a full discussion of all aspects of the law relating to these forms of security, see Gordon, *op. cit.*, Chap. 20.

Chapter 2

THE INITIAL STAGES—STANDARD SECURITIES

Initial Methods of Enforcement

Standard conditions 8 and 9[1] make clear that a creditor has two basic paths which he may follow in enforcing his rights under a standard security. First, he may call up the loan. Secondly, the creditor may compel performance by the debtor of any obligation due by him under the security. In either case, failure by the debtor to comply will entitle the creditor to seek possession and/or sale of the subjects. In any matter where the secured property remains occupied and the debtor refuses to co-operate, the creditor will require to serve court proceedings. The nature, content and interpretation of such court proceedings is considered below.[2] 2.1

The practical steps which a creditor must initially take in pursuing either of the potential routes are (a) where he wishes to call up the loan, to serve a calling-up notice; and (b) where he wishes to compel performance of any obligation, to serve a notice of default and/or to raise and serve a section 24 court action. The rules relating thereto and a consideration of the advantages and disadvantages of each procedure are considered below. This chapter also explores when each of these strategies is appropriate and what further steps may require to be taken to ensure compliance with the Consumer Credit Act 1974.

Calling-up Notice

The creditor (in the absence of contractual agreement to the contrary[3] or a requirement of law) may call-up the standard security in accordance with section 19 of the 1970 Act.[4] This applies even where there is no failure by the debtor to comply with the requirements of the security. Section 19 provides: 2.2

"Where a creditor in a standard security intends to require discharge of the debt thereby secured and, failing that discharge, to exercise any power conferred by the security to sell any subjects of the security or any other power which he may appropriately exercise on the default of the debtor within the meaning of standard

---

[1] See paras 13.8 and 13.9. References to statutory provisions in this chapter are to the Conveyancing and Feudal Reform (Scotland) Act 1970 (hereafter "the 1970 Act") (c.35) unless otherwise stated.

[2] See paras 2.2.10, 2.3.11 and 2.4.

[3] For a practical example of the terms of a standard security causing problems with the validity of a calling-up notice, see D. J. Cusine, *Standard Securities* (1991), para. 8–12, case 3.

[4] Standard condition 8.

condition 9(1)(a), he shall serve a notice calling-up the security in conformity with *Form A of Schedule 6* to this Act (hereinafter in this Act referred to as a 'calling-up notice')".

Content of the Calling-up Notice

2.2.1 The full text of Form A of Schedule 6, as revised by the Mortgage Rights (Scotland) Act 2001,[5] is repeated in the Appendix[6] but the key provisions include:

    (a) That repayment of the principal sum, interest and expenses is required within two months[7];

    (b) If such repayment is not made, the security subjects may be sold; and

    (c) An explanatory note added by the 2001 Act.[8]

Service of the Calling-up Notice

2.2.2 The rules in relation to service of notices, including the method of service and the persons on whom they should be served, are substantially changed by the 2001 Act and are considered below.[9]

Restriction of Period of Notice

2.2.3 The two month period of notice may be restricted in certain circumstances but complete waiver of the period is no longer possible. The law on this area has been changed by the 2001 Act and the matter is dealt with below.[10]

Failure to Comply with Calling-up Notice

2.2.4 If the debtor fails to comply with the calling-up notice and make payment of the sums specified therein within the timescale indicated, the debtor is held to be in default.[11] In these circumstances, the creditor is entitled to exercise such of his rights under the security as he considers appropriate.[12] Such rights are additional to any other rights the creditor may have under the contract to which the security relates or which are

---

[5] (asp 11), hereafter "the 2001 Act".

[6] See para. 13.14.

[7] If the security secures a non-monetary obligation, the calling-up notice requires to be adapted and would require to make clear the obligation of which the creditor sought performance: see Form A of Sched. 6 to the 1970 Act at para. 13.14 and the example provided in Talman (ed.), *Halliday's Conveyancing Law and Practice* (2nd ed., 1996) (hereafter "Halliday, *Conveyancing*") Vol. II, para. 54–09.

[8] Which informs recipients of their ability under the 2001 Act to make an application for suspension of the creditor's rights and the circumstances the court will take into account in determining the application.

[9] See para. 4.2.21.

[10] See para. 4.2.9.

[11] Standard condition 9(1)(a); this is a different form of default than that under standard condition 9(1)(b), a distinction with importance consequences: see para. 2.4.2.

[12] s.20(1).

conferred on the creditor by any other rule of law.[13] The rights include entering into possession, selling the subjects, letting the subjects (after entering into possession) and the remaining rights specified in standard condition 10.[14]

The calling-up notice ceases to have effect after five years from the date of the notice where the subjects have not been offered for or exposed to sale or, where there has been such offer or exposure, from the date of the last offer or exposure.[15] However, a calling-up notice will remain effective during the relevant five year period even if the original reason giving rise to its service has been superseded.[16] The calling-up notice could therefore be relied upon by the creditor at any time within the timescale indicated for any purpose but particularly with a view to compelling a debtor to remedy a later default. Where a calling-up notice is served and a court action subsequently raised which results in decree for warrant to exercise the powers of the creditor, the prescriptive period may not run from the date of the notice, even where there has been no exposure to sale.[17]

The Accuracy of Information in the Notice and any Appendix

The statutory style for the calling-up notice expects the level of outstanding debt to be stated on the notice. In the absence of a decided case, there was some debate as to whether a certificate of indebtedness required to be served with the calling-up notice and the extent to which the certificate required to be accurate. In *Royal Bank of Scotland v. Marshall*,[18] the creditor had served a calling-up notice without such a certificate. According to the terms of the standard security in that case, the amount due could be conclusively ascertained only by such a certificate. There was divided opinion in commentaries on the Act.[19] In the event, Sheriff Gordon Q.C. held that it was not necessary to serve a certificate with the calling-up notice. The debtor also argued that the notices were defective by reason of having failed to specify the debt

2.2.5

---

[13] s.20(1).
[14] s.20; see Chaps 7 and 8; the full text of the standard conditions is repeated in the Appendix at paras 13.1 *et seq.*
[15] s.19(11).
[16] For example, the creditor may have decided to call-up the loan as arrears had reached an unacceptable level (while a notice of default would also be competent in these circumstances, the creditor may call-up the loan whenever he chooses: see para. 2.7). In *Thomson v. Yorkshire Building Society* 1994, S.C.L.R. 1014, a creditor was not prevented from enforcing a decree obtained following expiry of a calling-up notice where the decree had been obtained two and a half years before.
[17] *Wilson v. Skipton Building Society,* 1995 G.W.D. 37–1895; but if the action is founded on the calling-up notices, they must not have expired before decree is granted: *Royal Bank of Scotland plc v. Clark,* 2000 S.L.T. (Sh.Ct) 101.
[18] Paisley & Cusine, *Unreported Property Cases from the Sheriff Courts* (W. Green and Son, Edinburgh 2000), p.445.
[19] On the one hand, Halliday, *Conveyancing*, at para. 39–06, Cusine, *Standard Securities*, at para. 8–05 and Wallace & McNeil, *Banking* (10th ed., 1991), p.157 favoured the view that the notices were defective without such a certificate, while a later opinion by Professor Halliday (in D.J. Cusine (ed.), *The Conveyancing Opinions of J. M. Halliday* (1992), (hereafter "Halliday, *Conveyancing Opinions*", p.333) indicated that the certificate did not require to be served along with the calling-up notices although it would require to be served thereafter.

secured as at the date of demand but rather as they stood at a date 28 days earlier.[20] The Sheriff preferred the creditor's submission that the reference in the style to a specific sum of interest as part of the principal was merely a way of giving information as to how the principal was made up.[21]

Even where a certificate of indebtedness has been served with the calling-up notice, it has been argued that inaccuracies within the certificate render the calling-up notice invalid. An important distinction must be drawn between inaccuracies in any appendix and inaccuracies in the notice itself. In *Royal Bank of Scotland v. Shanks*,[22] the creditor raised proceedings on the strength of a calling-up notice. The terms of the parties' contract[23] provided that the sum outstanding should be set out in a statement signed by a person within a designated class of authorised persons. One of the debtors argued that the correct procedure had not been followed in that the official of the bank who had signed the relevant documentation was not within the designated class of persons specified. It was argued by the debtor that the requirements were mandatory and, as they were drafted for the creditor's own use, could not be departed from, rendering the calling-up notice void. Lord Penrose found that the creditor had failed to follow the correct procedures but described the deficiency in the appendix as a minor matter which did not go to the root of liability. He found there to be "no reason why the deficiency in the appendix affects the validity of the notice".

Shanks is also useful authority to confirm that a creditor is not bound by or limited to the sum stated in the certificate[24]:

> "Form A includes language which was incorporated into the notice in this case: 'subject to such adjustment of the principal sum and the amount of interest as may subsequently be determined'. *Section 19(9)* confers on the debtor in that event the right to require a final statement.[25] That provision envisages a situation in which the debtor may call for final determination of the liability, typically where he intends to discharge it. But generally the scheme of the provisions allows for revision of the sum claimed, after service of the calling-up notice, at the instance of the creditor. In the case of a security for an account current it is not unlikely that there will be transactions on the account following service of a notice. There may be contributions from co-obligants; there may be credits and debits of principal sums in ordinary course which modify the balance due;

---

[20] It seems likely that the sum specified had been calculated at the date of the last payment due by the debtor.

[21] "i.e. of the original principal and accrued interest" *per* Sheriff Gordon Q.C. in *Marshall supra*.

[22] 1998 S.L.T. 355.

[23] But not the standard security itself.

[24] The standard security, of course, continues to secure the whole debt due irrespective of whether a calling-up notice has been served; see also *Hewit*, at para. 2.2.6, which confirmed that a statement provided under s.19(9) does not fix the sum outstanding to that specified.

[25] See para. 2.2.6.

and there almost certainly will be further accruals of interest. The Act does not require, nor in my opinion does it envisage, final determination of the debt at the date of service of the notice."[26]

Nonetheless, a creditor should not include any sums which are due to him but not covered by the standard security as he may only call-up the sums due under the security itself.[27]

It is permissible to include extra information in the calling-up notice[28] but a deficiency in the calling-up notice itself, as opposed to in any certificate accompanying the notice, will be a more serious matter for the creditor. This is particularly so if there is no agreement that the creditor's formal demand for payment will be conclusive evidence that the sum indicated is due and payable.[29] In that case, a much higher degree of accuracy may be required in the calling-up notice, having regard to the exercise of such summary procedure by the creditor. In *Gardiner, Petitioner,*[30] Lady Paton indicated that a discrepancy between the words and figures in the calling-up notice may raise serious doubts about the validity of calling-up notices[31] noting "a high degree of accuracy is required where any party uses any form of diligence or summary measure".

Similarly, an error in the manner of execution of the calling-up notice may be fatal.[32] In *Elswick Bay Shipping Co Ltd v. Royal Bank of Scotland plc*,[33] a notice preliminary to the appointment of a receiver required to be signed by one of five specified officials of the creditor. It was instead signed by a senior official of the creditor who was not one of those specified. The court held that the notice was rendered invalid and the deed appointing the receiver fell to be reduced.[34]

---

[26] *per* Lord Penrose at p.363C—E.

[27] Halliday, *Conveyancing,* para. 54–07.

[28] Cusine, *op. cit.*, para. 8–03 citing s.53(1) of the 1970 Act which states "nothing in this Act shall preclude the inclusion of any additional matter which the person . . . giving the notice . . . may consider relevant".

[29] *Gardiner, petr,* 2001 G.W.D. 38–1433, where Lady Paton in the Outer House expressly contrasted the contractual documentation there with the documentation normally seen with bank loans (as had been the case in *Marshall* and *Shanks, supra* nos 18 and 22) which allows the bank to conclusively determine the sum owing. Although the decision was reversed by the Inner House (see *infra* no. 48), it is submitted that this aspect of the decision remains valid. Cusine, *Standard Securities*, para. 8–05 describes the provision of such a certificate in security documentation as "almost universal practice". See also *Clydesdale Bank plc v. Adamson,* 2001 G.W.D. 27–1082 where the security had such provisions and a calling-up notice and Schedule 7 certificate (see para. 2.4.1) had been lodged in process and not challenged. The debtor argued that the creditor had failed to prove a debt was due by not having a witness speak to the terms of the calling-up notice and certificate but Sheriff Morris Q.C. found the notice to be conclusive evidence of its contents.

[30] 2001 G.W.D. 38–1433.

[31] Although the decision was successfully reclaimed, the Extra Division did not disapprove this aspect of the judgment.

[32] There is a rebuttable presumption that the officer of the creditor who signs the certificate has authority to do so: *Clydesdale Bank plc v. Mowbray,* 1988 G.W.D. 23–987.

[33] 1982 S.L.T. 62.

[34] Errors in the designation of the party on whom the notice is sought to be served may also be fatal: para. 4.2.29.

What can be done about a Calling-up Notice?

2.2.6 Even before the passing of the 2001 Act, it was possible for the debtor to challenge a calling-up notice under section 19(9) of the 1970 Act which states:

> "Where a creditor in a standard security has indicated in a calling-up notice that any sum and any interest thereon due under the contract may be subject to adjustment in amount, he shall, if the person on whom notice has been served so requests, furnish the debtor[35] with a statement of the amount as finally determined within a period of one month from the date of service of the calling-up notice,[36] and a failure by the creditor to comply with the provisions of this subsection shall cause the calling-up notice to be of no effect."[37]

This provision was tested before the courts in *Bank of Scotland v. Flett*,[38] where debtor had written to the creditor by letter 15 days after her receipt of a calling-up notice. The letter had been written in the context of an imminent proof in her divorce action. She intended to conduct the proof herself and asked the creditor to send her "an updated account of all outstanding monies relating to the above accounts at your earliest convenience as I shall require these details for the proof". The letter was not written to the creditor's legal department which had served the notice but to their residential mortgages department. It made no reference to the calling-up notice.[39] Sheriff Principal Nicholson[40] held it essential that any request for information under section 19(9) had to make it clear that it was a request under such subsection.[41] Otherwise, as in that case, the request would not fall to be classed as a section 19(9) request.[42]

---

[35] It is the debtor rather than the person requesting who is to receive the statement but it has been suggested that the prudent creditor will provide the statement to everyone who received the notice: Halliday, *Conveyancing*, para. 54–15. However, disclosure of financial information other than by requirement of law may cause difficulties for the creditor under the Data Protection Act 1998 (c.29). That Act is considered further at para. 4.2.27.

[36] It is a curious and unsatisfactory feature of s.19(9) that the time limit for compliance by the creditor runs from the date of the calling-up notice, not from the date of the request by the debtor. In theory, a debtor could make a request immediately before the expiry of the creditor's time limit. This possibility formed part of the basis for the decision in *Flett*, *infra* no. 38. It has been suggested that to counter this possibility, the creditor should prepare the s.19(9) statement in advance so that it may be handed over immediately if a request is made: Halliday, *Conveyancing*, para. 54–15. But in practice creditors with large books are unlikely to add to administration on many accounts when the incidence of such requests is extremely low.

[37] The importance of s.19(9) should not be overstated. Even if a creditor fails to comply with a request under the subsection, rendering that calling-up notice invalid, the creditor can then serve a further calling-up notice: *Flett* at p.594.

[38] 1995 S.C.L.R. 591.

[39] The letter also referred to another account number for a different property.

[40] at Edinburgh.

[41] Because of the prejudice the creditor will suffer if he fails to provide the specified information.

[42] As a result, there was no default by the creditor for failing to respond (in fact, it denied having received the letter) and decree was granted in its favour.

Similarly in *Clydesdale Bank plc v. Mowbray*,[43] a letter by the debtor calling for "amendment/adjustment of the sum . . . claimed" was held by the Inner House to be incapable of construction as a request under section 19(9). Further, if the terms of the agreement are such that the creditor may conclusively certify the amount due[44] and such a certificate is annexed to the calling-up notice, the debtor is disabled from relying on section 19(9).

Finally, section 19(9) was considered in *Hewit v. Williamson*.[45] In that case, a creditor brought an action against a debtor to determine the extent of the sums secured by a standard security. It was argued by the debtor, *inter alia*, that the sum which could be claimed under the security was restricted by the sum mentioned in the calling-up notice and it was too late to raise in this action the question of what debts were secured. Lord MacFadyen held the effect of section 19(9) to be that

> "[i]f a statement is provided, that fixes the amount which the debtor must pay to avoid default. If, however, the debtor does not request a statement, and fails to comply with the calling-up notice . . . I see no reason for construing Section 19(9) as having the effect of fixing the sum covered by the standard security."

Although the 2001 Act provides additional remedies for debtors and others on service of a calling-up notice,[46] it does not detract from the recipient's rights to challenge the amount stated as due under the calling-up notice in accordance with section 19(9).

Suspension of Calling-up Notice

A petition for suspension of the calling-up notice[47] may be the appropriate remedy for an aggrieved debtor to take in circumstances where there is genuine dispute as to the existence of the debt.[48] Such a genuine dispute will not include the situation where the contractual documentation allows the creditor to state conclusively what is owing by the debtor. The remedy of suspension therefore operates as a safeguard against the use of a summary procedure by a creditor to circumvent court proceedings in circumstances where the court might take a different view as to the creditor's entitlement. The granting or refusal of interim suspension

2.2.7

---

[43] 1988 G.W.D. 23–987.
[44] For further discussion of such certificates, see *supra*, no. 29.
[45] 1999 S.L.T. 313.
[46] See Chap. 4.
[47] Court of Session Act 1988 (c.36), s.47.
[48] *Gardiner, supra*, no. 29; but note that disputes as to the extent of the debt, where it is not suggested that no sum at all is due, will not suffice of themselves to preclude enforcement based on the calling-up notice. The contrary was implied by the decision at first instance but this aspect of the judgment was overturned by the Extra Division in a decision reported at 2002 G.W.D. 5–167. The Inner House, commenting on the petitioner's case, noted "[n]owhere in their pleadings was there any averment to the effect that no sum was due at the date of the issue of the calling-up notice". Accordingly, if it was not the case that no sum was due under the calling-up notice, then the debtor was in default by failure to comply with the notice and the creditor was entitled to rely on it. As a result, suspension was recalled.

is a matter for the discretion of the court but thereafter a proof on the merits may be necessary.[49] It is not a valid ground for suspension that professional agents appointed by the creditor to advise it are not independent.[50] Suspension is not a means to circumvent an unsuccessful appeal or application for legal aid by the debtor.[51] Suspension of a calling-up notice appears to be competent even after the two month period specified in the notice has expired.[52]

Expenses of Calling-up Procedure

2.2.8 The creditor is entitled to the expenses of the calling-up procedure under section 19 by virtue of standard condition 12 which expressly provides that the debtor is liable for "all expenses reasonably incurred by the creditor in calling-up the security".

Application for Suspension of the Creditor's Rights

2.2.9 The 2001 Act allows certain identified parties to apply to the sheriff court for suspension of the creditors' rights based on a calling-up notice. The permitted applicants, procedure for and determination of such an application are all considered below.[53]

Court Action in Relation to Calling-up Notice

2.2.10 If the debtor remains in the subjects and refuses to leave voluntarily, the creditor will require to raise a court action for ejection in order to be able to exercise his existing right of sale.[54] Although it is not strictly necessary for the exercise of his powers, a creditor may also consider it convenient to obtain a declarator from the court that the debtor is indeed in default[55] as this may make it easier to deal with tenants or prospective purchasers at a later stage. In the interim between the expiry of a calling-up notice and the debtor being ejected, it appears competent

---

[49] On the procedure for suspensions, see Jamieson, *Summary Applications and Suspensions* (2000), Chaps 27–29.

[50] *Grantly Developments v. Clydesdale Bank plc*, 2000 G.W.D. 6–213, where the court also rejected the argument that a creditor has an implied duty to do nothing that would prejudice the debtor's ability to meet his obligations under the agreement between creditor and debtor. Similarly, in a repossession context, the Court of Appeal in England rejected a defence that variation of the interest rate by the creditor worked to the detriment of the debtor, though a creditor is still under some duty to act reasonably: *Nash and Staunton v. Paragon Finance plc* [2002] 2 All E.R. 248.

[51] *Wilson v. Skipton Building Society*, 1995 G.W.D. 37–1895.

[52] *Gardiner*, at first instance, *supra*, no. 29; an argument was advanced, based on *Sutherland v. Sutherland* (1843) 5D. 544, that suspension of a calling-up notice was analogous to suspension of a charge and that once the days specified in either document had expired, an application for suspension was too late. The court indicated that it did not regard *Sutherland* as entirely in point although there were other considerations in *Gardiner* including that the two month period may not have expired. This aspect of the case was not considered by the Inner House.

[53] See Chap. 4.

[54] In *Cedar Holdings Ltd v. Iyyaz*, 1989 S.C.L.R. 236, Sheriff Principal Caplan Q.C. described this as (p.238) requiring "to enlist the help of the court to put a remedy into effect".

[55] Within the meaning of standard condition 9(1)(a).

for a creditor to obtain a court order requiring the debtor to allow prospective purchasers to view the subjects.[56]

The craves which would normally be included in an action relating to a calling-up notice would be for declarator in terms of section 20 of the 1970 Act that the defender (the debtor) is in default within the meaning of standard condition 9(1)(a) of Schedule 3 to the 1970 Act; for warrant to sell, repair, enter into possession and exercise all other powers competent to the heritable creditor on default by the defender; to ordain the defender and others[57] to vacate the security subjects and to grant warrant to officers of court to summarily eject the defender and others from the security subjects; and for expenses. The nature of the action focusing as it does on confirmation of the right to exercise powers of the creditor, in the form of declarator and warrant, rather than on the question of what and if so how much is due by the debtor, has been criticised.[58]

The warrant for ejection stems not from the 1970 Act but from section 5 of the Heritable Securities (Scotland) Act 1894.[59] Standard condition 10(1) permits the exercise by the creditor of any remedy including those "arising from any other enactment." It is of interest that there are two legs to section 5 of the 1894 Act and they apply differently to court actions related to calling-up notices and actions based on section 24 of the 1970 Act.[60] In the case of an action related to a calling-up notice, the right to eject under section 5 arises where the debtor has failed "in due payment of the principal after formal requisition".[61] The source of the remedy of ejection is important as it has a bearing on the notices which require to be served to comply with the 2001 Act.[62]

---

[56] Halliday, *Conveyancing Opinions*, p.131.

[57] On the inclusion of the words "and others", see para. 6.2.

[58] See for example Gretton & Reid, *Conveyancing* (1993), para 20–28.

[59] (c.44), hereafter "the 1894 Act"; although he did not expressly mention the 1894 Act, in *Hill Samuel v. Haas*, 1989 S.C.L.R. 210, Sheriff Principal Caplan Q.C. confirmed (p.212) "the 1970 Act nowhere provides for a creditor applying to the court for remedies of declarator or ejection" finding that an application for such declarator and ejection is not an action under the 1970 Act; see also *Iyyaz, supra*, no. 54. This issue was of great importance at the time (see *infra* no. 63) for reasons now superseded but remains relevant to the operation of the 2001 Act.

[60] For discussion of s.5 of the 1894 Act as it applies to actions under s.24 of the 1970 Act, see para. 2.4.2.

[61] For further discussion of the source of the remedy of ejection generally, see Jamieson, "Creditors' Remedies under a Standard Security", 1989 S.L.T. (News) 201; Gretton & Reid, *Conveyancing*, *op. cit.*, para. 20.30; Halliday, *Conveyancing*, para. 54–64; Braid, "Remedies on Default", 1999 PQLE 208 at p.8; *Haas, supra; Iyyaz, supra*; but it has been suggested that the crave for ejection is based on common law: *Provincial Building Society v. Menzies*, 1984 S.L.T. (Sh.Ct) 81 at p.82; *Mountstar Metal Corporation Ltd v. Cameron*, 1987 S.L.T. (Sh.Ct) 106 at p.108E; or that ejection is an essential and inseparable part of the remedy of taking possession, such that the crave for ejection is truly based on s.24(1): *National & Provincial Building Society v. Riddell*, 1986 S.L.T. (Sh.Ct) 6 at p.9A, a view not followed by Sheriff Principal O'Brien in *Clydesdale Bank plc v. R. Findlay & Co.*, 1989 S.L.T. (Sh.Ct) 77 at p.80.

[62] See para. 4.2.22.

Procedural Considerations for Court Action

2.2.11 After much debate and confusion in the 1980s,[63] the Sheriff Court Ordinary Cause Rules now provide that an application under any of the following provisions of Part II of the 1970 Act is by way of initial writ as an ordinary cause, where any other remedy (such as ejection) is craved; section 18(2) (declarator that obligations under contract performed); section 20(3) (application by creditor for warrant to let security subjects); section 22(1) (objections to notice of default); section 22(3) (counter-application for remedies under the Act); section 24(1) (application by a creditor for warrant to exercise remedies on default); and section 28(1) (decree of foreclosure).[64] The current Ordinary Cause Rules fail to specify the position where no other remedy is craved but their immediate predecessor stipulated that such proceedings should be by way of a summary application[65] and it is submitted that remains the correct course.[66] Jurisdiction for court proceedings under Part II of the 1970 Act is governed by section 29 of the 1970 Act which provides "[t]he court for the purposes of this Part of this Act ... in relation to a standard security, shall be the sheriff having jurisdiction over any part of the security subjects, and the sheriff shall be deemed to have such jurisdiction whatever the value of the subjects". The decision of the sheriff disposing of an application to court under Part II of the 1970 Act is final and not subject to appeal except as to a question of title or as to any other remedy granted.[67]

These rules apply without any difficulty to an application for warrant for the exercise of powers by a creditor under section 24 of the 1970 Act[68] but the position is, regrettably, more complicated in relation to proceedings for declarator and ejection relating to an expired calling-up notice. Although such actions certainly relate to Part II of the 1970 Act, which after all regulates enforcement of standard securities, there is judicial authority that they are not actions under Part II[69] which takes them outwith the clarifying provisions of the Ordinary Cause Rules discussed above.[70] Nonetheless, the procedure for such actions is still properly by way of an ordinary action,[71] the Inner House having

---

[63] See for example the discussion by Jamieson, "Creditors' Remedies under a Standard Security", 1989 S.L.T. (News) 201.

[64] r.34.10(1) of Ordinary Cause Rules, being Sched. 1 to the Sheriff Courts (Scotland) Act 1907 (c.51) (as inserted by S.I. 1993 No. 1956).

[65] r.107A(1) of the Ordinary Cause Rules as inserted by Act of Sederunt (Amendment of Sheriff Court Ordinary Cause, Summary Cause, and Small Claim, Rules) 1990 (S.I. 1990 No. 661), which still applies to any proceedings commenced before January 1, 1994.

[66] Jamieson, *op. cit.*, para. 17–112.

[67] r.34.10(2) of the Ordinary Cause Rules and r.3.4.2 of the Summary Applications Rules. *Scott v. Hawkins*, unreported, December 19, 1984 where Sheriff Principal Caplan held that an interlocutor refusing to receive answers late and granting decree could not be appealed.

[68] See para. 2.4.2.

[69] See *supra*, no. 59; in any event, such proceedings certainly do not fall within the specific types of action under Pt II of the 1970 Act listed above.

[70] Unless an application by the creditor for warrant to let the subjects under s.20(3) is expressly included, though it is suggested that the type of action envisaged by this provision is an application to allow the creditor to lease the subjects for more than the seven years to which he is automatically entitled: see para. 7.5.2.

[71] Jamieson, *op. cit.*, p.202.

confirmed that where a calling-up notice has expired, a creditor may competently combine a crave for declarator in relation to the powers thereby acquired with a crave for ejection.[72] Jurisdiction for such actions finds its basis in the Civil Jurisdiction and Judgments Act 1982.[73] As a matter of practice, such actions are now frequently raised under ordinary cause procedure without difficulty.[74]

Although actions under the 1970 Act must be raised in the sheriff court, it is possible for proceedings to be remitted to the Court of Session, where there are related proceedings there, *ob congintentiam*.[75]

Can Such Actions be Defended?

As with any court action for repossession, an application for an order under the 2001 Act can be made to suspend the creditors' rights.[76] Such an application is not the same, of course, as a defence. If no such application is made, or if it is made and refused,[77] the possible defences to a court action for repossession related to an expired calling-up notice are limited. A defence based on a failure to comply by the creditor with an objection under section 19(9) is clearly valid.[78] Until recently, a question remained as to whether, if no such objection had been taken, the debtor could advance any defence in a later court action. **2.2.12**

This question was specifically answered in the recent case *Sykes (J) & Sons (Fish Merchants) Ltd v. Grieve*.[79] The creditor had served a calling-up notice on the debtor and no objection was taken. The creditor raised proceedings and sought summary decree of declarator of default,[80] and for warrant to enter possession and to sell the security subjects.[81] The debtor opposed claiming that the sum referred to in the calling-up notice was in fact owed by a third party[82] and that no money had ever been advanced to the debtor. The creditor argued that, by having failed to comply with or object to the calling-up notice, the debtor should not be entitled to maintain any defence. The sheriff declined to grant summary decree and on appeal, Sheriff Principal MacInnes Q.C. adhered to that decision. It was held that a debtor was entitled to await court proceedings before stating a defence such as advanced here.[83]

---

[72] *Clydesdale Bank v. Mowbray*, 1988 G.W.D. 23–978.

[73] (c.27), Sched. 4, para. 11(a)(I) (as inserted by the Civil Jurisdiction and Judgments Order 2001) (S.I. 2001 No. 3929, effective March 1, 2002).

[74] See for example *Sykes*, *infra* no. 79.

[75] On account of the connection between them, as in *Royal Bank of Scotland plc v. Shanks*, 1998 S.L.T. 355.

[76] See Chap. 4.

[77] Or granted but later revoked.

[78] See para. 2.2.6.

[79] 2002 S.L.T. (Sh.Ct) 15.

[80] Within the meaning of standard condition 9(1)(a).

[81] Although the powers for which warrant was sought were in fact already available, a calling-up notice having expired: s.20(1).

[82] A company with a connection to the debtor.

[83] The Sheriff Principal stated (p.17L—18A): "There is no statutory provision nor judicial authority of which I am aware which requires a debtor to seek judicial interruption of the default procedure in respect of a standard security as a prerequisite of stating a defence to an action such as this. In my opinion a debtor in a standard security is entitled to await an action such as this before stating a defence such as the defence which is stated in this case."

Accordingly, the legislation does not work in such a way as to prohibit a debtor from advancing defences that, for example, the sum had been repaid or no money had ever been advanced, simply because a calling-up notice has not been objected to.[84] It must be correct that a defence which goes to the very heart of the issue, namely whether there is an outstanding secured debt due by the debtor, remains capable of being raised. Such a course is not without its dangers for the aggrieved party, however, by reason of the fact that the creditor is entitled to exercise his powers in terms of section 20 where a calling-up notice has not been complied with. It is not therefore strictly necessary for the creditor to raise an action of the type discussed in *Sykes*. Without the forum of such a court action to advance his position, a debtor might then be thrown back on the remedy of suspension.[85] Nonetheless, if court action is raised by the creditor, defences in relation to the existence of the debt or the validity of the security may still be advanced after the period of notice in a calling-up notice has expired.

Advantages and Disadvantages of Calling-up Notice

2.2.13 Naturally, whether one method is advantageous or not depends on whether one is the creditor or the debtor. As the creditor is the enforcing party, the matter is looked at from that perspective. The advantages for the creditor include a limitation on the defences available to the debtor whose only option in many cases (at least before the 2001 Act) was to pay the whole sum outstanding; even under the new law, the issuing of a calling-up notice may improve the creditor's position in consideration of an application under the 2001 Act as a formal two month period of notice will have been given to the debtor[86]; service of the notice may highlight the disappearance of the debtor at an advanced stage; and in the right circumstances, the property may be taken into possession on the strength of an expired calling-up notice and sold.[87]

Disadvantages for the creditor include a further two months delay in obtaining repossession if the debtor is not prepared to co-operate; under the 2001 Act, service of a calling-up notice may expose the creditor to a longer period within which the debtor can make an application for an order suspending the creditor's rights,[88] to the risk of a summary application against him[89] and to the possibility of the calling-up notice being set aside altogether[90]; service of the calling-up notice does not avoid the need for a court action to eject the debtor if he will not co-operate; and, for public relations reasons, creditors may try to avoid relying on calling-up notices because it highlights the reality that they can seek recovery of a heritably secured property at any time, even if the debtor is not in arrears.

---

[84] The wording of the judgment suggests that a defence challenging the amount of the debt, rather than its existence or the identity of the correct debtor, might not be stateable at this stage, reinforcing the importance of a timeous challenge under s.19(9) if the amount is at issue.
[85] See para. 2.2.7.
[86] See Chap. 4.
[87] See para. 2.7.1.
[88] See para. 4.2.9.
[89] See para. 4.2.8.
[90] See para. 4.2.18.

Summary

The most complete answer to a calling-up notice is to comply with its terms and pay the whole loan balance within two months. Assuming this is not possible, the debtor who disagrees with the amount stated on a calling-up notice should object to it under section 19(9) or he may find it difficult to challenge the level of debt later. However, other potential lines of defence, such as that the security was entirely invalid, that the sums were advanced to another party or that full payment had been made, could still lie in a later court action. In contrast to the limited defences available, the debtor and other identified parties have wide rights under the 2001 Act to seek suspension of the creditor's rights arising from a calling-up notice. 2.2.14

Notice of Default

Where the debtor has failed to comply with any requirement arising out of the security, he is held to be in default. In these circumstances, the creditor may use the second method of enforcement open to him by the service of a notice of default, which calls on the debtor and proprietor to purge the default.[91] Service of the notice in these circumstances is without prejudice to any other powers the creditor has and so it is open to the creditor to serve a calling-up notice instead of or in addition to the notice of default if he chooses.[92] 2.3

Nature of Default

"Default" in this context covers any default apart from failure to comply with a calling-up notice[93], provided that the default is "remediable".[94] If it is not, service of a notice of default is incompetent.[95] The procedure for service of a notice of default applies regardless of whether the default is monetary or not. For example, failure by the debtor to comply with any one of the conditions of the standard security[96] will entitle creditor under the 1970 Act to "perform any obligation imposed by the standard conditions on the debtor which the debtor has failed to perform".[97] The 2.3.1

---

[91] The format of the notice is considered at para. 2.3.2.

[92] s.21(1) and *Bank of Scotland v. Millward*, 1999 S.L.T. 901. See para. 2.7. Failure to comply with a calling-up notice is also a default but of a different type: see para. 2.2.4.

[93] *United Dominions Trust Ltd v. Site Preparations Ltd (No.2)*, 1978 S.L.T. (Sh.Ct) 21.

[94] s.21(1).

[95] In which case, the creditor must use one of the other two routes of enforcement. Payment of monetary arrears will always be remediable but that does not necessarily follow for all of the debtor's non-monetary obligations. For example, the obligation in standard condition 6 that the debtor must not let the security subjects without the prior consent in writing of the creditor is an obligation which the debtor, once he has breached it, cannot remedy as he cannot go back in time to obtain the creditor's consent. Of course there may be practical steps he can take to appease the creditor such as by trying to come to an arrangement that sees his tenant leave the subjects. Nonetheless, the wording suggests that service of a notice of default would be incompetent. A similar example of non-remediable default in relation to the requirements in relation to planning notices incumbent on the debtor in terms of standard condition 4 is provided in Halliday, *Conveyancing*, para. 54–21.

[96] Which are likely to be based on the standard conditions laid down by the 1970 Act. The standard conditions are repeated in the Appendix at paras 13.1 *et seq*.

[97] Standard condition 7.

correct procedure for a creditor wishing to enforce in these circumstances is to serve a notice of default.[98] While this applies to all conditions of the loan, such as keeping the property in good repair, insuring the property and so on, most commonly what goes wrong is the payment of the loan, resulting in arrears.

It has been argued that a failure to pay interest and/or capital is not a default at all, having regard to the wording of standard condition 9 which states "(1) The debtor shall be held to be in default ... (b) where there has been a failure to comply with any other requirement arising out of the security". In *United Dominions Trust Ltd v. Site Preparations Ltd (No.2)*,[99] the defender argued that the liability to pay interest and capital arose not out of "the security" but from the existence of the debt. The word "security" was contrasted with the term "standard security" used elsewhere in the 1970 Act to found an argument that the right created was different from the deed embodying the right. As a result, it was argued, a failure to pay interest and capital did not fall within standard condition 9(1)(b). While describing this as "an ingenious argument", Sheriff Henderson[1] rejected it holding that the condition "appears to cover any default apart from failure to comply with a calling-up notice. Payment of interest and capital seem to me to be of the essence of a heritable security".[2]

Content of Notice of Default

2.3.2 Where the creditor wishes to call on the debtor to purge the default, the notice of default he serves must be in accordance with Form B of Schedule 6 to the 1970 Act.[3] The key provisions of the notice are:

(a) That the creditor requires the default, as clearly specified, to be rectified within one month of service;

(b) That failing rectification the creditor will be entitled to exercise certain powers competent to him; and

(c) An explanatory note (added by the 2001 Act) which informs recipients of their ability to make applications under the 2001 Act.

Service of the Notice of Default

2.3.3 The rules in relation to service of notices, including the method of service and the persons on whom they should be served, are substantially changed by the 2001 Act and are considered below.[4]

Restriction of Period of Notice

2.3.4 The one month period of notice could formerly be restricted or waived but this is prohibited by the 2001 Act. The matter is dealt with in more detail below.[5]

---

[98] Subject to the comments at *supra*, no. 95.
[99] 1978 S.L.T. (Sh.Ct) 21.
[1] at Alloa.
[2] p.23.
[3] Repeated in full in the Appendix at para. 13.15.
[4] See para. 4.2.21.
[5] See para. 4.2.9.

Failure to Comply with Notice of Default

2.3.5 It is the duty of the debtor to comply with any requirement, due to be performed or fulfilled by him, contained in the notice of default.[6] The debtor may of course comply with his duty and purge the default by remedying it within the specified timescale. If that does not happen, the creditor is entitled to exercise such of his rights under standard conditions 10(2), (6) and (7) as he considers appropriate,[7] namely sale,[8] carrying out repairs and other works[9] and foreclosure.[10] These may be exercised without further procedure though as a matter of practicality, it may be necessary to raise court proceedings to allow the rights to be enforced. For example, while the creditor is entitled to exercise the power of sale where a debtor has not complied with the requirements in a notice of default, if the debtor does not co-operate, warrant will be required from the court to secure to the creditor certain other rights, such as entering into possession[11] or ejection of the debtor, which may be required as a matter of practicality for sale to take place.

The notice of default ceases to have effect after five years from its date.[12] However, a notice of default will remain effective during the relevant five year period even if the creditor does not immediately exercise rights such as where, for example, an arrangement is entered into with the debtor. If the debtor fails to adhere and the default remains, the creditor may rely on the existing notice of default.

The Accuracy of the Notice

2.3.6 As with calling-up notices, defects in the notice of default must be avoided to ensure that there is no question as to its validity.[13] Provided there is no inaccuracy and that the terms of the notice remain clear, it is possible to depart from the statutory style by including additional matters in the notice.[14]

What can be done about a Notice of Default?

2.3.7 Even before the passing of the 2001 Act, it was possible for the debtor to object to a notice of default. Section 22 of the 1970 Act provides that where a person on whom a notice of default has been served considers himself aggrieved by any requirement of that notice he may—within a

---

[6] Unless the notice has been set aside by the court: s.23(1); this may be the original notice or the notice as varied by the court under s.22: see para. 2.3.7.

[7] s.23(2).

[8] See Chap. 8.

[9] See para. 7.5.3.

[10] See para. 7.5.4. Sheriff Cusine has recommended that the law should be changed to allow a creditor proceeding by notice of default to exercise all of the powers in standard condition 10, though he also suggests the period of notice in a notice of default should be extended to two months: Cusine, "The Creditor's Remedies under a Standard Security" 1998 S.L.P.Q. 79.

[11] *Bank of Scotland v. Fernand*; and see para. 2.7.1.

[12] s.21(4).

[13] See para. 2.2.5 in relation to calling-up notices. It is submitted the provisions in relation to accuracy in the notice stated there apply equally to notices of default.

[14] Cusine, *op. cit.*, para. 8.13 referring to s.53(1) of the 1970 Act.

period of 14 days of the service of the notice—object to it by application to the court.[15] The application must be by way of summary application.[16]

This procedure is very rarely used but provides a method for a debtor to prevent a creditor pursuing remedies on the strength of the notice when the existence of the default is in dispute.[17] While the 2001 Act provides additional remedies to the debtor served with a notice of default, it does not in any way detract from the debtor's ability to proceed under section 22. A copy of the application must be served on the creditor and on anyone else on whom the notice has been served by the creditor before or when the application is lodged.[18]

After hearing the parties and making such inquiry as it may think fit, the court may order the notice appealed against to be set aside, in whole or in part, or otherwise to be varied, or to be upheld.[19] With a view to avoiding unnecessary delay, it is also open to the creditor on receipt of such an application to make a counter-application craving for any of the remedies conferred on him by the 1970 Act or by other legislation.[20] Again such application must be by way of summary application.[21] The creditor may lodge in court in these circumstances a certificate specifying the nature of the default which is *prima facie* evidence of the facts required to be stated in it.[22] The court is granted wide discretion to grant whatever remedy it thinks proper in relation to the section 22 application and any counter-application by the creditor.[23]

---

[15] s.22(1).

[16] Unless any other remedy is craved in which case the application must be by way of initial writ: r.34.10(1)(c) of Ordinary Cause Rules.

[17] It is perhaps more straightforward to understand how there could be a dispute as to the existence of a default if a non-monetary obligation is considered. The creditor could have served a notice of default based on a failure by the debtor to maintain the subjects as required by standard condition 1. As that provision judges the failure according to "the reasonable satisfaction of the creditor", the debtor might argue that the creditor's adopted stance is unreasonable. It is possible, though, that the section could be invoked in a monetary context where a debtor has several accounts or assets with a creditor and they have been transferred *inter se* in terms of security documentation with which the debtor might not be familiar or where the terms are ambiguous.

[18] s.22(1); this provision is unqualified but it might be that the debtor would be unaware of the identity of (all) those on whom the creditor had served the notice. As the provision is mandatory and there is no qualification, the sheriff would require the debtor to start again if he had failed to comply with its terms, but by that time the 14 day period might have expired making this impossible. Gordon, *Scottish Land Law* (2nd ed., 1999) para. 20-177, suggests that a creditor could not object to a service omission based on his own failure to inform the debtor of the parties on whom to serve it but the matter may be one of fundamental incompetency, of which the Court might take notice *ex proprio motu*, notwithstanding the creditor's attitude.

[19] s.22(2).

[20] s.22(3); this has the bizarre result that the creditor may obtain warrant to exercise his remedies under s.24 more quickly than if the debtor had not objected in the first place, a fact which does not sit very well with the intended protection of the debtor afforded by s.22. The provision may have been intended to deter vexatious applications by debtors.

[21] Unless any other remedy is craved in which case the application must be by way of initial writ: r.34.10(1)(d) of Ordinary Cause Rules.

[22] s.22(4); the certificate is in the same format as that discussed at para. 2.4.1.

[23] s.22(3).

Suspension of Notice of Default

2.3.8 As with calling-up notices, it is open to a debtor to seek suspension of the notice of default if there is genuine dispute as to the existence of the debt.[24] The discussion of the law on suspension of calling-up notices may be extended to notices of default.[25]

Expenses of Notice of Default Procedure

2.3.9 The creditor is entitled to recover the expenses of notice of default procedure on a proper reading of section 21 and standard condition 12 of the 1970 Act. The latter permits recovery of "all expenses reasonably incurred by the creditor in ... exercising any other powers conferred upon him by the security". Section 21 provides that a notice of default may be served "without prejudice to any other powers", supporting the view that service of a notice of default is a power within the meaning of standard condition 12.[26]

Application Under the 2001 Act

2.3.10 The 2001 Act allows certain identified parties to apply to the court for suspension of the creditor's rights based on a notice of default. The permitted applicants, procedure and determination of such an application are all considered below.[27]

Court Action Based on a Notice of Default

2.3.11 If the debtor remains in the subjects and refuses to leave voluntarily, the creditor will require to raise a court action in order to be able to exercise his right of sale. Such an action is based on section 24 of the 1970 Act. The procedural considerations for and possible defences to such an action are examined below.[28]

Advantages and Disadvantages of Notice of Default

2.3.12 As with calling-up notices, these are considered from the creditor's viewpoint. Advantages for the creditor include the possibility of setting up *prima facie* evidence of the default[29] if the notice is not objected to; that it is quicker than a calling-up notice; that the creditor may rely on the provision of an additional month's notice in the determination of an application for suspension of the creditor's rights under the 2001 Act; and that service of the notice may highlight the disappearance of the debtor at a relatively early stage.

---

[24] *Gardiner*, 2001 G.W.D. 38–1433.
[25] See para. 2.2.7.
[26] Cusine, "Expenses under a Standard Security", 1994 *Juridical Review* 18 at p.24.
[27] See Chap. 4.
[28] See para. 2.4.2.
[29] In Halliday, *Conveyancing*, para. 54–37 it is suggested that the service of an unchallenged notice of default "is more than merely *prima facie* evidence of default" but no authority is given for the proposition. While such service undoubtedly assists the creditor in a s.24 court action, the earlier service of the notice is not conclusive evidence of default by itself.

Disadvantages include the ability of the debtor to apply to the court against the procedure; that it is slower than simply proceeding straight to court by a section 24 action; that by itself, a notice of default never gives a creditor the right to enter into possession; that service of a notice of default may actually extend the period within which an application under the 2001 Act may be made and may expose the creditor to a summary application against him; that if the arrears are paid off, the default is usually considered purged and if arrears then reoccur, the creditor will require to start again; and that the debtor may redeem the security without notice of his intention to do so (compared to the two months notice required under other forms of enforcement) which, while usually welcome and at most a minor disadvantage, may cause inconvenience in certain respects.[30]

Summary

2.3.13 The debtor who considers himself aggrieved by a notice of default should object to it by application to the court under section 22 or he may find it more difficult to challenge later.[31] However, an uncooperative debtor cannot be ejected simply on the strength of a notice of default and it is open to him to remain in the security subjects (subject to any other action being taken by the creditor) while a court action is resolved. The debtor and other identified parties have wide rights under the 2001 Act to seek suspension of the creditor's rights arising from a notice of default, either following service of the notice or following the raising of court proceedings based on such a notice.

Section 24 Action

2.4 The third method of enforcement open to the creditor is to raise and serve a section 24 action, so called because it is founded on section 24 of the 1970 Act which provides:

"(1) Without prejudice to his proceeding by way of notice of default in respect of a default within the meaning of standard condition 9(1)(b), a creditor in a standard security, where the debtor is in default within the meaning of that standard condition or standard condition 9(1)(c)[32] may apply to the court for warrant to exercise any of the remedies which he is entitled to exercise on a default within the meaning of standard condition 9(1)(a)."

Although an action based on an expired notice of default is also based on the same section of the 1970 Act,[33] the method of enforcement considered here may be based on the simple fact of the default rather than on an expired notice of default.[34] The default may be either of the

---

[30] See s.23(3) and para. 6.4 for further discussion.
[31] In addition to relying on the absence of a challenge under s.22, the creditor may lodge in court a certificate as *prima facie* evidence of the fact of default (within the meaning of standard condition 9(1)(b)) in terms of s.24; see para. 2.4.1.
[32] On which see para. 2.7.2.
[33] s.24.
[34] For a practical example of the importance of this distinction, see Halliday, *Conveyancing Opinions*, p.318; for the avoidance of doubt, the action may also be based on an expired notice of default.

same type as led to the service of a notice of default, if any,[35] or may be related to the insolvency of the proprietor of the security subjects.[36] The action seeks the same remedies as are open to the creditor following expiry of a calling-up notice, including the power of sale.

Proof of Default

Section 24(2) provides that in a section 24 action,[37] a certificate which conforms with the requirements of Schedule 7 to the 1970 Act may be lodged in court by the creditor, and that certificate is *prima facie* evidence[38] of the facts in the Schedule. The Schedule is repeated in the Appendix[39] but, in brief, requires the creditor to specify his name and address, the details of the standard security and full details of the nature of the default, failing which it will not be received as evidence.

2.4.1

Procedural Considerations for a Section 24 Action

The proceedings are normally by way of ordinary cause, there are limited rights of appeal and the sheriff court where the subjects are situated has jurisdiction.[40] An action based on section 24, whether founding on an expired notice of default or simply the fact of default, will include the following craves; for declarator that the defender (the debtor) is in default under condition 9(1)(b) of the standard conditions in Schedule 3 to the 1970 Act[41]; for warrant under section 24 of the 1970 Act for the pursuer to sell, repair, enter into possession and exercise all other powers competent to the heritable creditor in possession; to ordain the defender, the defender's family and others[42] to vacate the subjects and to grant warrant to officers of court to summarily eject the defender; and for expenses. If the action is based on an expired notice of default, that will be narrated in the condescendence of the writ.

2.4.2

As with court actions related to calling-up notices, the warrant for ejection stems from section 5 of the Heritable Securities (Scotland) Act 1894.[43] In the case of court actions based on section 24, however, the relevant part of section 5 is a failure by the debtor to pay "the interest due under the security". The other part of section 5 relates only to a failure to pay principal which is less likely to apply in a section 24 context. While failure to pay interest is by far the most common reason for a section 24 application, problems may arise where the default under standard condition 9(1)(b) is a non-monetary one.[44] In that situation, the

---

[35] That is default within the meaning of standard condition 9(1)(b).
[36] Standard condition 9(1)(c): see para. 2.7.2.
[37] Where the default is within the meaning of standard condition 9(1)(b).
[38] In *Clydesdale Bank plc v. Adamson*, 2001 G.W.D. 27–1082, Sheriff Morris Q.C. at Airdrie indicated that a failure to suggest that the sums certified were not due and the absence of a defence to the action by one of the debtors implied that a debt existed.
[39] See paras 13.18–13.20.
[40] See para. 2.2.11. This is the practical position in almost all such actions now but if no other remedy is craved, such as ejection of the debtor, then the position is uncertain but probably by way of summary application.
[41] Or, alternatively, declarator in terms of standard condition 9(1)(c), which is less common: see para. 2.7.2.
[42] On use of the words "and others", see para. 6.2.
[43] See para. 2.2.10.
[44] As in *Bank of Scotland v. Fernand*, 1997 S.L.T. (Sh.Ct) 78, where the debtor had failed to maintain the garden and failed to insure the premises.

creditor will certainly be entitled to apply for declarator under section 24 that he is entitled to his remedies but he may not be entitled to have the debtor ejected which, of course, may give rise to difficulties in the practical exercise of certain remedies, such as sale.[44a] The source of the remedy of ejection also raises questions in relation to the correct service of notices under the 2001 Act.[45]

Expenses of Undefended Section 24 Action

2.4.3 As with any ordinary action, the creditor is entitled to judicial expenses. Consideration of the recoverability from the debtor of the difference between judicial expenses and those costs actually incurred (which is perhaps more common and certainly more significant in relation to defended actions) is dealt with below.[46]

Applications under the 2001 Act

2.4.4 The 2001 Act allows certain identified parties to apply to the court for suspension of the creditors' rights based on a section 24 action. The permitted applicants, procedure and determination of such an application are all considered below.[47]

Defence of Section 24 Action

2.4.5 It is certainly possible for a debtor to defend a section 24 action by the creditor, whether based on an expired notice of default or not. The defence may be to dispute the existence of any default or to question the validity of any notice served.[48] However, if the debtor has failed to respond to a notice of default,[49] a presumption may be raised that the creditor is correct to assert a default within the meaning of standard condition 9(1)(b). It will also be possible to contest the action with defences based on the existence of the debt itself or the validity of the security.[50] However, the right to enter into possession is clear and an objection to a crave for ejection where the debtor is admitted to be in monetary default is unstateable.[51] It was not possible to successfully defend an action on the basis that the court had discretion on whether or not to allow the creditor to proceed until the passing of the 2001 Act.[52]

Advantages and Disadvantages of Section 24 Action

2.4.6 Once again, these are viewed from the creditor's perspective. Advantages for the creditor include that it is the quickest method of enforcement; that it keeps the period within which an application under the

---

[44a] *Clydesdale Bank plc. v. R. Findlay & Co.*, 1989 S.L.T. (Sh.Ct) 77.
[45] See para. 4.2.22.
[46] See para. 5.17.
[47] See Chap. 4.
[48] Though note that even if the notice is defective, the creditor may still succeed in an action based on the fact of default in terms of s.24 of the 1970 Act: see para. 2.4.
[49] Under s.22.
[50] As with calling-up notices: *Sykes (J) & Sons (Fish Merchants) Ltd v. Grieve*, 2002 S.L.T. (Sh.Ct) 15.
[51] *Clydesdale Bank plc v. Mowbray*, 1988 G.W.D. 23–987; *Clydesdale Bank plc v. Mowbray*, 1989 G.W.D. 27–1212.
[52] *Halifax Building Society v. Gupta*, 1994 S.L.T. 339, considered in detail at para. 4.2.2.

2001 Act may be made to a minimum (unless the action is defended); and that all remedies available to the creditor under the 1970 Act remain open, should the court grant decree.

Disadvantages for the creditor are that it is slightly more likely to be defended than an action related to an expired calling-up notice or notice of default as the creditor cannot rely on presumptions created by such expired notices; and that, because it is quicker, an application for suspension of the creditor's rights under the 2001 Act may be more likely to be granted.

Consumer Credit Cases

A substantial number of secured loans, particularly granted by postponed security holders, are governed by the Consumer Credit Act 1974.[53] The object of such regulation is to provide consumer protection in circumstances where debtors may be more liable to expose themselves or be exposed to debt which they are unable to maintain. As the risk to the creditor is normally greater when taking a postponed security, so the interest rate on the loan advanced tends to be higher. The loans which fall within the ambit of the 1974 Act are those where the credit does not exceed 25,000[54] and where none of the exemptions from the 1974 Act apply. These exemptions can be significant. For example, loans by building societies and local authorities as creditor are largely exempt.[55]

The effect of the 1974 Act on repossessions falling within its regulation is fivefold. First, as with any loan regulated by the 1974 Act, any failure to comply with its terms on the constitution of the agreement may preclude the creditor from enforcing.[56] Secondly, an additional preliminary step must be taken when the creditor seeks to take action. Specifically, no matter which route of enforcement is chosen, a default notice under the 1974 Act[57] must also be served and should expire before any such further enforcement action.[58] Next, the creditor cannot proceed to sell where he might otherwise have done so[59] without a court order for exercise of his remedies.[60] There may be additional considerations in

2.5

---

[53] (c.39), hereafter referred to as "the 1974 Act"; as the 1974 Act obviously post-dates the 1970 Act, which provides for mandatory use of the standard security from its coming into effect (see para. 1.2), it is appropriate to consider its terms within this chapter, rather than that applying to the forms of security available for loans made before the 1970 Act.

[54] The Consumer Credit (Increase of Monetary Limits) Order 1983 (S.I. 1983 No. 1878) as amended by The Consumer Credit (Increase of Monetary Limits) (Amendment) Order (S.I. 1998 No. 996) but note that the European Commission has issued a consultation paper on the amendment of Directive 87/102/EEC which *inter alia* proposes that all thresholds and ceilings be removed.

[55] s.16 of the 1974 Act. A full list of the exemptions is beyond the scope of this work but may be found in s.16 and the Consumer Credit (Exempt Agreements) Order (S.I. 1989 No. 869).

[56] s.127 of the 1974 Act.

[57] Under ss. 87 and 88 of the 1974 Act; the default notice should not be confused with the notice of default under s.21 of the 1970 Act.

[58] Which will take at least seven days from the date of service of the notice: s.88 of the 1974 Act.

[59] For example on an expired calling-up notice.

[60] s.126 of the 1974 Act. If the creditor attempted to do so, the debtor would be entitled to interdict the sale: s.170(3). The creditor may not contract out of this provision: s.173 of the 1974 Act.

relation to redemption.[61] Finally, two additional means of challenging proceedings are available to debtors by virtue of the 1974 Act. The court, if it considers it just, may make an order under that Act suspending an order for possession until such time as the court directs or until the occurrence of a specified act or omission.[62] Alternatively, a time order[63] may be made allowing repayment by installments at such times as the court considers just and reasonable given the means of the debtor.[64] Although the Act refers expressly only to the position of the debtor, there is Court of Appeal authority that the requirement to act justly and reasonably entitles the court to also consider the position of the creditor.[65]

The first Scottish case to deal with this crossover between the 1970 Act and the 1974 Act confirms that debtors may invoke the 1974 Act, where it applies, to afford additional protection against creditors proceeding under the 1970 Act. In *Murie McDougall Ltd v. Sinclair*,[66] both a default notice[67] and a notice of default[68] had been served on the debtor separately and without objection being taken to either. Nonetheless, when the creditor raised a repossession action based on the notice of default, the debtor lodged an application with the court under section 129 of the 1974 Act seeking a time order to reduce the monthly payments. The creditor argued that such an application was incompetent as the debtor had failed to object to the notice of default. Sheriff Fitzsimons[69] disagreed finding that, even though it was an action of repossession, section 22 of the 1970 Act had no application to these circumstances.[70]

Other Preliminary Steps

2.6 Where a creditor has taken one of the routes described above as an initial step to exercise his rights, and has complied with any obligations under the Consumer Credit Act 1974, he need not provide any further notice to the debtor unless he is contractually obliged to do so. While it is open to the court to construe standard documents against the creditor *contra proferentem*, it appears that a term which may imply the requirement to give further notice will be interpreted narrowly. In *Clydesdale Bank plc v. Davidson*,[71] the defender relied on condition 6 of the security,

---

[61] See para. 6.4.

[62] s.135 of the 1974 Act; the procedure for the making of a time order is by way of summary application: Act of Sederunt 1985 No. 705.

[63] The 1974 Act uses the phrases "time order", "time to pay order" and "time to pay direction".

[64] s.129 of the 1974 Act.

[65] In *First National Bank plc v. Syed* [1991] 2 All E.R. 250, where there had been a fairly long history of default and only sporadic payments by the debtor, Dillon L.J. held (p.256) "consideration of what is just does not exclude consideration of the creditor's position; it is not limited to the debtor's position"; (the decision is in fact *per incuriam* by reason of a failure to consider s.38A of the Administration of Justice Act 1970). See Hickman (1994) 110 L.Q.R. 221.

[66] 1994 S.C.L.R. 805.

[67] Under s.87 of the 1974 Act.

[68] Under s.21 of the 1970 Act.

[69] at Dumbarton.

[70] As it transpired, the application was dismissed on the merits.

[71] 1993 S.C.L.R. 984.

which modified the standard conditions, stating: "The Bank may, at any time after it shall have become entitled to enter into possession of the security subjects, serve notice upon the debtor requiring him to vacate the security subjects within a period of 7 days". Although the creditor had served a calling-up notice which had expired before a writ was raised, the debtor argued that a separate seven day notice was required. In fact, the sheriff held that the condition simply permitted an optional alternative procedure which the creditor might follow and did not in any way derogate from its right to proceed with a calling-up notice.

Which Route is Appropriate?

The first point to be made is that each of the initial steps provided for by the 1970 Act may be used together. In *Bank of Scotland v. Millward*,[72] the Inner House confirmed that the remedies of calling-up notices and notices of default were not mutually exclusive and, as a matter of practice, acknowledged that it was obvious that practitioners used notices of default even where calling-up notices could have been used. The court held that a creditor in a standard security could serve a calling-up notice where it was looking for repayment of all sums outstanding but did not have to. If the debtor was in default, the creditor equally had the right to serve as an alternative (or indeed additionally) a notice of default.[73] Sections 19 and 21 of the Act did not permit the conclusion that the remedies were mutually exclusive, as had been argued by the debtor.[74]

2.7

Many creditors had, until the passing of the 2001 Act, proceeded on a "belt and braces approach"[75] of serving calling-up notices, notices of default and raising a section 24 action simultaneously. Such an approach allowed creditors to benefit from the speed of section 24 proceedings while allowing them to fall back on the notices if circumstances so required.[76] The passing of the 2001 Act, however, makes it disadvantageous for a creditor to adopt such an approach[77] and many creditors have already chosen to switch to the use of section 24 actions alone under the new regime.

Voluntary Surrender and Abandoned Properties

Calling-up notices are particularly useful when possession is being surrendered voluntarily or when the property is empty. This arises from an important difference between calling-up notices and notices of

2.7.1

---

[72] 1999 S.L.T. 901.

[73] This follows from the wording of standard condition 9 which holds the debtor in default "where a calling-up notice in respect of the security has been served and has not been complied with; . . . where there has been a failure to comply with any other requirement arising out of the security". The latter sentence clearly covers failure to pay arrears in addition to a failure to pay all sums due under the security.

[74] A further consequence of the decision is that the word "shall" in s.19 ("he shall serve a notice calling-up the security") is to be read in a permissive and not a mandatory sense.

[75] Urquhart, "Mortgage Rights (Scotland) Act 2001", Green's *Property Law Bulletin* 53–1.

[76] So, for example, even if the level of arrears under the writ was challenged successfully, the debtor would be unlikely to have a defence to an action related to a calling-up notice.

[77] See para. 2.2.13.

default. Any calling-up notice where the period of notice has expired (by waiver of notice or otherwise) gives the creditor the immediate right to enter into possession and sell the subjects.[78] This is not true of a notice of default, as there is no power to enter possession unless warrant[79] has been granted by the court to that effect.[80] In *Bank of Scotland v. Fernand*,[81] the creditor sought declarator that it was entitled to enter into possession of the security subjects on the defender's failure to comply with requirements arising out of the standard security granted by her. In other words, it did not seek authority to enter possession, simply declarator that it already had that right. The creditor did not adopt the calling-up notice procedure. Sheriff Principal Macleod[82] held that the remedy of entering possession is only available to a creditor by way of calling-up notice or by application to the court. Entering into possession is not one of the remedies available to a creditor, following service of a notice of default, under section 23(2), without thereafter an application to the court under section 24.

Prior to the passing of the 2001 Act, it was possible for a debtor who wished the creditor to take the subjects back to sign a waiver of the entire period of notice under a calling-up notice. Often, for a debtor with alternative accommodation available and whose only option to pay off or reduce the debt was sale of the subjects, voluntary surrender of the property was not an unattractive proposition. It prevented arrears mounting further, so far as possible. From the creditor's point of view, the delay and cost of court proceedings were avoided. The rules on waiver of periods of notice have been changed and are discussed more fully below.[83] The minimum period of notice in calling-up notice is now one month and the category of persons who must consent to waiver of any notice is extended. This makes a quick voluntary surrender of security subjects much more difficult. The use of the calling-up notice remains the quickest, cheapest and therefore most appropriate course of action, for both creditor and debtor, where the debtor wishes to hand over the property and the requisite waivers down to the minimum period of notice can be obtained. Surrender of the security subjects does not, of course, automatically relieve the debtor of all sums outstanding under the loan and it remains open to the creditor to pursue the debtor for any unsecured shortfall debt resulting after sale of the security subjects.

The position is more difficult, for creditors at least, in the case of abandoned properties. In this eventuality, there is unlikely to be a debtor available or willing to sign any waiver. There will therefore be a two

---

[78] s.20(2) of the 1970 Act; as a matter of practice, if the debtor is not prepared to vacate voluntarily, a court action will be required to eject the debtor. A court action based on a calling-up notice may also be desirable in other circumstances as where the creditor wishes to satisfy tenants in the subjects that rents may be paid to him: *Fernand* citing with approval Halliday, *The Conveyancing and Feudal Reform (Scotland) Act 1970* (2nd ed.), p.198.

[79] Under s.24 of the 1970 Act.

[80] Assuming that the standard conditions had not been varied. This would be competent as the power to enter into possession is not one where variation is prohibited: s.11(3) of the 1970 Act.

[81] 1997 S.L.T. (Sh.Ct) 78.

[82] at Glasgow.

[83] See para. 4.2.9.

month period between the creditor deciding to take action on the one hand and obtaining the legal rights to enter into possession and sell the subjects[84] on the other hand. As is clear from *Fernand*, there is no right to enter possession based on a notice of default alone.[85] While it is not a course technically open, there is no doubt that some creditors have considered recovering the subjects at an earlier stage, particularly if there are security concerns over the empty subjects. It is easy to understand this viewpoint as the creditor will often be faced with an account which is badly off the rails and a rapidly deteriorating asset. If the debtor re-appears and complains, the creditor may return the keys to him. In any case, the creditor is not entitled to sell until the preliminary steps have been completed but a creditor who follows this course[86] might make his presence apparent to the outside world and prevent further deterioration. The alternative is simply to carry out repairs, which does not require entry into possession,[87] but this power does not permit the creditor to install security guards or market the subjects.

Insolvent Proprietor

A section 24 writ is the correct way to proceed where the proprietor of the security subjects is insolvent and the creditor wishes to sell.[88] Such an action finds its basis in standard condition 9(1)(c) which provides that the debtor is in default "where the proprietor of the security subjects has become insolvent". Insolvency in these circumstances includes the situation where the proprietor has become apparently insolvent.[89] It has been confirmed that a limited company may fall within this definition of insolvency,[90] although the insolvency of a company is also dealt with expressly by reference, *inter alia*, to the making of a winding-up order or the appointment of a receiver.[91]

2.7.2

It should be noted that although the application in these circumstances is founded on the insolvency of the proprietor, the debtor (if not the proprietor) may be neither insolvent or in default of his obligations to the creditor. In that event, the debtor must try to make other arrangements with the creditor himself.

---

[84] Either under a calling-up notice, with its two month period, or a s.24 writ where the issuing of the writ, its service (which will probably require to be by sheriff officer or on the walls of court in these circumstances), craving for decree and the wait for the extract decree are unlikely to be completed much before two months if at all.

[85] Although the creditor may not need to enter into possession if he is simply selling the subjects: see para. 7.4.

[86] Which, for the avoidance of doubt, would not be in exercise of his powers under the 1970 Act.

[87] See para. 7.5.3.

[88] s.24(1).

[89] Standard condition 9(2)(a) uses the words "notour bankrupt" but s.75(9) of the Bankruptcy (Scotland) Act 1985 (c.66) provides that references in any enactment to notour bankruptcy shall be construed as references to apparent insolvency; the standard condition also includes the situations where the proprietor has executed a trust deed for creditors or has died and a judicial factor has been appointed. The full definition of insolvency for these purposes is found in standard condition 9(2).

[90] *United Dominions Trust Ltd v. Site Preparations Ltd (No.2)*, 1978 S.L.T. 21 at p.24 although the contrary view was taken in *United Dominions Trust Ltd v. Site Preparations Ltd (No.1)*, 1978 S.L.T. (Sh.Ct) 14; the decision in *(No.2)* is supported by Cusine, *op. cit.*, para. 8.21 and Gordon, *op. cit.*, para. 20–183 and is submitted to be correct.

[91] Standard condition 9(2)(c).

CHAPTER 3

THE INITIAL STAGES—PRE-EXISTING FORMS OF SECURITY[1]

The Nature of the Securities[2]

3.1 As noted above,[3] the existing forms of security before November 29, 1970 were the bond and disposition in security; the bond of cash credit and disposition in security; and the *ex facie* absolute disposition.

The bond and disposition in security and the bond of cash credit and disposition in security may be considered together as the same rules generally apply in relation to enforcement.[4] References hereafter to a bond and disposition in security may be taken to refer also to a bond of cash credit and disposition in security, unless otherwise indicated. In each case, the deed was a personal bond by the debtor with a disposition of the land in security of the personal obligation. Both the personal bond and disposition were in favour of the creditor and their effect amounted to the grant of rights by the debtor over subjects in security of the obligation due.

By contrast with the types of security described above, the third pre-existing form of security generally used before the 1970 Act, the *ex facie* absolute disposition, is an unusual concept. It is the most important of the three, having been the form most commonly in use before the coming into effect of the 1970 Act. As the name implies, the deed is, on the face of it, a complete transfer of ownership from the proprietor to a third party as with a normal disposition. In fact, the relationship is one of debtor and heritable creditor and the deed is qualified by a back letter or agreement in terms of which the true nature of the relationship and the terms of the security are set out.[5] Accordingly, notwithstanding its apparent terms, the effect of an *ex facie* absolution disposition is the same as that of the bond and disposition in security, namely a grant by the debtor of a right in favour of the creditor to secure an obligation due by the debtor.

---

[1] That is, forms of security which existed before the coming into effect of the Conveyancing and Feudal Reform (Scotland) Act 1970 (c.35), hereafter "the 1970 Act". See Chap. 1.

[2] For further discussion, see J.S. Talman (ed.), *Halliday's Conveyancing Law and Practice* (2nd ed., 1996), Vol. II (hereafter "Halliday, *Conveyancing*"), paras. 47–04 *et seq*.

[3] See para. 1.6.

[4] Except that in enforcement of the bond of cash credit and disposition in security, a certificate of the sums outstanding is required where a calling-up notice is served: Halliday, *Conveyancing*, para. 48–73; see also Gordon, *Scottish Land Law* (2nd ed., 1999), para. 20–84.

[5] For a full consideration of the law on *ex facie* absolute dispositions, see Gordon, *op. cit.*, para. 20–86 *et seq* and Halliday, *Conveyancing*, Chap. 49.

Enforcement of the Pre-existing Forms of Security

Each of the pre-existing forms of security entitles the creditor to exercise certain powers. To do so, certain preliminary steps may require to have been completed or the creditor may have entered into possession. As noted above,[6] forms of enforcement not specific to repossessions, such as personal diligence, are not considered here. **3.2**

Bond and Disposition in Security

The first option open to the holder of a bond and disposition in security is to serve a calling-up notice.[7] The procedural rules on service and on whom the notice should be served are regulated by statute and are similar to the provisions of the 1970 Act.[8] As with standard securities, the notice requires payment of all sums due to the creditor by the debtor, but the debtor is afforded three months within which to comply with the notice.[9] If the notice is not complied with, the creditor is entitled to exercise the remedy of sale.[10] The rules in relation to sales by a creditor in a bond and disposition in security are considered below.[11] A creditor in a bond and disposition in security may exercise the remedy of foreclosure if he is unable to sell the subjects.[12] **3.3**

Such a creditor also has the option, where there has been a default in payment of principal or interest, or where the proprietor is apparently insolvent or has granted a trust deed for creditors, to enter into possession and exercise further powers. These are considered further below but include the collection of rents,[13] carrying out repairs and renewals[14] and letting the subjects.[15] The creditor in a bond and disposition in security may raise an action of mails and duties which will allow him to enter into possession where the subjects are physically occupied by a third party, such as a tenant.[15a] Such an action allows the creditor to uplift the rents of the subjects.[16] As a matter of practicality it may be necessary to eject the debtor where he is in personal occupation of the subjects and for that a court action will be required. The action is based on section 5 of the Heritable Securities (Scotland) Act 1894 considered below.[17]

---

[6] See para. 1.3.

[7] Conveyancing (Scotland) Act 1924 (c.27), hereafter "the 1924 Act", s.33; the form of notice is Form 1 in Sched. M to the 1924 Act.

[8] 1924 Act ss.33 and 34; see Halliday, *Conveyancing*, paras. 48–22–48–26.

[9] 1924 Act s.33 and Form 1 of Sched. M thereto; the recipient of the notice may dispense with or shorten the *induciae*, subject to the consent of others specified, in accordance with s.35 of the 1924 Act.

[10] 1924 Act s.36.

[11] See Chap. 8.

[12] See para. 7.5.4.

[13] See para. 7.5.1.

[14] See para. 7.5.3.

[15] See para. 7.5.2.

[15a] The Scottish Executive has indicated that it is minded to abolish recourse to the diligence of mails and duties: *Enforcement of Civil Obligations in Scotland—A Consultation Paper*, April 2002, para. 5.311.

[16] See para. 7.5, where the provisions regulating procedure for such an action are set out.

[17] See para. 3.5; that Act (c.44) is hereafter referred to as "the 1894 Act".

Ex Facie Absolute Disposition

3.4 The creditor in an *ex facie* absolute disposition also has open to him the remedy of sale and, in that case, service of a calling-up notice is not required.[18] Where sale has proved impossible, the creditor again has the remedy of foreclosure.[19] As with the other forms of security, the creditor in an *ex facie* absolute disposition has the right to enter into possession. Generally, the conditions which must have occurred and the steps the creditor must take to do so will be the subject of agreement in the back letter or agreement to the disposition between the parties. If the issue is not otherwise agreed, the creditor may enter into possession on any default by the debtor under the security.[20] Having done so, the creditor may uplift the rents.[21]

If the debtor in an *ex facie* absolute disposition does not co-operate in allowing the creditor to enter into possession, the creditor may generally raise an action for ejection, again under section 5 of the 1894 Act.[22] This is competent on the basis that the debtor is regarded as an occupant whose right to occupy derives only from the permission of the creditor[23] and in any case a right to eject will usually be included in the back letter or agreement to the deed. In certain circumstances, however, an action under the 1894 Act is not competent[24] and, if that is the case, an action of declarator and removing will be required.[25]

Court Proceedings for Ejection

3.5 Section 5 of the 1894 Act provides:

> "Where a creditor desires to enter into possession of the lands disponed in security, and the proprietor thereof is in personal occupation of the same, or any part thereof, such proprietor shall be deemed to be an occupant without a title, and the creditor may take proceedings to eject him in all respects in the same way as if he were such occupant: Provided that this section shall not apply in any case unless such proprietor has made default in the punctual payment of the interest due under the security, or in due payment of the principal after formal requisition."

---

[18] See para. 8.
[19] See para. 7.5.4.
[20] Gordon, *op. cit.*, para. 20–100; Gloag & Irvine, *Rights in Security* (1897), p.159.
[21] See para. 7.5.1.
[22] See *Research Paper on Actions of Ejection and Removing*, A.G.M. Duncan, January 1984, para. 7.16 published by the Scottish Law Commission along with their Consultative Memorandum No.59 Recovery of Possession of Heritable Property.
[23] *Inglis' Trustees v. Macpherson* (1911) 2 S.L.T. 176 which makes clear, while being a case concerning a bond and disposition in security, that a party who occupies only with permission of the proprietor is effectively a squatter, being a person without any title at all; the earlier case of *Scottish Property Investment Company Building Society v. Horne* (1881) 8R. 737 held that an action of summary ejection by the creditor of the debtor in an *ex facie* absolute disposition was incompetent but the case pre-dated the 1894 Act, which restricted the debtor's rights, and the Sheriff Courts (Scotland) Act 1971 which now regulates such actions of ejection: see para. 3.5.
[24] Gordon, *op. cit.*, para. 20–48; Halliday, *Conveyancing*, para. 48–14.
[25] *Rankin v. Russell* (1868) 7M. 126; Gloag & Irvine, *op. cit.*, p.159.

The procedure for such an action has caused some difficulty. There are three possibilities for the form which such an action should take, namely summary application, ordinary action and summary cause. The issue was considered in *Prestwick Investment Trust v. Jones*,[26] where the pursuers, as creditors in a security[27] brought an action craving warrant for summary ejection of the defenders from the security subjects founding on their non-compliance with a calling-up notice served under the security. The pursuers sought to proceed under the 1894 Act by way of a summary application. The defender argued that the action could only be competently brought by way of summary cause.[28] Sheriff Grant[29] rejected that contention, holding that the action was properly by way of summary application.[30] The decision has been subject to criticism[31] and, in light of other decisions which make clear that summary application procedure is inappropriate,[32] it is submitted that it is incorrect.

The procedure for such an action of ejection prior to the passing of the 1970 Act was certainly by way of an ordinary action[33] but matters have been complicated by the Sheriff Courts (Scotland) Act 1971. Section 35(1)(c) thereof provides that all civil proceedings "for the recovery of possession of heritable ... property"[34] shall be by way of summary cause. In *Prestwick Investment*, the sheriff declined to hold that summary cause procedure was appropriate because he took the view that the word "recovery" implied that the pursuer had had possession at some time in the past. In *Bradford & Bingley Building Society v. Walker*,[35] Sheriff Kelbie[36] held that "getting or obtaining possession of something for the first time is a perfectly proper use of the word [recovery]". The sheriff, while not expressly ruling on this issue, said "I have to confess to some difficulty in seeing how a crave for ejection ... could be pursued by ordinary action".[37] The general uncertainty has led to a suggestion

---

[26] 1981 S.L.T. (Sh.Ct) 55.

[27] The security was a standard security but the creditor elected to pursue an action under s.5 of the 1894 Act. Section 20(1) of the 1970 Act confirms that the creditor's rights under that Act where a debtor has failed to comply with a calling-up notice are "in addition to and not in derogation from ... any right conferred by any enactment."

[28] Founding on s.35(1)(c) of the Sheriff Courts (Scotland) Act 1971, *infra*.

[29] at Ayr.

[30] Stating (p.56) "The essential point made for the pursuers was that they were not seeking recovery of possession of the subjects, because they had never had such possession. They were seeking to enter into possession by reasons of the ... default on the standard security."

[31] Jamieson, "Creditors' Remedies under a Standard Security" 1989 S.L.T. (News) 201 noting that the decision was based on the mistaken view that s.29 of the 1970 Act applied; *Research Paper on Actions of Ejection and Removing*, A.G.M. Duncan, January 1984, para. 7.16 published by the Scottish Law Commission along with their Consultative Memorandum No.59 Recovery of Possession of Heritable Property.

[32] *Provincial Building Society v. Menzies*, 1984 S.L.T. (Sh.Ct) 81 at p.82; *Mountstar Metal Corporation Ltd v. Cameron*, 1987 S.L.T. (Sh.Ct) 106 at p.108E; *Bradford & Bingley v. Walker*, 1988 S.L.T. (Sh.Ct) 33.

[33] Dobie, *Sheriff Court Practice* (1948), p.595; Jamieson, "Creditors' Remedies under a Standard Security" 1989 S.L.T. (News) 201.

[34] Unless there is also a crave for payment of more than £1,500 in which case it is by ordinary action.

[35] 1988 S.L.T. (Sh.Ct) 33.

[36] at Aberdeen.

[37] p.36G; but see the annotation to s.5 in R. Rennie (ed.), *Scottish Conveyancing Legislation* (W. Green and Son) para. A.309.1, where Sheriff Cusine submits that such a case should be brought by ordinary action.

that practitioners should inquire as to the practice of the particular sheriff court in which the proceedings are to be brought.[37a] There is no harm in such a course but it is unlikely that a sheriff considering the matter at debate would consider himself bound by an indication as to the correct procedure given by the clerk at the outset.

It is submitted that the correct procedure for an action of ejection under section 5 of the 1894 Act is indeed by way of summary cause procedure under the 1971 Act. The nature of the action is simply one of ejection,[38] no more, and is not disqualified from being a summary cause by reason of the incorporation of certain other craves.[39] However, the mere fact that the action is by way of summary cause does not disentitle an applicant from making an application for a section 2 order under the Mortgage Rights (Scotland) Act 2001[40] as the creditor will still have commenced proceedings relying on section 5 of the 1894 Act,[41] bringing the matter within the categories of action to which the 2001 Act applies.[42] The expenses of an action raised under this provision are recoverable by the creditor from the debtor.[43]

When decree for ejection has been obtained, it may be passed to sheriff officers to eject the debtor.[44] Once the debtor is ejected, the practical hurdle to the creditor selling the subjects or entering into possession and exercising his powers is overcome and he may proceed to do so in accordance with the rules thereon.[45]

[37a] Macphail, *Sheriff Court Practice* (2nd ed., 1998), para. 23–30.

[38] In *Milmor Properties Ltd v. W & T Investment Co Ltd*, 1999 S.C.L.R. 910, Sheriff Cowan, interpreting the phrase "actions *ad factum praestandum*" in s.35(1)(c) of the Sheriff Courts (Scotland) Act 1971, held (p.915B) "It is the nature of the action which is being described, not the content of the individual craves."

[39] *Stair Memorial Encyclopaedia*, Vol. 18, para. 154; *Research Paper on Actions of Ejection and Removing*, A.G.M. Duncan, January 1984, paras. 7.16 and 7.19 published by the Scottish Law Commission along with their Consultative Memorandum No.59 Recovery of Possession of Heritable Property; Deutsch "Circumventing the Mortgage Rights (Scotland) Act 2001", 2001 Civ.P.B. 43—1; but if a crave for interdict is desired in such circumstances, the safest course is to raise a separate ordinary action therefor: *Disblair Estates Ltd v. Jackson*, unreported, Aberdeen Sheriff Court, November 24, 1982 (the decision is referred to in said Research Paper); if the creditor sought any form of declarator, summary cause procedure would not be competent. Macphail, *Sheriff Court Practice* (2nd ed., 1998), para. 23–08 citing *Gerber v. Greggs Bakeries Ltd*, unreported, October 18, 1981.

[40] (asp 11), hereafter "the 2001 Act"; see Chap. 4.

[41] But the wording of the preamble to the 2001 Act does create some uncertainty: see para. 4.2.6.

[42] s.1(1)(c) of the 2001 Act; it is however unclear as a matter of practicality how the application would be made as the subordinate legislation made under the 2001 Act amends only the Ordinary Cause Rules and Summary Applications Rules: see para. 4.2.8.

[43] Cusine, "Expenses under a Standard Security" 1994 *Juridical Review* 18 at p.31.

[44] See para. 5.22.

[45] See Chaps 7 (recovering the subjects) and 8 (sale).

CHAPTER 4

DETERMINATION OF COURT PROCEEDINGS—PART I

Introduction

Possible defences to a court action based on an expired calling-up notice or section 24 action[1] have been considered above.[2] While the defences detailed there remain open to a debtor to advance, contested court proceedings for repossession will now largely fall into two categories: challenges under The Mortgage Rights (Scotland) Act 2001[3]; and proceedings which challenge the validity of the standard security itself.   **4.1**

This and the following chapter explore these two areas in depth and also consider the extent to which human rights legislation may have a bearing in defended repossession cases. To complete consideration of those aspects of the repossession process which are court rather than conveyancing related, the expenses of repossession actions are considered and the period between decree and eviction is reviewed.

The Mortgage Rights (Scotland) Act 2001   **4.2**

Introduction

The Mortgage Rights (Scotland) Act 2001[4] has radically changed the law on repossession by secured lenders in Scotland. The Act came into force on December 3, 2001.[5]   **4.2.1**

To ensure a full understanding of the scope of change brought in by the Act, it is worth examining the law as it stood prior to December 3, 2001 and the political climate which resulted in its reversal.

The Law Before the 2001 Act

The restricted response available to a debtor served with a calling-up notice or notice of default has been considered above.[6] The leading repossession case dealing with the debtor's general ability to challenge   **4.2.2**

---

[1] whether based on a notice of default or not.
[2] See Chap. 2.
[3] (asp 11).
[4] Throughout this Chapter, references to "the 2001 Act" and "the Act" are to the Mortgage Rights (Scotland) Act 2001 except where the context otherwise requires. The short title is confirmed by s.7(3). The choice of name, including as it does the word "mortgage", has been subject to not wholly favourable comment. See for example Morrison, Mortgage Rights (Scotland) Act 2001, 2001 Civil Practice Bulletin 42–2 and Gretton & Reid, Conveyancing 2000 (2001), p.91. However, Cathie Craigie M.S.P., who introduced the Bill, has supported the name noting that the public use the word mortgage and arguing that when legislating for ordinary people, their language should be used.
[5] The Mortgage Rights (Scotland) Act 2001 (Commencement and Transitional Provision) Order 2001 (S.S.I. 2001 No.418).
[6] See Chap. 2.

court proceedings raised by a secured creditor for recovery of the secured subjects was *Halifax Building Society v. Gupta*.[7]

This was—or at least should have been—a straightforward repossession action raised by the Halifax Building Society for recovery of subjects in Bathgate, West Lothian. In April 1990 the creditor had served a notice of default on the debtor on the ground that he had failed to make monthly payments due by him in terms of the standard security. The debtor did not comply with the default notice, with the result that he was in default within the meaning of standard condition 9(1)(b) of the 1970 Act. The creditor applied to the sheriff court at Linlithgow for a warrant under section 24 of the 1970 Act to enter into possession of and sell the security subjects. After sundry procedure the action came before the sheriff for a debate. He was invited by the creditor to repel the defences and grant decree *de plano* as the debtor had admitted on record that he was in arrears with his mortgage payments. The debtor informed the sheriff that he would resume these payments once the action had been sisted. He submitted that the court had a discretion to refuse the creditor its remedy and he invited the sheriff to take that course.

The sheriff held that the court did not have a discretion in the matter and he saw no reason why he should not grant the creditor's application. In his view the debtor had no relevant defence to the action and he repelled the defences. Following an unsuccessful appeal to the sheriff principal, the defender appealed to the Inner House, where Lord President Hope stated:

> "The complaint which underlies his whole approach to this case is that [the heritable creditor] ought not to have been allowed to proceed further with the action which he contends is for the exercise of a remedy which is discretionary. He maintains that it would be contrary to equity for them to be allowed to do this, since he is willing to purge his default provided he is given the same facilities for restructuring or rescheduling his obligations as are normally available to the pursuers' other borrowers."

The debtor was not contradicted on his argument that the creditor normally made a rescheduled programme of repayment available to other debtors. Nonetheless, the Inner House adhered to the decision of the sheriff principal. The court confirmed:

> "The defender is seeking to prevent the pursuers from exercising their powers, not to control them in the manner of their exercise. He has no legitimate interest to insist that the pursuers' exercise of their power of sale should be denied to them on the grounds which he has put forward in his defences, and the sheriff was in our opinion right to reject this argument on the ground that it was irrelevant."[8]

---

[7] 1994 S.L.T. 339

[8] The Inner House approved the earlier decision *United Dominions Trust Ltd v. Site Preparations Ltd (No.1)*, 1978 S.L.T. (Sh.Ct) 14, where Sheriff Smith (p.17) had stated "section 24 provides that the creditor may apply for a warrant: it does not provide that the sheriff may grant it. On the contrary, the wording of section 24(1) 'for warrant to exercise any of the remedies [to] which he is entitled,' makes it clear to me that the only discretion which exists is that of the creditor: he may apply to the court for a warrant if he thinks fit, in order to obtain a remedy to which he is entitled."

In short, provided there was no issue relating to the validity of the security courts had no discretion to refuse a creditor's application for decree in terms of section 24.[9]

The Political Climate

The background to the introduction of the Mortgage Rights (Scotland) Bill arose from the discretion available to English courts to stop repossession orders being implemented.[10] By contrast with the Scottish position, if the debtor is offering to repay arrears by installments, the English courts are provided with discretion when a creditor continues to seek recovery of possession. The 2001 Act, as enacted, gives courts discretion to allow them to suspend the rights of secured creditors, in certain circumstances, and so prevent repossession of the property secured.

4.2.3

The Bill was one of the first Member's bills[11] introduced in the Scottish Parliament. It quickly obtained the support of the Scottish Executive making its passing very likely from a relatively early stage. That turned out to be of some significance. It was apparent that, for those whose interests would be adversely affected, the best that could be achieved would be terms which reflected such interests more favourably, rather than successful opposition to the Bill itself.[12]

The stated policies of the Bill, in the words of the Member of the Scottish Parliament who introduced it, Cathie Craigie, were:

- "to enable a court to suspend certain rights of a mortgage lender . . . where the borrower is in default" and
- "to provide greater protection for tenants of borrowers in default."[13]

Ms Craigie suggested when the Bill was introduced that 60 per cent of repossession orders in England are suspended and that 75 per cent of debtors who benefited from such suspension subsequently maintained their payments.[14] During the year 2000, Scottish courts granted 4,922 repossession decrees.[15] Approximately 3,000 properties per year were

---

[9] It has been argued, however, that there is a distinction to be drawn between the lack of discretion formerly available to the courts at this stage and the ability of the court to restrain the creditor in the exercise of his powers. The former issue is rendered obsolete by the 2001 Act but the latter is discussed in detail at para. 7.6.1.

[10] A review of the similar legislation enacted in England is to be found at paras 4.3 *et seq.*

[11] The equivalent in the Scottish Parliament of a Private Member's Bill in the U.K. Parliament.

[12] To review the progress of the Bill, including a list of amendments for Stages 2 and 3, see www.scottish.parliament.uk/parl_bus/bill-final.htm#19.

[13] The Mortgage Rights (Scotland) Bill, as introduced. See also http://www.cathiecraigie.co.uk/.

[14] These figures also appear in Dailly, "Mortgage Rights (Scotland) Act 2001" *Scolag Legal Journal*, September 2001, p.157.

[15] Scottish Courts Service figure (confirmed by the *Draft Consultation Paper on Mortgage to Rent Scheme*, issued by the Scottish Executive in July 2001); the figure of 4,922 had dropped from a high of 5,952 in 1999, following a steep rise from 2,058 in 1994. The rise in recent years in the number of decrees does not sit well with the reduction in the number of mortgages in arrears (see para. 1.1) and suggests that creditors had become more aware of their rights in the intervening period.

actually repossessed at that time.[16] Prior to the passing of the 2001 Act, no more than two per cent of repossession actions in Scotland were defended at all. Of those, a minority made it to debate or proof. It has been predicted that the 2001 Act will lead to a "flood of applications"[17] as the applicant has little to lose and certainly if the English experience is anything to go by, the effect of the 2001 Act will be very significant indeed.

It is of some significance that there had been no concrete proposals to introduce this or similar legislation in the U.K. Parliament at any time since the passing of the 1970 Act itself. The apparent lack of Westminster time for such matters suggests that it is unlikely that, even now, steps would have been taken there to reform Scots law. The change in the law may therefore fairly be said to be a direct result of devolution. The 2001 Act was passed unanimously by the Scottish Parliament on June 20, 2001 and received Royal Assent on July 25, 2001.

Outline of Main Provisions

4.2.4 Where a heritable creditor[18] has taken action to enforce its rights, the 2001 Act makes provision for the sheriff court to suspend the enforcement process in appropriate cases. Suspension of enforcement, in this context, appears to mean mainly suspension of court proceedings though it is possible that suspension of enforcement of a decree will be possible.[19]

The Act applies where the property is used to any extent for residential purposes.[20] Accordingly, it does not apply to wholly commercial premises. Buy to let mortgages are likely to be covered, as in most cases, the property will be used for residential purposes. Similarly, it seems reasonable to suppose that a commercial property with residential accommodation for the owner and his family will be covered by the wording. Although domestic in nature, holiday homes are likely to be excluded by the legislation as applicants, to qualify, must be using the security subjects as their sole or main residence.[21]

In exercising its discretion, "the court is required to consider various issues including whether:

- "the applicant might be able to repay the debt or arrears, or fulfil the obligations under the standard security, within a reasonable time so as to keep their home; or

- the enforcement process should be delayed to give the applicant and others staying at the property time to find alternative accommodation."[22]

---

[16] Estimate of Council of Mortgage Lenders (hereafter "CML").
[17] Annotation by Sheriff Cusine to the 2001 Act in R. Rennie (ed.), *Scottish Conveyancing Legislation*, (W. Green and Son, Edinburgh), para. A.855.
[18] The Act uses the wording "a creditor in a standard security over an interest in land".
[19] See para. 4.2.8 below.
[20] s.1(1).
[21] s.1(2).
[22] Explanatory Notes to the Act; the full issues to be considered are set out in s.2 on which see para. 4.2.12, *infra*.

Procedural Considerations

4.2.5 The circumstances in which an application may be made are set out in section 1.[23] This section confirms the steps which must have been taken by the creditor before an application is competent; who may apply; the time limits within which an application must be made; and restricts the ability of the creditor to have the debtor waive time limits or to take action while an application is competent.

Steps Taken by Creditor

4.2.6 The 2001 Act applies[24] where the creditor has issued a calling-up notice[25] or a notice of default,[26] issued a section 24 writ[27] or has commenced proceedings under section 5 of the Heritable Securities (Scotland) Act 1894.[28] It should be noted at this stage that the Ordinary Cause Rules[29] have been amended to take account of repossession actions raised by creditors under section 24 of the 1970 Act.[30] It is now necessary for the initial writ to include averments about those persons who appear to the pursuer to be entitled to apply for a section 2 order and such persons, as far as they are known to the creditor, must be called as defenders.[31]

An interesting question is whether the 2001 Act only applies to enforcement by a creditor under a standard security. The preamble to the Act states:

> "An Act of the Scottish Parliament to provide for the suspension in certain circumstances of enforcement rights of a creditor in a *standard security* over property used for residential purposes and the continuation of proceedings relating to those rights; to make provision for notifying tenants and other occupiers of enforcement action by a creditor in a *standard security*; and for connected purposes."[32]

This suggests that a debtor in a bond and disposition in security or under an *ex facie* absolute disposition may not make an application under the Act for suspension of a creditor's rights. The preamble is of course part

---

[23] The full text of s.1 is set out in the Appendix at para. 10.1.
[24] s.1(1).
[25] Under s.19 of the 1970 Act.
[26] Under s.21 of the 1970 Act.
[27] Under s.24 of the 1970 Act.
[28] (c.44), hereafter "the 1894 Act"; the intention of the creditor in taking action under the security is entirely irrelevant, so it does not matter whether the creditor's action is truly to secure payment of arrears, or is a step on the road to sale, or is a precursor to one of the creditor's other remedies; it is at least questionable as to whether action by an adjudging creditor (even if related to a separately constituted obligation than that secured by the standard security) falls within this provision: Deutsch "Circumventing the Mortgage Rights (Scotland) Act 2001", 2002 Civ.P.B. 43—1.
[29] First Schedule to the Sheriff Courts (Scotland) Act 1907 (c.51).
[30] And indeed ordinary causes raised under s.5 of the 1894 Act but it is submitted that an action for ejection under that section with no other craves would not be competent as an ordinary action: see para. 3.5.
[31] r.3.2(3) of the Ordinary Cause Rules as amended by S.S.I. 2002 No. 7.
[32] Emphasis added.

of the Act and may assist in its explanation[33] but the references in the terms of the Act itself to a creditor taking action under the 1894 Act strongly suggest that a debtor would be entitled to make such an application even where the creditor's rights are based on a pre-existing form of security.[34]

Who May Apply?

4.2.7 The following persons are entitled to make an application under the 2001 Act[35]:

(1) The debtor in the standard security or the proprietor of the security subjects (where the proprietor is not the debtor) but only where the property subject to the security (in whole or in part) is that person's sole or main residence;

(2) the debtor or proprietor's non-entitled spouse,[36] where the property is a matrimonial home[37] and is that person's sole or main residence[38];

(3) the debtor or the proprietor's partner, whether same or opposite sex, where the property is that person's sole or main residence; and

(4) a partner of the debtor or proprietor who:
   (a) is of the same or opposite sex;
   (b) is living in the property as their sole or main residence but the property is not the sole or main residence of the debtor or proprietor;
   (c) lived with the debtor or proprietor for at least 6 months before the property ceased to be the sole or main residence of that person; and
   (d) has a child under the age of 16 years with the debtor or proprietor and the child's sole or main residence is the property subject to the security.

Although an applicant may become eligible to apply by any one of the four categories, if he is to qualify under the fourth category, he must satisfy all of the conditions set out in that paragraph. The fourth category is designed to cover the situation where the couple have separated and their child remains in the property.[39]

---

[33] *The County Council of the County of Renfrew v. Binnie* (1898) 1F. 186.

[34] The terms are sufficiently unambiguous that it is unlikely that they could be overcome by the wording of the preamble: *Binnie, supra* no. 33, at p.191.

[35] s.1(2).

[36] s.2(7) provides that "non-entitled spouse" is to be construed in accordance with the Matrimonial Homes (Family Protection) (Scotland) Act 1981 (c.59).

[37] s.2(7) provides that "matrimonial home" is to be construed in accordance with the Matrimonial Homes (Family Protection) (Scotland) Act 1981.

[38] It appears that even if the non-entitled spouse has signed a formal renunciation of occupancy rights, that will not bar an application under the 2001 Act.

[39] There was discussion of whether any ex-partner of the debtor should be entitled to apply, during the progress of the Bill. The Executive felt that such a measure was open to abuse which might work against the debtor's interests.

The term "debtor in the standard security" will hopefully not give rise to too many problems. "Proprietor" is not defined and may be more problematic. As property vests in the trustee from the date of sequestration,[40] the definition should include trustees in sequestration. It is unlikely, as a matter of practicality, that a trustee would wish to delay the sale of the security subjects.[41] There may be practical difficulties of proof in establishing, for non-married couples, that they are "partners" within the meaning of section 1(2) to allow them to qualify as applicants under the third or fourth categories. The person entitled to apply is defined as "a person living together with the debtor or the proprietor as husband or wife or in a relationship which has the characteristics of the relationship between husband and wife except that the persons are of the same sex".[42] For opposite sex couples, some guidance on "living together ... as husband and wife" might be gained from the caselaw on marriage by cohabitation with habit and repute.[43] For same sex couples, it is interesting to note that the wording "in a relationship which has the characteristics of the relationship between husband and wife except that the persons are of the same sex" appears identically in the Housing (Scotland) Act 2001[44] and in due course there may be guidance gained from the interpretation of that legislation.

A further question raised by the extension of rights to same sex couples arises from the quite different terms of the Matrimonial Homes (Family Protection) Act 1981. That Act does not provide any protection for non-entitled partners of same sex couples and it is not open for them to go to the courts under that Act to determine occupancy rights. The 2001 Act has created a situation where persons with no formal occupancy rights are permitted to make applications under the Act. While they should not do so according to wording of the legislation, it remains to be seen whether the courts will approach these applications differently from those of, say, a non-entitled spouse. Similarly, it remains to be seen whether there will be a difference in emphasis between the rights granted to spouses and those to partners. The courts have no power to transfer responsibility for the debt between partners as they do with spouses under the 1981 Act[45] but it is clear that spouses and partners should be treated in the same way under the 2001 Act.

There may also be a practical difficulty with proving that a child is that of the debtor or proprietor (if not registered as such). This becomes particularly an issue in relation to stepchildren and "any person brought up or treated by the person ... and the debtor or the proprietor ... as their child".[46] It is this same definition of "child", of course, which

---

[40] Bankruptcy (Scotland) Act 1985 (c.66), s.31.

[41] The relationship between trustees in sequestration and heritable creditors is examined in more detail at para. 6.3.

[42] s.1(2)(c).

[43] See Clive, *The Law of Husband and Wife in Scotland* (4th ed., 1997), paras. 5.019 *et seq.*

[44] (asp 10), Sched. 3, para. 2(1)(a)(ii) identifying qualified persons who may succeed to a Scottish Secure Tenancy. The Housing (Scotland) Act 2001 received Royal Assent on July 18, 2001 and this part of it must come into force by September 30, 2002, though the exact commencement date is not yet known.

[45] See para. 6.5.2.

[46] s.1(3).

affords the opportunity of protection to same sex couples through the fourth category of applicant.

Although such practical difficulties of proof exist, in relation to partners and children, the other side of the coin is more challenging still. How can a creditor challenge an assertion that two persons are enjoying a relationship where they live together as husband and wife?

The definition of persons entitled to apply under section 1 is limited. At stage 2 of the Bill, Robert Brown MSP[47] tabled amendments which tried to extend the Bill to allow any other persons who lawfully occupied[48] the security subjects as their sole or main residence to apply for a suspended order.[49] However, the view that the debtor should be the primary consideration prevailed amid concern that allowing other third parties to challenge might act against the debtor's interest as he remained liable for mounting arrears. There was particular concern expressed[50] at the potential knock on effect on the private rented sector. The proposed extension did not proceed.

Procedure for Application

4.2.8 Applications to the court, where the application challenges a calling-up notice or notice of default must be made by way of summary application.[51] Similarly, an application to vary or revoke an order, or to further continue proceedings, which relate to a creditor's rights under a calling-up notice or notice of default must be by way of summary application. Such applications proceed in accordance with the normal rules on summary application procedure, the full detail of which is beyond the scope of this work.[52]

Summary application procedure is also appropriate where the creditor applies to the court in certain circumstances under Part II of the 1970 Act[53] and in that case, the application under the 2001 Act must be made in accordance with the Summary Applications Rules[54] as amended by subordinate legislation which followed the Act.[55] New forms are introduced for warrants of citation[56] and for citation itself[57] by the creditor

---

[47] Who was also influential in bringing about the Family Homes and Homelessness (Scotland) Bill which covered some of the same issues as the Mortgage Rights (Scotland) Bill. The former was withdrawn on June 14, 2001 following widespread support for the latter but the full proposed text of the withdrawn Bill may be viewed at http://www.scottish.parliament.uk/parl_bus/bills/b13s1.pdf.

[48] Such as brothers or sisters, or lodgers.

[49] While they cannot make the applications, the interests of such people are nonetheless to be taken into account under s.2(2)(d) of the Act.

[50] Including by Cathie Craigie herself and by the Deputy First Minister.

[51] s.1(6).

[52] For discussion of summary application procedure, see Jamieson, *Summary Applications and Suspensions* (2000).

[53] These circumstances, which are rare, are detailed at para. 2.2.11.

[54] Act of Sederunt (Summary Applications, Statutory Applications and Appeals etc. Rules) 1999 (S.I. 1999 No. 929).

[55] Act of Sederunt (Amendment of Ordinary Cause Rules and Summary Applications, Statutory Applications and Appeals etc. Rules) (Applications under the Mortgage Rights (Scotland) Act 2001) 2002 (S.S.I. 2002 No. 7), effective January 17, 2002. It is remarkable that the Act came into force a full 45 days before any formal mechanism was introduced for applications to be made.

[56] Form 6A of the Summary Application Rules.

[57] Form 6B of the Summary Application Rules.

and there is a new certificate of citation for all summary applications.[58] These are repeated in the Appendix.[59] It is also provided that the new provisions apply where the creditor has commenced summary application proceedings under section 5 of the 1894 Act[60] but it is doubted that summary applications are the correct mode of procedure for such actions.[61] As a result, while the 2001 Act undoubtedly applies to a court action (of whatever nature) which the creditor has raised under section 5 of the 1894 Act,[62] there appears to be no procedural mechanism for an applicant to put forward his application.[63] It is submitted that in these circumstances a sheriff should allow the application to be made orally.[64]

Where a creditor has raised a summary application under Part II of the 1970 Act, the application under the 2001 Act may be lodged in the form of a minute in which case the applicant may appear or be represented at any hearing to determine the application made in the minute. Alternatively, an application for an order suspending a creditor's rights may be made orally when the summary application first calls in court or as the sheriff otherwise directs.[65]

The use of summary applications is clearly intended to provide an expedited procedure for debtors and others to use in challenging notices served on them.[66] Nonetheless, they are still separate court cases with formal written pleadings and court hearings. It remains to be seen how many potential applicants served with such notices under the 1970 Act will take the step of raising their own court actions before a creditor raises his writ. Matters become more complicated still if the creditor is pursuing the matter simultaneously by calling-up notice, notice of default and an ordinary action based on section 24.[67] If so, a summary application may be raised by the debtor (or other applicant) in response to the calling-up notice or notice of default, while an entirely separate court action continues against the debtor at the instance of the creditor. This very fact may deter lenders from continuing to serve calling-up notices or notices of default.

Applications to the court, where the application is in response to an ordinary action raised by a creditor are by minute[68] in that action.[69] This applies to applications for an order suspending the creditor's rights and applications to vary or revoke an existing order, or to further continue

---

[58] Form 7 of the Summary Application Rules.
[59] See para. 11.3.
[60] rr. 2.7(7A) and 2.22A(1) of the Summary Application Rules.
[61] See para. 3.5.
[62] s.1(1)(c) of the 2001 Act.
[63] As the Summary Cause Rules were not amended by the Act of Sederunt (Amendment of Ordinary Cause Rules and Summary Applications, Statutory Applications and Appeals, etc Rules) (Applications under the Mortgage Rights (Scotland) Act 2001) 2002 (S.S.I. 2002 No. 7). Similarly, the Act of Sederunt (Summary Cause Rules) 2002 (S.S.I. 2002 No. 132), effective June 10, 2002, make no provision for the lodging of a minute in terms of the 2001 Act.
[64] A preliminary hearing will take place after the creditor has raised a summary cause action for ejection whether or not a defence has been entered.
[65] r.2.22A(3) of the Summary Applications Rules.
[66] Summary applications raised by the creditor will be very much the exception.
[67] The remedies are not mutually exclusive—see para. 2.7. above.
[68] A style minute for such an application is set out in Appendix 3.
[69] r.34.12(1) of the Ordinary Cause Rules, inserted by S.S.I. 2002 No. 7.

proceedings raised by the creditor.[70] The experience to date has generally been that on receipt by the court of a minute from an applicant, a hearing is fixed three to four weeks distant and intimated to the creditor by the court. At the hearing, *ex parte* statements are advanced by each party. Usually at least one continuation is granted for investigation and at least one sheriff has adopted the position that determination of the application at the initial hearing is inappropriate. Standing the lack of any such direction in the Act, it is submitted that a blanket approach of that nature would be unfounded but the matter remains one of the sheriff's discretion.

As with summary applications, new forms are introduced for warrants of citation[71] and for citation itself[72] by the creditor and there is a new certificate of citation[73] style set down for all ordinary causes. These are repeated in the Appendix.[74] Although the potential applicants, if known to the creditor, will have been named in the initial writ,[75] it is specifically provided that a minute in support of an application may be lodged by a person entitled to do so even although that person has not been called as a defender and such a person may appear or be represented at any hearing to determine the application.[76] It is not, therefore, necessary to defend an action raised by a creditor to make an application under the Act but, as with any court action, it remains a possibility.

Indeed, it seems likely that there will soon be a large increase in the number of defended actions.[77] First, some cases were already defended before the Act came into force and many of those cases would not have been resolved by the procedure under the Act. Secondly, other developments in repossession law have suggested that it may be appropriate to defend actions in situations where there was at least doubt on that issue before.[78] Next, legal aid will be more readily available in the context of repossessions than before and that may encourage a more full investigation into the circumstances of the case than might previously have been the case. Finally, it is easy to imagine the situation where an applicant receives service papers but by the time he has read them and arranged an appointment with his solicitor, the time within which an application may be made has almost expired. For a solicitor who may have no experience of the Act, which in itself gives no indication of the procedure to be followed, the simplest course may be to lodge a notice of intention to defend to prevent decree passing and so extend the time within which an application may be made.[79]

---

[70] In relation to the application. In a defended court action, continuations may be granted for other reasons in accordance with the Ordinary Cause Rules.

[71] Form O2A of the Ordinary Cause Rules.

[72] Form O5A of the Ordinary Cause Rules.

[73] Form O6 of the Ordinary Cause Rules; while this form does not require the creditor to certify that the appropriate forms have been sent to "The Occupier" (see para. 4.2.30), some courts are now insisting that the following paragraph be added to the Certificate: "A copy of the court action together with Form [insert as appropriate] was sent to The Occupier by recorded delivery post. The counterfoil therefor is attached hereto."

[74] See para. 11.3.

[75] See para. 4.2.6.

[76] r.34.12(2) of the Ordinary Cause Rules, inserted by S.S.I. 2002 No. 7.

[77] A moderate increase has already been observed since the coming into effect of the 2001 Act.

[78] See for example *Sykes* at para. 2.2.12 and *Kinnear* at para. 5.19.

[79] s.1(4)(c).

It is essential to stress that the Scottish Executive envisages that the vast majority of the orders suspending creditors' rights which will be granted will be made during the course of the court action and not at the time of decree. In other words, successful applications under the Act will result in the suspension of creditors' rights within live court actions rather than the suspension of enforcement of a granted decree. Although it is not entirely clear, it does appear possible for the latter course to be adopted though in practice suspensions at decree are likely to form a minority of orders granted under the new regime.

Creditors will therefore not generally be in the position of having decrees on which to fall back if the applicant does not comply, as they do in England.[80] Rather, if there is non-compliance, creditors will require to return to court and persuade it at that stage to revoke the order and grant decree. This is a key difference with the English legislation and is an example of an area where, for all its intended effect, the 2001 Act has gone further than the equivalent English provisions.

Time Considerations

The Act does not apply in a case where a calling-up notice or notice of default is served or proceedings commenced[81] before December 3, 2001.[82] Generally, the time limits within which applications must be made are as follows:

4.2.9

(1) In response to a calling-up notice, before the expiry of the period of notice.[83] In other words, the application must be made within two months of service.[84]
(2) In response to a notice of default, not later than one month after the expiry of the period of notice.[85] Again, this means within two months of service of the notice.
(3) Where a section 24 writ or an action under section 5 of the 1894 Act have been raised, before the conclusion of proceedings. Although this is not defined, this presumably means before decree has been granted.[86]

The creditor is prohibited from exercising any of its rights (or rights which it may acquire) under the notices or court action at any time when an application is competent or while determination of an application is pending.[87] If the time limits for an application, which are mandatory,[88] are not complied with, there is no facility within the Act for the court to

---

[80] See para. 4.3.
[81] Under s.24 of the 1970 Act or s.5 of the 1894 Act.
[82] The Mortgage Rights (Scotland) Act 2001 (Commencement and Transitional Provisions) Order 2001 (S.S.I. 2001 No. 418).
[83] s.1(4)(a).
[84] For the date on which notice starts to run, see para. 4.2.25.
[85] s.1(4)(b).
[86] That is, final decree to include the issue of expenses. This interpretation is supported by Dailly, "Mortgage Rights (Scotland) Act 2001" *Scolag Legal Journal*, September 2001, p.158.
[87] s.1(7).
[88] s.1(4) uses the wording "must be made".

receive an application though late. If a court action raised by the creditor has been defended, the application may still be lodged after the *induciae* for the lodging of a notice of intention to defend has expired provided no decree has been obtained, as that will fall within the phrase "before the conclusion of proceedings".[89]

The law on waiver of periods of notice is revised by the 2001 Act. The 1970 Act formerly permitted the entire period of notice in either the calling-up notice or notice of default to be waived. The period of notice in the calling-up notice may no longer be shortened to a period of less than one month[90] and that only with the consent in writing of the recipient, the debtor, the proprietor,[91] the debtor's spouse (if the property is a matrimonial home), any other person entitled to make an application under the 2001 Act[92] and any creditors with *pari passu* or postponed ranking securities to that of the creditor serving the calling-up notice.[93] The form of waiver notice is set out in the 1970 Act.[94] The one month period of notice in a notice of default may not dispensed with or shortened[95] but the additional one month thereafter within which an application may be made[96] may be dispensed with or shortened provided the consent in writing is obtained of all recipients of the Notice[97]; if the security subjects are a matrimonial home, the spouses of all recipients; and any other person entitled to make an application under the 2001 Act.[98]

Proper Court for Applications

4.2.10 Although not a matter strictly dealt with in section 1 where the other procedural rules are found, it is convenient to consider the appropriate court at which to make applications during this discussion of procedural matters. Section 2(7) provides that "court" in sections 1 and 2 means the sheriff court. Accordingly, a mortgage rights application direct to the Court of Session would appear to be incompetent. This is a sensible provision having regard to the terms of section 29 of the 1970 Act which confers jurisdiction for repossession actions on the sheriff court.[99]

Disposal of Applications

4.2.11 Section 2 governs the powers of the court in determining applications and sets out in detail the issues which it must consider in exercising its discretion. Courts may make an order under this section only when it is

---

[89] s.1(4)(c).

[90] s.19(10) as revised by, and s.19(10A) of the 1970 Act as inserted by, s.1(8)(a) of the 2001 Act.

[91] These three will often of course be the same person.

[92] s.19(10B) of the 1970 Act as inserted by s.1(8)(a)(ii) of the 2001 Act.

[93] s.19(10); this allows such creditors an opportunity to make arrangements with the calling-up creditor if they do not wish the subjects to be sold: Halliday, *Conveyancing*, para. 54–17.

[94] Form C of Sched. 6; this form is repeated in the Appendix.

[95] s.1(8)(b).

[96] Under s.1(4)(b).

[97] That is, all proper recipients. Section 19(10) of the 1970 Act makes reference to the shortening of notice by the person "on whom it is served". If service is made on the wrong party, however, that party's inability to sufficiently bind others by his actions precludes him validly restricting the period of notice, at least as far as the Keeper is concerned: Cusine, *op. cit.*, para 8–12, Case 2.

[98] s.1(5).

[99] See para. 2.2.11.

considered reasonable in all circumstances to do so.[1] It is perhaps inevitable that such a sweeping piece of new legislation would include the undefined phrase "reasonable in all the circumstances", although further guidance is provided on when an order should be made in the Act.[2] The issue of reasonableness in recovery of property also crops up in the Housing (Scotland) Act 1988[3] and the Housing (Scotland) Act 2001[4] which may in the course of time have some influence on interpretation of the wording under the Act. Nonetheless, the phrase is likely to lead to inconsistency.[5]

If a Section 2 order is made, the court may suspend the exercise of the rights of the creditor[6] to such extent, for such period and subject to such conditions as it thinks fit.[7] If the application is made in proceedings under section 24 of the 1970 Act or section 5 of the 1894 Act, the court may continue the proceedings to such date as it thinks fit.[8] The Explanatory Notes to the Act,[9] prepared by the Scottish Executive, suggest that the main purpose of these provisions was twofold, namely to give the applicant reasonable time to remedy the default, where (in the view of the court) the applicant is likely to be able to achieve this, and/or to give the applicant and others staying at the property sufficient time to arrange alternative accommodation and avoid risking homelessness.

The Four-legged Test

4.2.12 Subject always to the stated caveats of reasonableness and taking into account all the circumstances, the Act currently provides that in assessing whether or not to make the order, the court must have regard to:

- the nature of and reasons for the default;
- the ability of the applicant[10] to fulfill within a reasonable period the obligations under the standard security in default;
- any action taken by the creditor to assist the debtor to fulfil those obligations; and
- the ability of the applicant and any other person residing at the subjects to secure reasonable alternative accommodation.[11]

Section 2 is of crucial importance as it is here that the law stated in *Halifax Building Society v. Gupta* is reversed. Each of the four legs of the test bears further examination.[12]

---

[1] s.2(2); the wording of the Act allows for the making of "an order under this section", referred to for convenience herein as a "Section 2 Order".
[2] See para. 4.2.12.
[3] (c.43), s.18.
[4] (asp 10), s.16.
[5] See para. 4.2.19 *infra*.
[6] Including rights which may be acquired.
[7] s.2(1)(a).
[8] s.2(1)(b).
[9] Available at www.scotland-legislation.hmso.gov.uk/legislation/scotland/en/2001en11.htm.
[10] Defined by s.2(7) as the person who makes an application under s.1(2).
[11] s.2(2).
[12] Though it must be remembered that the four legs are not an exhaustive list of what may be considered by the court.

Playing the First Leg at Home

4.2.13 It seems inevitable that guidelines will quickly be established on the phrase "the nature of and reasons for the default". On "nature", it seems logical to assume that the smaller the default—in most cases, the lower the monetary arrears—the more likely it will be that an application to suspend a creditor's rights will be granted. On "reasons", one may assume that a dramatic recent event in the debtor's life—for example, a marriage breakdown—will weigh more with the court than simple irresponsibility. The court may grant a section 2 order to allow a debtor a period within which to get his life back together. There is a similarity here with the terms of the Housing (Scotland) Act 2001 which provides that in deciding whether it is reasonable to terminate a Scottish Secure Tenancy, the court must take into account the nature, frequency and duration of the conduct forming the ground for recovery of possession.[13]

The Second Leg

4.2.14 In assessing "the applicant's ability to fulfill within a reasonable period the obligations . . . in default", the court in most cases is being asked to judge whether the arrears will be repaid within a reasonable period. In such monetary situations, the courts will presumably want to see some evidence of income and expenditure. It is important to note that the wording refers to the "applicant" rather than the "debtor". In a monetary situation, the court is being asked to consider the extent to which a party who may have no legal liability to the creditor under the standard security is able to pay for the obligations of another party. It remains to be seen how much emphasis will be placed by the courts on this leg in a situation where, for example, the applicant is an ex-partner of the debtor with care of their child.

Whatever information is put forward by the applicant, it may be difficult for a creditor to counter the details. In the case of an applicant who is the debtor, the creditor may refer to the mortgage application form though, of course, that could be long out of date. In the case of a non-debtor applicant, the creditor may have no information at all and may wish to instruct an enquiry agent. However, the expedited court procedure set down for disposal of applications may work against any attempt to ascertain the factual position by independent enquiry. There may be similarities, in relation to disposal of this leg, to the way in which applications for a time to pay direction[14] are currently dealt with in unsecured debt actions. In a non-monetary situation, the court may allow the debtor a fixed period within which to remedy—for example, to carry out repairs—under stipulation that the application for suspension will not be continued when the case next calls.

In the majority of cases, the courts to date have been prepared to accept *ex parte* statements at the bar in support of the income and expenditure details advanced by the parties. At most, the courts have

---

[13] Which is most likely to be non-payment of rent. The full provision is found at s.16(3)(a) of the Housing (Scotland) Act 2001.

[14] Under s.1 of the Debtors (Scotland) Act 1987 (c.18).

sought documentary evidence in relation to certain incomings or outgoings. It has been observed, however, in at least one case, that an affidavit should be completed by the creditor in terms of which the precise level of arrears on the account is formally confirmed to the court. It is submitted that such a course, other than where there is material and genuine dispute between the parties as to figures advanced, is unnecessary and inappropriate in the context of an expedited procedure. Nonetheless, as the matter is one of the sheriff's discretion, it is competent for the sheriff to order that formal affidavits be produced in support of figures put forward by the creditor or debtor.

Perhaps the most controversial aspect of this leg will prove to be the phrase "within a reasonable period". As noted above, the court may suspend the creditors' rights for such period as it thinks fit. There is no limitation on that period.[15] If there is to be a similar approach to time to pay applications, that might support the view that repayment of arrears within two years would be acceptable to the courts. It has been suggested that the same period of two years is generally acceptable in England[16] but there is Court of Appeal authority[17] that the two year period should be departed from and a move made towards accepting repayment of arrears over the whole of the remaining term of the mortgage.[18] It is to be hoped that guidelines will quickly be established.

The Third Leg

The third leg obliges the court to have regard to "any action taken by the creditor to assist the debtor to fulfill those obligations". In most cases, as with the second leg, the obligations in question will be the repayment of monetary arrears.

4.2.15

This wording was incorporated at Stage 2 of the Bill's progress through the Scottish Parliament following submissions made by the Council of Mortgage Lenders[19] to the Scottish Executive. The CML felt that the first draft of the Bill (where this leg did not appear) failed to recognize action already taken by creditors to assist debtors with repayment difficulties.

The CML considered it important that the court takes into account any alternative payment arrangements which the debtor had agreed with the creditor for clearing the arrears and whether the debtor had complied with these arrangements. This allows the court to judge what action has already been taken by the creditor to try and help the debtor with the arrears and if the debtor has met those payments. The provision seems reasonable. It would surely not be just that a debtor who has received no letters or telephone calls from a creditor should be treated

---

[15] Despite submissions during the progress of the Bill from the Council of Mortgage Lenders that there should be.
[16] Dailly, *op. cit.*, p.158.
[17] *Cheltenham and Gloucester Building Society v. Norgan* [1996] All E.R. 449; planned regulation by the Financial Services Authority ("the FSA") makes it more likely that *Norgan* will be followed in the future: see para. 4.3.1.
[18] See para. 4.3 for a full discussion of the English experience to date, and Urquhart, Green's *Property Law Bulletin*, 53–2.
[19] Hereafter "the CML".

the same as one who has consistently ignored relevant correspondence or has broken a repayment arrangement. If a debtor has persistently failed to adhere to repayment arrangements in the past, that might provide material for the court to judge how the debtor would comply with a section 2 order with repayment conditions. This of course ties in with the second leg on the applicant's ability to fulfill the obligations in default.

Generally, a creditor will have attempted to resolve the matter by telephone and letter at the very least. It is now common for creditors also to involve a debt counselor who will visit the debtor in person and attempt to come to an arrangement that is satisfactory to both creditor and debtor. The extent of forbearance to which a creditor will agree will often depend on a number of factors, such as the ratio of the outstanding loan to the value of the property. The time of year may also play a part as creditors are often reluctant to enforce securities during the Christmas holiday period with a view to avoiding negative publicity.

The wording of the third leg encourages all heritable creditors to comply with the Mortgage Code.[20] Section 8 of the Code, which is monitored by the independent Mortgage Code Compliance Board,[21] provides that creditors are to deal sympathetically and positively with debtors facing financial difficulty. In terms of the Code, mortgage lenders will lend responsibly at the outset and will offer mortgage repayment protection insurance.[22] If arrears do develop, the creditor must develop a plan with the debtor for dealing with the arrears and co-operate with any debt counselling agencies. In all cases, possession will only be taken as a last resort.[23] The wording also encourages compliance with the CML's Statement of Practice on Arrears and Possessions.[24] This includes development of a plan with the debtor for clearing the arrears and seeking possession only as a last resort where attempts to reach alternative arrangements have been unsuccessful.

Even outwith the terms of these regulations, the third leg allows the court to judge what action has already been taken by the creditor to try and help the debtor with the arrears and whether the debtor has

---

[20] This is a voluntary code setting standards of good lending practice with which virtually all mortgage lenders comply. The full text of the Mortgage Code is available at http://www.mortgagecode.co.uk/mortgagecode.html.

[21] Which may reprimand, fine, suspend or de-register creditors.

[22] The CML estimate that 31 per cent of debtors in securities held by their members now carry such insurance.

[23] A European Code of Conduct has also been developed by the European Mortgage Federation and has been signed up to by CML members in the U.K. Implementation of this code was due by September 2002 though this may be delayed due to the change in the timetable for regulation of the field by the FSA (see para. 9.4.5). Compliance with this code may be another issue to which a creditor may refer under this leg, though as a matter of practice, compliance with the European Code may not involve any further consultation than would be required by the U.K. Mortgage Code.

[24] For an example of a case where such a voluntary code was taken into account by the court, see para. 4.3.1. The CML represents 98 per cent of the residential lending sector. A Pre-Action Protocol has been drafted by the CML to standardise the dispute resolution procedure among creditors before legal action is taken. This is currently subject to consultation with consumer and related bodies.

complied with any alternative arrangements. Again, there are similarities with the terms of the Housing (Scotland) Act 2001.[25]

Homing in on the Last Leg

It will be particularly interesting to note the courts' attitude to the last leg of the test, namely the ability of the applicant and any other person living at the subjects to secure reasonable alternative accommodation. It seems certain that courts will request information about the efforts those living in the house have made to find other accommodation and how long it is likely to be before that can be obtained. The location of such other accommodation may be relevant in assessing whether it is "reasonable". For example, if it will require children to change school and lose contact with existing friends, some sheriffs may consider it appropriate to grant a section 2 order.

4.2.16

More generally, this leg has been criticised for going further than simply considering the position of the debtor and his immediate family. The Act fails to define the phrase "any other person" used in this leg. Although, as noted above, it is not open to "any other person" to make an application under the Act, it is clear from the wording of this leg that should that person make known through another applicant their potential homelessness, the court may suspend the creditor's rights. The CML have noted that one consequence of this wide wording is that if the ability of, for example, lodgers to find alternative accommodation is taken into account by the court in granting a possession order, creditors may be more reluctant to consent to such letting arrangements. Creditors may certainly face some practical difficulty in countering information put forward by an applicant in relation to this leg.

There is also a potential catch 22 situation here. Local authorities are often reluctant to make a decision on the provision of alternative housing until a repossession decree has been granted. On the other hand, the court requires to consider what alternative accommodation will be available if repossession is granted. It remains to be seen how this conflict will work in practice as there is no guidance in the 2001 Act itself, but it should be noted that the duties of local authorities to persons threatened with homelessness are changed by the Housing (Scotland) Act 2001 such that the authority's duties to take steps to prevent threatened homelessness are increased.[26]

A final comment on this leg is that it fails to take any account of the reasons for homelessness, though that may be covered by the catch all "reasonable in all the circumstances". If not, the wording might be construed in such a way that a particular type of person—say, for example a drug user or convicted paedophile—who might have more difficulty than most in obtaining alternative accommodation, will be in a

---

[25] In terms of s.16(3)(d) of that Act, in assessing whether it is reasonable to order eviction from a Scottish Secure Tenancy, the court must have regard to "any action taken by the landlord, before raising the proceedings, with a view to securing the cessation of [the tenant's] conduct".

[26] s.32 of the Housing (Scotland) Act 1987 (c.26) as amended by the Housing (Scotland) Act 2001, s.3; one of the key provisions is the extension of the period within which a person may be threatened with homelessness from one month to two months.

more favourable position than the average debtor. There is no political statement here but, if the demonstrations against paedophiles in Portsmouth during 2000 are any guide, it must be unlikely that such interpretation would be welcomed by the general public.

To Such Extent, for Such Period and Subject to Such Conditions

4.2.17 The wording used by the Act makes clear that the precise terms of the order made are a matter for the discretion of the sheriff and are likely to vary widely depending on individual circumstances. There is as yet no case law in Scotland to cast light on the meaning of the phrases "to such extent", "for such period" and "subject to such conditions" as they apply to suspension of creditors' rights. Some guidance may be gained from consideration of similar phrases in England.[27] For the time being, it seems reasonable to assume that the court may specify a certain amount for the debtor to repay for a specified period of time, with a stipulation that failure by the debtor to adhere could lead to the revocation or expiry of the section 2 order. Timescales may also be set by the court for the debtor and others to find alternative accommodation with the court making clear that decree will be granted in favour of the creditor once that time period has expired.

Further Provisions in Relation to Section 2 Orders

4.2.18 Where the applicant clears the default while an order is in force, the standard security has effect as if the default had not occurred.[28] Special power is granted to the court in relation to calling-up notices.[29] The effect of a calling-up notice is, of course, to seek repayment of all sums outstanding within two months, failing which extensive rights are made available to the creditor.[30] A suspension order granted by the court for a fixed period in relation to a calling-up notice might therefore have been of limited benefit to a debtor who would struggle to pay all principal, interest and expenses within that timescale. The Act makes special provision to ensure that creditors do not circumvent its terms by serving calling-up notices when they are truly seeking recovery of arrears. The provision set down is that the court may suspend enforcement of the calling-up notice until the notice expires under the 1970 Act.[31] This permits the court to allow the applicant to repay the arrears only rather than the whole debt as otherwise required by a calling-up notice.

The terms of a section 2 order are by no means final. First, there are rights of appeal.[32] Although the sheriff's power is discretionary, the

---

[27] See para. 4.3.2.

[28] s.2(3); Sheriff Cusine has noted that one possible interpretation of this provision is that the creditor may not recover any expense incurred in relation to the default: Annotation to the 2001 Act, R. Rennie (ed.), *Scottish Conveyancing Legislation*, para. A.859, but the other interpretation he states there, that it simply means the creditor may not found on the default again, is more likely.

[29] s.2(4).

[30] See para. 2.2 above.

[31] The expiry period of a calling-up notice is five years under s.19(11) of the 1970 Act. See para. 2.2.4.

[32] Though in an application by the creditor under s.24, these are limited by r.23.10(2) of the Ordinary Cause Rules: see para. 2.2.11.

sheriff will require in his consideration of the case and in his note to address all aspects of the four legged test, under the umbrella of reasonableness and taking into account all the circumstances, failing which grounds of appeal may lie on the basis that the sheriff has not properly addressed his mind to the requirements of the legislation. Usually, the sheriff's decision will not be a final judgment disposing of the subject matter of the cause and as a result leave to appeal will be required to challenge an interlocutor under section 2.[33]

Secondly, the Act allows the creditor or the applicant to apply to the court to change the terms of the order or revoke it, or to further continue proceedings to a future date.[34] It seems reasonable to assume that a variation of an order will only be made if there has been a material change in circumstances though the circumstances of when a variation may be granted are not in any way restricted by the terms of the Act. The ability to apply for revocation is certainly a sensible provision. If a debtor is granted a section 2 order allowing him six months to make regular payments to bring arrears up to date and then fails to make any payment in the first three months after the order is made, it must be fair that a creditor should be entitled to return to court before the expiry of the originally specified period and seek a revocation order.

There is no restriction on the number of times that a section 2 order, or consideration of an application for such an order, may be continued. Although this falls within the general discretion available to the sheriff under the Act, it is perhaps surprising, having regard to the general move towards more closed adjustment procedures, that there is no limit at all on continuations. Early indications show that the courts are prepared to grant one or more continuations simply to allow the full factual background to be established before the application is substantively determined.

Finally, section 2 provides that both sections 1 and 2 are without prejudice to any other rights available to debtors, proprietors or non-entitled spouses.[35]

General Comment on Section 2

There are certain key issues thrown up by section 2 in relation to differing interests, inconsistency and, should it proceed, the mortgage to rent scheme.[36]

4.2.19

There is no guidance in the Act or elsewhere on how courts are to deal with cases where the interests of the debtor and the applicant for a suspended order differ. The CML has cited the example of a debtor who has separated from his partner and left the property. He may have lost

---

[33] Macphail, *Sheriff Court Practice* (2nd ed., 1998), para. 18–34; but if the cause is simply a summary application instigated by the applicant to challenge a calling-up notice or notice of default, refusal of the application may well amount to final judgment, rendering the decision open to appeal without leave.

[34] s.2(5).

[35] s.2(6).

[36] A full discussion of this scheme and its interaction with the 2001 Act is set out at para. 9.2.5.

his job, be unable to pay the mortgage and want the property repossessed to stop arrears mounting further. However, his partner may still be living at the property with their children. Although the legislation is unclear on this, it may be that the problem will often be more illusory than real. A partner remaining in the subjects with a child may be entitled[37] to have the Benefits Agency pay the creditor[38] in which case the conflicting interest does not arise, as the debtor's liability for arrears will not increase.[39] However, it is true that if there is no support from the state, the debtor's position will be worsened. The question to be asked is whether the court would look favourably on an application by the partner in these circumstances if the applicant is unwilling to make payments towards the debtor's liability which of course is a consideration under the second leg of the four-legged test. The matter is discretionary so there is no certain answer but it seems likely that once again the principal issue to be considered will be the income and expenditure of the applicant. It does not necessarily follow that because someone does not qualify for support from the state, they have a high disposable income. Accordingly, the possibility of conflicting interests does remain and it seems reasonable to suppose that the interests of children will weigh heavily with the courts. Only time will tell.

The inclusion of undefined sweeping phrases such as "reasonable in all the circumstances" and "within a reasonable period" in section 2 seems likely, in the initial stages at least, to create inconsistency between the courts.[40] Certain courts may take the view that a creditor has complied with his obligations by seeking repayment in correspondence. A step further might see a creditor survive an application on the basis it has put forward the opportunity of debt counselling. It may be more likely, however, that the intended reversal of the pre-existing law will see many debtors afforded the benefit of the postponement procedures. Clearly, one sheriff is not bound by the decision of another sheriff at any time. Can it therefore be assumed that the superior courts, in the fullness of time, will sort out the guidelines? Even on appeal, the wide discretion permitted to sheriffs may be viewed in a similar way to the issue of expenses now, where the appeal courts are reluctant to interfere unless there has been an obvious error.

The subject of expenses in mortgage rights applications is not covered in the Act or the subordinate legislation and is discussed below.[41]

Registration of Section 2 Order

4.2.20 Where an order is made under section 2, the clerk of court must, as soon as possible, send a certified copy of the order to the Keeper of the

---

[37] Depending on financial circumstances; see para. 6.6.1.
[38] Such payments are made direct to the creditor, rather than through the debtor who might not apply the money to the loan.
[39] Or at the very least will increase to a limited extent.
[40] And indeed between sheriffs within the same court. Some practitioners in the larger courts take the view that the likelihood of an application being granted will be a matter of luck, depending on the sheriff allocated to determine it.
[41] See para. 5.1.7.

Register of Inhibitions and Adjudications for recording.[42] He is also obliged to send to the Keeper a notice in the following terms[43]:

NOTICE
SHERIFF COURT, (*insert place of sheriff court*)
Date of order, (*insert date*)

A.B. (*insert designation and address*), **PURSUER(S)**
against
C.D. (*insert designation and address*), **DEFENDER(S)**

The Sheriff of (*insert name of sheriffdom*) at (*insert place of sheriff court*) has made an order, (*insert date*) under section 2 of the Mortgage Rights (Scotland) Act 2001—

> (*to suspend*) suspending for a period of (*insert period of suspension*) from (*give date on which suspension begins*) the exercise of the rights which the said C.D has or may acquire by virtue of the Conveyancing and Feudal Reform (Scotland) Act 1970 or the Heritable Securities (Scotland) Act 1894
> (*to continue*) continuing proceedings under section 24 of the Conveyancing and Feudal Reform (Scotland) Act 1970 / section 5 of the Heritable Securities (Scotland) Act 1894 until (*insert date to which proceedings are continued*)
> (*to vary*) varying the order (*insert details of previous order*) as follows (*insert details of variation*)
> (*to revoke*) revoking the order (*insert details of previous order*)
> (*delete as appropriate*)
> in respect of Security Subjects (*enter address*) as referred to in Standard Security granted by (*insert name of Granter(s)*) in favour of (*insert name of Grantee(s)*), (*insert date of recording, specifying the Division of the General Register of Sasines, or the date of registration in the Land Register, as the case may be*),
> a copy of which Order is annexed.
> (*insert name*)
> Sheriff Clerk Depute

The purpose of section 3 is to avoid the risk of a fraudulent or accidental sale by a creditor in the face of a section 2 order. This section was added after adverse comment on the Bill as introduced from the Keeper of the Registers of Scotland. It was thought that a sale by a creditor in defiance or ignorance of a section 2 order, or while an application for such an order was pending, might create a risk on the Keeper's indemnity. It seems clear from submissions made by the Keeper that the principal area of concern related to "unscrupulous lenders" and it appears unlikely that section 3 will have major effect on high street lenders.

---

[42] s.3(1)(a); there is therefore no cost in recording to creditor or debtor.
[43] s.3(1)(b); the form of notice is set out by The Mortgage Rights (Scotland) Act 2001 (Prescribed Notice) Order 2001 (S.S.I. 2001 No. 419), as permitted by s.3(2).

The Scottish Executive has issued assurances that the Scottish Courts Service will have the resources to ensure these notices are registered promptly. This may prove to be of importance as it seems that any continuation ordered under the 2001 Act must be sent for registration. It is easy to imagine a case, particularly if it has been defended, where there are numerous continuations granted. It seems that notice of each of those continuations should be registered.

The effect of section 2 orders on the conveyancing practicalities of repossession sales is dealt with below.[44]

Notices to Debtors, Proprietors and Occupiers

4.2.21 The rules on service of notices and court proceedings are substantially changed by the 2001 Act. In addition to revisal of the styles set out in the 1970 Act, the 2001 Act introduces the new concept of service of forms on "The Occupier" and provides for service of notices along with the service copy of court proceedings raised under section 24 of the 1970 Act or section 5 of the 1894 Act. The new forms introduced by the 2001 Act are repeated in full in the Appendix,[45] as are the new styles for calling-up notices[46] and notices of default[47] to reflect the changes to those notices brought about by the 2001 Act.[48]

Which Notices must be Served?

4.2.22 An overview of the notices which must be served is as follows:

Type of Creditor Action	Documents to be Served on Existing Recipients[49]	Documents to be Served on the Occupier
Service of a calling-up notice	Form A of Schedule 6 to the 1970 Act	Copy Form A and Form BB of Schedule 6 to the 1970 Act
Service of a notice of default	Form B of Schedule 6 to the 1970 Act	Copy Form B and Form BB of Schedule 6 to the 1970 Act
Service of a writ under section 24 of the 1970 Act	Service copy writ, service papers[50] and Form E of Schedule 6 to the 1970 Act	Copy writ and Form F of Schedule 6 to the 1970 Act
Service of proceedings under Section 5 of the 1894 Act[51]	Service copy writ, service papers and Form 1 in Part 2 of the Schedule to the 2001 Act	Copy writ and Form 2 in Part 2 of the Schedule to the 2001 Act

---

[44] See para. 8.5.
[45] See Appendix 1.
[46] See para. 13.14.
[47] See para. 13.15.
[48] The changes to the existing styles are set out in Pt 1 of the Sched. to the Act (paras 1–3) and simply reflect the rights conferred on the recipient of the notice by the Act and possible eligibility for legal aid.
[49] In other words, this column identifies the documents which should now be served on all those who would have received service of papers prior to the Act coming into force. For further detail of the persons on whom service should be made, see para. 4.2.30 below.
[50] As specified by Chap. 5 of the Ordinary Cause Rules 1993 (being the first Sched. to the Sheriff Courts (Scotland) Act 1907 (c.51)).
[51] Including service of a writ related to an expired calling-up notice.

As discussed above, the crave for ejection which is likely to be included in the repossession writ is in fact based on section 5 of the 1894 Act.[52] The 2001 Act provides that one notice is to be served in the case of an application under section 24 of the 1970 Act and another where the application is under section 5 of the 1894 Act. In the case of a section 24 action, it is likely that craves will be brought under both sections within the same process. Does this mean both notices must be served? Although this is a possibility, the better view is surely that notification under the procedure for section 24 actions will be sufficient. To do otherwise will merely lead to repetition of documentation and confusion in the mind of the debtor. By providing the notice to accompany the section 24 action, the debtor will receive essentially the same notification of his rights as he would obtain on receipt of notices under both that section and section 5 of the 1894 Act.

There is no express reference, in relation to service of notices, in the 2001 Act to section 20 of the 1970 Act which regulates the remedies available to a creditor following the expiry of a calling-up notice. An action for declarator related to that section is not an application under section 24 or indeed any of the provisions of the 1970 Act.[53] Were it not for the 1894 Act, it appears that a court action related to an expired calling-up notice might not require to be accompanied by any notice under the 2001 Act. However, as that action is likely to include a crave for ejection which finds its legal basis in the 1894 Act, it appears that such an action should be accompanied by the notices provided for in relation to that legislation.[54]

The penalty for non-compliance with these rules is that the calling-up notice or notice of default is held to be of no effect.[55] The Act fails, however, to specify what happens in the event of non-compliance with the rules in the event of service of court proceedings, either under the 1970 Act or the 1894 Act. It may be that an occupier, for example, who has not been sent appropriate intimation papers would be entitled to interdict a creditor from taking possession on the basis of his failure under the 2001 Act.

When Should Notices be Served?

A further difficulty with the Act relates to the precise wording of when the notices to the debtor, the proprietor and the occupier, to complement court proceedings, are to be served. In the case of proceedings under the 1970 Act, the Act says simply that the notices are to be served "[w]here the creditor applies to the Court".[56] The implication of such wording is that the notice should be served at the time of raising the

4.2.23

---

[52] See para. 2.2.10.
[53] See para. 2.2.11.
[54] Although it appears from the presentation of the legislation that such a result is accidental, the provisions on notices to accompany an action under the 1894 Act truly being designed to ensure notice to debtors and others where pre-1970 Act securities are being enforced.
[55] ss.19A(3) and 21(2A) of the 1970 Act as inserted by s.4(1) and (2) of the 2001 Act.
[56] s.24(3) of the 1970 Act as inserted by s.4(3) of the 2001 Act; In the case of proceedings under the 1894 Act, the equivalent wording used is "[w]here a creditor . . . commences proceedings" which does mean the date of service: see n.57 below.

action rather than at the point of service. That would have the bizarre result, however, that the notice (which must include a copy of the application) would arrive before the formal service copy of the proceedings. It is submitted that such a result cannot have been the intention of Parliament and that service of the notice at the same time as service of proceedings should be sufficient. The matter is not altogether free from doubt, though, and will remain so until an authoritative ruling is laid down.[57]

Method of Service

4.2.24 Of all the matters changed by the 2001 Act, that which has received the most publicity is how notices will be served.[58] In particular, it has been suggested that debtors in arrears can avoid repossession by simply refusing to answer their door to receive a recorded delivery notice and cannot then receive service by way of sheriff officer. A distinction requires to be made between the service of a calling-up notice, notice of default or court proceedings on the one hand and service of notices to occupiers and explanatory notices to accompany court proceedings on the other. In other words, there is a difference in the law as it applies to the existing forms and procedures to be followed, which have been adjusted by the 2001 Act, and the new forms which have been introduced by the 2001 Act.

Service of Forms Adjusted by the 2001 Act and of Court Proceedings

4.2.25 The 1970 Act provides that service of a calling-up notice may be made by delivery to the person on whom it is desired to be served or the notice may be sent by registered or recorded delivery post to him at his last known address.[59] If the address of the person on whom the creditor wishes to serve is not known, or if it is not known whether the person is still alive, or if the packet containing a calling-up notice is returned to the creditor with an intimation that it could not be delivered, the notice must be sent to the extractor of the Court of Session.[60] Service on the extractor is equivalent to service of a calling-up notice in the primary

---

[57] Support from the interpretation submitted as correct is available from *Edinburgh D.C. v. Davies*, 1987 S.L.T. (Sh.Ct) 33 where the court considered the terms of s.14 of the Tenants' Rights etc. (Scotland) Act 1980 (c.52). In that case, it was held that commencement of action is certainly when the action is served and "raising proceedings" means "commencing an action by effectual citation". However the wording "applies to the court" does not appear to have been judicially considered in Scotland.

[58] See for example the lead story in *The Herald*, December 21, 2001.

[59] s.19(6); note that in *Household Mortgage Corporation plc v. Diggory*, reported at Paisley and Cusine, *Unreported Property Cases from the Sheriff Courts* (W. Green and Son, Edinburgh, 2001), p.455, Sheriff Principal Risk Q.C. made clear, in circumstances where properly addressed calling-up notices had been accepted by a neighbour who had failed to pass them on to the debtors, that it is not a defence to aver that service was accepted by a third party even where the notices do not later reach the debtors. As Paisley and Cusine point out (p.461) it is possible for debtors to protect themselves against this eventuality by varying the terms of the security to provide for service in a specified manner, though residential debtors may not be able to negotiate these terms in practice; if service is being made on the Lord Advocate, service is to him at the Crown Office, Edinburgh.

[60] s.19(6).

manner.[61] A calling-up notice served by post is held to have been served on the day after the day of posting.[62] Section 21(2) of the 1970 Act provides that the notice of default "shall be served in the like manner and with the like requirements as to proof of service as a calling-up notice". In the case of court proceedings under the 1970 Act, they may be served by the normal rules governing service of writs.[63] In the case of court proceedings under the 1894 Act, service of the writ again falls to be governed by the standard rules on service.[64] Although the form of calling-up notice and notice of default are revised by the 2001 Act,[65] none of the rules on service detailed above is changed.

It is therefore clear that service of calling-up notices and notices of default continue to be governed by the 1970 Act and that either recorded delivery[66] or personal service of those notices is entirely competent under section 19(6) of the 1970 Act. Similarly, as regards service of court writs (as opposed to the notices specified to accompany them[67]), there is nothing in the 2001 Act which precludes service by the normal service methods, including by sheriff officer.[68] It is therefore submitted that it is incorrect to say that personal service is now incompetent generally in repossession actions or, indeed, that there is any change to the existing methods of service of calling-up notices, notices of default or court proceedings.[69]

Service of Forms Introduced by the 2001 Act

These forms include, first, each of the forms which must be served on the occupier, namely Forms BB and F of Schedule 6 to the 1970 Act and Form 2 of Part 2 of the Schedule to the 2001 Act. Secondly, the forms include the forms which must be served along with court proceedings, namely Form E of Schedule 6 to the 1970 Act and Form 1 of Part 2 of the Schedule to the 2001 Act. There are in fact three arguments as to how service of these notices should be effected, each of which is considered below. Given the confusion which has arisen over this issue, it is worth repeating the relevant statutory provisions in full.

4.2.26

The first argument is based on a literal reading of the new provisions in relation to service, inserted into the 1970 Act by the 2001 Act. For example, section 24 of the 1970 Act[70] now provides:

---

[61] *ibid.*

[62] s.19(8). It is submitted this means business day; but even where it was averred that service had been made on the day of posting, that did not provide a defence to a creditor's action for repossession: *Royal Bank of Scotland plc v. Marshall*, Paisley and Cusine, *op. cit.*, p.445.

[63] Chap. 5 of the Ordinary Cause Rules.

[64] In terms of the Act of Sederunt (Summary Cause Rules, Sheriff Court) 1976 (S.I. 1976 No. 476), see para. 3.5. As of June 10, 2002, the Act of Sederunt is revoked and the Act of Sederunt (Summary Cause Rules) 2002 (S.S.I. 2002 No. 132) comes into force. If declarator is sought, the Ordinary Cause Rules apply.

[65] See para. 4.2.21.

[66] Note that special delivery post is incompetent—*Ross and Bonnyman Ltd v. Hawson Garner Ltd*, 2001 G.W.D. 25–921.

[67] On which see para. 4.2.26.

[68] s.23(4) of the 1970 Act and s.4(5) of the 2001 Act relate only to service of notices.

[69] The content of the service papers has however changed: see para. 4.2.8.

[70] As amended by s.4(3) of the 2001 Act.

"(3) Where the creditor applies to the court under subsection (1) above, he shall . . .—

    (a) serve on the debtor and (where the proprietor is not the debtor) on the proprietor a notice in conformity with Form E of Schedule 6 to this Act,[71] and

    (b) serve on the occupier of the security subjects a notice in conformity with Form F of that Schedule.

(4) Notices under subsection (3) above shall be sent by recorded delivery letter addressed—

    (a) in the case of a notice under subsection (3)(a), to the debtor or . . . proprietor

    (b) in the case of a notice under subsection (3)(b), to 'The Occupier'".[72]

The argument goes that as the Act simply requires the notices to be sent by recorded delivery, the creditor does not require to establish receipt by the debtor, whether through the recorded delivery service or otherwise. The creditor fulfils his requirements under the Act when the letter is sent. This argument is supported by Cathie Craigie[73] and by the Scottish Executive.[74]

This argument is an attractive proposition on a reading of section 24(4) but matters are complicated by the mandatory requirement on the creditor in terms of section 24(3) to "serve . . . a notice".[75] Nonetheless, it is submitted that the two subsections must be read together. Doing so suggests that the method of the service mentioned in section 24(3) is that provided for in section 24(4). This leads to the conclusion that a creditor will indeed have complied with his duties if he simply sends the notices in Forms E and F by recorded delivery irrespective of whether actual service results. The same argument appears to hold good in relation to the notice to the occupier[76] which must accompany service of a calling-up notice or notice of default.[77]

The effect of the second argument, if it was successful, would be to make repossession extremely difficult if a debtor did not answer his door

---

[71] That is, the 1970 Act.

[72] The only relevant difference to consider for these purposes (leaving aside the identity of the recipients and the notices themselves) where court proceedings are commenced under the 1894 Act rather than the 1970 Act is that the notices to be served "must be sent", rather than "shall be sent": ss.4(4) and (5) of 2001 Act. It is submitted that both "must" and "shall" are mandatory in their terms and that this discussion applies both to service of the new forms under s.24 of the 1970 Act and service of forms in relation to 1894 Act proceedings by virtue of s.4 of the 2001 Act.

[73] The M.S.P. who introduced the Bill which led to the 2001 Act.

[74] See for example the booklet "The Mortgage Rights (Scotland) Act 2001 and You", published by the Scottish Executive.

[75] The same wording appears in s.4(4) of the 2001 Act in relation to proceedings under the 1894 Act.

[76] Form BB of Sched. 6 to the 1970 Act.

[77] In relation to calling-up notices, s.19A(1) of the 1970 Act (inserted by s.4(1) of the 2001 Act) again talks of service of the form but s.19A(2) provides: "Notices under subsection (1) above shall be sent by recorded delivery letter". The provisions of s.19A in relation to calling-up notices are applied to notices of default by s.21(2A) of the 1970 Act (inserted by s.4(2) of the 2001 Act).

to accept recorded delivery packages, or if the debtor or occupier was not present at the subjects for any reason.[78] The nature of the second argument is simply to rebut the premise of the first that sending the explanatory notices which accompany proceedings or the notices to the occupier is sufficient service. If service cannot be effected by recorded delivery, the argument goes, it remains incumbent on the creditor to achieve service. However, as no other method of service is competently provided for in the new provisions, he is unable to comply with his service obligation. In the case of a calling-up notice or notice of default, the legislation expressly provides that if a creditor has failed to comply, the calling-up notice or notice of default are held to be of no effect.[79] In the case of court proceedings where, for example, Form F has not been properly served on the occupier, the argument would be that the action is premature due to the failure to serve the mandatory notice. This argument has been primarily advanced by Mike Dailly of Govan Law Centre, whose views have been promulgated by *The Herald* newspaper. There is support for the view that no other method of service is competent[80] and so the difference between the first and second arguments comes to be whether a creditor has fulfilled his obligations simply by sending the notices whether or not actual service results. The issue cannot be free from doubt but it is submitted that the first argument is to be preferred for the reasons stated above.[81]

The third argument, which has also been advanced by Ms Craigie and the Scottish Executive, is that the difference between the first and second arguments is academic as the Act does not in fact preclude service by other means, as it does not provide that notices may be issued *only* by recorded delivery post. It is certainly true that the 2001 Act does not expressly exclude service by other means. The view that service by sheriff officers remains competent has received some support from commentators on the Act.[82] Indeed, it appears that the drafters of the legislation envisaged that service might take place in an alternative manner. The new certificate of citation provides that court proceedings may be served by sheriff officer[83] and it may be assumed that the Executive proceeded on the basis that the court proceedings would be served at the same time as the explanatory notices in Forms E and F.[84] While that may well have been the state of mind which led to these provisions,[85] it is difficult to interpret "shall be sent by recorded delivery"[86] as meaning that other methods of service are permitted. It is submitted that there is insufficient

---

[78] See *The Herald*, December 21, 2001, p.1.

[79] s.19A(3) of 1970 Act, dealing with calling-up notices, which is applied to notices of default by s.21(2A) the 1970 Act.

[80] See *Kane, infra* no. 88.

[81] Namely a reading together of ss.24(3) and (14) of the 1970 Act.

[82] See for example comments in *The Herald*, December 22, 2001.

[83] Form O6 of the First Sched. to the Sheriff Courts (Scotland) Act 1907 as inserted by S.S.I. 2002 No. 7.

[84] Indeed, if this is not what the Scottish Parliament intended, this creates further difficulties with the Act: see para. 4.2.23.

[85] Although the Explanatory Notes to the Act are quite clear that the notices "will be sent by recorded delivery".

[86] s.24(4) of the 1970 Act; or "must be sent" for 1894 Act proceedings: s.4(5) of the 2001 Act.

ambiguity in the wording which would allow the courts to give creditors' latitude in their choice of method of service.[87]

In *Govan Housing Society v. Kane*,[88] Sheriff Johnston[89] found,

> "in my view the service of a notice to quit . . . is such a fundamental and important document for the purposes of recovery of heritable possession that it required to be served in the manner set out in [rule] 34.8.[[90]] and that this did not brook any other method of service. So the options were, recorded delivery by any of the persons mentioned in 34.8.1 or sheriff officers. In this case it was not sheriff officers who made the service and in my view it was therefore inept. Accordingly the foundation for the action having been withdrawn, it must fall".

Although the case was a dispute between landlord and tenant, it is submitted that the sheriff's findings are capable of extension to the relationship of creditor and debtor in standard security. It is accordingly submitted that this argument is wrong and that service of the notices to the occupier and to accompany court proceedings is not permitted by sheriff officer.[91]

Nevertheless, a creditor may take the view that the best option is a "belt and braces" approach where, having sent an unsuccessful recorded delivery notice to the occupier or notice accompanying court proceedings to the debtor or proprietor, the creditor then has the notice served by sheriff officer.[92] There are attractions to this approach. The creditor has sent the notices by recorded delivery and so, if the first argument is correct, he has fulfilled his obligations. If it is incorrect, but the third argument is correct, he meets his requirements by service by sheriff officer. If the second argument is correct, he has not validly complied with his obligations but it would have been impossible to do so and he has at least done all he can to try to bring the matter to the attention of the recipient of the notice. Regrettably, the matter may not be as simple as that. If the second argument is correct, then service of the notices has

---

[87] In *Bank of Scotland v. Millward*, 1999 S.L.T. 901, the Inner House was prepared to read the word "shall" in s.19 of the 1970 Act in a permissive and not a mandatory sense (see para. 2.7). However, that section deals with one of several remedies open to a creditor, whereas s.24(4) places an obligation, with no alternative, on the creditor. The distinction is important and, it is submitted, means that "shall" in s.24(4) must be read in the mandatory sense.

[88] July 6, 2001, unreported.

[89] at Glasgow.

[90] That is, r.34.8 of the first Sched. to the Sheriff Courts (Scotland) Act 1907 which provides "(1) A notice . . . may be given by—(a) a sheriff officer (b) the person entitled to give such notice, or (c) the solicitor or factor of such person, posting the notice by registered post or the first class recorded delivery service . . . (2) A sheriff officer may also give notice . . . in any manner in which he may serve an initial writ".

[91] It is true that neither Forms E nor F will form the foundation for the action (unlike, for example, a calling-up notice) but it is submitted that the decision in *Kane* confirms that, even for these forms, a creditor may not choose a method of service which is not provided for in the Act.

[92] It is certainly not appropriate to proceed directly to sheriff officer without first attempting recorded delivery service, standing the wording of ss.19A(2) and 24(4) of the 1970 Act and s.4(4) of the 2001 Act.

not been made and, despite what the creditor may have tried to do, there may be a fundamental problem with his right to proceed further. If that was all, there might be no real downside in this approach, other than the additional cost of sheriff officers. However, serving the notices by sheriff officer where the creditor is not entitled to do so may give rise to a claim by the recipient that the creditor has wrongfully instructed sheriff officers to serve a document on him when he has no power to do so. Such service might be argued to be akin to wrongful diligence[93] or a breach of Article 8 and Article 1 of the First Protocol to the European Convention on Human Rights.[94]

Practical Issues of Service

4.2.27 Very often the debtor will be the same person as the occupier and so the difficulty over service of notices on the occupier may be overcome if service is made on the debtor. However, that does not assist in resolving the difficulties in relation to service of explanatory notices, such as Form E,[95] on the debtor himself.

It is undoubtedly the case that the difficulties over these provisions will soon be the subject of court decision. Even before the 2001 Act, recorded delivery service was unsuccessful in approximately one third of repossession actions. Requiring recording delivery service on an unnamed occupier, under the new regime, is likely to see the number of bounced recorded deliveries rise still higher. As service of the explanatory notice forms which accompany court proceedings[96] should be served with the service copy court papers,[97] a common occurrence will be that the creditor has both the form and the service copy court papers returned to him together where the recorded delivery attempt has been unsuccessful. Standing the views expressed above, the appropriate course for the creditor to adopt in these circumstances is to remove the explanatory notice form from the package and thereafter have the service copy court papers served by sheriff officers (as would have been done before the 2001 Act), counter-intuitive as that at first may seem. The alternative, in terms of the third argument, is to have all the papers served by sheriff officers. Even if the explanatory notice (such as Form E) is not served by sheriff officers, the defender will still have notice of his right to make an application for a section 2 order as the new form of citation for such actions[98] makes reference to his ability to do so and the procedure therefor.

---

[93] See Maher & Cusine, *The Law and Practice of Diligence* (1990), para. 12–18 citing *Fairbairn v. Cockburn's Trustees* (1878) 15 S.L.R. 705, though in that case, only nominal damages were awarded in a situation where a party had been ejected from premises under illegal warrant.
[94] On which see paras. 5.13 *et seq.*
[95] Of Sched. 6 to the 1970 Act.
[96] Form E of Sched. 6 to the 1970 Act and Form 1 of Pt 2 of the Sched. to the 2001 Act.
[97] See para. 4.2.23.
[98] Form O5A of the Ordinary Cause Rules in relation to actions under s.24 of the 1970 Act and Form 6B of the Summary Applications Rules in relation to summary applications under the 1970 Act, in terms of r.34.10(1) of the Ordinary Cause Rules and r.3.4.1 of the Summary Applications Rules. If the problem relates to a defect in a notice of default, that may not be fatal: para. 2.4.

Notwithstanding the difficulties on service, it may be possible for a creditor to argue that appearance by a debtor or applicant cures any defect in service of the court proceedings.[99] However, if the defect relates to service of a notice on which the action is based, such as where a calling-up notice has been raised and followed by court proceedings related thereto, appearance in the court action will not remedy the defect.[1]

A final concern in relation to service of notices on the occupier is whether they breach data protection legislation by disclosing confidential banking information of the debtor to third parties such as the occupier. However, the mandatory requirements of the Act suggest that no duty is breached.[2]

Conclusion on Method of Service

4.2.28 It is submitted that the creditor fulfils with his obligations in relation to service on the occupier and service of accompanying notices to court proceedings if he sends the notices by recorded delivery, irrespective of whether actual service results. The alternative for a creditor is to instruct sheriff officers to serve these notices. It is difficult to criticise a creditor who so acts or, standing the confusion and the view of the Scottish Executive that this is valid, a solicitor who advises his client to proceed in this manner. However, such a course may give rise to further problems for the creditor and, it is submitted, does not in fact cure any problems with service.

On any view, it is difficult to disagree with one description of the Act as "an absolute dog's breakfast".[3] A rumour was advanced that emergency legislation was being rushed through to remedy the alleged defect but that proved to be unfounded. The Scottish Executive has said that there is no difficulty with the current legislation and that no amendment legislation is being drafted or indeed necessary. Clearly an authoritative ruling will be required before there is certainty in this area too.

---

[99] Macphail, *op. cit.*, para. 6–04; Ordinary Cause r.5.10; but appearance in this context means the lodging of a notice of intention to defend: *Cairney v. Bulloch*, 1994 S.L.T. (Sh.Ct) 37. Accordingly, this argument will not be open to a creditor where the applicant is simply making an application for a section 2 order.

[1] This may follow by implication from *Hill Samuel* and *Gallagher infra*, nos 5 and 6, though in those cases the error was in the designation of the notice rather than the manner of service. However, the issue of defective manner of service was expressly considered by Sheriff Johnston at Glasgow in *Govan Housing Society v. Kane*, *supra* no. 88 which confirms the position.

[2] The Data Protection Act 1998 (c.29) provides that all processing of personal data must be done fairly and lawfully: Sched. 1, Pt I, para. 1. Part II, para. 1(2) of the same Sched. provides that information will be treated as fairly obtained if it is obtained from a person who is authorised by or under any enactment to supply it. Schedule 1 also directs that one of the conditions in Scheds 2 or 3 must be met for the processing of data to take place. Schedule 2, para. 3 provides: "The processing is necessary for compliance with any legal obligation to which the data controller is subject". Schedule 3, para. 7(1)(b) provides: "The processing is necessary for the exercise of any functions conferred on any person by or under an enactment".

[3] Mike Dailly, *The Herald*, December 21, 2001.

Importance of Observance of Rules on Service

4.2.29 It is tempting to dismiss much of the argument here as pedantry.[4] In fact, the importance of accuracy in service of notices in this area cannot be overstated as demonstrated by *Govan Housing Society v. Kane*, and two cases where errors in the designation of the recipient of the notice were held to be fatal to the pursuers' claims. In *Hill Samuel & Co Ltd v. Haas and Haas*,[5] Sheriff Principal Caplan dismissed the pursuers' claims seeking repossession. Both defenders had executed guarantees in favour of the pursuers in respect of borrowings by limited companies. The second defender also granted a standard security over certain heritable property in favour of the pursuers. She alone was the proprietor of the security subjects. The pursuers sought to call up their security by issuing a calling-up notice addressed to both defenders. The court held that if the foundation of the action was the calling-up notice, it was necessary for the notice to follow the requirements of the 1970 Act. That Act requires that such a notice be served on the proprietor. By addressing the notice to both defenders, the pursuers had failed to follow the Act.

A similarly strict view was taken in *Gallagher v. Ferns*[6] where a standard security had been granted by trustees over a farm. After alleged default of payment, calling-up notices were served on the trustees. The notices were addressed to them as individuals. No reference was made to the trustees' fiduciary capacity. Payment was not made and an action raised by the creditor against the surviving trustees based on the calling-up notice served on him. Sheriff Principal Cox upheld the sheriff's decision that the calling-up notices should have been served on the trustees specifically in that capacity, because, as individuals, they were neither the debtor under the security nor the proprietor of the subjects.[7] As the pursuer had failed to do so the action was incompetent and irrelevant.

By and On Whom should Service be Made?

4.2.30 The *Hill Samuel* and *Gallagher* cases[8] serve as a reminder of the care which must be taken in this area. Service will be made by the creditor seeking to secure performance under the security. If the creditor is a body of trustees, service must be by or for all of them. If he is a trustee in sequestration, the notice should be served by or for him in that capacity. If there is more than one creditor, each should serve a notice for the sum due to him.[9] It is not necessary that the creditor serving such a notice has a recorded or registered title to the security.[10]

---

[4] Though the terms of s.19A(3) of the 1970 Act, set out above, make clear that failure to deal properly with the occupier notice and other provisions will render the calling-up notice and notice of default invalid.

[5] 1989 S.C.L.R. 210.

[6] 1998 S.L.T. (Sh.Ct) 79.

[7] s.19(4) of the 1970 Act provides that if the proprietor is a body of trustees, it is sufficient for the calling-up notice to be served on a majority of the trustees infeft in the security subjects. An argument in *Gallagher* that proper service had been made because s.19 makes no reference to a requirement to serve on "a representative qua representative" failed, despite an observation that no commentators on the Act had suggested that trustees be designed as such.

[8] See para. 4.2.9.

[9] Halliday, *Conveyancing*, para. 54–10 where further examples of such special cases are given.

[10] *ibid.*

Calling-up notices must be served "on the person last infeft in the security subjects and appearing on the record as the proprietor"[11] and on any other person against whom the creditor wishes to preserve any right of recourse in respect of the debt.[12] Accordingly, service on the proprietor, the debtor and any guarantor is always necessary.[13] If the security or the title is in the name of two or more people, service must be made on each.[14] As a matter of practicality, it is wise to carry out a search as near to the date of service of the calling-up notice as is possible. A notice of default must be served on the debtor and on the proprietor but not on the other parties specified in relation to calling-up notices.[15] Nonetheless, a prudent creditor will serve on those other parties with a view to avoiding later difficulty[16] and, possibly, in the hope that receipt by such other persons will in some cases bring forward proposals which might not otherwise have been forthcoming.

In addition, in all cases where a creditor serves a calling-up notice on any of the persons specified by the 1970 Act, he must also send a notice[17] by recorded delivery addressed to "The Occupier"[18] at the security subjects together with a copy of the calling-up notice.[19] Failure to comply with this rule renders the calling-up notice of no effect.[20] These rules on providing notice to "The Occupier" apply equally to the situation where the creditor has served a notice of default as when a calling-up notice is served.[21]

In relation to specific cases of service outwith the norm, then in the event that the proprietor is deceased, service should be made on that person's representative or the person entitled to the subjects in terms of the last recorded title thereto.[22] If the proprietor was a deceased person with no representatives, service should be made on the Lord Advocate.[23]

---

[11] s.19(2) of the 1970 Act.

[12] s.19(5) of the 1970 Act.

[13] And on any former owners of the subjects whose personal obligations remain outstanding: Halliday, *Conveyancing*, para. 54–12.

[14] It has been suggested as prudent to include service on a non-entitled spouse whose consent to restriction of the period of notice may be required: Cusine, *op. cit.*, 8–07.

[15] s.21(1) of the 1970 Act.

[16] Halliday, *Conveyancing*, para. 54–26; but the same comments as made, *supra* no. 2, apply in relation to data protection issues.

[17] in Form BB of Sched. 6 to the 1970 Act (as inserted by s.4(1) of the 2001 Act). The form is repeated in the Appendix at para. 10.13.

[18] For the avoidance of doubt, the notice should simply be addressed to "The Occupier" followed by the address of the security subjects. It remains to be seen how persistent Consignia will be in obtaining a signature for a recorded delivery addressed to no specifically named person but there may be problems for creditors if the recorded delivery is indeed returned: see para. 4.2.27.

[19] s.19A of the 1970 Act; see para. 4.2.22.

[20] s.19A(3) of the 1970 Act.

[21] s.21(2A) of the 1970 Act, as inserted by s.4(2) of the 2001 Act.

[22] Even if there has been an alteration of the succession which does not appear in the Register of Sasines: s.19(2) of the 1970 Act. There is a difference of opinion as to who is the "representative" in these circumstances, the term not being defined in the Act. The view that it means the executor is supported by Halliday, *Conveyancing*, para. 54–11 and Braid, "Remedies on Default", 1999 PQLE 208 at 209, but it is noted in the latter publication that the office of the Queen's and Lord Treasurer's Remembrancer, which deals with such matters, takes the view that the term means the beneficiary under the will. It is submitted that the former view is correct.

[23] s.19(3) of the 1970 Act; but if it is not known if he is still alive, notice should be sent to the Extractor: s.19(6).

If the proprietor has been made bankrupt, the notice must be served on the trustee in sequestration[24] and on the bankrupt himself.[25] If the proprietor is a body of trustees, service on a majority of those infeft is sufficient.[26] If the proprietor is a partnership, service should be made on the firm and the individual partners who hold property for the firm.[27] If the proprietor is a company, service should be made on the company at its registered office and on any receiver, liquidator or administrator at his place of business.[28] If the company has been removed from the Register of Companies, service should be made on the Lord Advocate.[29] The standard conditions may be varied to provide different rules in relation to who should receive notices.

Where should Service be Made?

4.2.31 Service, whether by recorded delivery or personal service, should be to the recipient's last known address.[30] If the address is not known, or if it is not known if the person is still alive, or if attempted service is unsuccessful, a calling-up notice or notice of default must be sent to the Extractor of the Court of Session, which is equivalent in these circumstances to normal service by the postal or personal method.[31]

Proof of Service

4.2.32 The following are proof of service of a calling-up notice or notice of default[32]: an acknowledgement of service signed by the person served[33]; a certificate of posting[34] signed by the creditor or his agent together with the postal receipt; or in the case of service on the Extractor, an acknowledgement of receipt by the Extractor on a copy of the notice. In the absence of proof of service of a notice of default by recorded delivery, the Keeper has apparently been willing to accept a letter from a debtor to a creditor which relinquished his rights in the subjects and referred to service of the notice, but such a letter might not bind a trustee in sequestration.[35]

---

[24] Unless he has been discharged.

[25] s.19(3) of the 1970 Act; the 1970 Act does not deal with the signing of a trust deed but it would seem prudent standing the decision in *Gallagher* to serve on the trustee in those circumstances. The same view is given in Halliday, *Conveyancing*, para. 54–11.

[26] s.19(4) of the 1970 Act; the notice must make reference to their capacity as trustees: *Gallagher v. Ferns*, 1998 S.L.T. (Sh.Ct) 79.

[27] If the constitution of the partnership has changed, service should be made on all existing partners, including those assumed after the standard security was granted, and on any partners who granted the security who are no longer partners: Cusine, *op. cit.*, 8–07.

[28] Cusine, *op. cit.*, 8–07.

[29] s.19(3) of the 1970 Act.

[30] ss.19(6), 21(2) and 24(4)(a) of the 1970 Act but note that service on the Lord Advocate is to be made at the Crown Office in Edinburgh.

[31] ss.19(6) and 21(2) of the 1970 Act.

[32] Under ss.19(6), (7) and 21(2) of the 1970 Act.

[33] In Form C of Sched. 6, the style for which is repeated in the Appendix at para. 13–16; the acknowledgement of receipt of the notice need not be within any specified time after service or even prior to sale: C. Waelde (ed.), *Professor McDonald's Conveyancing Opinions* (1998), p.169. However, if the notice is served personally then, while the notice might be validly served, there may be difficulties in providing evidence of service in the absence of acknowledgement by the recipient: *ibid.*, p.170.

[34] In Form D of Sched. 6, the style for which is repeated in the Appendix at para. 13–17.

[35] Cusine, *op. cit.*, para. 8–18, Case 3.

Formal Provisions of the 2001 Act

4.2.33 The 2001 Act provides that it binds the Crown[36] and that expressions in the Act have the same meaning as those in Part II of the 1970 Act, except as the context otherwise requires.[37]

Practical Effects of the 2001 Act

4.2.34 The Act is likely to have far reaching consequences in relation to the cost of repossessing property and the cost to the public purse; on the time it takes creditors to obtain decree, if they manage to do so at all; and, as a result, on the attitude of creditors towards debtors.

Cost

4.2.35 It seems inevitable that there will soon be a large increase in the number of challenged repossession actions. This will involve additional work and representation at hearings for both parties to the action and any applicants who are not designed in the instance. As far as creditors are concerned, this will drive up their costs. The bigger banks, in particular, have been used to pursuing repossession actions on a fixed fee basis and the Act makes such arrangements more difficult, though not impossible. The Explanatory Notes, put together by the Scottish Executive, already predict increased expenditure for the public purse on legal aid of £250,000 as a result of the Act becoming law. The CML have said this figure could prove to be a significant underestimate. It must not be assumed, of course, that all applicants will qualify for legal aid. In many cases, the debtor will be in employment and, at best, any legal aid award will be subject to a large contribution. Nonetheless, the estimated figure does seem likely to rise. Interestingly, the initial reaction of the Scottish Legal Aid Board has been to decline permission under emergency legal aid to deal with application for a section 2 order. On receiving the full application, the Board have adopted a policy of granting permission to draft a minute for an application but declining cover for the hearing which will inevitably follow. As there is no point in drafting the minute without also appearing at the hearing, it seems certain that this approach will change sooner rather than later. Certain cases have already been continued by the courts to allow this apparent discrepancy to be resolved.

Time

4.2.36 In addition to added expense, the other obvious practical effect will be a delay in the average time it takes to obtain possession as section 2 orders are granted. This is likely to rise very significantly. Ignoring the actual periods of suspension of rights themselves, there will be delay caused by the time to fix a hearing for the application and, if further information is requested, for that to be obtained. Any application for legal aid in proceedings will only delay matters further even if the application under

---

[36] s.5.
[37] s.6.

the 2001 Act is ultimately unsuccessful,[38] as many cases will be sisted pending determination of the legal aid application.

It has been predicted that suspensions will be for months rather than years.[39] That remains to be seen[40] but, even if correct, will mean much longer timescales than creditors have been used to. Although that does not conflict with the intention of the Act, creditors who are the subject of mortgage fraud may feel aggrieved in a situation where they may have received no repayments at all, only to be faced with substantial delay when they attempt to recover possession.

It was suggested during the course of the Bill that, to avoid excessive delays, there should be a restriction on the number of times an order could be suspended. However, no such restriction has been enacted. On the contrary, the Act expressly allows the court to continue application proceedings which have already been continued.[41]

The Reaction from the Lending Industry

Creditors are likely to review the terms of their offers of advance and mortgage conditions to ensure that debtors will be responsible for any and all additional costs (both internal and external) arising from the changes, though in the majority of cases, the wording of security documentation will already allow recovery of those charges. Creditors are also likely to review their solicitor panel agreements which, generally, do not provide much comfort for creditors once actions are defended or challenged. With the sharp rise expected, creditors may consider it worthwhile seeking agreements on capped fees, at least up to certain points in the proceedings, for defended or challenged cases. **4.2.37**

As the Explanatory Notes to the Bill expressly acknowledged, while creditors will generally look to add costs to the debt, they are often only able to recover part of the outstanding balance, writing off the remainder. Underwriting of Scottish cases is likely to be reviewed and, for existing loans, pursuit of shortfalls may become more common north of the border than it has been to date. Many creditors are considering a new series of warning notices. There can be no doubt that the extent to which information is given to the debtor will be relevant. On a similar footing, staff in arrears departments are likely to be instructed to keep full records of all rescheduling arrangements which are entered into with debtor, as would be normal practice, but also of the breaches in arrangements and all efforts made to assist, however trivial.

Creditors are likely to review how long they will wait before starting possession proceedings. The desire of the creditor to press on at an earlier stage has to be weighed against the fact that too much aggression here may work against the creditor when the sheriff reviews whether suspension should be granted. One of the grounds to be considered is, of course, the nature of the default.

---

[38] Until the 2001 Act was passed, it had been relatively difficult to obtain legal aid to defend a repossession on the basis that the court had no discretion in the matter and, therefore, in most cases there was little prospect of a successful defence.

[39] Gretton & Reid, *Conveyancing 2000* (2001), p.92.

[40] The terms of s.2(4) make clear that the possibility of longer suspensions is a live issue.

[41] s.2(5)(b).

The continued use of calling-up notices and notices of default instead of section 24 writs has been called into question. An approach of covering the bases by proceeding with all three measures has been used to date by some of the biggest names in the lending industry. It now appears that serving the notices, which are very rarely of relevance under this approach, will actually extend the period within which the debtor can apply for a section 2 order.[42] That in turn precludes action even under the fastest of the routes adopted until the period within which an application is competent—under any of those routes—has expired.[43] Service of these notices also exposes the creditor to a possible summary application against it.

It will be interesting to examine the extent to which creditors challenge the information put forward in support of an application under the 2001 Act. This will again largely depend on whether the creditor is seeking repayment of arrears or recovery of the subjects. In either case, given the likely speed with which applications will be dealt, creditors have required to put in place procedures that ensure they can respond with the relevant information within a short time frame.

English Guidance on the Terms of the Act

4.3 One of the objectives of the 2001 Act was to bring Scots law more into line with English law. Some guidance on when the courts might grant section 2 orders may therefore be gained by looking at the law south of the border. The starting point for consideration here is section 36 of the Administration of Justice Act 1970[44] which provides:

> "(1)...if it appears to the court that in the event of its exercising the power the mortgagor is likely to be able *within a reasonable period* to pay any sums due under the mortgage or to remedy a default consisting of a breach of any other obligation arising under or by virtue of the mortgage.
> (2) The court—
>> (a) may adjourn the proceedings, or
>> (b) on giving judgment, or making an order, for delivery of possession of the mortgaged property, or at any time before the execution of such judgment or order, may—
>>> (i) stay or suspend execution of the judgment or order, or
>>> (ii) postpone the date for delivery of possession,
>
> *for such period* or periods as the court thinks reasonable.
> (3) *subject to such conditions* with regard to payment by the mortgagor of any sum secured by the mortgage or the remedying of any default as the court thinks fit."[45]

---

[42] From three weeks (between service and craving decree, unless of course the action is defended) in the case of a s.24 writ to two months in the case of service of these notices.

[43] s.1(7).

[44] As extended by the Administration of Justice Act 1973, s.8 which sets down that "sums due" in s.36 means installments or arrears and not the whole capital sum. This has some similarity with the reasoning behind the passing of s.2(4) of the 2001 Act.

[45] Emphasis added.

The terms italicised are all to be found, in similar contexts, in the 2001 Act.[46]

Within a Reasonable Period

4.3.1 In relation to interpretation of "within a reasonable period", the leading case is *Cheltenham and Gloucester Building Society v. Norgan*.[47] The Court of Appeal found that the starting point for a reasonable period should be the outstanding term of the mortgage. It should then be determined whether the debtor[48] could maintain the paying off of the arrears by installments over that period. In support of this view, it was noted that this should reduce the frequency with which cases such as this came before the courts, in turn keeping down the costs which would otherwise be applied to the loan account. It was also said that if such an opportunity was provided to the debtor, who failed to maintain the arrangement, the creditor would be entitled to say that the debtor had had his chance and that there should not be repeated capitalisations of arrears to the prejudice of the creditor.[49] In reaching its decision, the court noted the terms of a CML statement which made clear that creditors only sought possession as a last resort.[50]

In practical terms, the Court of Appeal noted this approach would require detailed analysis, by district judges, of budgets and future projections to determine whether the debtor would be able to meet the payments and when the creditor's security would be put at risk by postponement of arrears. More specifically, Lord Justice Evans said[51] the following considerations were relevant when determining a "reasonable period": (a) How much can the debtor reasonably afford to pay at the time of the application and in the future? (b) How long are the debtor's temporary difficulties in meeting his obligations likely to last? (c) Why have arrears accumulated? (d) How much of the original repayment term is left? (e) What type of loan is involved and when is the principal due to be repaid? (f) Should the court exercise its power to disregard accelerated payment provisions? (g) Is it reasonable to expect the creditor to recoup the arrears of interest either over the whole of the original term, or within a shorter period, or within a longer period? Is it reasonable to expect the creditor to capitalise the interest?[52] (h) Does anything, affecting the security, influence the length of the period for payment?

---

[46] At ss.2(2)(b), 2(1)(a)(ii) and 2(1)(a)(iii) respectively.
[47] [1996] 1 All E.R. 449.
[48] Or "mortgagor" to use the wording of the court.
[49] *per* Waite L.J. at p.460A; the effect of *Norgan* has been described as giving debtors a "once and for all" opportunity to get back on track with repayments: Morgan, "Mortgage Arrears and the Family Home" (1996) 112 L.Q.R. 553.
[50] The wording in question (set out at p.462D) was very similar to that of The Mortgage Code discussed at para. 4.2.15.
[51] p.463B—D.
[52] If this direction was followed in Scotland, it might lead to an increased liability on the part of the Benefits Agency as the interest proportion of the mortgage repayment would be augmented. It is unclear how a Scottish court which had ordered capitalisation of arrears would treat a further application if the debtor once again got into difficulties. The matter would be within the discretion of the sheriff under s.2 of the 2001 Act. It is submitted, from both a proper reading of *Norgan* and in the interests of justice to both parties, that it would be unreasonable to order capitalisation of arrears more than once.

Norgan was greeted with some dismay by the lending industry, notwithstanding the court's view that there should not be repeated capitalisation and the clear indications that the creditor's interests require to be taken into account. Creditors are hoping that it will not be followed in Scotland. However, the passing of the Human Rights Act 1998 may give *Norgan* even greater significance than before[53] and future regulation of the area by the Financial Services Authority is also likely to increase the importance of this case.[54] If the courts in Scotland do take a similar line to *Norgan*, disposal of applications may take rather longer than has been anticipated to date as each of the various branches of the test are considered by the court.

In *Norgan*, there was very substantial equity in the property[55] and a prospect that the arrears could be cleared. The English courts have approached the interpretation of a "reasonable period" differently in circumstances where a sale of the security subjects is the only realistic option to repay the creditor in full.[56] In these circumstances, a year appears to be the maximum period of delay permitted by the courts,[57] though it has been noted that there is no fixed rule.[58] As noted above,[59] the protection offered by the 2001 Act was designed to assist the debtor or other applicant where in the opinion of the court it is likely that the arrears will be repaid. Accordingly, in Scotland, if there is no prospect of repayment without sale, then in theory at least a section 2 order should not be granted. However, the terms of the Act do suggest that if a court was persuaded that sale would repay the creditor in full within a reasonable period, an order could nonetheless be granted.

For Such Period

4.3.2 The English courts have made it quite clear that an indefinite period of time is not an acceptable interpretation of the phrase "for such period". In one case, it was said that the time period must be "a stretch of time ending with some specified or ascertainable date".[60] This is a sensible approach but, if followed in Scotland, would preclude determination of

---

[53] For further discussion of human rights and repossessions, see paras 5.13 *et seq.*
[54] See para. 9.4.2.
[55] A loan of £90,000 had been taken out in 1986. The arrears appear to have reached a peak of £15,000 in 1992 but had fallen back to a lower sum by the time the case reached the Court of Appeal in 1995, by which time the mortgage had a further 11 years to run. At that time, the security subjects were said to have a value of £225,000.
[56] For the position where even sale will not repay the debt in full, see para. 4.3.3.
[57] *National and Provincial Building Society v. Lloyd* [1996] 1 All E.R. 630, where there was insufficient evidence that the debt could be repaid without the sale of the security subjects. Neill L.J. held (p.638B) "if there were, in a hypothetical case clear evidence that the completion of the sale of a property . . . could take place in six or nine months or even a year, I see no reason why a court could not come to the conclusion . . . the [debtor] was likely to be able within a reasonable period to pay any sums due under the mortgage".
[58] *Bristol & West Building Society v. Ellis* (1997) 29 H.L.R. 282, where the Court of Appeal held that a reasonable period was not strictly definable and depended on the facts of the case. The court found there was insufficient evidence to justify any order other than for immediate possession.
[59] See para. 4.2.11.
[60] *Royal Trust Co. of Canada v. Markham* [1975] 3 All E.R. 433 (CA) *per* Sir John Pennycuick at p.438D.

an application under the 2001 Act by the sisting of actions (if defended) or continuations *sine die* (if undefended). In England, beyond what is stated above, the matter is one within the discretion of the court. Generally, the courts are not prepared to set down fixed guidelines as to how discretion should be exercised.[61]

Subject to Such Conditions

There is little guidance available on the nature of conditions which may be attached. Of each of the phrases common to the jurisdictions, this is the term which will most often depend on individual facts and circumstances. The English courts' unwillingness to lay down fixed guidelines also precludes detailed consideration of what conditions may be involved. The legislation does however envisage payment of all overdue sums within the "reasonable period" discussed above.[62] In this, the English legislation is on all fours with the Scottish legislation which refers to fulfillment of the obligation in default within a reasonable period.[63] There is no reference in either text to part fulfilment.

4.3.3

Accordingly, while conditions may be attached, no order should be granted by the court unless the default is likely to be remedied within the period or, indeed, at all. In *Cheltenham and Gloucester Plc v. Krausz*,[64] the debtors had defaulted on their mortgage and a possession order was obtained against them. Warrant for execution (to evict) was set aside on four occasions, but the debtors breached the terms of each occasion. A fifth warrant fell due for execution on June 12, 1995. By that time, the mortgage debt amounted to £83,000. The debtors had obtained a written valuation on the property of £65,000, but they did not accept that, asserting the property had a value of about £90,000. The debtors applied for an order suspending the warrant on the grounds of having found a purchaser. This was successful and execution of the warrant was stayed. The bank appealed. The Court of Appeal allowed the appeal holding that the legislation[65] did not empower the court to suspend the creditors' rights where there were insufficient funds to discharge the mortgage debt in full.[66]

Similarly, no order should be granted on terms which the debtor will be unable to fulfil because, for example, he cannot afford the payments.[67] However, suspension of rights has been ordered in the case of an endowment mortgage where interest only payments were due and no capital was due to be repaid for 23 years at the time of decision.[68]

---

[61] *Cheltenham and Gloucester BS v. Grant* (1994) 26 H.L.R. 703.
[62] s.36 of the Administration of Justice Act 1970.
[63] s.2(2)(b) of the 2001 Act.
[64] [1997] 1 All E.R. 21.
[65] s.36 of the Administration of Justice Act 1970.
[66] *Krausz* is important for considering and doubting *Barrett v. Halifax Building Society* (1995) 28 H.L.R. 634, a case which generated huge publicity for appearing to suggest that debtors in a negative equity position (the Barretts were facing a shortfall of £85,000) could retain their properties to allow them to find a buyer themselves; for further discussion of *Barrett* and the then Scottish position, see Urquhart, "Enforcing Standard Securities", 1995 J.L.S.S. 400.
[67] *First National Bank plc v. Syed* [1991] 2 All E.R. 250, p.255.
[68] *Bank of Scotland v. Grimes* [1985] Q.B. 1179. The decision was made even though the endowment policy securing the loan had lapsed.

Further, the court may only exercise its powers to suspend the creditor's rights if it is likely that the debtor will be able to pay the further amounts which will fall due after the authorised "reasonable period" for clearing the arrears has expired.[69]

---

[69] s.8(2) of the Administration of Justice Act 1973.

CHAPTER 5

DETERMINATION OF COURT PROCEEDINGS— PART II

Challenges to the Validity of the Security

As set out above, a challenge to the validity of the security which the **5.1** creditor seeks to enforce is a matter which goes to the root of his dispute with the debtor and is one of the grounds on which a repossession action may be opposed.

Within the context of a sheriff court action brought by the creditor for warrant to exercise his remedies under the security, a debtor has two options. The first is to defend the sheriff court action and object to the deed in question by way of exception.[1] Such a course is available even though the sheriff court does not have jurisdiction to entertain actions of reduction relating to questions of heritable right and title.[2] This option may be used by a debtor where a deed is void or *ipso jure* null, such as where it has not been executed properly.

The second option, in the context of a sheriff court repossession action, is for the debtor to defend (irrespective of whether an action of reduction is to be commenced) on the basis of a failure by the creditor to comply with his obligation of good faith in circumstances when he was obliged to do so. This argument is based on *Smith v. Bank of Scotland*.[3] Such a challenge does not seek to set aside the security *per se* but amounts to a defence that the creditor may not enforce the security terms. The basis of such a challenge, in the context of defence of a repossession action, is identical to a challenge based on the *Smith* doctrine in the context of an action of reduction.[4]

An alternative route to challenge the validity of the security, and the only method by which the security can be set aside, is for the debtor to pursue an action of reduction itself. An action of reduction may only be raised in the Court of Session,[5] with the result that it cannot *per se* form a defence to a sheriff court action. Nonetheless, ongoing sheriff court actions will often be sisted until an action for reduction is determined. If the debtor or other obligant succeeds in the application for reduction[6] that will effectively dispose of the creditor's repossession action in the

---

[1] Or *ope exceptionis;* for discussion of the competency and procedure for such a defence, see Macphail, *Sheriff Court Practice* (2nd ed., 1998), paras. 12.66 *et seq.*

[2] Macphail, *ibid.*, para. 12–69; Sheriff Courts (Scotland) Act 1907 (c.51) s.5(4).

[3] 1997 S.L.T. 1061; 1997 S.C. (HL) 111.

[4] See para. 5.4. For examples of cases where the doctrine has been advanced as a defence to a sheriff court action by the creditor, rather than to found an action of reduction, see *Royal Bank of Scotland plc v. Clark*, 2000 S.L.T. (Sh.Ct) 101 and *Royal Bank of Scotland plc v. Wilson*, 2001 S.L.T. (Sh.Ct) 2.

[5] *Donald v. Donald*, 1913 S.C. 274.

[6] Or partial reduction.

sheriff court, at least as far as that defender is concerned. If the application for reduction is unsuccessful, the creditor whose action for repossession has been sisted will be entitled to enroll a motion in the sheriff court for recall of the sist and to proceed as he would have done had the challenge not been made. Reduction of a disposition, where the security remains in place, does not affect the security or the rights of the creditor thereunder.[7]

Grounds of Reduction

5.2 There are many grounds on which a challenge to the validity of the security by the reduction route may be based, but anything more than a cursory review of all such bases is beyond the scope of this work. Most of these grounds are as applicable to contract law in general as they are to heritable securities and have no particular relevance or special importance to Scottish repossession law.

The general grounds for seeking reduction of the security include: fraud,[8] a contract so induced being voidable; error,[9] including misrepresentation, provided that *restitutio in integrum* is possible[10]; force and fear,[11] an obligation being void[12] if it is proved that one of the parties was induced to consent by force or threats of force; facility and circumvention,[13] a contract being reducible if it is proved that one of the parties was in a state of material mental weakness at the time of contracting and the other party took advantage of his weakness to obtain consent; forgery, an apparent contract being a nullity if the signature is not genuine but forged[14]; and undue influence,[15] in the long established sense, a contract being liable to be set aside where it is proved that one party relied on the advice of the other and was subject to the influence of that other whose self-interest coloured his advice. These concepts will be familiar to anyone with a solid grounding in Scots law having been largely established by the end of the nineteenth century.

Much more recently, and in the specific context of heritable securities,[16] a new ground of challenge has opened up to those who provide security to a creditor for the debts of another.[17] This doctrine, as

---

[7] *Leslie v. Leslie*, 1987 S.L.T. 232 at p.238E where it was held that security holders would not suffer prejudice if decree of reduction was granted in terms of s.6 of the Divorce (Scotland) Act 1976.

[8] For further discussion, see McBryde, *The Law of Contract in Scotland* (2nd ed., W. Green and Son, Edinburgh, 2001), Chap. 14.

[9] For a recent example of a discharge of a standard security sought to be reduced on the basis of error, see *Security Pacific Finance Ltd v. Graham*, 1995 G.W.D. 29–1545.

[10] McBryde, *op. cit.*, Chap. 15.

[11] McBryde, *op. cit.*, Chap. 17.

[12] While it is theoretically unnecessary to reduce a void contract, as it is null *ab initio*, it would be unwise not to seek its reduction: see McBryde, *op. cit.*, para. 13–15.

[13] McBryde, *op. cit.*, Chap. 16.

[14] For a recent example of a standard security partially reduced on the ground of forgery, see *McLeod v. Cedar Holdings Ltd*, 1989 S.L.T. 620.

[15] McBryde, *op. cit.*, Chap. 16.

[16] And particularly standard securities; the doctrine is not however limited only to security transactions: see para. 5.11.

[17] The doctrine does not generally apply where joint debtors acquire joint benefit from

it applies in Scotland, is based on the longstanding obligation of the creditor to act in good faith but this obligation has been extended in the field of secured lending within the last five years. The new approach is a rapidly developing area of the law and the frequency with which it has recently been invoked merits a full discussion of the current legal position and the manner in which it has been reached.

The Origin of the Doctrine

For the origin of this recent extension of the law, it is necessary to look to England where a similar duty on creditors has been developed over recent years, most notably since the House of Lords considered the case *Barclays Bank plc v. O'Brien*.[18] In that case, a husband and wife had agreed to execute a second mortgage of their matrimonial home as security for overdraft facilities extended by the bank to a company in which the husband, but not the wife, had an interest. The branch manager of the bank sent the documents to another branch for execution with instructions to ensure that both were fully aware of the nature of the documents and that, if in doubt, they should consult their solicitors before signing. The instructions were not carried out and the wife signed the deed without reading it, based on her husband's false representation that it was limited to £60,000 and would last only three weeks. When the company's overdraft exceeded £154,000 the bank sought to enforce the mortgage and obtained an order for possession. The judge at first instance dismissed the wife's appeal, holding that since there was no evidence that in deceiving his wife the husband was acting on behalf of the bank, they could not be held responsible for his misrepresentation and, therefore, the charge was enforceable against her. The Court of Appeal allowed an appeal by the wife. The bank appealed to the House of Lords which upheld the Court of Appeal decision albeit on different grounds.

5.3

The court found that where a wife had been induced to stand as surety (cautioner) for her husband's debt by his undue influence, misrepresentation (as here) or some other legal wrong, she had an equity as against him to set aside that transaction. The surety's right to set aside the transaction would be enforceable against a third party who had actual or constructive notice of the circumstances giving rise to her equity. On the facts, the bank was found to have had constructive notice of the misrepresentation and the security was held to be unenforceable against the surety.

---

the security as, for example, where the loan is used to finance a joint house purchase. This was confirmed by the House of Lords in *CIBC Mortgages v. Pitt* [1994] 1 A.C. 200 and the same point was made by Lord Macfadyen in Scotland in *Ahmed v. Clydesdale Bank plc*, 2001 S.L.T. 423. In *Royal Bank of Scotland plc v. Etridge (No.2)* [2001] 3 W.L.R. 1021, *infra*, Lord Nicholls confirmed: "On the other side of the line [from the situation where the wife stands surety—cautioner—for her husband's debts] is the case where money is being advanced or has been advanced, to husband and wife jointly. In such a case the bank is not put on inquiry, unless the bank is aware the loan is being made for the husband's purposes, as distinct from their joint purposes." But distinguishing whether the case is an *O'Brien* type or a *Pitt* type may be difficult: Gretton, "Sexually Transmitted Debt" 1997 S.L.T. (News) 197. It is not, however, essential for the cause of action that the transaction is disadvantageous to the influenced person: *Etridge (No.2)*.

[18] [1994] 1 A.C. 180 (HL).

The Creditor's Duty of Good Faith

5.4 The leading Scottish case on this issue is *Smith v. Bank of Scotland*.[19] In *Smith*, a wife sought reduction of a standard security which she and her husband had executed in favour of the creditor. The security subjects were the jointly owned matrimonial home. The secured debt was a business loan to a firm in which the pursuer's husband was a partner. Mrs Smith averred that she, as cautioner[20] for the advance, was induced to grant the standard security by misrepresentation on the part of her husband. The cautioner had obtained no independent advice, nor had she been given any warning as to the consequences of the document she was signing. She was given no opportunity to peruse the document which she signed at the office of the creditor's solicitors. The granting of the security was essential to obtaining the finance. It was not averred that the creditor had had any actual knowledge of the husband's misrepresentation.[21] The Scottish courts consistently declined to follow *O'Brien* as *Smith* made its way towards the House of Lords.[22] The existing Scots law was that voluntary obligations were not rendered open to challenge due to misrepresentation by a third party.[23] Such obligations could only be challenged where the misrepresentation had been effected by the other party to the contract who had benefited.

When the case reached the House of Lords, the court achieved the same result as would have obtained in England under *O'Brien* by a

---

[19] 1997 S.L.T. 1061; 1997 S.C. (HL) 111.

[20] It is important to appreciate that the use of the word cautioner by the House of Lords in *Smith* is used in a wide sense to denote a person who exposes his assets to secure another's debts, whereas the traditional narrower use of the term is where a personal obligation is granted by a cautioner to pay a creditor if and when the principal debtor defaults. For further discussion, see the analysis by Lord Macfadyen in *Hewit v. Williamson*, 1999 S.L.T. 313, pp.316L–317D and the commentary by Professor Gretton at 1998 S.C.L.R. 616–618.

[21] It is of course open to a debtor to seek reduction on the basis of a legally wrongful act, such as undue influence or misrepresentation, by the creditor. In certain cases, a cautioner has sought to argue that although the wrongful act was carried out by the debtor (for example, a husband improperly procuring the consent of a wife), the debtor in so acting was the agent of the creditor: see for example *Royal Bank of Scotland plc v. Shanks*, 1998 S.L.T. 355 (where the case failed for lack of relevant averment) and *McCabe v. Skipton Building Society*, 1994 S.C.L.R. 501 (where the court found that in making false representations to his wife, a debtor could not properly be regarded as acting as agent for the creditor); such an argument is based on the long established ground for seeking reduction that the person who has obtained the benefit (in these cases, the creditor who has obtained the security) is the same person who perpetrated the legally wrongful act. The argument is therefore quite a distinct ground of attack from the doctrine in *Smith*. But *Shanks* and *McCabe* were both argued before the House of Lords had ruled in *Smith* and it is more likely that similar facts would now be argued on the creditor's duty of good faith as laid down there. Indeed, the decision in *Smith* potentially weakens the agency argument as in *O'Brien* (on which the court in *Smith* relied), the court ruled (p.198) that such agency cases "will be of very rare occurrence".

[22] Namely the Outer House, 1994 S.L.T. 1288, and the First Division, 1996 S.L.T. 392; the Second Division had referred to *O'Brien* in *McCabe* without disapproval as far as the law of Scotland is concerned, but *McCabe* turned on another point and it would be going too far to say that the court accepted its application. In consideration of *Smith* in the Outer House, the comments in *McCabe* were rightly distinguished as *obiter*, Lord Johnston holding that the question of whether *O'Brien* should be part of the law of Scotland had not been under consideration.

[23] Lord Clyde in *Smith* at p.1065D–E.

solution based on the creditor's obligation of good faith. Lord Clyde in delivering the leading judgment held:

> "In circumstances where the creditor should reasonably suspect that there may be factors bearing on the participation of the cautioner which might undermine the validity of the contract through his or her intimate relationship with the debtor the duty [to remain in good faith] would arise and would have to be fulfilled if the creditor is not to be prevented from later enforcing the contract . . . This is simply a duty arising out of the good faith of the contract to give advice . . . In the first place, the duty which arises on the creditor at the stage of the negotiation of the contract should only arise on the creditor if the circumstances of the case are such as to lead a reasonable man to believe that owing to the personal relationship between the debtor and the proposed cautioner the latter's consent may not be fully informed or freely given . . . Secondly, if the duty arises, then it requires that the creditor should take certain steps to secure that he remains in good faith so far as the proposed transaction is concerned . . . All that is required of him is that he should take reasonable steps to secure that in relation to the proposed contract he acts throughout in good faith. So far as the substance of those steps is concerned it seems to me that it would be sufficient for the creditor to warn the potential cautioner of the consequences of entering into the proposed cautionary obligation and to advise him or her to take independent advice."[24]

The importance of the decision in *Smith* cannot be overstated and it is worth emphasising the results of the judgment:

- where a cautioner could demonstrate that her consent to the granting of security was wrongly obtained[25] by the principal debtor[26]; and
- where a creditor should reasonably suspect that, because of the relationship between the principal debtor and the cautioner, the

---

[24] p.1068C–H.

[25] Such as by undue influence or misrepresentation; the essence of the act giving rise to a claim under the doctrine was described by Lord Macfadyen as "the abuse of a relationship of trust and confidence" in *Broadway v. Clydesdale Bank plc (No.2), infra*. For ease of reading, such an act is referred to hereafter as "undue influence" but it may equally include misrepresentation. The doctrine is also capable of extension to cases involving facility and circumvention: *Wright v. Cotias Investments Inc.*, 2000 S.C.L.R. 324 and see McKendrick, "The Undue Influence of English Law?" in *Scots Law into the 21st Century* (H. MacQueen ed., 1996), p.214 at pp.222–223. Finally, the doctrine applies to cases where the cautioner is subject to force and fear at the instance of the principal debtor: *Smith* (p.1065G), *Royal Bank of Scotland plc v. Clark*, 2000 S.L.T. (Sh.Ct) 101. Indeed, such securities could be challenged before *Smith*, on the basis that the deed was void rather than voidable, whether or not the creditor knew of or was implicated in the force and fear: *Trustee Savings Bank v. Balloch*, 1983 S.L.T. 240. But the test may be different in these circumstances: see Gretton & Reid, *Conveyancing 2000* (2001), pp.86 and 89 and Dickson, "Good Faith in Contract, Spousal Guarantees and *Smith v. Bank of Scotland*" 1998 S.L.T. (News) 39, p.44.

[26] This aspect of the decision was not immediately clear from *Smith* itself but *Smith* has been interpreted in this way in the subsequent cases: see *Braithwaite v. Bank of Scotland*, 1999 S.L.T. 25.

consent of that other party might not be fully informed or freely given; then[27]

- the creditor has a duty to remain in good faith with which he requires to comply to resist reduction of his security; but
- to preserve that duty of good faith, all that is required of the creditor is that he takes reasonable steps such as warning the cautioner of the consequences of the transaction and advising her to take independent advice.

The decision to bring Scots law more into line with English law was very much a conscious one. Lord Clyde stated:

"[The Court of Session] correctly recognised that the decision goes beyond the present situation in the law of Scotland, and applying the existing Scottish law, declined to follow [*O'Brien*] . . . I have not been persuaded that there are sufficiently cogent grounds for refusing the extension to Scotland of the development which has been achieved in England by the decision there in *Barclays Bank plc v O'Brien*. On the contrary I take the view that it is desirable to recognise a corresponding extension of the law in Scotland."[28]

Lord Jauncey in *Smith* confirmed the existing legal position, going so far as to say "[a]pplying the principles of Scots law alone I would therefore have been disposed to dismiss this appeal"[29] though in the event the decision of the court was unanimous. This issue is an important consideration as it has a bearing on the extent to which Scottish courts will look to English decisions for guidance. However, it must be remembered that the doctrines in the two jurisdictions are not identical.[30]

Proof of Undue Influence

5.5 The doctrine was considered further in *Braithwaite v. Bank of Scotland*,[31] where both the pursuer and her husband had been customers of the bank from 1989 to 1995. The case came before the Outer House for procedure roll debate. The wife had a current account and her husband had a business account. That business account became overdrawn and the husband (the principal debtor) requested an additional overdraft

---

[27] And only then: as Sheriff Fletcher said, interpreting *Smith*, in *Royal Bank of Scotland plc v. Clark*, 2000 S.L.T. (Sh.Ct) 101, p.105 "the duty arises only if the circumstances are such as to lead a reasonable man to believe that the consent may not be freely given."

[28] p.1067K. This judicial activism in making new law rather than interpreting existing law has been widely criticised. See for example Macgregor, "The House of Lords 'Applies' *O'Brien* North of the Border" (1998) 2 *Edinburgh Law Review* 90 and Dickson, "Good Faith in Contract, Spousal Guarantees and *Smith v. Bank of Scotland*" 1998 S.L.T. (News) 39.

[29] p.1064G.

[30] See for example *Royal Bank of Scotland plc v. Clark, supra* at para. 5.1 and para. 5.12 on differences between the two jurisdictions on the steps which a creditor must take to preserve his right to rely on the security.

[31] 1999 S.L.T. 25.

facility. In 1991, according to her averments, the wife as cautioner lodged a portfolio of shares and unit trusts with the bank and signed a document purporting to be a letter of pledge in its favour.[32] The issue before the court was whether it was necessary, as the creditor claimed, for the cautioner to establish that she had in fact acted under undue influence of her husband or a misrepresentation by him. The cautioner argued that the decision in *O'Brien* had been made on constructive notice and that the House of Lords in *Smith* had adopted the same policy as lay behind its decision in *O'Brien*. Further, a failure of the creditor to advise the pursuer, in circumstances where they knew the relationship between the cautioner and their principal debtor was one of husband and wife, was sufficient without proof in fact of undue influence and its effect. Lord Hamilton[33] held that

> "[t]he concept of good faith is used in the sense that a party may not be entitled to enforce his apparent rights because he is aware of or is put on enquiry to discover some prior vitiating factor. The existence in fact of such a factor is a prerequisite to the applicability of that concept."[34]

Accordingly, in addition to the creditor being put on notice of a requirement to preserve his good faith, proof is always required that undue influence has actually been exercised.[35]

Reliance on Undue Influence

Similarly, in addition to the existence of a vitiating factor, a cautioner **5.6** must prove that the execution of the deed complained of was as a result of undue influence. In *Ahmed v. Clydesdale Bank plc*,[36] a husband and wife purchased subjects with the assistance of a secured loan from the creditor. The standard security was an all sums security. Thereafter, the

---

[32] The use of the word pledge caused difficulties in itself as shares and similar securities cannot be the subject of a contract of pledge. In fact, the document involved an undertaking of obligations by the pursuer but not cautionary obligations.

[33] Relying on the speech of Lord Clyde in *Smith*.

[34] p.33C; it was not in fact altogether clear before *Braithwaite* that such a factor was required: see for example Dunlop, "*Smith v. Bank of Scotland*" 1997 J.L.S.S. 446, p.447 and Dickson, "Good Faith in Contract, Spousal Guarantees and *Smith v. Bank of Scotland*" 1998 S.L.T. (News) 39, pp.43–44, where both authors suggest that a proper reading of Lord Clyde's judgment in *Smith* is that no undue influence requires to be proved. But for support that *Smith* means a proof is required, see Gretton, "Sexually Transmitted Debt", 1997 S.L.T. (News) 195. *Braithwaite* and the authorities since (*infra*) suggest that Professor Gretton's view is correct. However, it must be accepted that since *Smith* the issue has not yet gone past courts of first instance in Scotland and the point cannot therefore be regarded as finally settled. Nonetheless, the English House of Lords decision in *Etridge (No.2)*, *infra*, lends support to the view taken in *Braithwaite*.

[35] It follows from the decision in *Braithwaite* that there must be sufficient averment of the perpetration of such a wrong if the case is to survive debate and the cautioner is to have the opportunity of proving it. In *Wright v. Cotias Investments Inc.*, 2000 S.C.L.R. 324, Lord Macfadyen stated (p.332) "To make a relevant case there must, in my view, be . . . averments of misrepresentation, or undue influence, or facility and circumvention, by a third party". The same point is also made specifically in *Royal Bank of Scotland v. Wilson*, 2001 S.L.T. (Sh.Ct.) 2, pp.5–6.

[36] 2001 S.L.T. 423.

husband borrowed further from the creditor without the wife's knowledge. She sought partial reduction of the security on the basis that the effect of the further advance was to render her a cautioner of her husband's business liabilities. Lord Macfadyen stated, "[t]he obligation which the pursuer seeks to set aside, namely the standard security, was entered into by her, in circumstances which are not impugned, long before the alleged acts of bad faith."[37] He found that even if the circumstances averred to support the cautioner's claim of a legally wrongful act had not occurred, the cautioner's position would have been the same, and so dismissed the action. The onus of proof rests on the cautioner, where the claim is made against the creditor, to show that the security was granted in reliance on the wrongful act.[38]

The Cautioner's Legal Advice

5.7 The majority of litigation in Scotland since the decisions in *Smith* and *Braithwaite* has focused on what reasonable steps the creditor requires to take to comply with his obligation of good faith. Much argument has centered round the provision of legal advice to the cautioner and the extent to which that affects the creditor's duty towards her.[39] The Scottish courts have, to date, favoured the view expressed in the English courts at least in relation to this aspect of the concept,[40] the most notable decision there having been that of the Court of Appeal in *Royal Bank of Scotland plc v. Etridge (No.2)*.[41] This decision has since been reviewed by the House of Lords[42] and is considered in more detail below.[43] In short, the Court of Appeal held that where a surety is being advised by a solicitor, to the knowledge of the creditor, the creditor is permitted to rely on the solicitor carrying out his obligations to give proper advice and so is not put on notice. As a result, no further steps are required of the creditor to preserve his duty of good faith.[44]

Etridge (No.2) was quoted with approval in Scotland in *Forsyth v. The Royal Bank of Scotland plc*,[45] where a wife sought reduction of a standard security granted by her and her husband to the bank to the extent it had

---

[37] p.427F.

[38] *Broadway v. Clydesdale Bank plc (No. 2)*, 2001 G.W.D. 14–552, where Lord Macfadyen preferred *Gray v. Binny* (1879) 7R. 332 on this point to *Chitty on Contracts* (28th ed., 1999), para. 7–050.

[39] Or him, but the cautioner is invariably the wife or mother.

[40] The Court of Appeal decision in *Etridge (No.2)* was cited with approval in *Forsyth, Clark, Wright* and *Broadway, infra*. The House of Lords' express wish to bring the law in the two jurisdictions together (see para. 5.4) makes English decisions of importance in this field, even if the two doctrines are not identical.

[41] [1998] 4 All E.R. 705.

[42] 2001 3 W.L.R. 1021.

[43] See para. 5.9.

[44] In "Good News for Bankers—Bad News for Lawyers?" 1999 S.L.T. (News) 53, reviewing the Court of Appeal decision in *Etridge (No.2)*, Professor Gretton said: "It now appears that it matters very little what form the law firm's certificate may take. Nor does it matter that the law firm acts for the wicked husband. All that is needed is a current practising certificate. The lawyer is a sort of priest. His intervention washes away all stain of sin, at least as far as the bank is concerned." The House of Lords in *Etridge (No.2)* has reined in the extent of duties on solicitors advising in these circumstances but much is still required: see para. 5.9.

[45] 2000 S.L.T. 1295.

been granted by her. The security covered sums advanced to the pursuer's husband for his business and did not relate to her borrowings. The pursuer averred that her husband had told her the subjects would not be at risk if she signed and that in signing she had relied on this misrepresentation. The creditor had not advised her of the risks of signing the deed or to obtain independent advice. However, the issue in *Forsyth* was one which had not been decided in *O'Brien* or *Smith*, namely to what extent did the provision of legal advice affect the creditor's duty to take "reasonable steps to secure that in relation to the proposed contract he acts throughout in good faith".[46] In the circumstances which led to *Forsyth*, the creditor had instructed a firm of solicitors to act on its behalf. The pursuer had not given instructions to that firm to act on her behalf but the creditor had reasonably perceived that the solicitors were so acting. There was no doubt[47] that, if the issue of legal advice had not been brought out, the creditor would have had a duty to warn the pursuer of the consequences of granting the standard security and to advise her to take independent advice. Failing that, reduction of the security would follow if it was established in fact that the pursuer had granted it on the basis of the misrepresentation by her husband.[48] Lord Macfadyen held, first, that the requirement of good faith on the creditor in cautionary obligations does not arise only where the cautioner who grants the obligation is without legal advice.[49] However, the extent of a creditor's duty may differ depending on whether the cautioner has had legal advice, the answer being dependent on what assumptions a creditor is entitled to make about the information and advice given by the solicitor to the cautioner.[50] On the parties' averments in *Forsyth*, the solicitors had been acting, as the creditor understood it, for the cautioner, her husband and the creditor. The court found that the creditor was entitled to infer from the fact that solicitors had acted for the cautioner that she would be properly advised as to the nature and consequences of the transaction.[51] Accordingly, on the basis of this assumption which the creditor was entitled to make, the creditor did not require to advise the cautioner (or even to establish that the solicitors had done so) to preserve its good faith.[52]

In fulfilling the duty of good faith, the creditor is not required to take into account the possibility that the solicitor will fail to fulfil his

---

[46] *per* Lord Clyde in *Smith* at p.1068H.

[47] Having regard to *O'Brien* and *Smith*.

[48] *per* Lord Macfadyen in *Forsyth* at p.1303G–H.

[49] In which case, the full extent of the duty of good faith is on the creditor, who must warn the cautioner of the nature and effect of the transaction and advise her to obtain independent legal advice.

[50] The same principle is brought out in *Broadway, supra* no. 38, and in *Royal Bank of Scotland plc v. Wilson*, 2001 S.L.T. (Sh.Ct) 2, where Sheriff Craik Q.C. stated (p.6): "The factor that independent legal advice was involved and available to the [cautioners] must weigh against the line of defence now tabled."

[51] p.1305K, relying on *Etridge (No.2)* in the Court of Appeal; the fact that the solicitors acted for both the cautioner and her husband was not sufficient to disentitle the creditor from relying on the involvement of the solicitors: p.1305A–B. The ability of the creditor to rely on advice tendered by a solicitor advising both husband and wife was confirmed in *Royal Bank of Scotland plc v. Clark*, 2000 S.L.T. (Sh.Ct) 101, p.105; see also para. 5.9.

[52] This point in *Forsyth* was followed in *Clydesdale Bank plc v. Adamson*, 2001 G.W.D. 27–1082, where the cautioner's case also failed on the basis that the creditor had by its own actions fulfilled its duty of good faith.

professional obligations. However, there may be circumstances where the creditor is aware of specific facts which suggest the solicitor has not fulfilled or will fail to fulfil his duties, in which case the creditor will require to take further steps to satisfy the duty of good faith incumbent on it.[53]

Lord Macfadyen followed his own decision in *Forsyth* in *Broadway v. Clydesdale Bank plc (No.2)*,[54] and provided further invaluable guidance on the creditor's duty of good faith. The facts were similar to those in *Smith* and *Forsyth*, the cautioner averring that she had executed a standard security in favour of the creditor for business debts under and as a result of undue influence from both her husband and her son. A solicitor had been involved and had sent a letter to the cautioner though it was not clear on the facts whether that letter had ever reached her. The creditor defended the claim relying on *Forsyth* in relation to the involvement of the solicitor and on the absence of undue influence on the facts. The cautioner relied heavily on English cases, including *O'Brien*, which supported strict classification of types of undue influence and a presumption of undue influence in similar circumstances to those averred by the pursuer.[55] Lord Macfadyen rejected the English approach holding:

> "There is, it seems to me, a risk that undue reliance on the categorisation developed in the English authorities ... may obscure the essential nature of undue influence ... I prefer the ... approach ... that it is undesirable and probably impossible to frame a comprehensive statement of what does and what does not constitute undue influence. The answer to the question whether the requisite abuse of a relationship of trust may be held to have occurred in a particular case must in my view depend on a consideration of the whole circumstances established in evidence."

The case also confirms that it is not an essential element of the doctrine that the perpetrator of the undue influence[56] personally benefits.[57] It was held on the facts that undue influence had not been established and so

---

[53] *Forsyth*, p.1304D.

[54] 2001 G.W.D. 14–552; the decision has been reclaimed and is due to be heard by the Inner House in October 2002. The same judge also followed *Forsyth* in *Wright v. Cotias Investments Inc.*, 2000 S.C.L.R. 324.

[55] In *Bank of Credit and Commerce International SA v. Aboody* [1990] 1 Q.B. 923, p.953, quoted with approval by Lord Browne-Wilkinson in the House of Lords in *O'Brien* and relied on by the pursuer in *Broadway*, the Court of Appeal had classified cases according to actual undue influence (Class 1), and presumed undue influence (Class 2, itself split into Class 2A and Class 2B). In the latter case, the surety required only to show a relationship of trust and confidence between surety and wrongdoer of such nature that it would be fair to presume abuse in having the security executed, the burden of proof then being transferred to the creditor to show that the obligation was entered freely. But even in England much more weight must now be placed on actual proof of undue influence following the House of Lords decision in *Etridge (No.2)*, [2001] 3 W.L.R. 1021.

[56] The decision refers only to undue influence in this respect but it is submitted that the principle may be extended to other forms of legally wrongful act, such as misrepresentation.

[57] Although the judge indicated that, having not heard full argument on the point, a concluded opinion could not be expressed.

the action failed. The judge considered the issue of the creditor's good faith nonetheless, particularly in the context of legal advice having been provided to the cautioner. Once again, the involvement of a solicitor was sufficient to preserve the creditor's good faith. Moreover, the court confirmed the point made in earlier cases[58] that "[t]he issue is not, of course, whether the [cautioner] in fact had a solicitor acting for her, but rather whether the defenders knew or had reasonable ground for believing that she did".[59] On the facts of *Broadway*, advice from a solicitor to the cautioner did not reach her. It was also held that knowledge on the part of the creditor's solicitor, who had believed that he was acting for the cautioner too, that the cautioner had had legal advice,[60] would have been sufficient to regard the creditor as having had knowledge of the cautioner's exposure to legal advice. In other words, the knowledge of an agent of the creditor that the cautioner has had certain advice is knowledge of the creditor himself.[61]

No Presumption of Undue Influence

Broadway is an important decision as the major difference for practical **5.8** purposes between the two jurisdictions at that time was whether the nature of the relationship between principal debtor and cautioner gives rise to a presumption of undue influence. The Scottish position has consistently been that no such presumption should be inferred, the matter always depending on proof of the actual circumstances prevailing at the time. In *Smith*, Lord Clyde said: "It is not to be supposed or presumed that, simply because there is a close personal relationship the security will be given otherwise that with a full and free consent." Lord Macfadyen's decision in *Broadway* confirms the position. Once again, if the cautioner is to succeed there must be relevant averments that the creditor was in bad faith,[62] including a narration in the averments of the factual circumstances from which that conclusion can be drawn.[63] Interestingly, while Scots law has been catching up with the law in England, albeit by means of a different doctrine, since the decision in *Smith* in 1997, the English courts have now retreated from the classification approach back towards the Scottish position where no presumption of a wrongful act is made.[64]

---

[58] *Forsyth* and *Wright*.

[59] Lord Macfadyen made the same point in similar terms later in his judgment: "What matters is the [creditor's] knowledge or reasonable belief that the [cautioner] had a solicitor acting for her in the matter, not whether she actually received from that solicitor appropriate advice about the risks of the transaction." This approach is supported by Gretton and Reid, *Conveyancing 2000*, pp.87–88 where it is observed that as the issue is the creditor's good faith, "that is to a substantial extent how matters *appeared*" to the creditor.

[60] From himself.

[61] The same applies of course to knowledge held by employees of the creditor.

[62] *Wright v. Cotias Investments Inc.*, 2000 S.C.L.R. 324.

[63] For a detailed review of averments of such nature, see the decision of Lord Macfadyen following procedure roll debate in *Broadway v. Clydesdale Bank plc*, 2000 G.W.D. 19–763.

[64] The Scottish approach has been described as simpler and more direct than the English doctrine with the benefit of avoiding the potentially misleading route of constructive notice: Megarry and Wade, *The Law of Real Property* (C. Harpum ed., 6th ed., 2000), para. 19–177; and Rickett, "The Financier's Duty of Care to a Surety" (1998) 114 L.Q.R. 17, which also reviews a third approach, favoured by the Australian courts, of "unconscientious dealing".

Etridge (No.2)

5.9 This significant change was effected in *Royal Bank of Scotland plc v. Etridge (No.2)*,[65] where the House of Lords reviewed the whole law in this field as it applies in England. The leading speech is that of Lord Nicholls. He confirmed firstly that a bank is put on inquiry whenever a wife offers to stand surety for her husband's debts[66] and then turned to consider what steps the creditor must take when it is put on inquiry. Lord Nicholls said,

> "it is plainly neither desirable nor practicable that banks should be required to discover for themselves whether a wife's consent is being procured by the exercise of undue influence of her husband. This is not a step the banks should be expected to take ... The furthest a bank can be expected to go is to take reasonable steps to satisfy itself that the wife has had brought home to her, in a meaningful way, the practical implication of the proposed transaction ... It is not unreasonable for the banks to prefer that this task should be undertaken by an independent legal adviser."[67]

Ordinarily it is reasonable for a creditor to rely on confirmation from a solicitor, acting for the surety, that he has advised her properly but the House of Lords laid down detailed guidelines which a creditor must follow in future cases[68] if he is to gain protection from the solicitor's advice to the surety.[69] First, the creditor must check *directly with the wife*[70] the name of the solicitor she wishes to act. As part of this direct communication, the creditor must advise the surety that he will be obtaining written confirmation from a solicitor that the nature and effect of the transaction has been fully explained and that the purpose for the creditor in obtaining such confirmation is to prevent the surety later disputing the documentation. Next, the creditor must provide the solicitor with the necessary financial information for the solicitor to properly explain the transaction to the wife. While this will to some extent depend on the individual facts, it will normally include such factors as the current level of the husband's indebtedness. If the creditor has information from which it suspects that there has been a legally wrongful act, the creditor must advise the solicitor of that information. Finally, according to Lord Nicholls, the creditor must always obtain written confirmation from the solicitor that he has duly advised the surety of the nature and effect of the transaction. Interestingly, it is on this last point that differences are most likely to emerge between the two jurisdictions. Lord Clyde in the same case said

---

[65] [2001] 3 W.L.R. 1021; the decision was issued on October 11, 2001.

[66] Overruling the Court of Appeal on this point which had suggested a more complex assessment.

[67] pp.1039F–1040E.

[68] The court effectively drew a line in the sand as at October 11, 2001. For transactions before that date, the creditor is normally protected if a solicitor acting for the surety confirmed to the creditor that he had explained the risks. For transactions after that date, the detailed steps set out by Lord Nicholls must be followed, at least in England.

[69] The sentences which follow are necessarily a summary but the full text of this part of Lord Nicholls' speech is repeated in the Appendix at para. 14.2.

[70] Lord Nicholls' emphasis.

"Necessarily the precise course to be adopted will depend upon the circumstances. In ... Forsyth ..., it appeared to the creditor that the wife had already had the benefit of professional legal advice. In such a case, it may well be that no further steps need be taken by the creditor to safeguard his rights."[71]

These comments may be construed in such a way as to support an argument in Scotland that the creditor's reasonable belief that legal advice has been provided remains sufficient to preserve good faith, even if there has been no express written confirmation to that effect. This issue is considered further below.[72]

The position is always different if the creditor knows that the solicitor has failed in his duties or if there are facts from which the creditor should have realised that appropriate advice has not been provided. In such a case, the security will be open to challenge unless the creditor has taken further steps to comply with the duty incumbent on him. The court also set out detailed guidelines on the advice which solicitors should provide when they accept instructions to advise a surety.[73] It is not, however, necessary that in all cases a separate solicitor must act for husband and wife. If at any stage the solicitor is concerned that a conflict of interest may develop, he must cease to act for the wife.[74]

Policy Issues

The decisions in *O'Brien* and *Smith*, and the clarification provided by the various decisions above, are no accident. This is apparent from the manner in which Lord Clyde in *Smith* sought to bring Scottish law into line with English law.[75] More generally, there has been a clear strategy pursued by the courts to protect cautioners in circumstances where no protection existed previously but only within reason.[76] In *Royal Bank of Scotland plc v. Wilson*,[77] Sheriff Craik Q.C. provided a useful summary of the basis on which the doctrine has been advanced:

"In Forsyth's case counsel for the defenders had reminded the court that: 'The English courts recognised that what is involved is a balancing exercise, maintaining proper equilibrium between, on the

5.10

---

[71] p.1051H.
[72] See para. 5.12.
[73] Once again overruling the Court of Appeal which had gone "much too far". It is submitted that it is inappropriate to consider these guidelines in full here as they do not directly affect the relationship between the surety and the creditor, though of course there could be circumstances where the security might be open to challenge if the creditor is aware that one of the steps has not been fulfilled by the solicitor. Given their importance to solicitors generally, the text of Lord Nicholls' speech on this point is repeated in full in the Appendix at para. 14.1. See also Sim, "Risks in Advising Spouses—the *Etridge* effect", 2001 J.L.S.S. 42.
[74] The same point has been made in Scotland in *Forsyth* and *Clark*: see *supra* no. 50.
[75] See para. 5.4.
[76] For example, in *O'Brien*, [1994] 1 A.C. 180 (H.L.), Lord Browne-Wilkinson said (p.188H) "it is essential that a law designed to protect the vulnerable does not render the matrimonial home unacceptable as security to financial institutions."
[77] 2001 S.L.T. (Sh.Ct) 2.

one hand, the protection of those who may be susceptible to misrepresentation or undue influence, and, on the other hand, the desirability of certainty in commercial transactions and the avoidance of the stifling of the legitimate use of resources to support borrowing.' Various English decisions were cited in this connection and the court in Forsyth's case did not demur from that proposition. I think this must be so".[78]

This is undoubtedly a correct summary of the policy behind the doctrine and was confirmed in *Etridge (No.2)*, where Lord Bingham of Cornhill stated:

"The transactions which give rise to these appeals are commonplace but of great social and economic importance. It is important that a wife (or anyone in a like position) should not charge her interest in the matrimonial home to secure the borrowing of her husband (or anyone in a like position) without fully understanding the nature and effect of the proposed transaction and that the decision is hers, to agree or not to agree. It is important that lenders should feel able to advance money, in run-of-the-mill cases with no abnormal purpose."

In the same case, Lord Nicholls said:

"For most home-owning couples, their homes are their most valuable asset. They must surely be free, if they so wish, to use this asset as a means of raising money, whether for the purpose of the husband's business or for any other business . . . If the freedom of home-owners to make economic use of their homes is not to be frustrated, a bank must be able to have confidence that a wife's signature of the necessary guarantee and charge will be as binding upon her as is the signature of anyone else on documents which he or she may sign."

Broad Applicability of Doctrine

5.11 It is important to emphasise that, while the majority of cases involve wives subjected to undue influence by husbands, the doctrine applies to any relationship of trust and confidence which has been abused. In *Etridge (No.2)*, Lord Nicholls said "[t]he position is likewise if the husband stands surety for his wife's debts. Similarly, in the case of unmarried couples, whether heterosexual or homosexual, where the bank is aware of the relationship". The judge also confirmed that a relationship of parent and child is one where trust and confidence exists but said that it is not "possible to produce a comprehensive list of relationships where there is a substantial risk of the exercise of undue influence, all others being excluded from the ambit of the *O'Brien* principle". On the

---

[78] p.5.

same issue, referring to the classification approach adopted by the English courts hitherto, Lord Clyde stated "[a]ll these classifications to my mind add mystery rather than illumination", emphasising that whether or not there has been undue influence is a matter of evidence and proof. In these findings, the House of Lords has moved irrefutably away from the strict categorisations favoured by the Court of Appeal in *Etridge (No.2)* towards the decisions in Scotland of *Forsyth* and *Broadway*. This, and the Scottish courts' existing reliance on proof of undue influence, mean that the doctrine in Scotland can fairly be said to apply to any relationship of trust and confidence which has been abused and not merely to husband and wife cases.[79] However, the position may be different in commercial cases and the rule does not include the situation where the principal debtor is a company and the cautioner is a shareholder and director of the company.[80]

Further, while its major effect to date has been in security transactions (hence its inclusion here), the doctrine is capable of extension to a wider range of obligations taken on by a cautioner as the result of undue influence.

Summary

Summarising the law as it stands in Scotland at this stage is no easy matter. *Etridge (No.2)*, as an English decision of the House of Lords, is not strictly binding but would in the normal case be regarded as highly persuasive. However, it is not at all clear that the Scottish courts will follow *Etridge (No.2)* on all its findings. The Inner House has already expressed reservations about certain aspects of the decision in *Clydesdale Bank plc v. Black*[81] and there has been commentary to the effect that the duties on solicitors advising may be more onerous in Scotland than in England.[82] It must always be remembered that the two doctrines are not identical. The Scottish emphasis on good faith cannot be discounted. If a creditor has acted in accordance with the law as it stood at a particular time (say, for example, as confirmed by the Inner House in *Smith*), can he be criticised for a breach of good faith if the law is subsequently determined by the House of Lords to be different? Even if *Etridge (No.2)* is followed in Scotland on all its points, the extent to which the creditor is protected depends on whether the transaction pre-dated or post-dated October 11, 2001.[83] Certain aspects of the decision in *Etridge (No.2)* are unquestionably compatible with Scots law and, unless specifically indicated, it is submitted that the principles enunciated below reflect the position in Scotland at present with reasonable certainty.

5.12

---

[79] *Broadway* and *Wright* both included consideration of averred undue influence by a son; the doctrine will also extend to homosexual couples where there is the requisite relationship of trust and confidence: *Etridge (No.2)*, Thomson; "Misplaced Concern?" 1997 S.L.G. 124.

[80] *Wright, supra,* p.335 where Lord Macfadyen stated "[t]o apply the rule in such circumstances would go very far beyond the circumstances contemplated in *Smith* . . . and would have a very serious impact on commercial lending practice."

[81] Heard on February 26 and 27, 2002 and currently at *avizandum*.

[82] Sim, "Risks in Advising Spouses—the *Etridge* effect", 2001 J.L.S.S. 42.

[83] See para. 5.9.

The cautioner is entitled to protection from undue influence,[84] the purpose of which is to have her provide security to a creditor for the debts of another. Undue influence must always have taken place before the cautioner is entitled to rely on a failure by the creditor to comply with his duty of good faith. The cautioner's decision to make available security must be based on the undue influence. The onus of proving that the security was executed in reliance on undue influence rests on the cautioner. The undue influence may be effected by either the creditor or the other whose debts are being secured.[85] It is not essential that the perpetrator of the undue influence should benefit from it. In an action against the creditor based on the undue influence, there must be specific and relevant averments of the act complained of. No presumption is raised that undue influence has taken place simply because of the nature of the relationship between the cautioner and the principal debtor. The question of whether undue influence has taken place will always be a matter for proof which will depend on the individual circumstances of each case.

The creditor has a duty of good faith, where he should reasonably suspect, because of the relationship between the principal debtor and the cautioner, that the cautioner's consent to the security in his favour might not be fully informed or freely given. This will include the situation whenever a wife offers to stand as cautioner for her husband's debts.[86] To preserve his good faith, the creditor must take reasonable steps to ensure that the cautioner is protected. If a cautioner seeks to prove that the creditor has not complied with his duty of good faith, there must be specific and relevant averments to support that aspect of the claim.

The reasonable steps which a creditor must take include warning the cautioner of the nature and consequence of providing the security and ensuring that the cautioner is offered the benefit of independent legal advice. If the cautioner is legally represented, then for transactions before October 11, 2001, that will normally suffice in itself to preserve the creditor's good faith and so preclude a challenge to the security. For transactions thereafter, the position depends on whether the Scottish courts will follow *Etridge (No.2)*. If they do, the creditor (and the solicitor) will require to take the very much more detailed steps detailed there if the creditor's good faith is to be preserved. If not, the position remains as for pre-*Etridge* transactions.

For transactions before October 11, 2001, then even if the cautioner is not legally represented, provided the creditor had reasonable cause to believe that the cautioner had the benefit of legal advice[87] in connection with the transaction, his good faith will be preserved. The creditor's

---

[84] "undue influence" is again used here (as stated *supra* no. 25) for convenience to describe any act in consequence of which the cautioner's consent to the granting of the security is improperly obtained.

[85] Although strictly for the applicability of the doctrine in *Smith*, the undue influence will have been exercised by someone other than the holder of the security, who will be innocent of that act.

[86] Assuming the Scottish courts follow *Etridge (No.2)*. It is possible that the Scottish courts will require that there be a higher threshold before the creditor's duty is triggered.

[87] Assuming there is no reason for the creditor to believe that the advice has been defective.

knowledge or reasonable belief may be acquired through information held by agents of the creditor rather than directly held by the creditor himself. This will remain the law if the Scottish courts do not follow Lord Nicholls' views in *Etridge (No.2)* and it is perhaps on this very point that a different view in Scotland may prevail. The reasons are, first, the difference in the doctrines and the emphasis in Scotland on good faith. If a creditor genuinely believes that a cautioner has had full and independent legal advice about the transaction, can he really be said not to have complied with his duty of good faith? There is little or no room for the application of the English concept of equity in these circumstances. Secondly, Lord Clyde's views in *Etridge (No.2)* appear closer to the existing Scottish model than to Lord Nicholls' comments on this point.[88] If, however, the Scottish courts follow Lord Nicholls without question, then the issue of reasonable belief so clearly enunciated in *Broadway* is no longer relevant, the creditor requiring instead to take very much more detailed steps himself and to obtain written confirmation from the solicitor that the nature and effect of the transaction have been explained to the cautioner.

In either event, in the normal case, it makes no difference that the solicitor acts for the creditor and for the principal debtor, as the creditor is entitled to assume that the solicitor will comply with his duties to avoid conflicts of interest and to see that the cautioner understands the nature and consequence of providing security.

There is an exception to these general rules where the creditor is aware of facts which suggest that the cautioner's consent might not be fully informed or freely given, such as where he knows that the cautioner's legal advice has not been appropriate. In such circumstances, unless the creditor takes steps to ensure that such consent is valid and informed, the creditor's security will be open to challenge. However, there may be cases where the position cannot be rectified in that manner and so the transaction should not proceed. If it does, the creditor proceeds at his own risk.

If the creditor complies with his duty of good faith, his security will not to be open to challenge. The cautioner will accordingly remain liable to the creditor, though she may have a claim (usually worthless) against the perpetrator of the undue influence.

Human Rights and Repossessions

The Human Rights Act 1998[89] came into force on October 2, 2000. The 1998 Act gives effect to the substantive rights created by the European Convention on Human Rights.[90] The 1998 Act itself is merely a framework. What is important is the Convention itself and the whole body of law based on the interpretation of the Convention. A full consideration of the terms of the 1998 Act and the Convention is beyond the scope of this work but a consideration of the salient issues affecting repossession follows below.

5.13

---

[88] See para. 5.9.
[89] (c.42), hereafter "the 1998 Act".
[90] The full title is "European Convention for the Protection of Human Rights and Fundamental Freedoms", hereafter "the Convention".

Under the 1998 Act, courts must interpret, so far as is possible to do so, Acts of Parliament in a way that is compatible with the Convention rights.[91] It is further provided that "it is unlawful for a public authority to act in a way which is incompatible with a Convention right".[92]

The term "public authority" is expressly defined to include courts and tribunals.[93] These provisions made it clear that courts require to apply the Convention in disputes involving public authorities and so it has proved in practice.[94] However, heritable creditors are not public authorities within the meaning in the Act. The full extent to which Convention rights will be applied by courts in disputes between private parties remains unclear[95] but the imposition of the duty on courts not to act incompatibly with the Convention has already resulted in the application of the Convention in Scotland where neither party to the action is a public authority.[96]

Application of the Convention in Repossessions

5.14 It appears that the provisions of the Convention most likely to be of relevance in this area are Article 6 providing the right to a fair trial; Article 8 providing the right to respect for private and family life; and Article 1 of the First Protocol, providing for the protection of property.[97]

Article 6 provides, *inter alia*, "[i]n the determination of his civil rights and obligations . . ., everyone is entitled to a fair and public hearing within a reasonable time by an independent and impartial tribunal established by law".

It is not suggested that in this context the sheriff court will fall foul of the definition "independent and impartial tribunal".[98] However, there may be circumstances in which the "fair and public hearing" is not obtained. Imagine that a decree is granted by the court for repossession[99] but enforcement is suspended[1] on condition that the debtor maintains a repayment arrangement. If the debtor fails to so maintain payments, and the decree becomes immediately enforceable without further discussion,

---

[91] s.3 of the 1998 Act.
[92] s.6 of the 1998 Act.
[93] s.6(3)(a) of the 1998 Act.
[94] See for example *County Properties Ltd v. The Scottish Ministers*, 2001 S.L.T. 1125, a Scottish case which also illustrates that not only natural persons have human rights. In theory, this might open the door for a heritable creditor to claim in certain circumstances that his rights were being breached.
[95] For a restrictive view of the application of the Convention to private law, see Buxton, "The Human Rights Act and Private Law" (2000) 116 L.Q.R. 48.
[96] *Karl Construction Ltd v. Palisade Properties plc*, 2002 G.W.D. 7–212, Lord Drummond Young.
[97] An argument has been advanced that unsympathetic pursuit of debtors by creditors may be a breach of Article 3 ("No one shall be subjected to . . . degrading treatment") but the Article is headed "Prohibition of Torture" and it is highly unlikely that it applies to repossessions.
[98] *Clancy v. Caird*, 2000 S.L.T. 546.
[99] Under s.24 of the 1970 Act.
[1] Under s.2 of the 2001 Act; although this is likely to be less common than suspension before decree, it appears possible—see para. 4.2.8.

has the debtor had a fair and public hearing?[2] What too of service on the walls of court in the case of a disappeared debtor? The terms of the Convention suggest creditors should ensure all possible avenues of enquiry have been exhausted before that mode of notification is adopted. Article 6 may also offer debtors the right to challenge enforcement of apparently purged decrees.[3]

Article 8 provides, *inter alia*:

> "(1) Everyone has the right to respect for his private and family life, his home and his correspondence.
> (2) There shall be no interference by a public authority with the exercise of this right except such as is in accordance with the law and is necessary in a democratic society in the interests of . . . the economic well-being of the country . . ., or for the protection of the rights and freedoms of others."

It is clear that eviction will have an impact on family life and respect for the home.[4] The question is to what extent interference with the right is justified. Article 8 has been considered in England in the context of repossessions, albeit in a case before the 1998 Act came into force. In *Albany Homes Loans Ltd v. Massey*,[5] possession was refused against one debtor where the other debtor (the wife) had the right to remain in occupation. This situation arose because she was maintaining an *O'Brien* defence to the action[6] and the court would not permit possession against her until that issue was determined. In the Court of Appeal, Lord Justice Schiemann described Article 8 as "a clue to the solution to the problems posed by this case".[7] It was common ground that the making of the order

---

[2] The creditor would argue that he had, the fair and public hearing having come before the suspension. Support for this view is found in *St Brice v. Southwark London B.C.* [2001] E.W.C.A. Civ. 1138. In that case, it was argued that that the decision of a creditor to proceed, when decree has been granted earlier but the creditor has shown latitude or the debtor has failed to comply with conditions imposed at the time of decree being granted (such as where a s.2 order with conditions is made under the 2001 Act at the time of decree), was contrary to Arts 6 and 8 of the Convention as possession proceeded on the basis of an administrative rather than judicial act. The Court of Appeal dismissed this argument holding that the step of proceeding further was one which had already been authorised by the court and did not alter the legal status of the party affected (in this case a tenant) or make any decision in relation to his rights. Leave to appeal to the House of Lords was sought but refused. It may also be argued by a debtor that each party must have the right to see and challenge all the evidence on which the court will rely. That could suggest that a revisiting of the reasons for the debtor's failure might be required.

[3] In some cases, where further arrears have accrued, a decree may remain enforceable even if the sum originally specified as outstanding in the writ has been repaid.

[4] *Poplar Housing and Regeneration Community Association Ltd v. Donoghue* [2002] Q.B. 48. In that case, the Court of Appeal in a landlord and tenant case found that Art. 8 of the Convention applied but that the Housing Act 1988 did not conflict with its terms on the basis that Parliament had intended preference to be given to those who were not intentionally homeless; the Court further held that s.21(4) of that Act was necessary in a democratic society because a procedure was required to allow recovery of property at the end of a tenancy, a finding which may give comfort to creditors faced with a human rights challenge to the terms of the 1970 Act.

[5] [1997] 2 All E.R. 609.

[6] See para 5.3.

[7] p.612H.

for possession, at the time it was made and at the time of the appeal, was not necessary for the protection of the rights of the creditor. In the event, an undertaking was provided by the security holder not to seek possession until the wife's case had been heard.

In addition to possible challenge to repossession orders themselves, it is thought that Article 8 may also be used in an attempt to prevent disclosure of otherwise confidential information[8] on the basis that such disclosure would be a breach of the right to respect for private life.

Article 8 is a qualified right. It may be departed from if certain conditions so justify. In these circumstances, the principle of proportionality comes into play. In considering this principle, there must be struck "a fair balance between the rights of the individual and the needs of society".[9] Heritable creditors could argue that a legal system which precluded them from repossessing properties or made it unfeasibly difficult to do so would act against the interests of the community as a whole by reason of the consequential effect that would have on the ability to obtain secured loans and the cost of borrowing.[10] On the other hand, debtors may argue that the individual's right to home ownership is of such fundamental importance that it may not be overridden other than in exceptional circumstances. A debtor may argue that, in the case of a few months arrears, an ordinary court action for payment of the debt would be a more proportionate response from a creditor than an action to recover the security subjects.

The court will also have regard here to the margin of appreciation allowed to the states who are party to the Convention. This doctrine provides that states have latitude in determining the balance between the public interest and the interests of individuals. A creditor may be able to find support for the existing law in previous decisions of the European Court of Human Rights which indicate that it will only interfere with the state's determination of the balancing exercise if the state has acted in a way which is "manifestly without reasonable foundation".[11]

Finally, on the subject of Article 8, it should be noted that the although it refers to "home", in certain circumstances this may be capable of extension to business premises if the debtor carries on non-business related activities from the commercial property.[12]

Article 1 of the First Protocol provides:

> "Every natural or legal person is entitled to the peaceful enjoyment of his possessions. No one shall be deprived of his possessions except in the public interest and subject to the conditions provided for by law...The preceding provisions shall not, however, in any

---

[8] As is likely to be required in a consideration of a section 2 order under the 2001 Act. See para. 4.2.14.

[9] Lord President Rodger in *A (A Mental Patient) v. The Scottish Ministers,* 2000 S.L.T. 873, p.900F.

[10] See *Poplar, supra* no. 4; and *Fredin v. Sweden* (1991) 13 E.H.R.R. 784 where the European Court of Human Rights held "an interference [with Article 1 of the First Protocol] must achieve a 'fair balance' between the demands of the general interest of the community and the requirements of the protection of the individual's fundamental rights."

[11] *Mellacher v. Austria* (1990) 12 E.H.R.R. 391.

[12] *Niemitz v. Germany,* 1992 A. 251–B.

way impair the right of a State to enforce such laws as it deems necessary to control the use of property in accordance with the general interest".

The word "possessions" has been held to include security rights *in rem*.[13] The term also includes money advanced by a creditor to a debtor.[14] Article 1 of the First Protocol has obvious similarities with Article 8 and, like that, is qualified, meaning that action by a creditor must be proportionate.[14a] It is likely that arguments advanced under Article 8 will also rely on the terms of this provision.[15] The effect of Article 1 of the First Protocol to date has been most notable in the field of unsecured debt recovery where it has been relied upon to curtail the use of inhibition on the dependence.[16]

Remedies for Breach of the Convention

5.15 The courts may not override primary legislation and in these circumstances must make a declaration of incompatibility.[17] Such a declaration does not affect the validity of the existing United Kingdom legislation.[18] By contrast, subordinate legislation must be struck down by the courts in favour of the Convention if there is a conflict.

Damages may be awarded under the 1998 Act but only if courts are satisfied that an award is necessary to afford just satisfaction.[19] In practice, damages have been awarded infrequently and, where awards have been made, they have been low. A more realistic remedy in a repossession setting is likely to be an interdict.

---

[13] *Gasus Dosier-und Fodertechnik v. Netherlands*, 1995 A 306–B *Strathclyde Joint Police Board v. The Elderslie Estates Ltd*, 2002 S.L.T. (Land Ct) 2 at p.7.

[14] In *Wilson v. First County Trust Ltd* [2001] Q.B. 407, Sir Andrew Morritt V.-C. in the Court of Appeal held, on a consideration of Art. 1 of the First Protocol: "The money advanced by [the creditor] to [the debtor] was its possession. It lent that money to [the debtor] on terms, as it thought, that it should be repaid in six months time. It has been deprived of that possession as provided for by law". The appeal was adjourned following an indication by the court that s.127(3) of the Consumer Credit Act 1974 might be incompatible with Art. 6 and Art. 1 of the First Protocol to the Convention. When the appeal hearing was resumed (reported at [2002] Q.B. 74), a declaration of incompatibility was made but the terms of the judgment set out above remain valid.

[14a] In *Strathclyde Joint Police Board v. The Elderslie Estates Ltd*, 2002 S.L.T. (Land Ct) 2 at p.12C, a remedy provided by s.1(4) of the 1970 Act was found "proportional to the needs of the situation".

[15] As in *Chapman v. U.K.*, Appl. No. 27238/95 where, having been moved on from temporary sites repeatedly, the applicant alleged violations of Art. 8 and Art. 1 of the First Protocol when she was denied planning permission to live in a mobile home on land she had purchased. The application was unsuccessful.

[16] *Karl Construction Ltd v. Palisade Properties plc*, 2002 G.W.D. 7–212, where the court held that the automatic right to inhibit on the dependence of an action was contrary to this provision of the Convention.

[17] s.4 of the 1998 Act though note that only the superior courts may do so. For an example involving a creditor, see *supra* no. 14.

[18] But note that the Scottish Parliament and Scottish Executive have no power to act incompatibly with the Convention: ss.29 and 57 of the Scotland Act 1998 (c.46).

[19] s.8(3) of the 1998 Act.

Conclusion

5.16 A final consideration, in relation to the applicability of each of these provisions, is that the 1998 Act is part of a bigger picture. In the English case *Daniels v. Walker*,[20] Lord Woolf M.R. made it clear that where the applicable court rules had been followed, defendants should not be allowed to raise arguments under the 1998 Act as a form of "last ditch" defence.[21] It is submitted, on a consideration of human rights and repossessions as a whole, that in the ordinary case a heritable creditor who has taken steps to resolve the problems with the debtor and, thereafter, has followed the appropriate court procedure is unlikely to face a successful challenge under the Convention.

The Expenses of Court Proceedings[22]

5.17 As with the general rule on expenses in any litigation,[23] legal expenses in repossessions have tended to follow success. Given the lack of discretion available to the court to refuse repossession, until the passing of the 2001 Act, it is not surprising that in the overwhelming majority of cases, expenses were awarded in favour of the creditor. That much has been relatively uncontroversial to date.

How Much can be Recovered?

5.18 Of more interest is the question of how much the creditor is entitled to recover from the debtor by way of expenses and, in particular, whether the creditor is entitled to seek recovery of expenses on a party/party basis or an agent/client basis.[24] In the former scenario, only those expenses recoverable by way of judicial expenses could be sought from the debtor. In the latter, all reasonable expenses, whether they would be recoverable by way of judicial expenses or not, would be properly chargeable to the debtor. A normal litigation would see expenses awarded on a party/party basis unless there were special circumstances justifying an agent/client award.

The complication in a repossession arises from the terms of standard condition 12[25] which provides,

> "[t]he debtor shall be personally liable to the creditor for . . . all expenses reasonably incurred by the creditor in calling-up the security and realising or attempting to realise the security subjects,

---

[20] (2000) 1 W.L.R. 1382.

[21] Stating "if the court is not going to be taken down blind alleys it is essential that counsel, and those who instruct counsel, take a responsible attitude as to when it is right to raise a Human Rights Act point".

[22] For consideration of the expenses which a creditor is generally entitled to pass on to a debtor (both legal and otherwise) under the security, see Cusine, "Expenses under a Standard Security", 1994 *Juridical Review* 18.

[23] Macphail, *Sheriff Court Practice* (2nd ed., 1998), para. 19–07.

[24] For further discussion of the distinction between the two types of expenses, see Macphail, *op. cit.*, paras. 19–43 *et seq.*

[25] Sched. 3 to the 1970 Act, para. 12.

or any part thereof, and exercising any other powers conferred upon him by the security."[26]

Although standard condition 12 is capable of variation, in practice[27] the creditor would be unlikely to accept a variation which diminished his right to recover expenses.

The issue is accordingly whether the creditor has a contractual right to recover the legal expenses of enforcement, above and in addition to any judicial expenses awarded by the court. To put it another way, is the creditor restricted only to expenses on the judicial scale, no matter what it may have actually incurred in legal costs in reality?

This question was addressed in *Clydesdale Bank plc v. Mowbray*. The creditor had previously raised various proceedings against the debtor to realise security subjects. Two awards of judicial expenses had been made on a party/party basis in favour of the creditor but the creditor did not have its accounts taxed. In a further two court processes, the creditor was not awarded expenses. The creditor raised this action for recovery of all expenses in respect of the two matters where expenses had been awarded in its favour, but for an amount to include both the judicial expenses for which the defender had been found liable previously and the agent/client expenses which could not have been recovered at taxation or by enforcement of the existing awards of expenses. Further non-legal costs, such as advertising and clearing costs, were included in the claim.

At first instance,[28] Lord Maclean relied heavily on standard condition 12 in rejecting the defender's argument that a separate action for the recovery of expenses of process was incompetent, having regard to the earlier award of judicial expenses on a party/party basis by the courts: "[The court must determine] what expenses the pursuers have reasonably incurred in calling-up the securities and realising or attempting to realise the security subjects. These expenses, in my opinion, are not restricted in the way which the defender maintained before me."

The matter was reclaimed and the defender's argument repeated. The proper remedy, he maintained, was to enforce the existing decrees for expenses. The Extra Division, indicating that the competency issue had not been fully argued, reserved the question of whether the creditor was limited to judicial expenses.[29] Rather, they found that because the sum concluded for included non-litigation costs, the competency of which was not in issue, and as even the level of judicial expenses was uncertain (the accounts not having been taxed), a proof before answer would be necessary, whether or not the defender's argument was correct. It should be noted that, while the reclaiming motion was refused, the repelling of the defender's plea in law was recalled.

The question therefore remains unanswered, leaving the law in an unsatisfactorily uncertain state. It is submitted on a full consideration of

---

[26] The creditor is also given the right to expenses under standard condition 7(3) and ss.10, 13, 14 and 27 of the 1970 Act, the last providing that a creditor may use the sale proceeds "in payment of all expenses properly incurred by him in connection with the sale", which might be taken to include those steps such as court proceedings which led to the sale.
[27] In a residential loan context at least.
[28] 1998 Green's *Property Law Bulletin* 37–7.
[29] 2000 S.C. 151.

standard condition 12 and the other provisions on expenses in the 1970 Act that the creditor is entitled to more than judicial expenses. As a matter of practice, creditors almost invariably add all costs, judicial and otherwise, to the loan account although in many cases they benefit from wider protection in the contractual provisions than is afforded by standard condition 12. In such circumstances, creditors may even decline to seek judicial expenses to ensure they are not barred from insisting on a higher sum in terms of the contract.

Reasonably Incurred

5.19 It must always be remembered that standard condition 12 only entitles the creditor to expenses "reasonably incurred." In *Royal Bank of Scotland plc v. Kinnear*,[30] expenses were awarded against the heritable creditor on the basis that it had acted unreasonably in raising proceedings where the debtor was willing to effect a sale voluntarily. Before seeking decree, the subjects had been marketed and three offers received which exceeded the exposure of the creditor. To prevent decree passing, which would have affected the debtor's ability to obtain a further loan, the action was defended but it was conceded that there was no valid defence to the merits. In due course, the sale went through and the debt was repaid. On appeal, Sheriff Principal Kerr Q.C.,[31] while indicating that every case turned on its own facts, adhered to the judgment describing the decision at first instance as entirely appropriate. The court indicated that it was not reasonable for the creditor to require the comfort of a decree in circumstances such as these.

Expenses Under the 2001 Act

5.20 The 2001 Act does not address the issue of expenses of applications for a section 2 order. The matter will be one within the discretion of the sheriff but it seems reasonable to assume that expenses will follow success. Generally, the passing of the 2001 Act is unlikely to deter further challenges on the subject of expenses as in *Mowbray* and *Kinnear*.

The Repossession Decree

5.21 After the *induciae*[32] has expired following service of a repossession writ,[33] the creditor will be entitled to apply for decree, assuming that no application under the 2001 Act has been made or the application has been unsuccessful. If an application succeeds, the creditor may later apply for revocation or variation of the order and that, in turn, may lead to the position where the creditor may apply for decree. Generally, decree will be granted without any conditions attached but it appears possible for the sheriff to grant decree and, contemporaneously, make a section 2 order under the 2001 Act.[34] In the latter case, enforcement of

---

[30] 2001 G.W.D. 3–124.
[31] in North Strathclyde.
[32] Usually a period of 21 days from the date of service by the creditor.
[33] Whether related to a calling-up notice or based on s.24 of the 1970 Act.
[34] See para. 4.2.8.

the decree will be subject to the terms of that order. In the former instance, the question arises as to whether, leaving aside the possibility of appeal which applies as in any sheriff court matter,[35] there are any steps the debtor may take to prevent the creditor repossessing the security subjects.

This issue was addressed in *Thomson v. Yorkshire Building Society*.[36] In that case, the defender was the creditor of the pursuers in terms of a standard security. The debtors had defaulted and the creditor had obtained decree in an earlier process. Thereafter the debtors became bankrupt. The debtors sought warrant to raise an action and to obtain an interdict preventing the creditor from exercising its rights and enforcing the decree. Sheriff Principal Nicholson Q.C.[37] upheld the sheriff's refusal of warrant to raise and of interim interdict. He held that the remedies sought by the debtors were those which would compete with the right of their creditor. It was observed by the court that the action taken by the debtors suggested that the decree granted was in some way subject to supervision by another court before it could be enforced, which could not be correct. Further, it would be perverse to hold that the creditor had waived its right to enforce the decree because it had shown latitude to the pursuers.[38]

Accordingly, leaving aside the possibility of a decree granted alongside a section 2 order, the court will not prevent a creditor from enforcing a decree which has been granted. There is no reason why the passing of the 2001 Act will change that as regards decrees which are granted without attached conditions.

Eviction

Having obtained decree for the ejection of the debtor, it is open to the creditor to arrange an eviction as soon as the extract decree is made available by the court.[38a] Sheriff officers may evict on the strength of the decree having simply provided notification to the debtor that they intend to do so. Alternatively, sheriff officers may serve a pre-eviction charge, but it does not appear necessary to do so and many creditors now proceed without such charges.[39] Similarly, if a charge is used, it is unclear what period of charge should apply.[39a] The Scottish Executive has indicated that it considers it appropriate to make service of a charge a requirement before eviction may proceed. The period of charge and the days on which eviction may take place are also likely to be clarified.[39b]

Frequently, a creditor will enter into an arrangement with the debtor after an eviction date has been fixed as a result of which the eviction will

5.22

---

[35] But see para. 2.2.11.
[36] 1994 S.C.L.R. 1014.
[37] at Edinburgh.
[38] On which see para. 5.14.
[38a] Though rejection may not be carried out at night.
[39] There is no statutory requirement to do so but the matter has not been authoritatively decided; the position may be different if the creditor wishes to proceed on a summary cause decree (for example, under the circumstances set out at para. 3.5): Lewis "Is a Charge Necessary for Recovery of Possession of Heritable Property?" 1997 Civ.P.B. 15—8.
[39a] See also *Enforcement of Civil Obligations in Scotland—A Consultation Paper*, April 2002, para. 5.315.
[39b] *ibid.*, paras 5.322 and 5.323.

be cancelled. There is no bar to the number of times an eviction may be cancelled but creditors generally have internal guidelines which will require the full arrears to be paid off if an eviction has been cancelled twice before.

If the eviction proceeds, the sheriff officers eject the debtor and are likely to immediately take or organise some of the steps considered below in relation to the recovery of the subjects,[40] most notably the changing of the locks to ensure the debtor does not re-enter the subjects. The English concept of "passive resistance", where the debtor remains in the subjects and will not be ejected by the bailiff, does not apply in Scotland where, if the debtor does not co-operate with sheriff officers, they will call the police for assistance.

---

[40] See para. 7.2.

CHAPTER 6

SPECIAL CASES

Introduction

Special considerations apply to repossessions where the debtor has 6.1
leased the subjects to a tenant, or has been made bankrupt. Similarly,
there are particular issues for a creditor to consider when a debtor seeks
to redeem the security during the repossession process or where the
debtor has a non-entitled spouse. These considerations, and certain
practical issues such as the receipt by the debtor of state benefits, are
considered below.

Tenants of Debtors

Under standard condition 6,[1] the debtor is obliged not to let the security 6.2
subjects without the prior written consent of the heritable creditor.
Nonetheless, a common problem creditors encounter is that the debtor
without obtaining their approval has indeed let the subjects to a third
party. Such an arrangement does not affect the creditor's rights to
recover the security subjects from the debtor, other than to provide an
additional factor, in the form of the interests of the tenant and anyone
else living at the property, which the court must take into account in
determining an application under the 2001 Act.[2]

The relationship between the creditor and the debtor's tenant is more
difficult, unless the creditor has adopted the terms of the lease or other
tenancy agreement and become the landlord of the debtor's tenant.[3]
That is the exception rather than the rule. If a debtor in a standard
security has entered into a lease with a third party, of which the creditor
is unaware and to which when it is brought to his knowledge he does not
wish to consent, the lease is voidable at the instance of the heritable
creditor.[4]

The basis of the decision which confirmed this *Trade Development
Bank v. Warriner and Mason (Scotland) Ltd*,[5] is that the terms of the
standard security[6] should have put the tenant of the debtor on notice

---

[1] Para. 12 of Sched. 3 to the 1970 Act; references to statutory provisions in this Chapter are to the 1970 Act except where the context otherwise requires.

[2] s.2(2)(d) of the 2001 Act, though the tenant himself does not have the right to make the application unless he qualifies on another ground (for example, if he is the partner of the debtor).

[3] This situation is discussed at para. 7.5.2.

[4] For consideration of the position where the creditor is aware of the lease at the time it is entered into, see para. 7.5.2.

[5] 1980 S.L.T. 223.

[6] And in particular standard condition 6. The decision was made even though the standard security provided "we agree that the standard conditions shall be varied in accordance with the said minute of agreement" and the minute of agreement was unrecorded.

that the consent of the heritable creditor was required. Lord President Emslie said

> "since [the tenant] took the lease of 1975 from [the debtor] without the prior consent of the [heritable creditor] and without either searching the record or making any other inquiry, they would in law fall to be treated as having taken their lease from [the debtor] in *mala fide* and upon that ground the lease is reducible[7] at the instance of the [heritable creditor]".[8]

In *Trade Development Bank Ltd v. David W. Haig (Bellshill) Ltd*,[9] a tenant of a debtor sought to argue that there was "excusable ignorance" on its part of the standard security between debtor and heritable creditor.[10] The tenant argued that it had had no reason to search the registers for a standard security and so was justifiably ignorant of its terms, including standard condition 6. It was put forward that sub-tenancy arrangements, as existed here, strengthened this argument as only certain leases can be registered and subjected to a standard security.[11] This too was rejected by the Inner House on the basis that the Register of Sasines gave public notice of the existence of the standard security. Lord President Emslie stated

> "I have no hesitation in saying that 'excusable ignorance' on the part of sub-lessees cannot prevent a security holder from objecting successfully to the validity of the sub-lease upon the ground that it was granted by his debtor in contravention of standard condition 6."[12]

The creditor was found entitled to decree of reduction, declarator and removing.

However, where the tenant has special statutory protection, such as by way of an assured tenancy, the matter is more complicated. The procedural way forward in this situation where the creditor does not wish to adopt the terms of his debtor's lease and the tenant remains in

---

[7] The lease is voidable not void. In *Warriner*, Lord Cameron held (p.233): "If [the lease] were null and void *ab initio* it could never be saved by any subsequent action or agreement of parties. [A lease] entered into without prior written consent is one which is voidable at the instance of the party whose consent is required but has not been obtained."

[8] p.229, the court noting further that if tenants were not put on inquiry, the protection which the 1970 Act intended to confer on heritable creditors would be constantly at risk; but the decision has been criticised as wrongly decided and that standard condition 6, which should have been viewed as a real condition, was unenforceable against the tenant: Reid, "Real Conditions in Standard Securities" 1983 S.L.T. 169; for a response to that argument, see Cusine, *Standard Securities*, para. 5–34; a lease granted by a debtor may also be voidable on the basis of the more general proposition that it is granted to the prejudice of the heritable creditor. This argument was made by the creditor in *Warriner and Mason*, *supra* no. 5 but the court (p.229) found it unnecessary to decide the point.

[9] 1983 S.L.T. 510.

[10] "excusable ignorance" had also been advanced as a defence in *Warriner and Mason*, *supra*, but was rejected for lack of sufficient averment rather than on principle (p.230).

[11] See para. 7.5.2.

[12] p.515.

physical possession was considered in *Tamroui v. Clydesdale Bank plc.*[13] In that case, the pursuer, unaware of a standard security by her landlord in favour of the creditor, had entered into a short assured tenancy of subjects in Dundee with the debtor. The standard security, which predated the tenancy agreement, did not permit the creation of the lease without the consent of the creditor. Following default by the debtor, the creditor obtained decree allowing it to enter possession and eject the debtor. The creditor instructed sheriff officers to enforce the decree against the debtor's tenant, who raised an action against the creditor seeking to interdict it from ejecting her from the property.

The creditor argued that the tenant was in occupation in breach of the conditions of the standard security and that, as it predated the tenancy and had been recorded, the tenant must be taken to have knowledge of the terms of the security.[14] The tenant argued that the creditor did not have a decree to eject the tenant[15] and that a fresh action was necessary by the creditor against her. The court considered the terms of section 18 of the Housing (Scotland) Act 1988[16] which regulate the circumstances in which recovery of possession may be ordered under a short assured tenancy. The section provides "[i]f the sheriff is satisfied that any of the grounds in Part I of Schedule 5 to this Act are established then ... he shall make an order for possession."[17] Part I of Schedule 5 includes Ground 2 as follows:

> "The house is subject to a heritable security granted before the creation of the tenancy and
> (a) as a result of a default by the debtor the creditor is entitled to sell the house and requires it for the purpose of disposing of it with vacant possession in exercise of that entitlement; and
> (b) either notice was given in writing to the tenant not later than the date of commencement of the tenancy that possession might be recovered on this Ground or the sheriff is satisfied that it is reasonable to dispense with the requirement of notice."

Sheriff Davidson granted interim interdict on the assumption that this legislation is for the benefit and protection of tenants and, being later in

---

[13] 1997 S.L.T. (Sh.Ct.) 20.

[14] As in *Warriner and Mason*; it was suggested during the course through Parliament of the Housing (Scotland) Act 1988 (c.43), which regulates short assured tenancies, that tenants should check for the existence of standard securities at the time of constitution of the tenancy agreement but that appears wholly impractical having regard to lack of knowledge and perhaps lack of funds on the part of the tenant: see 1996 Hous.L.R. 42, p.46 for further discussion.

[15] The warrant for ejection craved by heritable creditors commonly seeks removing of the debtor, the debtor's family "and others". It is believed the decree the creditor held against the debtor in *Tamroui* did not include the words "and others". Some creditors continue to seek ejection of assured tenants, against whom they have no decree, on the basis of these words in the decree against the debtor but it seems likely from the reasoning in *Tamroui* that an application for interdict at the instance of the tenant would be successful.

[16] Hereafter "the 1988 Act".

[17] s.18(3) of the 1988 Act.

date, takes account of the provisions of the 1970 Act. The pursuer's tenancy was voidable but not void. That being so, the court ordered that there required to be an application under section 18 of the Housing (Scotland) Act 1988 for an order for possession, in addition to the repossession action under the 1970 Act against the debtor, before the tenant could be evicted from the subjects.[18] The sheriff noted that this may give rise to difficulties for heritable creditors:

> "As Mr Cusine points out, having a tenant in possession rather than the debtor/proprietor will affect the insurance premium payable in respect of the property. Indubitably, the heritable creditor's right to sell will be more difficult to effect with a tenant in possession and the provisions of the Housing (Scotland) Act 1988 appear to give some scope for unscrupulous debtor/proprietors to be paid rent without paying the mortgage at least for a period. However, the terms of the Act appear to me to be extremely clear in requiring that a tenant can only be removed from a short assured tenancy in terms of the Housing (Scotland) Act 1988, and heritable creditors will have to take separate action for their removal."[19]

Interim interdict was also granted in favour of a tenant in *Cameron v. Abbey National plc*[20] where again the creditor had taken decree against the debtor but not the tenant. The tenant was served with a charge for ejection by sheriff officers. Sheriff MacFarlane at Glasgow held it was plain that the pursuer's tenancy[21] was voidable and that a separate action required to be brought under the 1988 Act.

While these decisions are clearly beneficial for tenants with statutory protection whose agreements post-date the terms of the security, there is a twist in the tale. While the 2001 Act was enacted, *inter alia*, to give greater protection to tenants,[22] Mrs Tamroui, as a tenant, would not have been entitled to make an application for a section 2 order herself.[23] This is despite the fact that she was a single mother with two children aged six and two with nowhere else to go. A further consideration is that the position remains uncertain in relation to tenancies created prior to the constitution of the standard security and unknown to the heritable creditor.[24] Although less common than tenancies post-dating the security, these have become more prevalent as a result of the increase in re-mortgaging.[25] If the creditor then obtains decree against the debtor,

---

[18] The court expressly approved Cusine, *Standard Securities* at para. 5–08.

[19] An appeal was marked to the sheriff principal but did not proceed.

[20] 1999 Hous. L.R. 19.

[21] Which, while *ex facie* a protected tenancy under the Rent (Scotland) Act 1984 (c.58), was argued to be a an assured tenancy under the 1988 Act. This argument appears to have been accepted.

[22] See para. 4.2.3.

[23] *Qua* tenant; it would always be possible for a tenant, like anyone else, to qualify under another ground such as if the tenant was the partner of the debtor.

[24] If the creditor knows of the lease at the time of taking the standard security, he cannot insist on vacant possession on taking decree against the debtor: *Trade Development Bank v. Warriner and Mason (Scotland) Ltd*, 1980 S.L.T. 223.

[25] The debtor should, of course, have disclosed the existence of the tenancy at the time of re-mortgaging but this does not always happen.

he will find himself in the same practical position as the creditor in *Tamroui* but without the ability to rely on Ground 2 of Part 1 of Schedule 5 to the 1988 Act, which makes clear that it applies only to securities granted before the creation of the tenancy. Similarly, even if the tenant has no statutory protection, the provision in the security which prohibits creation of a lease without the consent of the creditor, so rendering later leases voidable, will post-date the lease creation itself.[26] It appears that a creditor in these circumstances may be left with little option but to adopt the terms of the tenancy at least in the short term.[27] The relationship between heritable creditors and their tenants is discussed elsewhere.[28]

The Housing (Scotland) Act 2001[29] does not include private landlords[30] within the definition of registered social landlord[31] meaning that it has no effect on assured tenancies where the landlord is other than a housing association, local authority or similar body. Tenancies under a shared ownership agreement are also excluded from the terms of the Act,[32] as are existing short assured tenancies even where the landlord is a registered social landlord. These provisions mean that the Housing (Scotland) Act 2001 will have no impact of any consequence on tenancies of debtors which heritable creditors require to address after evicting the debtor. This fact will be of some relief to heritable creditors as the Act will give[33] greater protection to tenants under the new Scottish secure tenancy than was available under assured tenancies. The one repossession area where this Act may come into play is where the debtor, which fails in its obligations, is a housing association itself. In this context, the heritable creditor is likely to have taken security over various subjects in relation to which there are Scottish secure tenancy agreements between the housing association as landlord and its tenant. A heritable creditor in these circumstances will be unable to recover vacant possession of the secured subjects as the Scottish secure tenancy does not include any equivalent provision, in the grounds for obtaining possession, as that specified in Ground 2 of Part 1 of Schedule 5 to the 1988 Act.[34] Such occurrences will be very rare and the possibility will in any event have been taken into account, at least in relation to future advances, at the time of constitution of the loan. It is therefore safe to say that the impact of the Housing (Scotland) Act 2001 on repossessing heritable creditors will be very limited indeed.

Nonetheless, for the reasons discussed, it is possible by reason of the operation of the 1988 Act for a debtor to limit or at least delay the rights

---

[26] Such a lease or tenancy agreement would not fall within the type of voidable lease described in *Trade Development Bank v. Warriner and Mason (Scotland) Ltd*, 1980 S.L.T. 223, on the basis that no consent was required from the creditor at the time the lease was entered into. Halliday, *Conveyancing*, para. 52–06, confirms that a tenant whose right has been made real will have preferential rights to any security later created.

[27] By s.20(5) of the 1970 Act.

[28] See para. 7.5.2.

[29] (asp 10).

[30] As defined in s.11(1).

[31] Defined in ss.57 and 111.

[32] s.11(4) and Sched. 1 para. 7; "shared ownership agreement" is defined in s.83(3).

[33] The Act received Royal Assent on July 18, 2001. The substantive provisions will be in force by September 30, 2002 but the exact commencement date is not yet known.

[34] See para. p.103.

of a creditor to recover the subjects under the standard security even after decree has been granted. However, it is not possible for *pro indiviso* proprietors who are debtors of a secured creditor to avoid repossession of the subjects by a lease to one of their own number.[35] Similarly, where the proprietor of the subjects was a tenant who had purchased his landlord's interest before granting the standard security, the lease was held to have ended and did not revive to disentitle the creditor from recovering possession.[36] In the case of croft land, while a debtor will not be a legal tenant with a right to protection under the Crofters (Scotland) Act 1955,[37] compulsory re-letting provisions may cause difficulties for heritable creditors.[38]

Insolvent Debtors

6.3 It is a relatively common occurrence that a creditor wishing to repossess or sell the subjects will find that the debtor is insolvent for the obvious reason that debtors in that position are less likely to maintain payments to the heritable creditor. The initial procedure which a creditor must follow where the proprietor is insolvent has already been considered.[39] Special considerations apply in the substantive law where the debtor is insolvent. As most insolvent debtors are individuals, the relevant provisions are considered mainly by reference to sequestration with references to insolvency legislation where appropriate.

The Bankruptcy (Scotland) Act 1985[40] provides guidance on the relationship between the trustee in sequestration, the heritable creditor and the debtor in these circumstances. The whole of the debtor's estate vests in the permanent trustee in sequestration for the benefit of the creditors as at the date of sequestration.[41] However, section 33(3) of the 1985 Act provides that "*sections 31 and 32* of this Act are without prejudice to the right of any secured creditor which is preferable to the rights of the permanent trustee".[42]

This section was considered by the Inner House in *Abbey National plc v. Arthur and Sutherland*.[43] The pursuers were holders of a standard security granted in their favour by the defenders. On the basis that the

---

[35] *Clydesdale Bank plc v. Davidson*, 1998 S.L.T. 522, where an attempt to create protection of occupancy under the Agricultural Holdings Acts failed on the basis that as *pro indiviso* proprietors each had a right to occupy common property, they could not validly confer on any of their own number the separate real right of occupancy (to be effective against a third party) which derived from a lease.

[36] *Bank of Scotland v. Cameron*, 1989 S.L.T. (Land Ct) 38.

[37] s.3(3).

[38] *Cameron, supra* no. 36.

[39] See para. 2.7.2.

[40] (c.66), hereafter referred to as "the 1985 Act".

[41] s.31 of the 1985 Act; s.145(1) of the Insolvency Act 1986 (c.45) provides that where a company is being wound up, the court may order that all property of the company shall vest in the liquidator.

[42] A similar provision is made where the debtor is a company. In that case, the Insolvency (Scotland) Rules 1986 (S.I. 1986 No. 1915) provide that the rights of a secured creditor over the subjects are normally preferable to those of a liquidator: see r.4.66(6).

[43] 1999 G.W.D. 34–1640; this decision did not conclude the difficulties experienced by the heritable creditors in this case. For a review of subsequent events see Maclean "Penalty for Breach of Interdict where Prior Criminal Sentence", 2002 Civ.P.B. 43–5.

defenders were in default with payments, the pursuers obtained decree and evicted the defenders from the property. Thereafter, the defenders broke into the property. Further evictions and break-ins were said to have occurred at subsequent dates. They craved and were granted interdict against the ejected debtors from entering the property. On appeal, the second defender argued that the decree had been obtained "on an improper basis". It was argued that the action of possession should have been brought against the trustee in sequestration on the basis that the subjects now vested in him. The Inner House rejected the appeal, founding on section 33(3). The court confirmed that the rights of the heritable creditor did not in any way depend on whether or not the debtor was divested of the subjects or of any residual right to the free proceeds of sale.

While the 2001 Act does not deal expressly with trustees in sequestration, the fact that the Act allows the proprietor to apply for a suspension of creditor's rights suggests that a trustee in sequestration[44] could so apply. However, it seems likely that section 33(3)[45] would have a bearing on the disposal of any such application. The court would also be likely to take into account the terms of section 39 of the 1985 Act which regulate the potential conflict between the rights of sale available to both the secured creditor and the trustee in sequestration. As either party may sell, this provision resolves the issue of who may proceed by stating that whoever first intimates an intention to sell to the other may then sell the subjects without interference thereafter.[46] However, where there has been undue delay by either party, the other may apply to the court for authorisation to sell instead.[47]

Although each party has the right to sell, the trustee's right is qualified to the extent that he may sell only with the concurrence of all secured creditors unless he obtains a sufficiently high price to discharge every security. If the creditor sells where a trustee in sequestration is in place, the net free proceeds of sale should be paid to the trustee in all cases,[48] to avoid a claim against the creditor for wrongful disposal of the free proceeds. It appears that if the creditor enforces his security but then chooses to enter into possession, or exercise another remedy other than sale, the trustee in sequestration may not interfere with the choice by the creditor or force a sale.[49] It may be dangerous for a creditor to take steps to enforce his security when an interim trustee in sequestration is in place, as the creditor may not validly intimate an intention to sell to the

---

[44] Or liquidator.

[45] Or in the case of a liquidator, r.4.66(6) of the Insolvency (Scotland) Rules 1986.

[46] s.39(4) of the 1985 Act, but note that the heritable creditor must intimate to the permanent trustee; s.185(1)(b) of the Insolvency Act 1986 provides that s.39(4) of the 1985 Act applies in like manner to insolvencies as it applies to the sequestration of a debtor's estate, with any necessary modifications; if a judicial factor has been appointed, there are no fixed rules as to preference on who may sell. In one case, the creditor was found entitled to declarator of the right to sell but the factor was later permitted to effect the sale: *G Dunlop & Son's Judicial Factor v. Armstrong*, 1994 S.L.T. 199 and 1995 S.L.T. 645.

[47] s.39(4); there is no Scottish case law to provide guidance on what might amount to undue delay.

[48] *Alliance & Leicester Building Society v. Hecht*, 1991 S.C.L.R. 562, discussed further at para. 8.17.

[49] McBryde, *Bankruptcy* (1st ed., 1989), p.133.

interim trustee.[50] If the trustee in sequestration intimates his intention while the creditor is selling (assuming the creditor has not yet validly intimated) then the matter is likely to be determined by whether the creditor has concluded missives. If he has, it is submitted that he would be entitled to proceed to sell.[51] If he has not, the creditor cannot proceed to sell.[52] There are no fixed rules on who should pay the expenses of sale but as a matter of practicality agreement is usually reached to the effect that the party or parties who have benefited from the sale bear the expenses.

There may be circumstances in which no sale takes place, at least initially, because on the one hand there is insufficient equity to justify the permanent trustee taking steps and on the other the creditor is continuing to receive repayments. Such a situation does not work to the advantage of the debtor as he is, in fact, only contributing further funds to the creditors in his sequestration, either directly to the secured creditor by payment of interest, or indirectly to the creditors as a whole by reducing the value of the security over the subjects and so increasing the equity. There were dangers too for the creditor in this situation. If the creditor continued to accept payments to the point[53] where the debtor was discharged from the sequestration, it was uncertain but at the very least arguable that the formal discharge would have the effect of extinguishing the debt, no matter what sums might otherwise have been repayable to the creditor.[54] Heritable creditors are now protected against this eventuality. The 1985 Act now provides[55] that a discharge of the debtor does not affect the rights of a secured creditor to enforce his security in respect of a debt or obligation for which the debtor has been discharged.[56]

Redemption Before Sale

6.4 It is appropriate to consider in detail the issue of redemption within the process of repossession as a whole. Frequently, debtors will seek to redeem the security before the subjects are repossessed and/or sold. The rules governing this area are complex[57] and, in the context of repossessions, depend to some extent on the nature of enforcement action taken by the creditor.

In all cases involving a standard security, the debtor is entitled to exercise his right (if any) to redeem the standard security on giving notice of his intention to do so.[58] To validly redeem the security, the

---

[50] For further discussion, see McBryde, *Bankruptcy* (2nd ed., 1995), para. 9–53.
[51] As with a debtor seeking to redeem: see *G. Dunlop & Sons v. Armstrong*, 1994 S.L.T. 199 and para. 6.4. But the position is uncertain: McBryde, *op. cit.*, para. 9–53.
[52] *ibid*.
[53] Usually three years.
[54] See McBryde, "The Discharge of a Debtor and Securities" 1991 S.L.T. (News) 195.
[55] s.55(3) and Sched. 4 para. 16 as amended by the Bankruptcy (Scotland) Act 1993.
[56] Discharge in this context meaning of course discharge in the sequestration rather than discharge of the security.
[57] And, other than where they are likely to be relevant in a repossession setting, are not considered in full here. For further detail of the law on redemption of standard securities generally, see Halliday, *Conveyancing*, para. 55–53 *et seq*.
[58] Standard condition 11(1).

debtor must repay all sums due to the creditor thereunder. A similar right exists in relation to a bond and disposition in security.[59] There are no special rules on redemption in relation to an *ex facie* absolute disposition unless they are expressly provided for in the security. The issue of redemption of the pre-existing forms of security is not considered further here.[60]

A creditor exercising the power of sale over subjects in relation to which there is a prior security has the same right as the debtor to redeem[61]. In either case, the notice must be in writing[62] though the creditor whose security is being redeemed may waive that requirement.[63] That creditor may also agree to waive or reduce the amount of notice from that which he would be otherwise entitled to receive under the Act[64] or the terms of the standard security.[65] The rules on service of notices of redemption are similar to those which apply to service of a calling-up notice.[66] As with certificates attached to calling-up notices,[67] errors in the amount stated in the notice of redemption do not affect its validity and it is effective for the amount due as subsequently ascertained.[68] Where the debtor redeems, the creditor is obliged to grant a discharge.[69]

The provisions in standard condition 11 dealing with redemption may not be varied but, entailing as they do repayment of the creditor's whole outstanding debt, will usually not be a right to which the creditor will object or one which will give rise to litigation. Nonetheless, the uneasy relationship between certain terms of the 1970 Act contrived to clarify this potentially important issue. The decision in *G. Dunlop & Son's Judicial Factor v. Armstrong*[70] considered sections 18(1) and 23(3) of the 1970 Act which respectively provide:

> "18(1) . . . The debtor in a standard security or, where the debtor is not the proprietor, the proprietor of the security subjects shall be

---

[59] Conveyancing (Scotland) Act 1924 (c.27), s.32 but three months notice must be given of the intention to redeem a bond and disposition in security. See Halliday, *Conveyancing*, paras. 48–63—48–66.

[60] For discussion of the law as it applies to such securities, see Gordon, *Scottish Land Law* (2nd ed., 1999), paras. 20—26 and 20—97.

[61] s.26(2); see para. **.; in the case of a bond and disposition in security, the postponed creditor's right is based on common law: Gordon, *op. cit.*, para. 20–26.

[62] Standard condition 11(1); the form of notice is Form A in Sched. 5.

[63] Standard condition 11(2); as a matter of practice, a creditor seeking to repossess will generally be happy to see the security redeemed and may be flexible to secure that result.

[64] Normally two months under s.18(1) (as amended by the Redemption of Standard Securities (Scotland) Act 1971 (c.45)) but see *G. Dunlop, infra* no. 70.

[65] Standard condition 11(2).

[66] The detailed rules on service are set out in standard condition 11(3); see also Forms B and C in Sched. 5.

[67] See para. 2.25.

[68] Standard condition 11(4).

[69] Standard condition 11(5); the discharge must be in the form set out by s.17 of the 1970 Act; if for any reason the debtor cannot obtain a discharge, he may consign the funds for the person appearing to have the best right thereto or may apply to the court for declarator of performance of obligations under the standard security (s.18(3) of the 1970 Act) and in either case, procedure may follow which disburdens the subjects of the security: s.18(4) of the 1970 Act.

[70] 1994 S.L.T. 199; also reported *sub nom, Forbes v. Armstrong,* 1993 S.C.L.R. 204.

> entitled to redeem the security on giving two months' notice of his intention so to do ...
> 23(3)[71] At any time after the expiry of the period stated in a notice of default ... but before the conclusion of any enforceable contract to sell the security subjects ... the debtor or proprietor (being in either case a person entitled to redeem the security) may ... redeem the security without the necessity of observance of any requirement as to notice."

A farming partnership granted standard securities in favour of a bank over various farms. In due course the bank called up the standard securities. The calling-up notices were not complied with and the bank exposed the security subjects for sale. Before a sale was effected, the pursuer was appointed as judicial factor on the sequestrated estates of the firm. The bank assigned its interest to a third party in return for payment. The pursuer then served notices of redemption in terms of section 18 of the 1970 Act on the then creditor. The creditor required that, in addition to principal and interest, the debtor pay certain expenses but the creditor refused to give details (other than an amount) or to vouch the expenses. The pursuer then tendered payment of the agreed principal and interest, together with a certain payment in expenses and an offer of a formal undertaking to pay such other expenses as were found to be lawfully due to the creditor. The creditor refused to grant a discharge. The judicial factor withdrew the tender and then raised the action seeking to have the creditor ordained to discharge the securities on payment on the terms previously tendered. The creditor counterclaimed for declarator that he was entitled to sell the subjects.

Lord Kirkwood held that the judicial factor was entitled to redeem the securities even though the calling-up notices had not been complied with. The debtor's right to redeem in section 18(1) was "not qualified in any way", although it was noted that section 23(3) only applies where a notice of default has been served and there is no corresponding provision in relation to calling-up notices. Further, there was no reason in principle why the creditor's right to sell and the debtor's right to serve a notice of redemption could not co-exist. However, mere service of a notice of redemption would not have the effect of preventing the creditor from exercising his power of sale. It remains open to the creditor to conclude an enforceable contract of sale before the expiry of the two month period in the notice of redemption or in the event of non-payment by the debtor at the end of that period. If the security is redeemed before the creditor has concluded an enforceable contract of sale, the creditor is entitled to recover from the debtor the expenses occasioned by the abortive attempt to sell the subjects. On the facts, it was established that the creditor should have accepted the tendered payment, with consequences for recovery of further interest, but that the judicial factor's withdrawal of the tender meant that there was no longer an offer of redemption which could be accepted and his action therefore failed. As the calling-up notices served by the bank had not expired, the creditor was granted his declarator of the entitlement to sell.

---

[71] As amended by the Redemption of Standard Securities (Scotland) Act 1971.

The decision in *Dunlop* has received widespread support[72] but it has also been noted that it has strange consequences. As section 23(3) applies only after service of a notice of default, a debtor who has been served with a notice of default may redeem at any time before an enforceable contract of sale is concluded without giving notice. By contrast, if the debtor has been served with a calling-up notice or if the creditor has simply raised a section 24 action without first serving a notice of default, it appears from *Dunlop* that the debtor requires to give two months notice of redemption.[73] If the creditor has opted for service of both of the notices, then it appears the debtor, having received a notice of default, may redeem without notice.[74]

In addition, where the security is more than 20 years old and any part of the security is used as a dwellinghouse, the debtor has a right to redeem under the Land Tenure Reform (Scotland) Act 1974.[75] The debtor must give two months notice to the creditor of his intention to redeem. There are detailed rules as to the calculation of the redemption figure due to the creditor in these circumstances.[76]

Spouses

6.5 The 2001 Act permits non-entitled spouses to apply to the court for suspension of the rights of a heritable creditor[77] but, in certain circumstances, a non-entitled spouse[78] may have additional remedies against a secured creditor under the Matrimonial Homes (Family Protection) (Scotland) Act 1981.

Matrimonial Homes (Family Protection) (Scotland) Act 1981

6.5.1 As with all dealings under the 1981 Act, a creditor will not fall foul of occupancy rights if he has protected himself at the outset by obtaining the consent in writing of the non-entitled spouse to the security or a renunciation from that person of any occupancy rights[79]. Additionally, section 8 of the 1981 Act expressly provides that the rights of a creditor under a secured loan, where there has been non-performance of an obligation (most commonly failure to pay installments), shall not be prejudiced by the occupancy rights of a non-entitled spouse.[80]

---

[72] See the references *infra* no. 74, and the discussion of the decision, without criticism, in *Hewit v. Williamson*, 1999 S.L.T. 313.

[73] Though Gretton and Reid, *Conveyancing* (1993), para. 20–32 suggest that the same rule may apply with calling-up notices and s.24 writs, as it does to notices of default, on the grounds of reasonableness. In any case involving a regulated agreement under the Consumer Credit Act 1974, the debtor may rely on s.94 thereof which permits him to complete payments ahead of time on the provision of notice to the creditor. Such a notice may take effect immediately on receipt.

[74] For further discussion, see the commentary by Sheriff Cusine to the case report at 1993 S.C.L.R. 204 at p.217 and Green's *Property Law Bulletin* 2–3.

[75] s.11, provided that the security was created after September 1, 1974; s.12 of that Act also deals with the issue of redemption and includes within its scope commercial property.

[76] s.11(4) of the Land Tenure Reform (Scotland) Act 1974.

[77] s.1(2)(b) of the 2001 Act.

[78] as defined in s.1(1) of the Matrimonial Homes (Family Protection) (Scotland) Act 1981 (c. 59). The 1981 Act does not offer equal protection to cohabiting partners, whether same or opposite sex, as it does to spouses, in contrast to the wider provisions of the 2001 Act.

[79] s.6(3) of the 1981 Act.

[80] s.8(1).

However, the secured creditor only acquires protection where he has acted in good faith and at or before the granting of the security there was granted to the secured creditor by the grantor:

(1) an affidavit sworn or affirmed by the grantor of the security which confirms that the security subjects are not a matrimonial home in relation to which a spouse of the grantor has occupancy rights; or

(2) a renunciation of occupancy rights or a consent to the granting of the security which bears to have been properly made or given by the non-entitled spouse.[81]

What if none of the documents has been obtained?

6.5.2 The 1981 Act is designed in such a way as to protect non-entitled spouses from homelessness. As a result, there are certain features in the Act which prevent circumvention of the occupancy rights. If occupancy rights exist which the non-entitled spouse wishes to exercise and the creditor does not have the documentary protection referred to above, the secured creditor may not be able to obtain vacant possession on repossession.

The creditor would be entitled to evict the debtor and exercise the power of sale in these circumstances[82] but would not be entitled to eject the non-entitled spouse. As a matter of practicality, the creditor is unlikely to wish to exercise his remedies even against the debtor given the negative publicity which might arise from forcing a couple apart. In circumstances where the secured creditor has formally taken possession but the non-entitled spouse remains in occupation, the creditor without the necessary protection will therefore be entitled to sell but without vacant possession. That will of course have a highly detrimental effect on the sale price[83] and might even raise questions under section 25 of the 1970 Act.[84]

The creditor is also entitled to apply to the court for an order to have the non-entitled spouse perform the obligation due by the debtor. The creditor is only entitled to apply where the non-entitled spouse is in

---

[81] s.8(2A) of the 1981 Act. This is the law as it applies to securities granted after 30 December 1985, when section 13 of the Law Reform (Miscellaneous Provisions)(Scotland) Act 1985 came into force, introducing s.8(2A) of the 1981 Act. For securities granted before that date, but after the coming into effect of the 1981 Act, see s.8(2) of the 1981 Act (as amended). The 1981 Act does not apply to securities granted before it came into force on September 1, 1982; it should be noted that a heritable creditor should also obtain an affidavit, consent or renunciation from joint proprietors, who are not spouses, at the time of the granting of the security. This arises from the fact that the definition of "entitled spouse" in s.6(2) of the 1981 Act, which applies to ss.6 and 7 of the 1981 Act and allows such parties to sell without such a document, does not apply to s.8 of the 1981 Act which deals with the interests of heritable creditors.

[82] Subject to any other circumstances, such as the 2001 Act.

[83] But note that a purchaser from the heritable creditor in these circumstances could eject the non-entitled spouse after purchase on the basis that the occupancy rights of a non-entitled spouse are not protected against subsequent dealings by third parties: see Clive, *The Law of Husband and Wife* (4th ed., 1997), para. 15.084.

[84] See para. 8.10.

occupation of the subjects and the debtor is not.[85] This option, when it is available, would be attractive to a creditor seeking to have arrears repaid, which failing to recover the subjects from the non-entitled spouse.

The non-entitled spouse is protected against the possibility of the creditor seeking to circumvent occupancy rights by sequestrating the debtor. Such a sequestration would not be a dealing within the meaning of the 1981 Act giving rise to occupancy rights[86] but the Court of Session may recall the sequestration or make such order as it thinks appropriate to protect the occupancy rights of the non-entitled spouse. To do so, the court must be satisfied that the purpose of the petition for sequestration was wholly or mainly to defeat the occupancy rights of the non-entitled spouse.[87]

Although such protection is available to non-entitled spouses, the 1981 Act is invoked as a matter of practice very rarely and then generally as a delaying measure. If anything, the widening of rights offered by the 2001 Act is likely to render the 1981 Act of even less significance.

Miscellaneous Cases

6.6 In some situations, there will be practical rather than legal considerations which may influence the repossession process. For example, there may be a contribution towards the debtor's obligations by the Benefits Agency or there may be media interest in the matter.

Debtors on Benefits

6.6.1 Unless there is a contractual obligation to the contrary, the creditor is not obliged to forego possession proceedings if benefits payments are being received.[88] Nonetheless, the applicant's ability to fulfil the obligations in default[89] is a key consideration for the court under the 2001 Act. This would appear to include circumstances where the obligation is fulfilled with the assistance of a third party, as the source of funds may be largely irrelevant to the court. Often the source of funds may be a

---

[85] s.8(1); see also Clive, *op. cit.*, para. 15.086, where it is suggested that for the section to apply the non-entitled spouse must also have granted a consent to the security or renunciation of occupancy rights and where the limitations on this provision are criticised. The position is not entirely clear as s.8 appears to be untested by the courts.

[86] s.6.

[87] Bankruptcy (Scotland) Act 1985 (c.66), s.41(1)(b).

[88] For the circumstances in which the Benefits Agency will make payments towards the loan, see the Income Support (General) Regulations 1987 (S.I. 1987 No. 1967) (as amended). The basic rules at present are that income support for mortgage interest payments (commonly known as "ISMI") is not provided, where the advance was made on or after October 2, 1995, when the debtor has savings of more than £8,000. If he does not, ISMI will start to pay all allowable mortgage interest from the 40th week of the debtor's claim. For advances prior to October 2, 1995, ISMI does not pay for the first eight weeks of the claim. Thereafter payments of 50 per cent of the allowable mortgage interest are made for the next 18 weeks before full allowable mortgage interest payments commence in the 26th week of the claim. All payments are made direct to creditors. Payments are calculated having regard to a standard rate of interest which is, as at the date of publication, 5.34 per cent: Income Support (General) (Standard Interest Rate Amendment) (No. 2) Regulations 2002 (S.I. 2002 No. 338), effective March 24, 2002.

[89] s.2(2)(b) of the 2001 Act.

relative or friend but the principle applies equally to payments made to the creditor by the Benefits Agency. Accordingly, receipt of benefits may support application for a section 2 order under the 2001 Act.

Media Interest

6.6.2 On occasion, the identity of the debtor, the location of the security subjects, the manner in which the creditor has proceeded or other factors may give rise to media interest in the repossession process. It goes without saying that such interest does not alter in any way the legal rights and responsibilities of both parties. That said, it is often the case in such matters that one or other of the parties may choose to act other than it would normally have done. For example, a high-profile debtor may seek to resolve matters before court proceedings are raised. More commonly, a creditor whose public image may influence many thousands of potential customers may seek to agree less advantageous terms to see the matter resolved without adverse publicity.

Arrangements

6.6.3 It is very common that a debtor on receipt of a formal notice or court proceedings will acknowledge the seriousness of the matter and take steps to enter into an arrangement with the creditor for payment of the arrears. Prior to the introduction of the 2001 Act, creditors generally agreed to alternative payment arrangements, once court proceedings had been raised, on the expressly stated basis that decree would still be taken in the court proceedings but not enforced provided the debtor agreed to certain terms. These included the maintaining of the arrangement; the making of all payments on time; that the debtor would not defend the action; and, where appropriate, that the level of payment would be reviewed at an agreed future date.

Although such terms remain possible, the terms of the 2001 Act suggest that, even if the debtor has agreed not to make an application for a section 2 order under that Act thereafter, if he defaults on the arrangement and then does so apply, the court will still consider the application. It is of course relevant for the court to consider what efforts the creditor has made to assist the debtor in complying with his obligations.[90] A sheriff, in exercise of his discretion, may be less willing to grant an order where a debtor has failed already to comply with a rescheduling arrangement.

---

[90] s.2(2)(c) of the 2001 Act.

CHAPTER 7

RECOVERING THE SUBJECTS

Introduction

Of all the remedies open to a heritable creditor, that which is exercised **7.1** most commonly is sale. The duties of the creditor in relation to sale and special considerations which apply then are considered elsewhere.[1] The purpose of this chapter is to explore what happens following eviction and the remedies, other than sale, which are at that time open to the creditor.[2] It would have been more convenient to title this chapter "taking possession" or even "entering into possession", but it does not necessarily follow that a creditor who has merely evicted the debtor and taken no further steps to control the subjects possesses them or has entered into possession thereof, even if thereafter he sells the subjects.[3]

The remedies available to the creditor in a standard security, leaving aside sale, are set out in the Conveyancing and Feudal Reform (Scotland) Act 1970[4] and include entering into possession; granting leases; carrying out repairs, alterations and improvements; and foreclosure. Before becoming entitled to exercise these rights, the debtor must be in default and the creditor must have taken the necessary preliminary steps to set up the exercise of his rights.[5] Each of these rights is considered below.

Where the creditor has acquired rights under a bond and disposition in security, he may enter into possession and uplift the rents, make all necessary repairs and renewals and let the subjects. He also acquires the right to insure against various risks.[6] Similarly, a creditor under an *ex facie* absolute disposition may enter into possession and uplift the rents. Again, these rights are considered below.

---

[1] See Chap. 8.
[2] As heritable creditor. The heritable creditor will also have the normal range of options open to any creditor, such as an ordinary action with a pecuniary crave for payment, or summary enforcement of contractual terms where there is a warrant for execution, but as these are not remedies specific to repossession law and are in any event rarely used in this context (see para. 1.3), they are not considered further here.
[3] See para. 7.4.
[4] (c.35), hereafter "the 1970 Act", s.20 and standard condition 10; all references to statutory provisions in this chapter are to the 1970 Act except as the context otherwise requires.
[5] That is, a calling-up notice must have been served and not complied with; or the creditor has obtained a warrant to exercise his remedies under s.24 of the Act; or in relation to sale, carrying out repairs and foreclosure, a notice of default has been served and the default specified not remedied. See Chap. 2. It has been argued that ss.20(3),(4) and (5), *infra*, are only applicable where the default is within the meaning of standard condition 9(1)(a) (that is, failure to comply with a calling-up notice) but this was rejected by the Inner House in *David Watson Property Management v. Woolwich Equitable Building Society*, 1990 S.C.L.R. 517, pp.520E and 521C.
[6] The Conveyancing (Scotland) Act 1924 (c.27), s.25(1)(a), hereafter "the 1924 Act".

Practical Issues

7.2 On taking possession, a heritable creditor is likely to change the locks, for the simple reason that this will usually prevent or dissuade the evicted debtor from resuming physical possession of the subjects.[7] The creditor will also notify the utilities of the change in control of the subjects (to ensure that liability for bills is apportioned) and will often instruct that the plumbing is drained down in case of accidental damage during the period in which the creditor has control. The creditor will normally take any other steps necessary to secure the property, such as the replacement of broken windows.[8] Insurance will be taken out in case of damage or destruction to the subjects though many major secured creditors carry block insurance policies to cover all properties they have in possession at any one time, or in some cases, are self-insured. The local police station will be notified, the idea being that there may be heightened vigilance which may benefit the creditor if it is known that the subjects are empty. At least one and often two valuations will be carried out.[9] If the creditor intends to sell the subjects, steps will quickly be taken to market them as the creditor will be keen to recover his money and limit any potential loss on which interest will be accruing.

The recovery of the subjects will often be a source of some relief to the creditor, particularly if matters have been protracted by applications under the Mortgage Rights (Scotland) Act 2001.[10] It is, however, not uncommon on recovering the subjects to find that matters may be rather more difficult for the creditor than had been anticipated. The extensive powers available to the heritable creditor, both in statute and at common law, assist in resolving such problems. It may be discovered that there have been unauthorised works or repairs or that there is a title defect[11] in which case the conveyancing will be complicated.[12] Repairs may be necessary.[13] The property may not be as marketable as had been hoped.[14] There may be difficulty in securing the subjects including as noted above from the debtor. Third parties may seek to recover liabilities due to them by the debtor from the heritable creditor.[15] Frequently, the creditor will find that there is moveable property, belonging to the debtor or others, remaining in the subjects following eviction.

---

[7] Though this does not always work, in which case the creditor may require to re-eject and then interdict the debtor. For a practical example, see *Abbey National plc v. Sutherland*, 1999 G.W.D. 34–1640.

[8] The power to do so derives from standard condition 10(6), on which see para. 7.5.3.

[9] To identify the value of the subjects which will assist the creditor in complying with his duty under s.25 and may prove important if a claim for breach of that duty is made. See para. 8.8. The valuations may also suggest a marketing strategy.

[10] (asp 11), hereafter "the 2001 Act".

[11] Although some creditors now have the title examined during the litigation process to highlight potential problems at the earliest possible stage and prevent unnecessary delay later.

[12] See para. 8.6.

[13] See para. 7.5.3.

[14] For any number of reasons; in a recent case in which the author was involved, a murder had been committed at the subjects. This fact, and the debtor's stated resolve to recover the subjects on his release from prison, was duly relayed to potential purchasers by neighbours with predictable results.

[15] See para. 7.7.

The Creditor's Duty in Relation to Moveables

Moveable items left in the subjects do not, of course, form part of the security subjects and continue to belong to the debtor.[16] If the creditor does not dispose of the goods as soon as he recovers the security subjects, he owes a duty of care. This is not a duty of care in relation to the sale of the security subjects or the heritable property generally but is nonetheless a consideration which must be taken into account by a heritable creditor following eviction of the debtor.

7.3

There has been considerable discussion as to the precise legal categorisation of the duty[17] but in essence if the creditor is in a position where he knows or ought to have known that moveable property is in his possession or under his control, he has a duty to take reasonable care for the safekeeping and disposal of that property.[18] The duty is owed to the owner of the moveable goods, whether he was the creditor's debtor or not.[19] It is not a defence, however, for the creditor simply to deny responsibility on the basis of lack of knowledge of the existence of the moveable items.[20] In one case, a creditor whose agents disposed of a former occupant's goods at a tip required to pay for goods which were in a locked cupboard and of which the creditor and its agents were initially unaware following repossession.[21] The reasoning is that if the creditor makes it clear that he intends to exercise control over anything on the premises, he can possess items of which he has no knowledge. This creates a difficulty for creditors as the very fact of repossession itself will

---

[16] Unless there has been a poinding of the ground which, unlike an action of maills and duties, may be raised by a creditor under a standard security: for further detail of the action, see Maher & Cusine, *The Law and Practice of Diligence* (1990), para. 8–56.

[17] In *Harris v. Abbey National plc*, 1997 S.C.L.R. 359, Sheriff Craik Q.C. rejected a claim against a heritable creditor based on theft and spuilzie in favour of an implied contract of gratuitous deposit by the owner and an assumption of the responsibilities of a depository by the creditor. Spuilzie was also argued as being the appropriate remedy in *Gemmell v. Bank of Scotland*, 1998 S.C.L.R. 144 but Sheriff Gordon Q.C. disagreed and dismissed the action. However, it has been argued that spuilzie is the appropriate concept for cases such as these: Green's *Reparation Law Bulletin* 13–9; and that the basing of the decision in *Harris* on implied contract was unnecessary: Stewart, *Reparation* (2000), para. 6–8. The full findings in fact in *Harris* are repeated at 1996 Hous. L.R. 100.

[18] The duty arises by the creditor agreeing to take the moveable property on deposit, even if he does so by implication in allowing the owner of the moveable property an opportunity to collect it at a later date. The debtors in a security will be required by the decree on which the creditor founds in repossessing to leave the subjects void and redd, and failure to do so permits the creditor to remove the property provided he does so immediately: *Gemmell* at p.146F. This has the interesting consequence that the creditor may fulfil his obligations by disposing of the goods without liability as soon as he recovers the subjects, as in these circumstances he does not assume the responsibilities of a depository: see *infra* no. 23.

[19] In *Gemmell*, an action in relation to moveable property was brought by the debtors but in *Harris*, the duty was owed to a former occupant of the subjects who had no legal relationship with the creditor and had left the subjects some time before repossession took place.

[20] *Harris*, following *Parker v. British Airways Board* [1982] 1 Q.B. 1004.

[21] *Harris*; it was proved that the existence of the goods was brought to the attention of the creditors' agents within a week or so of repossession and that knowledge was imputed to the creditor. The decision makes clear, though, that even without such imputed knowledge, the creditor would have been liable.

invariably be an indication that control over the premises is to be exercised.[22]

It appears that the creditor may be entitled to avoid liability by putting all residual moveable items out in the street at the time of repossession.[23] If the goods remain in the subjects then once their existence comes to the attention of the creditor, he should confirm their existence and location at the subjects and contact their owner (or his agents) to determine what should be done with the goods. The doctrine of contributory negligence has been applied to the duty of the creditor in these circumstances.[24] Contributory negligence may arise from the fact of leaving the goods in the subjects without authority or permission; from delaying bringing the existence of the goods to the attention of the creditor; and from delaying to resolve the matter with the creditor thereafter.[25]

There is a practical consideration which, in many cases, will weigh more heavily with the creditor than the legal issues discussed above. It is very unusual for moveable goods of any substantial value to be left in the subjects when the creditor takes possession.[26] The cost to the creditor of searching and clearing the premises and then liasing with the debtor on the manner of disposal may outweigh the value of the goods left behind[27] and, in any event, actions against creditors of this type are rare. Although the cost of removing and dealing with the moveable property thereafter may be passed on to the debtor,[28] it is often the case that the debtor will not be in a financial position to meet the obligation. It is undoubtedly the case that many creditors "take a view" on the disposal of such goods. In some cases, creditors may have been granted the right to sell such movables in the security documentation but the legal basis for such a sale is as agent of the debtor.[29] Any such expressed right would not be enforceable against the debtor's trustee in bankruptcy.[30]

The Scottish Executive has sought views on whether formal provision should be made for disposal of possessions left in the subjects but has

---

[22] For example, by changing of the locks.

[23] *Harris* at p.361C, the duty only arising where the creditor accepts the moveable property on deposit to give the debtors or others an opportunity to collect; it is unlikely that primary lenders would wish to adopt the course of disposing of goods immediately given the potential for adverse publicity and for conflict with the local authority. **RIDER BS MISSING**

[24] *Harris* at p.361.

[25] *Harris* p.362 where each of these factors applied, the pursuer having been described as "a somewhat hapless individual" by the sheriff. A finding of 60 per cent contributory negligence was made where the pursuer had delayed resolving the matter until three months after the eviction.

[26] It is probably more common for heritable property to have been dismantled by the debtor instead.

[27] In *Harris*, the goods were found to have a value of £900 and after a finding of contributory negligence, decree was granted for £360.

[28] Cusine, "Expenses under a Standard Security", 1994 *Juridical Review* 18.

[29] Gretton and Reid, *Conveyancing* (1993), para. 20–30; an example of a variation of the standard conditions which would permit the creditor to sell on this basis is provided by Cusine, *Standard Securities* (1991), para. 5–25; there would not be a valid right of sale in the case of movables belonging to a party other than the debtor.

[30] Paisley, "Standard Conditions", 1999 PQLE 208, p.26.

noted that making this a requirement would place "a substantial and unreasonable burden on heritable proprietors".[30a]

Entering into Possession

7.4 Certain powers of the heritable creditor are only open to him to exercise where he has entered into possession[31] or is in lawful possession of the subjects.[32] The right to enter into possession is only available[33] to a creditor in a standard security where the debtor is in default[34] and either a calling-up notice has expired, which is a default in itself, or the creditor has obtained a warrant from the court in terms of section 24 of the 1970 Act to enter into possession.[35]

The meaning of the term "entered into possession" remains unclear more than 30 years after the coming into force of the 1970 Act.[36] It is commonly assumed that entering into possession means simply taking the standard steps on the road to sale of evicting the debtor, changing the locks and marketing the subjects.[37] It has been submitted that this is incorrect[38] and that the term implies much greater control of the subjects[39] and an intention to exercise a longer term interest than proceeding to sale. This view receives support from the decision of Sheriff Allan[40] in *Ascot Inns Ltd (in receivership) v. Braidwood Estates Ltd.*[41] In this unusual case, the proprietors of a hotel had granted a standard security in favour of a creditor. They had also entered into a tenancy arrangement in relation to the hotel with a third party. On default by the proprietor, the creditor obtained decree for warrant to enter into possession but did not take any action on the strength of it.

[30a] *Enforcement of Civil Obligations in Scotland—A Consultation Paper*, April 2002, para. 5.325.

[31] For example, those specified in standard conditions 10(3), (4) and (5).

[32] For example those specified in ss.20(3) and (5); it is submitted this phrase has the same meaning as "entered into possession" see para. 7.7.1.

[33] Subject to the terms of any other agreement between the parties.

[34] Within the meaning of standard condition 9.

[35] See Chap. 2.

[36] It has been argued that the same interpretation should be applied for the term whether relating to the provisions for bonds and dispositions in security on the one hand or standard securities on the other. It is certainly the case that the 1970 Act was not intended to innovate on the general law relating to heritable securities: *per* Lord Chancellor in *David Watson Property Management v. Woolwich Equitable Building Society*, 1992 S.L.T. 430, at pp.434–435. It therefore appears valid to consider the legal position on "entering into possession" as it applies to the pre-existing forms of security in interpreting the phrase in cases involving standard securities. For further detail of these earlier authorities, see Halliday's *Conveyancing Law and Practice* (J.S. Talman ed.), Vol. II (hereafter "Halliday, *Conveyancing*"), paras. 48–10 *et seq*. It is submitted that such earlier authorities lend support to the view taken here that a longer term interest in the subjects than sale is required for the creditor to have entered into possession.

[37] There is some support for this view: see, for example, Braid, "Remedies on Default", 1999 PQLE 208 at p.14; Paisley, *Land Law* (2001), para. 11–21 describes it as "an open question" whether such steps amount to entering into possession.

[38] Cusine, "The Creditor's Remedies under a Standard Security", 1998 S.L.P.Q. 79 at p.82.

[39] In Cusine, *Standard Securities* (1991), para. 8–40, the author suggests that to be in possession "there will be some degree of management of the subjects".

[40] at Lanark.

[41] 1995 S.C.L.R. 390.

The creditor entered into negotiations with the tenant for the tenant to purchase the subjects but these proved abortive and the tenant vacated the subjects, leaving five months rent unpaid. The proprietors, now in receivership, raised an action against the tenant for payment of the arrears of rent. The tenant defended claiming that any arrears of rent were due to the creditor who, they argued, had entered into constructive possession of the subjects. This argument was rejected by the sheriff who found in favour of the pursuers,[42] holding that "a creditor proceeding to sell is quite separate and distinct from a creditor entering into possession".[43] Further, the unsuccessful negotiation between the creditor and the tenant "in no way involves, even by implication, the heritable creditors entering into possession".[44]

It was held in *Skipton Building Society v. Wain*[45] that where a heritable creditor had changed the locks and given instructions that the subjects be marketed but thereafter allowed the debtors to remain physically in possession and to run a business from the subjects with their permission, they had nonetheless entered into possession in terms of the 1970 Act. On balance, it is submitted that entering into possession must mean more than changing the locks and proceeding to sell.[46] A longer term interest in the subjects is required, though it is clear that physical possession is not necessary. The view that the phrase means more than a step on the road to sale by a heritable creditor might also be capable of support by interpretation of similar terms in other heritable property legislation.[47]

---

[42] The decision is clearly the correct one but, if it can be faulted at all, it is in the court's finding that because the creditors had not entered into possession on the strength of the decree, the subjects "reverted to the owner" (or its successor). In fact, the decree obtained by the creditor was never sufficient to disburden the debtor of his proprietorial interest without further action by the creditor (for example, the exercise of the powers of sale or foreclosure) and accordingly it is submitted that the use of the word "reverted" is misplaced.

[43] p.392E; the sheriff appears to have placed considerable reliance on the fact that standard conditions 10(3)–(5) mention entering into possession while standard condition 10(2), dealing with sale, does not.

[44] p.392F.

[45] 1986 S.L.T. 96, Outer House.

[46] See also the apparently conflicting views on this subject in *Northern Rock Building Society v. J.W. Wood, Community Charges Registration Officer*, 1990 S.L.T. (Sh.Ct) 109 and *Bank of Scotland v. Community Charges Registration Officer for Central Region* at para. 7.7.2, *infra*.

[47] In *Kaur v. Singh*, 1998 S.C.L.R. 849, the Inner House considered the term "proprietor in possession" in s.9(3) of the Law Reform (Miscellaneous Provisions) (Scotland) Act 1985 (c.73) in a context which involved a heritable creditor. Lord President Rodger stated (p.860A–B): "In interpreting the expression 'in possession' as referring to possession of the subjects, we are again conscious that the legislator has used the term 'possession' without any qualification and that it is the term so used which we have to interpret. In our view, used in that way, the expression suggests possession of land or other heritable subjects rather than possession of a legal interest." The heritable creditor was found not to have been a proprietor in possession as there had been no suggestion that they were physically in possession of the subjects. But the analogy cannot be taken too far and *Kaur* certainly does not mean that for a heritable creditor to enter into possession, he must physically take possession.

Only One Creditor May Enter Into Possession

7.4.1 It is not competent for more than one heritable creditor to enter into possession of security subjects.[48] In the event of a dispute between heritable creditors, the courts will have regard to who has taken action first. In *Skipton*,[49] the pursuers, as heritable creditors, had entered into possession by changing the locks but, as noted above, had allowed the owner to remain in order to sell the subjects as a going concern. They then sought to interdict the holder of a postponed security, who had obtained a later decree than their own from disturbing their position as heritable creditor in possession or otherwise enforcing that decree. The court granted interim interdict, holding that as only one heritable creditor could enter into possession, it would be wrong for the postponed security holder now to do so and, in any event, the balance of convenience favoured continuation of the interdict.

Powers of Heritable Creditor in Possession

7.5 In addition to the powers which a creditor may exercise generally,[50] certain powers are only available to the creditor who has entered into possession. These powers include the right to recover rents and the right to let the security subjects. Certain powers, while competent without formally entering into possession, are rarely exercised other than when the creditor has done so. These include the right to repair, construct, alter or improve the subjects and the right to apply to the court for a decree of foreclosure. These various powers which must be or are usually exercised when the heritable creditor has entered into possession are considered below.

Right to Collect Rents and Other Sums

7.5.1 Where the heritable creditor in a standard security has entered into possession of the security subjects, he may receive or recover feuduties, ground annuals or, most significantly, the rents of all or part of the subjects.[51] As a matter of practicality, the creditor should intimate his expired calling-up notice or decree with warrant to enter into possession to the tenant, and advise the tenant or make clear by his actions that he has entered into possession in place of the debtor and that the rents should be paid to him and not the debtor.[52] Should the tenant thereafter

---

[48] *Skipton Building Society v. Wain*, 1986 S.L.T. 96, p.97; It has been suggested that if a postponed security holder takes possession, the prior security holder may exercise a preferential right to take possession: Halliday, *Conveyancing*, para. 54–61 citing *Northern Rock Building Society v. Barclays Bank plc* (a case wrongly cited as having been reported at 1986 S.L.T. 109 and which it has not been possible to trace) but it is submitted that this is incorrect on a proper reading of *Skipton*.

[49] *Skipton Building Society v. Wain*, 1986 S.L.T. 96.

[50] Such as sale.

[51] Standard condition 10(3); as with all the powers of the creditor considered in this chapter, this depends on the creditor having taken the necessary preliminary steps, such as service of a calling-up notice which has expired, or the obtaining of a decree entitling him to exercise the power in terms of s.24; on the forthcoming abolition of feuduty, see para. 7.7.1.

[52] As was the case with intimation of a decree in an action of maills and duties under a bond and disposition in security. The tenant cannot be expected to know without notice that the creditor has taken possession and it is only by intimation that he is precluded from making payment to the debtor, as he would have done before.

pay the debtor, that will not meet his liability to the creditor who may insist on a further payment by the tenant. Rental may not be recovered where the creditor has not entered into possession.[53]

A creditor under a bond and disposition in security has the right, where the debtor has defaulted in payment of principal or interest, or where the proprietor is apparently insolvent, to enter into possession of such land and uplift the rents and other duties thereof.[54] The right is exercised by an action of mails and duties brought by the creditor against the proprietor.[55] The procedure is governed by sections 3 and 15 of the Heritable Securities (Scotland) Act 1894.[56] As soon as decree is obtained in such an action, the creditor is held to have entered into possession.[57] In the case of a creditor in an *ex facie* absolute disposition, the creditor may collect rents from tenants without further procedure and an action of mails and duties is not necessary.[58]

It was unclear until recently whether by entering into possession a heritable creditor in a standard security could collect only the rents from that date or whether rent from an earlier date, such as from the date of creation of the security, could also be recovered.[59] This question was answered by the Extra Division in *UCB Bank Ltd v. Hire Foulis Ltd (in liquidation)*.[60] In that case, a liquidator had been appointed to the debtor company. The liquidator collected certain sums from third party companies in respect of rights of occupancy in the subjects which had previously been granted by the debtor company. The heritable creditor then entered into possession and sought recovery of all rents received from the constitution of the security on the basis that they formed part of the security which they had been granted. The court rejected this argument, holding that section 20(5) made it clear that the assignation of proprietorial rights—including the right to rents—to the creditor takes place when and not before the creditor takes possession. Accordingly, the rents already paid did not form part of the security subjects.[61] This

---

[53] Standard condition 10(3) and *Ascot Inns Ltd (in receivership) v. Braidwood Estates Ltd*, 1995 S.C.L.R. 390; Halliday, *Conveyancing*, para. 54–58 suggests that a creditor making a s.24 application may notify tenants of the proprietor before decree of his action to interpel them from paying rents to the proprietor but the decision in *UCB Bank plc v. Hire Foulis Ltd (in liquidation)*, 1999 S.L.T. 950, which postdates that work, makes clear that the heritable creditor is only entitled to rents from the time he enters possession.

[54] Conveyancing (Scotland) Act 1924 (c.27), s.25(1)(a), hereafter "the 1924 Act".

[55] It is not necessary to call the tenants as defenders: s.3 of the Heritable Securities (Scotland) Act 1894 (c.44), hereafter "the 1894 Act", but if that is not done, the tenants should be given intimation of the action. The Scottish Executive has indicated that it is minded to abolish recourse to the diligence of mails and duties: *Enforcement of Civil Obligations in Scotland—A Consultation Paper*, April 2002, para. 5.311.

[56] The action may be raised in the sheriff court or the Court of Session for further discussion, see Maher and Cusine, *The Law and Practice of Diligence* (1990), paras. 8–65 *et seq*; Macphail, *Sheriff Court Practice* (2nd ed., 1998), paras 23–29 *et seq*; the form of action existing before the 1894 Act remains competent but is no longer used: Gordon, *Scottish Land Law* (2nd ed., 1999), para. 20–44; Gloag and Irvine, *Rights in Security* (1897), p.103.

[57] Gloag and Irvine, *op. cit.*, p.104.

[58] Indeed it may be incompetent: Maher and Cusine, *op. cit.*, para. 8.65.

[59] Whether already paid or unpaid.

[60] 1999 S.L.T. 950.

[61] The court also considered that the common law was that once rents were paid to the person entitled, they no longer formed part of the security subjects.

finding clearly accords with that of the House of Lords in *David Watson Property Management*.[62]

As the relationship between creditor and debtor is, at least in some respects, similar to that of a quasi-trustee,[63] the creditor should keep detailed records of the sums received as these will require to be taken into account in the calculation of any surplus or shortfall on the secured debt. In all cases, rents recovered should be applied first towards interest and then to capital.[64] The creditor must account to the debtor for any balance of rents recovered beyond what is necessary to discharge the liability under the security.[65] As with any collection of rent, the creditor will also require to meet any tax liability from the rents received, including VAT under the Value Added Tax Act 1994.[66]

Leases

The existence of a lease over the subjects between the debtor and a third party, to which the creditor has not consented and does not wish to consent, may give rise to difficulties for a heritable creditor which are considered elsewhere.[67] In such cases, the creditor will simply seek ejection of the unauthorised tenant and detailed consideration of the terms under which the lease was held may be unnecessary. There are however many cases, in relation to commercial subjects in particular, where the issue of leasehold rights and obligations requires to be considered by a heritable creditor. There are several situations where this may happen.

7.5.2

First, where the creditor's debtor is the landlord under a lease with a third party, the creditor on entering into possession of the security subjects has transferred to him all the rights of his debtor in relation to the granting of leases.[68] As state of knowledge is crucial to the question of whether a lease granted by his debtor is voidable,[69] it may determine and limit the creditor's rights against the third party who acquired rights in terms of the lease. In *Trade Development Bank v. Crittal Windows Ltd*,[70] Lord President Emslie held[71]:

"I see no reason why, if it is established that the [heritable creditor] had knowledge[72] that some sort of right, which might be capable of

---

[62] *supra* no. 36 that case was cited in *UCB* on a different point.

[63] See para. 8.8.

[64] Cusine, Annotation to Heritable Securities (Scotland) Act 1894 in *Scottish Conveyancing Legislation* (R. Rennie ed.), para. A.311.1.

[65] s.25(1)(a) of the 1924 Act (bonds and dispositions in security); Gloag and Irvine, *op. cit.*, p.159 (*ex facie* absolute dispositions).

[66] Halliday, *Conveyancing*, para. 54–69.

[67] See para. 6.2.

[68] Standard condition 10(5); as with all the powers in this chapter, this depends on the creditor having taken the necessary preliminary steps, such as service of a calling-up notice which has expired, or a decree entitling him to exercise the power in terms of s.24; the creditor in a bond and disposition in security also has this right: *Macrae v. Leith*, 1913 S.C. 901.

[69] See para. 6.2.

[70] 1983 S.L.T. 510.

[71] p.517.

[72] At or before the time his security is constituted.

becoming a real right in the security subjects, had already been conferred upon the [tenant], the [tenant] should not be entitled to ... prevent the [heritable creditor] from exercising their rights in security".

Accordingly, if the creditor at the outset is aware of or consented to a tenancy arrangement between his debtor and a third party, or even knows of rights which might become real, he is not permitted to insist on removal of the tenant when he recovers the subjects from his debtor.[73] If on the other hand the creditor was unaware of the arrangements between his debtor and the tenant,[74] but agrees to the tenant's continuing presence, the creditor takes on the terms of the existing lease.[75] He is entitled to issue new leases between himself and the tenant.[76]

Secondly, where the creditor's debtor is the tenant under a lease with a third party, a security over the tenant's interest under the lease in favour of the creditor may be granted. The heritable creditor will require that the lease is capable of being recorded, to allow the standard security to be recorded.[77] This means that the lease must be probative[78] and for more than 20 years.[79] To preserve its value to the creditor, the lease should also be capable of being absolutely assigned.[80]

Should the debtor default in these circumstances then, as with any security, the creditor may enter into possession of his debtor's interest. The creditor on entering into possession has transferred to him the debtor's rights of occupancy over the security subjects.[81] This means that he may not remain in possession beyond the expiry of his debtor's lease. However, for the same reason, he may challenge any attempt to terminate the lease by the landlord on the same basis that his debtor could have done so. There is, however, a practical difficulty for heritable creditors here. The tenant may receive notification of breach of the lease terms prior to the recovery of possession by the heritable creditor. While the tenant will likely be obligated to advise the creditor of receipt of such a notice in terms of the security in which he is the debtor, he may not

---

[73] *Trade Development Bank v. Crittal Windows Ltd*, 1983 S.L.T. 510; *Trade Development Bank v. Warriner and Mason (Scotland) Ltd*, 1980 S.L.T. 223.

[74] Which would be a breach of standard condition 6 but is a regular occurrence in practice.

[75] s.20(5)(a) which provides that there are deemed to be assigned to a creditor who is in possession all rights and obligations of the proprietor relating to leases, and standard conditions 10(4) and (5).

[76] Standard conditions 10(4) and (5).

[77] In addition to allowing enforcement by the creditor of his rights, this avoids the alternative of an assignation in security (under the Registration of Leases (Scotland) Act 1857 (c.26), s.4) which may impose undesirable obligations of the tenant on the creditor.

[78] If before the coming into effect of the Requirements of Writing (Scotland) Act 1995 (c.7) on August 1, 1995 or self-proving thereafter.

[79] Registration of Leases (Scotland) Act 1857, s.1, as amended; but the lease need not be recorded immediately. Accordingly, the creditor could procure an interest during the course of the lease, provided its total duration exceeds 20 years, and at that time have the lease and standard security recorded. The necessary length of the lease in effect limits the issue to commercial property as the Land Tenure Reform (Scotland) Act 1974 (c.38), s.8 prohibits the creation of leases for more than 20 years over domestic property.

[80] See Halliday, *Conveyancing Opinions* (1992), p.287.

[81] Standard condition 10(5).

always do so. The creditor, on seeking to enter into possession, may find that steps have already been taken to irritate the lease which will affect the value of or potentially remove from his control the subjects of his security. The potential danger to the creditor is so great that a prudent heritable creditor in these circumstances will ensure that the lease allows him, in addition to his debtor, to remedy any default by the tenant under the lease, failing which to take on or dispose of the tenant's interest under the lease.[82] If the heritable creditor has been in a security relationship with the tenant since the time the lease was entered into, the lease may also stipulate that the landlord must serve a copy of an irritancy notice on the heritable creditor in addition to the debtor.[83] In addition to his rights of occupancy, the heritable creditor who enters into possession on the basis of his security over the tenant's interest requires to observe his obligations to the landlord as the tenant's interest is acquired *tantum et tale*.[84] However, in the absence of specific agreement, the heritable creditor is not responsible for any liabilities under the lease unless and until he enters into possession.[85] Once the creditor has entered into possession in such circumstances, he may challenge or respond to any notice served by the landlord in the same way that the tenant could have done[86] but it is not certain, unless terms have been specifically agreed, that the landlord is obliged to serve notice on the heritable creditor rather than the tenant in these circumstances. The Scottish Law Commission have proposed that the law be clarified on this point.[87]

---

[82] For an example of this in practice, see *Holt Leisure Parks Ltd v. Scottish & Newcastle Breweries plc,* 1996 G.W.D. 22–1284; an example of the style wording of such a provision is given in Halliday, *Conveyancing Opinions,* p.289; at one stage, consideration was given to the passing of a legislative provision which would protect creditors who had been unable to negotiate such protective arrangements by the use of formal procedure to be followed. In the event, the Scottish Law Commission decided that the area was not an appropriate area for legislative intervention: *Irritancies in Leases,* Scot. Law Com. Report No. 75, February 1983, paras. 5.10 and 5.13.

[83] The tenant is protected to a limited extent by the minimum provisions in relation to irritancy which are mandated by ss.4 and 5 of the Law Reform (Miscellaneous Provisions) (Scotland) Act 1985 but it is very doubtful that these provisions can be extended to the tenant's creditor. This makes it an essential requirement for the heritable creditor to have such an express provision in the lease to protect him.

[84] s.20(5) as interpreted by Lord President Hope in *David Watson Property Management v. Woolwich Equitable Building Society,* 1992 S.L.T. 430, this decision being reported at 1990 S.C.L.R. 517, p.521B (a finding not interfered with by the House of Lords when considering the same case); but this also means that if there were grounds for the tenant to withhold rent, the creditor may also do so. The same position obtains in relation to the pre-existing forms of security: *Marshall's Trustees v. Banks,* 1934 S.C. 405. A further consequence is that where the lease contains a keep-open clause, the heritable creditor should seek to exclude from its obligations any requirements to occupy and trade from the premises.

[85] *Holt, supra* no. 82; the same point (that the heritable creditor is only responsible for obligations during the period in which he is in possession) on s.20(5) was made in relation to non-leasehold obligations by the House of Lords in *David Watson,* ibid.

[86] Standard condition 10(5).

[87] *Recovery of Possession of Heritable Property* (Scot. Law Com. No. 118), 1989. At para. 4.95, the Commission recommended that where the creditor has entered into possession security subjects, a notice served by the landlord should not be effective unless it is given to the creditor, in which case it should not be necessary to serve notice on the tenant. But no legislation has followed on the report and the position remains unclear.

Thirdly, the heritable creditor, on entering into possession, is entitled to let the subjects or any part thereof, even if the debtor had not previously done so.[88] However, the creditor's power in this respect is limited, unless there is express provision on the matter in his agreement with the debtor.[89] In terms of the statutory provisions, the lease may be granted for a period of up to seven years without difficulty, but if the creditor wishes to let for a longer period, he must apply to the court for permission.[90] The court has wide discretion to dispose of any such application as it sees fit.[91]

Repairs and Other Works

7.5.3 There are two principal, but separate, bases in the 1970 Act which permit the creditor in a standard security to carry out repairs. First, an obligation on the debtor is imposed to maintain the security subjects in good and sufficient repair to the reasonable satisfaction of the creditor.[92] In pursuance of that obligation, the debtor must make all necessary repairs and make good all defects.[93] If the debtor fails in the obligation, the creditor is entitled to perform it.[94] Under these provisions, the creditor must give the debtor seven days clear notice in writing before entering on the subjects.[95] All expenses and charges reasonably incurred by the creditor in carrying out such repairs and making good such defects are recoverable from the debtor and are secured by the security subjects.[96]

Secondly, where the debtor is in default, the creditor is given the express right to effect all such repairs and make good such defects as are either necessary[97] or reasonably required[98] to maintain the security subjects. These provisions go further than the first in two respects; (a)

---

[88] Standard condition 10(4) and s.20(3). The latter uses the wording "is in lawful possession" but it is submitted this has the same meaning as having "entered into possession": see para. 7.71.

[89] Halliday, *Conveyancing Opinions*, p.383, relying on the terms of s.20(1) of the 1970 Act. In that case, the creditor was given express right in terms of the security to grant leases "for any term of years" and Professor Halliday agreed that it would be competent for the creditor to grant a lease of 125 years in the event of default by the debtor.

[90] s.20(3); this provision also details the rules for the application which must state the proposed tenant and the duration and conditions of the proposed lease. The application must be served on the proprietor and any other heritable creditor with an interest in the subjects. The procedure for such an application is by way of summary application unless any other remedy is craved in which case the application must be by way of initial writ: r.34.10(1)(b) of the Ordinary Cause Rules.

[91] s.20(4); but if the creditor's security is one of the forms pre-existing before the 1970 Act, the sheriff's power is limited so that any lease for longer than seven years approved by the court must not exceed 21 years (or 31 years in the case of minerals): s.7 Heritable Securities (Scotland) Act 1894.

[92] Standard condition 1(a).

[93] Standard condition 1(c).

[94] Standard condition 7(1).

[95] Standard conditions 1(b) and 7(2).

[96] Standard condition 7(3); by contrast, the cost of repair works carried out by the debtor are irrelevant to his relationship with the creditor as they do not affect the level of the debt and the creditor, no matter the value of the subjects, may not recover more than that: Stair Memorial Encyclopaedia, Vol. 20 para. 166 citing *Selby's Heirs v. Jollie* [1795] Mor. 13438.

[97] Standard condition 10(6).

[98] s.20(5)(b).

the creditor may carry out other works, in addition to or as alternative to repair. He may effect such reconstruction, alteration and improvement in the subjects as would be expected of a prudent proprietor to maintain the market value of the subjects[99]; (b) the creditor may enter on the subjects at all reasonable times,[1] without giving notice or having entered into possession although as a matter of practicality it might be necessary to do so, or at least to have the debtor ejected, if the debtor was unco-operative.[2]

Before exercising rights under standard condition 10(6), as with the other remedies discussed in this chapter, the creditor must have taken the appropriate preliminary steps, in this case being service of a calling-up notice or notice of default and allowing the period of notice thereunder to expire, or obtaining a warrant from the court to exercise the remedies under section 24 of the Act. As stated above, in the case of his rights under standard condition 10(6), he need not first have entered into possession, though he will usually have done so.

If the creditor has entered into possession, that will impose certain liabilities as well as rights in relation to the maintenance of the subjects, and a creditor may require to carry out works to the subjects in circumstances when he might have preferred not to do so if, for example, there is vandalism to the security subjects. This follows from the wording of section 20(5)(b) that the creditor has assigned to him in these circumstances

> "all ... obligations of the proprietor relating to ... (b) the management and maintenance of the subjects and the effecting of any reconstructions, alteration or improvement reasonably required for the purpose of maintaining the market value of the subjects."[3]

There is also a common law duty to maintain the subjects in this situation[4] and to ensure that the security subjects do not suffer avoidable damage.[5]

---

[99] Standard condition 10(6); s.20(5)(b) imports the same right but instead provides that the works must be "reasonably required for the purpose of maintaining the market value of the subjects". The creditor may also have the right to carry out these further forms of works on a reading of standard conditions 2 and 7, as the former obliges the debtor to complete unfinished buildings to the reasonable satisfaction of the creditor (standard condition 2(a)) and not to demolish, alter or add to the security subjects (standard condition 2(b)), apparently without qualification. While it would be unusual, the differences in these provisions could be of importance if the creditor could not satisfy the test of "prudent proprietor" under standard condition 10(6).

[1] Standard condition 10(6).

[2] And as a matter of practice, it would be unusual for a creditor to exercise the rights before having entered into possession. The right might be exercised to repair the subjects before they are sold by the heritable creditor, but only if the cost of the repairs would materially outweigh the diminution in sale price which would otherwise result.

[3] The same principle applies to pre-existing securities: In *Baillie v. Shearer's Judicial Factor* [1894] 21R. 498, the debtor's title obliged him to maintain the pavement in front of his house. When the heritable creditor entered into possession and a third party was injured because of the defective condition of the payment, the creditor was found liable.

[4] Junor, "The Heritable Creditor's Right to Sell—The Arising Obligations?" 1997 S.L.G. 159, p.161; *Baillie, ibid.*

[5] Halliday, *Conveyancing Opinions*, p.328.

A creditor under a bond and disposition in security has the right, where the debtor has defaulted in payment of principal or interest, or where the proprietor is apparently insolvent, to enter into possession and make all necessary renewals and repairs but he may not improve the subjects, in contrast to the position of a creditor in a standard security.[6]

Foreclosure

7.5.4 In terms of standard condition 10(7), where the debtor in a standard security is in default,[7] the creditor may apply to the court for a decree of foreclosure. Before doing so, the creditor must have exposed the subjects to sale, by public roup, for at least two months at a price no higher than the sum due under his own and any prior or *pari passu* securities and failed to find a purchaser.[8] The subjects must be exposed, at least initially, in their entirety in one lot.[9] Foreclosure covers the situation where sale is impossible and is effectively the remedy of last resort. As a matter of practice, it is very rarely used. The effect of foreclosure is to transfer a full title to the heritable creditor, changing his interest from creditor to owner.[10] As such a strategy might possibly appeal to an unscrupulous creditor who seeks to recover an asset greater than the debt owed, detailed provision is made to ensure that the debtor is not prejudiced.[11]

On application to the court,[12] the creditor must lodge a statement setting out the whole amount due under the security.[13] Service of the application must be effected on the debtor, proprietor and any heritable creditor who has had an interest in the security subjects recorded in the Register of Sasines or registered in the Land Register of Scotland during the preceding 20 years.[14] Interestingly, the court has discretion under this section to allow the debtor a period of up to three months to pay the whole amount due. This contrasts with the lack of discretion available to the court elsewhere in the 1970 Act but is comparable to the new provisions of the 2001 Act.[15] As an alternative to decree, the court may also order such further intimation or inquiry as it thinks fit, which will

---

[6] s.25(1)(a) of the 1924 Act.

[7] And in terms of the 1970 Act the creditor has taken the necessary preliminary steps, of service of a calling-up notice or notice of default, or the obtaining of a warrant under s.24, to entitle him to exercise this remedy.

[8] s.28(1).

[9] Halliday, *Conveyancing*, para. 54–76.

[10] This is generally the only way in which the creditor can become a "full" owner of the subjects, although it is possible for a creditor to purchase the property subject to his security at a sale by another creditor. For an example, see *Begbie v. Boyd* [1837] 16S. 232. It is submitted that such a course remains competent under the 1970 Act though care would require to be taken to demonstrate a sale at arms length to preclude a possible claim against the selling creditor by the debtor under s.25.

[11] In addition to the provisions set out here, the creditor may not vary standard condition 10(7): see para. 1.5.

[12] The application is by way of summary application unless any other remedy is craved in which case the application must be by way of initial writ: r.34.10(1)(e) of Ordinary Cause Rules; a style is provided in Halliday, *Conveyancing*, para. 54–79.

[13] s.28(2).

[14] s.28(3).

[15] See Chap. 4.

usually involve remit to a man of skill,[16] or make an order that the security subjects should be resold at a price it fixes.[17] Even if there is later found to be an irregularity in the foreclosure proceedings, or indeed in the repossession procedure which preceded it, that does not affect the title obtained by the creditor from the decree of foreclosure.[18]

Once such a decree of foreclosure is granted, the creditor is found entitled to the subjects at the price at which they were last exposed and an appropriate entry made in the relevant property register.[19] This has the effect of extinguishing any rights to redeem the security, fully vesting the subjects in the creditor[20] and disburdening the subjects of the security and all securities and diligences postponed to it.[21] Stamp duty is payable on an extract decree of sale as it amounts to a conveyance.[22] The level of duty is based on the value of the subjects. Foreclosure does not affect any outstanding personal obligation due by the debtor.[23]

A creditor in a bond and disposition in security has a similar ability to exercise a right of foreclosure.[24] There is no legal reason why the creditor under an *ex facie* absolute disposition cannot exercise a right of foreclosure but there may be practical difficulties in obtaining the necessary discharge of the debtor's right of redemption.[25]

Restrictions on Exercise or Choice of Remedy by Creditor

The creditor in a standard security has the range of remedies considered **7.6** above, in addition to sale,[26] available to him in terms of the 1970 Act. In certain specific instances, considered below, the creditor is precluded from acting however he chooses to procure repayment of the debt secured.[27] A more difficult question is whether the creditor is generally limited in his choice of remedy.[28]

General Discussion

In *Armstrong, Petitioner*,[29] a farming partnership had become unworkable **7.6.1** after the partners' marriage had broken down. A judicial factor was appointed but a heritable creditor under standard securities sought to interdict the factor from selling, letting or otherwise marketing the subjects averring that he would be prejudiced if the factor sold. Interim interdict was granted but later recalled by Lord Jauncey who held

---

[16] Gordon, *op. cit.*, para. 20–200; Halliday, *Conveyancing*, para. 54–81.
[17] s.28(4).
[18] s.28(8) but a claim for damages could be brought against the creditor in these circumstances if a loss could be established.
[19] s.28(5).
[20] As at the date of recording or registration.
[21] s.28(6).
[22] Stamp Act 1891 (c.39), s.54; Halliday, *Conveyancing*, para. 54–85.
[23] s.28(7).
[24] s.8 of the 1894 Act, but the rules are not identical to those under the 1970 Act. For further detail, see Gordon, *op. cit.*, para. 20–79 *et seq.*
[25] Gordon, *op. cit.*, para. 20–102.
[26] Considered in Chap. 8.
[27] See para. 7.6.2.
[28] See also Gretton and Reid, *Conveyancing* (1993), para. 20.28.
[29] 1988 S.L.T. 255.

> "while I consider that the petitioner is not disabled from exercising the rights of a heritable creditor, he must exercise those rights *civiliter*[30] and with proper regard to the interests of the debtors. A creditor's primary interest will normally be the recovery of the debt due to him and I do not consider that he has unlimited discretion as to which one or more of the powers he exercises. If the value of the heritage is likely to exceed the sum of the debt, his interest is to have the heritage sold and thereafter to account for the surplus to the debtor. If in such a situation he elected to exercise the powers in condition 10 in a manner which did not result in money being available for the debtor he might very well be restrained from so acting. A heritable creditor cannot use his powers for the primary purpose of advancing his own interests at the expense of the debtor when he has the alternative of proceeding in a more equitable manner."[31]

The decision in *Armstrong* was relied upon by the defender in *Halifax Building Society v. Gupta*[32] to support his argument that the court had discretion in the circumstances prevailing there to refuse the creditor's application for warrant to exercise remedies. In that case, Lord President Hope said of the decision in *Armstrong*:

> "It is implicit in [Lord Jauncey's] discussion of the matter that he recognised that the heritable creditor has a right to exercise his powers in terms of the standard security . . . [His] point was that, in a situation where the value of the heritage was likely to exceed the amount of the debt, the creditor's obligation to account to the debtor for the surplus was a matter which ought also to be taken into account . . . The situation which Lord Jauncey was considering was far removed from that in the present case, and we do not consider that his observations about the way in which the creditor must exercise the rights conferred on him by the security can be applied for in the way contended for here by the defender."[33]

It is submitted that, on a proper reading of *Armstrong*[34] and *Gupta*, and having regard to the authorities on attempts by a debtor to interdict sale,[35] the creditor cannot be prevented from exercising the power of sale if he chooses to do so.[36] Although there is no magic wording in the Act which expressly distinguishes the power of sale from the creditor's other remedies,[37] it is the primary method by which the creditor may procure

---

[30] civilly.
[31] p.258.
[32] 1994 S.L.T. 339; see para. 4.2.2 for a full consideration of the case.
[33] pp.345K—346A; this interpretation of the decision in *Armstrong* has been criticised: see Guthrie, "Controlling Creditors' Rights under Standard Securities", 1994 S.L.T. (News) 93, p.95.
[34] Even if it is accepted as a correct decision, on which see *infra*.
[35] See para. 8.11.
[36] At least under a standard security. In *Kerr v. McArthur's Trustees* [1848] 11D. 301, interdict was granted against a creditor who sought to sell under a bond and disposition in security at under-value. This issue is considered further at para. 8.11.
[37] Although, with sale, the debtor has the further protection of s.25 which does not cover the other remedies open to the creditor.

redemption of the security, or at least the maximum sum possible towards the debt. Sale does not work in such a way that the debtor is unfairly prejudiced by it, even if sale will not realise sufficient funds to pay off the debt secured.[38]

The position is more difficult in relation to the exercise of remedies other than sale. It has been argued that *Armstrong* stands for the view that in certain circumstances, the creditor can be prevented from exercising certain remedies under standard condition 10[39] and that is certainly the natural reading of the judgment on that point. But the decision in *Armstrong* has been heavily criticised and it has been argued that it was wrongly decided.[40] In support of that view, Sheriff Cusine has noted that many relevant authorities were not referred to and that there is an apparent contradiction in requiring a creditor to consider the debtor's best interests.[41] It has been argued that the decision in *Gupta* effectively overruled *Armstrong* and that the approval of the decision in *United Dominions Trust Ltd v. Site Preparations Ltd (No.1)*[42] by the Inner House in *Gupta* means that a creditor may choose to exercise whichever of his remedies he wishes.[43]

There is no question that, before the passing of the 2001 Act, *Gupta* confirmed that the court could not refuse an application for decree by a creditor but that is not necessarily the same thing as to say that the choice of exercise of remedies, to which the creditor is entitled, cannot be controlled by the court.[44] In *G. Dunlop and Sons' Judicial Factor v. Armstrong*,[45] Lord Penrose considered the above comments of Lord Jauncey in *Armstrong* and expressly agreed with them.[46]

The conflicting views on Lord Jauncey's decision in *Armstrong* make the position uncertain but it seems likely, standing the decision of Lord Penrose, that there will be circumstances where a particular choice of

---

[38] Unless the sale is at under-value in which the debtor has a claim for damages: see para. 8.11; for the sake of completeness, it should be noted that the petition for interim interdict in *Armstrong* did not state which powers the creditor wished to exercise.

[39] Guthrie, *supra* no. 33, an article which also supports the view, rejected here, that interdict of a sale at under-value is competent (although the author of that article accepts that the creditor will not be prevented from selling where there will be no surplus).

[40] A reclaiming motion was marked but the appeal did not proceed.

[41] Cusine, *op. cit.*, para. 8–25 (in consideration of whether *Armstrong* allows the Court to prevent sale rather than the exercise of other remedies), where there is a useful review of the omitted authorities; but see Guthrie, *supra* no. 33, in response; interestingly, at para. A.482.2, *Scottish Conveyancing Statutes* (R. Rennie ed.), as annotated by Cusine and Guthrie, *Armstrong* is cited as continuing authority for the proposition that in exercising his remedies, the creditor "must bear the debtor's interests in mind".

[42] 1978 S.L.T. (Sh.Ct) 14.

[43] Urquhart, "Enforcing Standard Securities" 1995 J.L.S.S. 400.

[44] The discussion in *Armstrong* took place against the background of served calling-up notices which had not been complied with. Accordingly, as with a decree granted under s.24, the creditor had already reached the stage where he was on the face of it entitled to exercise the remedies set out in standard condition 10.

[45] 1995 S.L.T. 645; the views of Lord Penrose were expressed in the context of a heritable creditor seeking to interdict a judicial factor from selling the subjects. The refusal of the petition was based on a solution of allowing the asset to be realised at an early opportunity, supporting the view that attempts to interdict sale are in a different category. Although it is the same court action, this is a quite separate decision in the case from that reported at 1994 S.L.T. 199 and discussed at para. 6.4.

[46] p.648J.

remedy other than sale is so far removed from the position which would be adopted by a reasonable creditor, that the court will impose a degree of control on the exercise by the creditor of his powers. Nonetheless, it is submitted that, as the overriding purpose of the standard security is to provide an effective means for the creditor to recover the debt secured and as the remedies in standard condition 10 can only be exercised where the debtor is in default, the court should be very slow to grant any petition interfering with the creditor's choice of remedy.[47]

7.6.2 Specific Instances

7.6.2.1 Catholic and secondary securities. Most notably, a creditor seeking to exercise his remedies over security subjects will require to have regard to the interests of another creditor where he holds security over other subjects owned by the same debtor and the other creditor does not. This is the doctrine of catholic and secondary securities[48] which provides that the catholic creditor must seek to procure payment from the subjects over which the other creditor has no security.[49] In the event that he obtains full payment there, he must assign his rights in the subjects over which there had been two securities to the other security holder. The doctrine is a limitation on the creditor's choice of remedy as he is precluded from an unfettered choice of which security to enforce and, if he enforces both securities, there may be limitations on his choice of remedy in relation to one of the securities. As a matter of practice, the doctrine is often excluded by ranking agreements.

7.6.2.2 Security over a security. If a person has put up the standard security in which he is the creditor as security for an obligation in which he is the debtor, the creditor in that security will not be entitled to recover the security subjects from the debtor in the original security. This is not a restriction on that creditor's rights of enforcement *per se*, as he will still be entitled to recover the subject of his security (namely the secured creditor's interest in the other security relationship) but it is mentioned here as an example of a situation where the creditor in a standard security does not have an unfettered choice of the normal remedies open to a creditor under the 1970 Act.[50]

7.6.2.3 Contractual provisions. It was not possible to limit the choice of exercise of powers by a creditor on the basis of earlier contractual provisions, even if the security (including standard securities) was granted in furtherance of those provisions.[51] The provisions were ineffec-

---

[47] The right of creditors to invoke all or any of their remedies to obtain payment is one which was recognised before the 1970 Act: Junor, "The Heritable Creditor's Right to Sell—The Arising Obligations", 1997 S.L.G. 159, citing *McWhirter v. McCulloch's Trustees* [1887] 14R. 918, and *McNab v. Clark* [1889] 16R. 610.
[48] The creditor with the plurality of securities is the catholic creditor.
[49] Bell, *Commentaries*, II, 417.
[50] This issue is dealt with comprehensively by Gretton and Reid, *op. cit.*, para. 20.16.
[51] *Hambros Bank Ltd v. Lloyds Bank plc*, 1999 S.L.T. 49; this was a case dealing with the extent of obligations of the debtor but it is submitted that the principle applies equally to the powers which a creditor may exercise, should those be the subject of an earlier agreement superseded by the express security terms.

tual to qualify a matter expressly dealt with in security deeds which themselves stood unreduced.[52] The correct remedy for a debtor who considered that the security did not accurately reflect the parties' agreement was rectification of the security deed or reduction thereof. However, the coming effect of the Contract (Scotland) Act 1997[53] opens the door to a debtor to claim that a creditor may be limited in the exercise of his choice of powers by earlier express contractual provisions, even if those are not reflected in the standard security. However, the courts will be very slow to imply contractual terms which would impinge on a creditor's right to enforce a standard security.[54]

Potential Liabilities of Heritable Creditor in Possession

It is not altogether straightforward to reconcile the various decisions which give insight into the potential liabilities of a heritable creditor who has evicted his debtor from the security subjects. There are several important issues to be considered. The first is the time at which the liability is incurred. Next, consideration requires to be given to whether the heritable creditor, on recovering the subjects, can be equated to the owner. It may also be important to compare and contrast the position of a heritable creditor with that of an occupier. Finally, there are miscellaneous cases, such as where the land is contaminated, where the question of whether the heritable creditor has entered into possession may be of crucial importance.

7.7

The Timing of the Liability

Section 20(5) of the 1970 Act provides:

7.7.1

"(5) There shall be deemed to be assigned to a creditor who is in lawful possession of the security subjects all rights and obligations of the proprietor relating to—

(a) leases, or any permission or right of occupancy, granted in respect of those subjects or any part thereof, and
(b) the management and maintenance of the subjects and the effecting of any reconstruction, alteration or improvement reasonably required for the purpose of maintaining the market value of the subjects."

The words "and obligations" might suggest that the heritable creditor in possession inherits liabilities of the debtor, incurred prior to recovery of the subjects by the creditor. This issue was most authoritatively examined in relation to common repairs in *David Watson Property Management v. Woolwich Equitable Building Society*.[55] A debtor in a standard security was the proprietor of certain subjects in Glasgow. Following his

---

[52] *ibid*.
[53] s.2.
[54] See for example *Wilson v. Target Holdings*, 1995 G.W.D. 31–1599.
[55] 1992 S.L.T. 430; 1992 S.C. (HL) 21; 1992 S.C.L.R. 357.

default and due procedure, he was evicted by the heritable creditor.[56] At that time, the debtor was in arrears of common charges, feuduty, insurance premiums and management charges amounting to £182.27. The pursuers were the factors of the subjects and sought recovery of these arrears from the heritable creditor. The creditor agreed to accept responsibility for the arrears of feuduty of £3.20 and paid that sum, leaving a balance of £179.07. The creditor also accepted liability for charges incurred subsequent to the date of eviction but refused to pay any further sums in relation to the period prior to eviction. The factors accordingly raised proceedings for the sums relating to that period. Both the sheriff and sheriff principal held that the outstanding sum was an obligation relating to "the management and maintenance of the subjects" in terms of section 20(5)(b) of the 1970 Act. Accordingly, they held that the heritable creditor was obliged to make payment of the sums outstanding by their debtor as at the date they recovered the subjects. This result was reversed on appeal to the Inner House where the court distinguished the word "proprietor" used in section 20(5) from the word "debtor" used elsewhere in the Act, particularly in standard condition 10(5).[57] Further, the court held that the obligations at issue in the action were personal rather than real and, accordingly, liability therefor did not transmit to the heritable creditor following eviction of the debtor.[58] The Inner House placed these obligations in the same category as any personal obligation owed by the debtor to any other third party before the creditor entered into possession. The factors appealed to the House of Lords which, recognising the general importance of the matter, notwithstanding the small sum sued for, agreed to consider the case.[59] The parties were divided as to whether the pre-existing law relating to heritable securities[60] was relevant to consideration of the issue. The House of Lords declined to rule on this issue expressly, finding it unnecessary in the consideration of the dispute, but holding that the result would have been the same had the case been considered in relation to the earlier legislation. The case was decided on the wording "who is in lawful possession of the security subjects", found in section 20(5), which the House held "necessarily refers to those rights and obligations subsisting during the period for which the creditor is in

---

[56] Finding in fact seven of the sheriff, reported at 1989 S.C.L.R. 111 (at p.112) states: "Following default of his payments to the [heritable creditor] in respect of their loan to him secured over the property, the [heritable creditor] put in hand the appropriate default procedure and then took possession of the property from the said [debtor]". In consideration of the case by the Inner House, reported at 1990 S.C.L.R. 517, Lord President Hope stated that the heritable creditor (p.518C) "entered into possession of the flat". The wording of s.20(5) refers to a creditor "who is in lawful possession" which was viewed by the Lord President as having the same meaning as "entered into possession". However, it is submitted that the creditor may not have been in lawful possession at all if the creditor had simply changed the locks (see para. 7.4). The wording of the finding in fact is likely to leave unclear whether the creditor had simply changed the locks or had in fact entered into possession.

[57] But note that the Lord Chancellor (Lord MacKay) in the House of Lords indicated that he did not find that distinction "helpful in determining the issue" (p.359).

[58] The decision of the Inner House is reported at 1990 S.C.L.R. 517.

[59] It is interesting to note that each side had agreed to bear their own costs to the stage of the Inner House but this agreement was not extended to the final appeal.

[60] That is, the law relating to securities before the coming into effect of the 1970 Act.

lawful possession of the security subjects".[61] The provision was accordingly not effective until the period begins and ceases to have effect when the period ends. As the outstanding sums sued for were due before the creditor entered possession, they were not liable and the appeal was dismissed. A final issue, helpfully addressed by the court, related to the nature of the obligation, personal or real. The factors had accepted that the debt was personal before the Inner House. In the House of Lords they claimed that the obligation to pay the debt was transmissible from proprietor to proprietor in terms of the deed of conditions for the subjects, which having included reference to the factors' charges and so on elsewhere, included the term, "[t]he whole burdens . . . above written are hereby created and declared to be real liens, burdens and conditions". Notwithstanding that wording, the court held by reference to existing authority that the obligations in question would not transmit to a successor in title.

The effect of this decision is therefore that a heritable creditor in possession will only assume responsibility for personal debts incurred from the date on which it takes possession, even where earlier debts of that nature are expressed as real burdens. Such debts would include works to the security subjects instructed by the debtor prior to the heritable creditor taking possession. This principle also extends to obligations of a tenant incurred prior to the creditor taking possession,[62] such as rent arrears, unless there is specific agreement between the creditor and the landlord to the contrary.[63] It was, however, accepted by both parties in *David Watson* that unallocated ground burdens would transmit if unpaid and these are therefore an exception to the general rule that the heritable creditor will not be responsible.[64]

Distinction Between Heritable Creditor and Owner

The distinction between the position of a true proprietor and that of a heritable creditor in possession is nowhere more starkly illustrated than in the area of potential liability to third parties. The matter was addressed in two cases dealing with taxation obligations to local government, the first being *Northern Rock Building Society v. J.W. Wood, Community Charges Registration Officer.*[65]

The debtor had been evicted by the heritable creditor who then advertised and sold the subjects. The heritable creditor was entered on the Community Charges Register as "owner"[66] following conclusion of

7.7.2

---

[61] *per* Lord MacKay, p.359.

[62] Of the tenant's interest under the lease.

[63] *Holt Leisure Parks Ltd v. Scottish & Newcastle Breweries plc*, 1996 G.W.D. 22–1284.

[64] The debtor is of course obliged to make due and punctual payment of any ground burden under standard condition 3(b) but will not always perform this obligation as a matter of practice. If he fails to do so, the creditor may pay and the expense of doing so will be secured by the subjects (standard condition 7). This issue will shortly be rendered largely academic as the most common unallocated ground annual was feuduty which will be abolished when s.13(2) of the Abolition of Feudal Tenure etc. (Scotland) Act 2000 (asp 5) comes into force (no date has yet been fixed).

[65] 1990 S.L.T. (Sh.Ct) 109, a decision of Sheriff McEwan Q.C. at Ayr Sheriff Court; an appeal to the Court of Session was marked but abandoned.

[66] The term used in the relevant statute, namely the Abolition of Domestic Rates (Scotland) Act 1987 (c.47), and undefined therein.

the missives from sale and deleted therefrom with effect from the date of entry of the sale by the creditor, rendering it liable for the community charge in respect of the property during that period.[67] The creditor appealed under section 16(1) of the Abolition of Domestic Rates (Scotland) Act 1987 to the sheriff. The court reversed the decision of the deputy community charges registration officer and directed deletion of the entry listing the creditor as responsible, holding that the creditor was not at any time the "owner" of the subjects. That determination is of fundamental importance for heritable creditors generally.

The court held that the creditors would only be in the position of owners if they had exercised the remedy of foreclosure and that there was nothing in Scots law which suggested that the creditor in possession, before foreclosure, should be regarded as the owner.[68] The court also placed reliance on the absence of a definition of "owner" in the 1987 Act.[69] The creditor also argued that it was not in possession but, rather, was exercising its right of sale, which was quite distinct from its right to enter into possession. The sheriff did not expressly answer this argument but implied that the heritable creditor's argument was correct and it had not entered into possession[70]:

> "although they had a right to enter into possession and sell, the building society were never physically in possession of the subjects. The mere fact that they employed agents to advertise and ultimately to sell them to a third party is not in my view indicative of possession."[71]

Finally, the court also took the view that a heritable creditor who had entered into possession by virtue of a decree of mails and duties was in a far greater position of power and authority, and much closer to the position of an owner, than the heritable creditors in this case.[72] While

---

[67] Standing the eventual decision, the wording used by the registration order is of some significance: "The Building Society, as the heritable creditor, having entered into possession under Section 20 should be treated as the owner of the subjects".

[68] In support of this position, the successful appellants had founded, *inter alia*, on the wording of standard conditions 3(b), 7, 9 and 10; to s.20(5)(b) and its interpretation in *David Watson, supra*; to the restrictions, compared with an owner, on a heritable creditor granting leases under s.20; to s.25 and the proposition that a heritable creditor could not, in contrast to an owner, give the property away; to s.27 where it is clear that the heritable creditor holds funds in trust for the person ultimately entitled; and to the wording of s.28 dealing with foreclosure.

[69] Which as a taxing statute had to be considered strictly in favour of the potential taxpayer.

[70] This interpretation of the judgment in *Northern Rock* was certainly that taken by Sheriff Crowe in *Bank of Scotland, infra*, at p.399G, albeit he did not necessarily agree with it.

[71] p.111I; this finding also supported the heritable creditor as the purposes of the 1987 Act, found in s.7 thereof, clearly intended those living locally to be beneficiaries of local authority services and the court found that was the basis on which the charge under that Act was levied.

[72] The sheriff drew support for his conclusions from Gloag and Irvine, *Rights in Security*, (1897). On this subject, the learned authors stated (p.100): "[The position of heritable creditor in possession] is in several respects to be distinguished from that of a proprietor.

the debtors themselves, having been evicted, might also not be liable for the community charge,[73] that did not affect the issue of whether the creditor was liable.

This approach was confirmed by the later case *Bank of Scotland v. Community Charges Registration Officer for Central Region*.[74] Again, the heritable creditor had evicted a debtor in default and there had been a period between eviction and sale in respect of which the registration officer sought to have the heritable creditor pay the community charge. Sheriff Crowe, for the same reasons as Sheriff McEwan, found that ownership could not be equated with simple possession and the entry in the Community Charges Register was therefore deleted. The decision in this respect is on all fours with that in *Northern Rock*.[75]

However, the thorny question of whether the heritable creditors had entered into possession, by having evicted the debtors (but done no more than sought to sell), was further muddied by the sheriff's observation on that aspect of the decision in *Northern Rock*, "[t]he circumstances of that case were similar and in broad terms I would agree with his views. I am not sure that I would agree that the appellants in both cases did not enter into possession."[76]

The community charge was of course abolished shortly after these cases[77] but the principles remain valid in relation to council tax. Section 75 of the Local Government Finance Act 1992 provides that the primary person responsible for council tax is "the resident owner of the whole or any part of the dwelling".[78] Such a term, including as it does the word "resident"[79] could not include a heritable creditor who has simply changed the locks and is proceeding to sell. Neither will it include the debtor who, having been evicted, will no longer be resident. Section 75 then lists various persons who, in turn, will be liable for council tax, concluding with "the owner of any part of the dwelling which is not subject to a lease granted for a term of 6 months or more".[80] Once again,

---

Thus he retains the right to poind the ground, which a proprietor cannot do. He is not entitled to be enrolled as a voter, nor to exercise the rights of a proprietor in parish or county government. The proper criterion as to the limits of his rights would seem to be found in the consideration of the legitimate interest of a creditor in entering into possession. These are solely to obtain payment of his debt, principal and interest, out of the proceeds of the subjects. Whatever powers may be necessary for that purposes he would seem entitled to exercise; but he is not, it is submitted, entitled to use the subjects for his own convenience or enjoyment in any manner which has no effect in reducing his debt." While the days of parish government are past, there is much in this summary which remains valid today.

[73] Though this was not conclusively determined.

[74] 1991 S.C.L.R. 394.

[75] The court placed reliance on the decision in *Skipton Building Society v. Wain*, 1986 S.L.T. 96 where Lord Stewart stated (p.97G) "[The heritable creditors] have changed the locks and the owners presently run the hotel only by their leave", so drawing a clear distinction between a heritable creditor and an owner. Similarly, in *Royal Bank of Scotland plc v. Macbeth Currie*, 2002 G.W.D. 10–326, Sheriff Forbes held "it is quite clear from the authorities . . . that the heritable creditor is not the owner of the property".

[76] p.399F–G.

[77] Local Government Finance Act 1992 (c.14), s.100.

[78] s.75(2)(a).

[79] Defined in s.99(1) as "sole or main residence".

[80] s.75(2)(f)(iii); note also that s.76 allows the Secretary of State to prescribe that for certain classes of dwelling, liability will fall on "the owner of the dwelling" instead of being determined by s.75 but the same point applies as in relation to s.75.

the term "owner" is not defined and the question is therefore identical to that considered in the two cases considered above, namely can the heritable creditor who has evicted the debtor be equated with the owner? The answer is just as strongly no for council tax as it is for community charge. Where the creditor has entered into possession, rather than simply changed the locks,[81] the matter is put beyond doubt by subordinate legislation which confirms that no council tax or council water charge is payable for such repossessed properties.[82]

A heritable creditor does remain liable for the rates of commercial premises where he has entered into possession,[83] but is not liable where he has simply advertised the subjects for sale.[84] This point also has a bearing on sewerage charges in terms of the Local Government Finance Act 1992 which provides that such costs are payable by the person who is liable to pay the rates.[85] Once again, entering into possession exposes the creditor to the liability.

The importance of the distinction between "heritable creditor in possession" and "owner" does not stop at local government charges. As Sheriff Cusine notes,[86] the term "owner" appears in the Civic Government (Scotland) Act 1982[87] under which that person may be liable for the costs of works done by local authorities. The heritable creditor is not liable for such costs.[88]

However, where the term "owner" is defined by a particular statute, the position may be different. In terms of the Roads (Scotland) Act 1984,[89] the local roads authority may serve a notice on the frontagers of a private road requiring them to make up the road to a reasonable standard and maintain that standard thereafter. "Frontager" is defined[90] as the owner of the land fronting or abutting a road but "owner" in turn is defined[91] for the purposes of the 1984 Act as the person entitled to receive the rents.[92] Accordingly, a creditor will be liable under this provision if, but only if, he has entered into possession of the subjects.[93]

---

[81] For the distinction, see para. 7.4.

[82] The Council Tax (Exempt Dwellings) (Scotland) Order 1992 (S.I. 1992 No. 1333), the Schedule to which includes within the category of exempt dwellings (at para. 14): "[a] dwelling (a) which is not the sole or main residence of any person; (b) in respect of which the qualifying person . . . is a debtor . . . in a heritable security secured over the dwelling; and (c) lawful possession of which has been entered into by the creditor in that heritable security."

[83] s.16 of Valuation and Rating (Scotland) Act 1956 (c.60); Gordon, *op. cit.*, para. 20–53.

[84] *Armour on Valuation for Rating* (5th ed., W. Green and Son, Edinburgh, 1985), para. 12–05.

[85] Sched. 11, Pt II, para. 22.

[86] Cusine, *Standard Securities* (1991), para. 8–38.

[87] s.87.

[88] Cusine, *supra*; the same position in relation to similar terms found in s.10 of the Building (Scotland) Act 1959 was confirmed there by Sheriff Cusine and is also supported at Halliday, *Conveyancing Opinions*, p.337 where the similar distinction applied between heritable creditor and owner in *Spiers and Knox v. Marshall's Trustees* (1904) 11 S.L.T. 599 is noted.

[89] s.13.

[90] s.151.

[91] s.151.

[92] Or who would be entitled to receive the rents if the land was let.

[93] Halliday, *Conveyancing*, para. 49–21.

Liabilities of Heritable Creditor as Occupier

7.7.3 A heritable creditor in possession may be held to be an occupier within the meaning of the Occupiers Liability (Scotland) Act 1960[94] and it is submitted that remains true even where the creditor has done no more than change the locks.[95] The creditor in such circumstances should avail himself of insurance to cover an occupiers' liability claim.

The same is likely to apply to consideration of whether heritable creditors are liable under the Explosives Act 1875, section 23 of which provides that the occupier of certain premises must take all due precaution for the prevention of accidents by fire or explosion. In *Lord Advocate v. Aero Technologies Ltd (in receivership)*,[96] Lord Sutherland noted that it was the receivers who had been attending to the proper security of the premises and held that they could be regarded as occupiers finding that "in deciding who is the occupier of this factory the reality of the situation must be looked at".[97] It therefore seems likely that heritable creditors who have repossessed, whether or not they have entered into possession, may be held liable under this provision.

The Local Government Finance Act 1992 provides that an occupier is liable to pay a water charge if a water authority supplies a dwelling with a supply of water.[98] It is likely that a heritable creditor who had entered into possession could be held as falling into this category but in that situation the subjects are made an exempt dwelling from the council water charge by subordinate legislation.[99] The position is unclear where the creditor has simply changed the locks and is proceeding to sell.[1]

Contaminated Land

7.7.4 The question of when a heritable creditor enters into possession has been considered above.[2] This is potentially of great significance in the area of contaminated land, which is a problem faced from time to time

---

[94] (c.30); Cusine, *Standard Securities*, para. 8–37; Maher and Cusine, *op. cit.*, para. 8–70.

[95] The term "occupier" might give rise to the assumption that the heritable creditor would only be responsible where he enters into possession (see para. 7.4) but in *Telfer v. Glasgow Corp.*, 1974 S.L.T. (Notes) 51, the court held a company liable as occupiers within the meaning of the Occupiers Liability (Scotland) Act 1960 where they were retaining the keys of the building even though they had negotiated its sale to the local authority. The reasoning was that they were the party with authority and the power *de facto* to exclude others. Lord Stott stated: "All the evidence indicated that the place attracted hordes of children of all ages . . . In a situation of that kind when the [company] were leaving such a building standing unoccupied and derelict for a period of months or years there was, as I think, a very high onus on them to make strenuous efforts to keep it reasonably secure." This view is supported by the decision of Sheriff Forbes in *Royal Bank of Scotland plc v. Macbeth Currie*, 2002 G.W.D. 10–326, where the court held that possession of the keys by the heritable creditor was "tantamount to their having control of the premises".

[96] 1991 S.L.T. 134.

[97] p.136.

[98] Sched. 11, Pt I, paras. 7 and 8.

[99] The Council Tax (Exempt Dwellings) (Scotland) Order 1992 (S.I. 1992 No. 1333); see *supra* no. 82.

[1] As the creditor has not entered into possession: see para. 7.4.

[2] Although it is worth adding here that during the progress of the Environment Bill through Parliament, the government expressed the view that the surrender of keys by the debtor was not such as to put the heritable creditor in possession of the subjects: see Garner, *Environmental Law*, Vol. 2, IIA 20.

by both creditors who recover security subjects constructed before the issue was considered in depth[3] and by creditors who recover commercial subjects where there have been chemical or other works capable of causing contamination.

Legal liability for remediation of contaminated land is governed by Part IIA of the Environmental Protection Act 1990.[4] In certain circumstances, the person who has caused the pollution will not be the person who pays for the cleaning up. The Act deals with this by the concept of identifying the "appropriate person" to bear responsibility for remediation. The definition of the "appropriate person" is obviously of key importance and is found in section 78F of the 1990 Act. Two different categories of appropriate person are set down. First, the appropriate person may be "any person . . . who caused or knowingly permitted the substances . . . by reason of which the contaminated land in question is such land to be in, on or under that land is an appropriate person".[5] It is submitted a heritable creditor will not fall into this definition, known as a Class A person.[6]

However, a second category exists where it is not possible to find a Class A person.[7] This is of more significance than might first appear, as the debtor may have disappeared or, in the case of a corporate debtor, may have ceased to exist.[8] In such a situation, a Class B person may be liable for remediation of the contaminated land by virtue of section 78F(4) of the 1990 Act which provides: "If no person has, after reasonable inquiry, been found who is [a Class A person], the owner or occupier for the time being of the contaminated land in question is an appropriate person." In contrast to many statutes, "owner" is in fact defined. In this Act, the owner

> "in relation to any land in Scotland, means a person (other than a creditor in a heritable security not in possession of the security subjects) for the time being entitled to receive or who would, if the land were let, be entitled to receive, the rents of the land in connection with which the word is used".[9]

---

[3] It has been estimated that the issue of contaminated land may affect up to five per cent of all properties.

[4] (c.43), hereafter "the 1990 Act".

[5] s.78F(2) of 1990 Act.

[6] Although during the progress of the Environmental Bill which led to Pt IIA of the 1990 Act, it was questioned whether a heritable creditor might fall within the definition of a Class A person where the debtor had caused or knowingly permitted the contamination. In the House of Lords, Earl Ferrers said "I am advised that there is no judicial decision which supports the contention that a lender, by virtue of the act of lending the money only, could be said to have 'knowingly permitted' the substances to be in, on or under the land such that it is contaminated land. This would be the case if for no other reason than the lender irrespective of any convenants it may have required from the polluter as to environmental behaviour, would have no permissive rights over the land in question to prevent contamination occurring or continuing." (*Hansard*, H.L., 11 July 1995, col. 1497).

[7] The concept of holding someone other than the polluter liable is also known as "the deep pocket theory".

[8] In which case service of a remediation notice, which establishes the responsibility of remediation on the appropriate person, on a Class A person will be impossible: Scottish Executive Rural Affairs Department Circular 1/2000, unless of course the company is restored to the Register of Companies by an application under s.653 of the Companies Act 1985 (c.6).

[9] s.78A(9); the same subsection confirms that "creditor" and "heritable security" have the same meaning as in the 1970 Act.

The word "possession" is not defined but it is submitted it may be used in its natural meaning of physical possession. If the heritable creditor has not entered into possession, he will be neither physically "in possession" not legally so. If he has entered possession, he will qualify under the reference to letting and, in certain cases, may be physically in possession. "Occupier" is not defined in Part IIA and carries its ordinary meaning.[10] In both cases, a heritable creditor who has not entered into possession will not be liable for remediation of contaminated land under Part IIA of the 1990 Act, in contrast to the position if he has entered into possession.

Given the very substantial costs of decontamination,[11] the potential exposure to decontamination must always be considered by creditors seeking to take properties into possession, particularly where the subjects are commercial in nature. In determining whether to serve a remediation notice on a party identified as an "appropriate person" to be called upon to remedy the pollution, the authority must consider the cost caused to such a person.[12] While authorities have discretion in the matter, there is at least a possibility that the authority would perceive there to be less hardship to a national mortgage lender, in the service of a remediation notice, than on a private individual. Accordingly, it does not necessarily follow that because the debtor has not been served with a remediation notice, the heritable creditor who recovers the subjects from him and enters into possession will also escape potential liability.

Creditors must therefore be wary of the possibility of exposing themselves to the obligations imposed by environmental legislation. In practice, this will mean carrying out environmental audits in advance of issuing commercial loans and consideration of whether it is prudent to enter into possession. In extreme cases, there may be circumstances when the cost of remediation outweighs the value of the subjects in which case the creditor would require to walk away from the subjects rather than take them into possession or sell them without any remediation having been carried out. Certainly, a creditor may be willing to show more latitude with a debtor where there is a contaminated land issue identified before the creditor enters into possession. In addition to rescheduling of arrears repayments, the creditor may offer to assist the debtor in the costs of remediation as, otherwise, he may be left with a bankrupt debtor or a worthless security. Generally, creditors will often seek environmental insurance for protection.

Other Liabilities

Under the Housing (Scotland) Act 1987,[13] a local authority may serve a repair notice on a person "having control of the house" where it is satisfied that the house is in a state of serious disrepair.[14] The recipient must execute the works necessary to rectify the defects or the local

7.7.5

---

[10] Scottish Executive Rural Affairs Department Circular 1/2000.
[11] For land to be defined as contaminated, the harm that arises or will possibly result must be significant: s.78A(2) of the 1990 Act.
[12] s.78E of the 1990 Act.
[13] (c.26).
[14] s.108(1).

authority may do so.[15] In that event, the local authority may recover its expenses from the person having control of house or from a person who receives the rent of the house.[16] Once again, it is submitted that there is a key distinction between a heritable creditor who has entered into possession and one who has simply changed the locks, the former being potentially liable and the latter not.

The creditor may be liable for tax on rents received from tenants at the security subjects.[17] Having entered into possession, the creditor may also incur liabilities in respect of his obligation to maintain the subjects.[18]

Avoidance of Liabilities

7.8 If the creditor has entered into possession or otherwise exposed himself to liabilities, his only potential remedy appears to be to register a deed of disburdenment removing the property element from the standard security. Such a move, however, might be challenged by the person to whom the liability is owed. First, the creditor will be responsible for liabilities such as in *David Watson* for the period during which he is in possession. Secondly, there is the doctrine of personal bar. Having inherited the liability, it could be argued that the heritable creditor may not unilaterally avoid its obligation particularly if the party owed the liability has incurred expense in the knowledge that the creditor had entered or intended to enter into possession. Such an argument appears valid and that reinforces the care which must be taken by the heritable creditor when considering whether to enter into possession. In most cases, of course, disburdenment is simply not an option as it removes any interest the heritable creditor has in the subjects, leaving him without a security. In the event that the heritable creditor has not entered into possession, it is open to him to abandon and reject the asset.[19]

---

[15] s.108(2) and (3).
[16] s.109(1).
[17] See para. 7.5.1.
[18] For further detail, see para. 7.5.3.
[19] For an example, see *Ascot Inns Ltd (in receivership) v. Braidwood Estates Ltd*, 1995 S.C.L.R. 390.

CHAPTER 8

REPOSSESSION SALES

The Power of Sale

The power of sale is open to the creditor in a standard security in three 8.1
circumstances; first, where the debtor has failed to comply with a calling-up notice[1]; secondly, where the debtor has failed to comply with the requirement specified in a notice of default[2]; and thirdly where the creditor has obtained a warrant to exercise the power of sale from the court.[3] In any of these situations, the creditor may proceed to sell all or any part of the security subjects.[4] The sale may be either by private bargain or public auction.[5]

If the power of sale is being exercised under a bond and disposition in security, the creditor must have served a calling-up notice which has expired.[6] Sale in these circumstances may be by public auction or private bargain[7] but if the latter, it must be for the best price that can be reasonably obtained.[8] A creditor selling under an *ex facie* absolute disposition has an implied power of sale[9] which does not stem from the terms of the back letter or agreement setting out the terms of the security though of course the circumstances in which the creditor may sell may be set out there.[10] The creditor may sell by private bargain or public auction unless there is a specific agreement to the contrary in terms of the security arrangements.[11]

General Issues on Sale

The purpose of this discussion is to identify special considerations which 8.2
apply to sale by a heritable creditor rather than to review sales in general. It must always be remembered that the creditor in selling is

---

[1] s.20(2) of the Conveyancing and Feudal Reform (Scotland) Act 1970 (c.35), hereafter "the 1970 Act"; references to statutory provisions in this chapter are to the 1970 Act unless the context otherwise requires.

[2] s.23(2).

[3] s.24.

[4] Standard condition 10(2); the creditor may sell the subjects in lots: s.40 of Conveyancing (Scotland) Act 1924 (as amended) (c.27), hereafter "the 1924 Act".

[5] s.25, which uses the words "exposure to sale" meaning public auction.

[6] See para. 3.3 for further detail.

[7] Unless it is a sale by a *pari passu* creditor in which case sale must be by public auction: s.35(3) of the 1924 Act.

[8] s.36 of the 1924 Act and s.35(1) of the 1970 Act.

[9] *Aberdeen Trades Council v. Shipconstructors and Shipwrights Association*, 1949 S.C. (HL) 45.

[10] Gloag and Irvine, *Rights in Security* (1897), p.160; the sale may be conducted without notice to the debtor, but in all cases, the implied power may be overcome by express terms of the *ex facie* absolute disposition which debar the creditor from selling: *Aberdeen Trades Council, ibid.*

[11] *Duncan v. Mitchell & Co.* [1893] 21R. 37.

bound by the same restrictions in title as would have affected the debtor, had he been selling, such as a right of pre-emption.[12] Generally, however, the stance taken by a heritable creditor selling the subjects will differ in a number of important respects from that of a normal, private seller. There will be significant differences in the missives, compared to an ordinary sale. For example, the selling creditor will not undertake warranties or guarantees in the sale, for the simple reason that he is unlikely to have been in physical possession of the subjects at any time and will therefore have much less actual knowledge of the condition of the subjects than the ordinary seller. In relation to the conveyancing, the creditor will generally exhibit all documentation he holds and allow the purchaser or his agents to satisfy themselves as to matters of title and compliance with the preliminary procedure and to ensure that the necessary consents are available. Once security subjects have been marketed and an offer received, the heritable creditor may have a duty to effect a complete settlement as soon as possible to minimise the period during which there may be a risk of adverse consequences to the security subjects but the issue is unclear.[13]

The Format of the Missives

8.3 The absence of liability on the part of the heritable creditor in relation to certain obligations,[14] combined with a general lack of knowledge the creditor will have about alterations and so on, means that there is limited information which a creditor will be willing or able to give as part of the sale process. This has led to the development of an offer to sell by those acting for heritable creditors which is, in effect, a substitute for a qualified acceptance. Rather than responding point by point to an offer by a potential purchaser, the offer to sell will highlight the areas where the heritable creditor can offer comfort but leaves the remainder to the purchaser who then requires to make a decision on whether to take or leave the property on that basis.

The Content of the Missives[15]

8.4 It would be unusual for a heritable creditor to sell movables for the simple reason that they do not form part of the security subjects and, accordingly, it is not generally within the creditor's power to sell them.[16] If they are sold, the creditor's lack of physical possession and detailed knowledge about them means that no warranties will be given. For similar reasons, the heritable creditor will not provide warranties or agree to obtain the necessary consents in relation to any of the following:

---

[12] Halliday, *Conveyancing Opinions*, pp.478–479.

[13] *ibid*, p.328; this was certainly the case under bonds and dispositions in security but the view expressed in *Dick, infra*, that a creditor may sell at a time of his own choosing, may extend beyond advertisement and the initial stages of sale to the whole sale process.

[14] See para. 7.7.

[15] See also the very useful discussion on this subject at Cusine, *Standard Securities* (1991), para. 8.31.

[16] It is possible for the creditor to sell movables as an agent of the debtor if that is permitted by the standard conditions but this may give rise to problems: see Gretton & Reid, *Conveyancing* (1993), para. 20–30; Cusine, *op. cit.*, para. 5.25; and para. 7.3.

alterations (including building warrants, certificates of completion or planning permission); superior's consent[17]; and title to or the condition of fixtures and fittings (including any central heating system). In the event that an impasse is reached, the matter may be resolved by the use of indemnity insurance.[18]

Another issue in the missives for sale of a repossessed property relates to the situation where the heritable creditor declines to provide an undertaking to clear any inhibitions against the debtor which are postponed to the security under which sale is being effected. In fact, any such qualification has no practical effect (other than avoiding legal debate between the practitioners) as the subjects are disburdened of the inhibition once the disposition by the heritable creditor is recorded.[19]

The passing of risk under the missives may also be a matter of difficulty. A heritable creditor, not having physical possession, will be reluctant to assume the risk of destruction or damage to the subjects for the period between conclusion of missives and the date of entry. Equally, however, the purchaser, who will also not have had physical possession (nor even any form of legal interest in the subjects, other than an enforceable contract to purchase them), will be reluctant to assume this risk. The matter is one for negotiation and again the creditor's attitude will be of paramount importance. If the creditor, as is frequently the case, insists on relinquishing the risk on conclusion of missives, the purchaser will require to carry insurance to protect against any adverse occurrence before taking entry.[20]

Searches

The usual searches will be required as in any conveyance but the issue of searching when the sale is by a heritable creditor is complicated by the passing of the Mortgage Rights (Scotland) Act 2001.[21] One of the documents which a purchaser will examine in these circumstances will be that giving the heritable creditor his power of sale. This may be an expired calling-up notice but is more likely to be an extract decree containing a warrant to sell.[22] In the vast majority of cases, consideration, if any, will have been given to an application under the 2001 Act prior to the granting of such a decree.[23] However, it appears possible for a decree to be granted by the court at the same time as a section 2 order suspending the creditor's rights.[24] Certainly, an *ex facie* expired calling-up notice may have been subject to a section 2 order which will not be apparent from the terms of the notice. Accordingly, one effect of the 2001 Act is to cast the possibility of doubt on the documentation which would formerly have sufficed to evidence the creditor's power of sale.

8.5

---

[17] Though this will shortly be abolished when s.17 of the Abolition of Feudal Tenure etc. (Scotland) Act 2000 (asp 5) comes into force (no date has yet been fixed).

[18] See para. 8.6.

[19] s.26(1) of 1970 Act and see para. 8.15.

[20] For further discussion, see Cusine and Rennie, *Missives* (2nd ed., 1999), para. 4–27.

[21] (asp 11), hereafter "the 2001 Act"; the clerk of court is obliged to register any section 2 order in the Register of Inhibitions and Adjudications under s.3 of the 2001 Act: see para. 4.2.20.

[22] In terms of s.24 of the 1970 Act.

[23] See para. 4.2.8.

[24] See para. 4.2.8.

The wisest and indeed only safe course for conveyancing practitioners, even where it seems likely that the overwhelming majority of, for example, decrees will not be subject to section 2 orders, is to satisfy themselves that the creditor does indeed have the power of sale. The first option is to seek a warranty from the creditor that there is no section 2 order in force. However, in practice creditors are unlikely to reverse the position adopted to date of declining to provide any warranties. More likely is the second option which will see the creditor agreeing to exhibit, or the purchaser agreeing to obtain, a search in appropriate terms confirming that the power of sale contained in the exhibited documentation is unaffected by a section 2 order under the 2001 Act.

Care will be required in the instruction of the search. The form of order which will be entered in the Register has been considered above[25] and will include the address of the security subjects, the name of the pursuer in the court action and the identity of the parties to the standard security. These details appear to address earlier concerns which had been expressed[26] over the changing identities of heritable creditors (at least in terms of their names) and should prove sufficient for the searchers to identify whether the power of sale has been affected, particularly given that the pursuer in the action will almost invariably be the party selling. Further comfort may be drawn from the fact that the Keeper has had sight of most major creditors' deductions of title and would be likely to declare results against earlier names of a creditor even if the search is only worded in the most recent name of the creditor.[27]

The final searching issue relates to the length of the search. To date, it has been sufficient to search back for five years. That remains the case, at least for the time being, but once the 2001 Act has been in force for five years,[28] it may be that a longer search will be required having regard to the ability of the court to make a section 2 order "for such period"[29] as it thinks fit. It has been suggested that the search at that time should be from the date of registration of the security[30] but if the creditor is willing to provide the date on which it commenced enforcement action then, as an application under the 2001 Act can only be made in response to action taken by a creditor, it may be sufficient to search from that date.

---

[25] See para. 4.2.20.

[26] See for example, Urquhart, "Mortgage Rights (Scotland) Act 2001", *Green's Property Law Bulletin* 53–1.

[27] But note that the Keeper, if challenged, may rely on the answers provided to Form 1 or 2 submitted to the Keeper by the purchaser's agents (having been revised by the seller's agents). If the question as to whether any party to the dealing is subject to any legal incapacity or disability not already disclosed on the Land Certificate is answered in the negative, the Keeper may rely on that to avoid indemnity if that is incorrect. The same may apply in relation to the question of whether the statutory procedures necessary for the proper exercise of a power of sale under a heritable security have been followed.

[28] That is, on December 3, 2006.

[29] s.2(1)(a)(ii) of the 2001 Act.

[30] Urquhart, *supra* no. 26.

Matrimonial Homes Affidavits and Other Documentation

8.6 The heritable creditor, not being an owner in the true sense,[31] cannot have a non-entitled spouse[32] and in any event the subjects will not be a matrimonial home[33] in respect of which occupancy rights may exist. No affidavit is therefore required in the usual sale in relation to occupancy rights in terms of the Matrimonial Homes (Family Protection) (Scotland) Act 1981[34] arising from the interest of the creditor. In the extremely rare event that the heritable creditor has previously foreclosed,[35] and is a natural person now selling, an affidavit under the 1981 Act would be required but in such a situation the seller is effectively selling as any other would do so, rather than in the capacity of heritable creditor. In all cases, however, matrimonial homes affidavits should be obtained in relation to the debtor of the heritable creditor as the mere fact of repossession does not disentitle the non-entitled spouse of his or her occupancy rights.

As liability for unallocated ground burdens will become the responsibility of the purchaser,[36] it would be normal for the purchaser's solicitor to ensure that these are paid up as close to the date of sale as possible. Generally, it may be more difficult for selling heritable creditors to exhibit documentation than it would be for an owner who sells. Although this is reflected in creditors' attitudes to warranties[37] and warrandice, there may be occasions when the absence of documentation creates a real barrier to the progress of the matter. To obviate this, it is possible for creditors to obtain insurance indemnity cover which protects them in circumstances where, to ensure a sale may take place, they have no choice but to offer guarantees they would otherwise decline to make available. Such insurance cover may cover any or all of the following potential problems; failure to obtain planning permission or building regulation consent for works previously carried out to the subjects or the absence of a completion certification in relation to planning permission or building regulation; the existing breach of any title condition or burden; the existence of unknown rights, servitudes, burdens or other conditions in any deed to which the property may be subject and which are still capable to taking effect; the absence of a legally declared right of servitude (whether for pedestrian or vehicular access, or for services or drainage) where there is existing physical use of the rights which would be covered by such a declared servitude; and the absence of documentation required under the 1981 Act. It is also possible to obtain cover against a possible challenge by a trustee in sequestration on the basis of an earlier disposal of the subjects by the debtor.

---

[31] See para. 7.7.2.

[32] In most cases, of course, the heritable creditor will not be a natural person and will not have a spouse.

[33] As defined in s.22 of the Matrimonial Homes (Family Protection) (Scotland) Act 1981.

[34] (c.59), hereafter "the 1981 Act".

[35] See para. 7.5.4.

[36] *David Watson Property Management v. Woolwich Equitable Building Society*: see para. 7.7.1; but the issue will soon be obsolete: para. 7.7.1.

[37] Discussed at para. 8.4.

The Disposition

8.7 On sale, the creditor will grant a disposition the effect of which is considered below.[38] In common with heritable creditors' general reluctance to grant warranties in missives,[39] the creditor will usually decline to grant absolute warrandice in the disposition, preferring instead to offer fact and deed warrandice only.[40] The standardised approach adopted by creditors and their strong wish to ensure there is no possibility of a later claim usually means that negotiation on this point is impossible, the creditor effectively adopting a "take it or leave it" stance.

There are special provisions in relation to VAT where a heritable creditor effects a sale.[41] The supply is deemed to be made to the debtor with the creditor acting as a tax collector for Customs and Excise. Any VAT collected must be paid to Customs and Excise with Form VAT 833.[42]

The Creditor's Duty to Advertise and to Obtain the Best Price

8.8 Section 25 of the 1970 Act imposes a duty[43] on heritable creditors in standard securities to publicise the sale and not to prejudice the debtor or another creditor by accepting a low price.[44] The section provides:

> "A creditor in a standard security having right to sell the security subjects may exercise that right either by private bargain or by exposure to sale, and in either event it shall be the duty of the creditor to advertise the sale and to take all reasonable steps to

---

[38] See para. 8.15.

[39] See para. 8.4.

[40] For a style disposition, see Halliday's *Conveyancing Law and Practice* (J.S. Talman ed.), Vol. II (hereafter "Halliday, Conveyancing"), para. 54–47.

[41] Value Added Tax Act 1994 (c.23), Sched. 4 para. 7; Value Added Tax Regulations 1995 (S.I. 1995 No. 2518) reg. 27.

[42] For further detail, see Halliday, *Conveyancing*, para. 54–45.

[43] There is a difference of opinion as to whether the wording of s.25 imposes one duty or two. Sheriff Cusine provides a practical example of the potential significance of the distinction in relation to advertising requirements at *Standard Securities*, para. 8–29 and favours a construction of separate duties. Gretton and Reid, *op. cit.*, para. 20–30 also take the view that there are two separate duties and the same is implied in Halliday, *Conveyancing*, para. 54–43. But Lord MacFadyen implies a single duty in *Bisset v. Standard Property Investment plc*, 1999 G.W.D. 26–1253: "There is some force in the distinction . . . between the choice . . . conferred on the creditor in the first part of the section and the duty imposed on him in the second." There is also reference to a singular duty in *Gordaviran Ltd v. Clydesdale Bank plc*, 1994 S.C.L.R. 248.

[44] The debtor would of course remain liable for any shortfall on the account if the sale price was insufficient to clear his liability. Alternatively, if a surplus resulted from the sale, it would be the debtor rather than the creditor who lost out by the low sale price. This relationship was described in Halliday, *The Conveyancing Feudal Reform (Scotland) Act 1970* (2nd ed.), para. 5–11 as placing the heritable creditor in the position of quasi-trustee for the debtor. The Lord President agreed with this analysis in *Dick* although the analogy must not be taken too far: *Bisset*. The word trust is also used in s.27 (see para. 8.16) but it is important to distinguish this concept of trusteeship for the sale proceeds from the concept of the heritable creditor being trustee for the security subjects, which he is not: Hood, "The Duties of A Standard Security Holder" 1994 J.L.S.S. 257.

ensure that the price at which all or any of the subjects are sold is the best that can be reasonably obtained."[45]

Advertising the Sale

There are no fixed rules on the manner of advertisement[46] but the subjects must be identified. It is insufficient to advertise for sale unidentified subjects within the locality.[47] It is clear that advertisement under the 1970 Act may take place by a number of different avenues outwith the commonly accepted method of a public newspaper. These include advertisement by a widely read solicitors' property guide[48]; the window of an estate agent's office[49]; and circulation of details on the mailing list of an estate agent together with particulars being made available in the estate agent's office.[50] It may be that publication on the internet could be sufficient in the case of widespread exposure but regard must always be had to individual circumstances.[51] As with the method adopted, there is no fixed rule on the number of times a property must be advertised.[52]

8.9

Any special features pertaining to the subjects, such as that they are licensed premises, must be included in the advertisement.[53] In *Bank of Credit v. Thompson*,[54] two guarantors called on to pay a balance due following sale of security subjects claimed that the bank had failed in its duty under section 25.[55] In particular, they alleged the bank had advertised only in local and not in national newspapers. Further, they said, it had failed to state that the property had planning permission for

---

[45] The advertising duties of creditors selling under a bond in disposition and security are still governed by s.38 of the 1924 Act (as amended) which provides more rigorous rules than the 1970 Act. The rarity of these sales is such that the matter is not considered further here. For full details see s.38 of the 1924 Act and Halliday, *Conveyancing*, paras. 48–27 and 48–28. A creditor selling by private bargain under such a bond also has a duty to obtain the best price that can reasonably be obtained: s.40(1) of the 1924 Act. For a favourable comparison of Scots law on this topic generally with other jurisdictions see Gretton and Reid, *op. cit.*, para. 20–28.

[46] Cusine, *op. cit.*, para. 8–27.

[47] Halliday, *Conveyancing Opinions*, p.314.

[48] McDonald, "Advertising Requirements on a Sale by a Heritable Creditor", *Green's Property Law Bulletin* 7–5.

[49] Cusine, *op. cit.*, para. 8–28, Case 2.

[50] Cusine, *op. cit.*, para. 8–28, Case 3.

[51] In *Gordaviran Ltd v. Clydesdale Bank plc*, 1994 S.C.L.R. 248, advertisement of farmland had taken place in a local daily newspaper and a farming journal. The debtors claimed, *inter alia*, that advertisement should have taken place in a national newspaper and golf publications. The creditor submitted that the advertising used had gone "far beyond the minimum required" which appears correct although no express comment was made on that submission by the court. For practical issues relating to the sale of property on the internet, see de Went, "The Internet and its Future Role in Selling Property" (1997) 42 J.L.S.S. 242.

[52] Cusine, *op. cit.*, para. 8–28, Case 1; Halliday, *Conveyancing Opinions*, p.316 suggests for three or possibly only two consecutive weeks provided this is followed by an opportunity to inspect and survey the subjects.

[53] Halliday, *Conveyancing Opinions*, p.314.

[54] 1987 G.W.D. 10–341.

[55] The defenders' position was principally that the best price had not been obtained but the case provides some insight into the issue of advertisement.

office as well as shop use (although the subjects had in fact eventually been sold to a non-local firm for office use). The Sheriff Principal at Airdrie rejected this defence, noting that there was no cogent evidence that the premises would have been more attractive to potential buyers if they had been advertised as an office. Moreover, advertising in a national rather than a local newspaper would have added significantly to the costs of sale and there was no substantial evidence that businessmen out of the locality would have been interested.

In *Davidson v. Clydesdale Bank plc*,[55a] the court found that the sale of minerals had not been advertised in an appropriate publication, the one advertisement placed having been in a "cheaply produced document ... which carried virtually no advertising at all of any kind". Evidence was available that an advertisement could have been placed in an alternative and more appropriate publication.

The Best Price that can be Reasonably Obtained[56]

8.10 Certain fundamental principles were laid down by the Inner House in *Dick v. Clydesdale Bank plc*[57] in relation to this aspect of the creditor's duty towards the debtor. The creditor is entitled to sell at a time of his own choosing,[58] provided all reasonable steps are taken to ensure that the price is the best that can be reasonably obtained at that time.[58a] If all reasonable steps are taken to attract competition, the market should establish what the property is worth. The creditor may only be criticised for not taking certain steps if it can be proved that those further steps would have resulted in a higher sale price.[59] On the other hand, there may be circumstances where it is appropriate for the creditor, while having formally taken possession, to allow the debtor to physically

---

[55a] 2002 G.W.D. 13–426, a decision of Temporary Judge Coutts Q.C.

[56] There was formerly a further statutory duty on building societies, where they sold as heritable creditor in possession, "to take reasonable care to ensure that the price at which the land is sold is the best price that can be reasonably obtained": Building Societies Act 1986 (c.53), Sched. 4, paras. 1(1)(a) and s.119(2). This provision was repealed by the Building Societies Act 1997 (c. 32) s.12(2) but does not affect the remaining duty in terms of s.25 of the 1970 Act on building societies selling as heritable creditors.

[57] 1991 S.L.T. 678; for further discussion of the case, see Hood, "The Duties of A Standard Security Holder" 1994 J.L.S.S. 257.

[58] Though in *Bisset*, Lord Hamilton noted the lack of authority cited in *Dick* for this proposition and noted the earlier possibly contradictory decisions in *Kerr v. McArthur's Trustees* (1848) 11D. 301 and *Stewart v. Brown* (1882) 10R. 192; planned regulation of the area by the FSA may limit the creditor's rights in this respect: see para. 9.4.5.

[58a] This was described as a "high statutory duty" in *Davidson v. Clydesdale Bank plc*, 2002 G.W.D. 13–426

[59] He need not necessarily accept the price which is the highest if that is subject to suspensive or resolutive conditions, as the best price refers to the net realisable sum: Halliday, Conveyancing, para. 54–44. See also *Davidson, supra* no. 58a, where Temporary Judge Coutts Q.C. found that the creditor's agents (surveyors) had failed to take all reasonable steps but that these failures had had no effect on the sale price realised, meaning that no loss was established by the debtor of the creditor. In that case, the reasonable steps which were not taken included failures to critically analyse a mining engineers' report; to ascertain the reason for differences between various expert reports; to mention minerals on the title page of sale particulars; to place any reasonable emphasis in the sale particulars on the availability of planning permission; to lot the minerals separately; and to advertise the subjects in an appropriate manner.

remain in and run a business from the subjects.[60] It is incumbent on a debtor relying on section 25 to prove the identity of an alternative purchaser, and to show that that person would have been willing to pay a higher price at the relevant time than that obtained by the creditor.

In *Dick*, the creditor held a security over two pieces of land, one used for commercial purposes, the other larger part agricultural. The creditor repossessed and sold the land as a whole. The debtor brought an action for damages claiming that the larger piece of ground had been sold without regard to the hope value of the land for development. A proof before answer was allowed at first instance. The defenders successfully reclaimed, Lord President Hope finding:

> "The creditor is not to be subjected to the risk of challenge simply on the theory that the subjects may have had a greater value than was realised by the sale. What matters is the reality of the market place in which the subjects are exposed at the time when he decided to sell."

The open market value of the subjects may assist in the determination of the best price that could reasonably be obtained.[61] If the sale by the heritable creditor was the first of a series of two or more sale transactions, it is thought that the prices paid later in the chain could reflect on whether the best price had been obtained by the creditor.[62] The creditor also has the right, subject in the ordinary case only to the exercise of good faith, to choose which mode of sale to adopt.[63]

The Remedy of the Debtor

If the debtor is dissatisfied with the sale by the creditor, his remedy under section 25 is an action of damages[64] and not interdict.[65] In

8.11

---

[60] As argued for the successful petitioner in *Skipton Building Society v. Wain*, 1986 S.L.T. 96. This situation appears to have arisen where an empty property would have diminished the sale price (as is often the case) but could also have led to loss of the liquor license. The result is analogous to a receivership.

[61] In *Bisset*, the open market value was expressly distinguished from the theoretical hope value referred to in *Dick*. In *Royal Bank of Scotland v. Johnston*, 1987 G.W.D. 1–5, a proof on quantum had been allowed where debtors claimed as a loss the difference between the actual sale price and the price which would have been achieved if the subjects had been sold properly.

[62] *Stair Memorial Encyclopaedia*, Vol. 20, para. 204.

[63] This follows from the use of the word "may" in s.25 where the creditor is permitted the choice of private bargain or exposure to sale (*i.e.* sale by auction). Note though that the argument advanced in *Bisset* was only ever qualified by good faith was rejected. There may be cases where a mode of selection is so bizarre as to be outwith the creditor's power of selection, even if there is no bad faith. The court allowed averments that disposal of a trading hotel by public auction in 1993 and 1996 was "extremely unusual" to proceed to proof before answer.

[64] As in *Dick* and *Bisset*.

[65] It has been argued that interdict against sale at under value remains competent, notwithstanding the decision in *Associated Displays*: Guthrie, "Controlling Creditors' Rights under Standard Securities" 1994 S.L.T. (News) 93 at p.95 but it is submitted this is incorrect. That discussion centres on the decision in *Armstrong, Petr*, 1988 S.L.T. 255, which may have a bearing on the creditor's choice of remedy, where he is not selling but, it

Associated Displays Ltd (in liquidation) v. Turnbeam Ltd,[66] the debtors were liquidated and their heritable creditors sought to sell the property. They advertised it for sale and received an offer of £20,000. The liquidator of the debtor obtained a valuation of £180,000 and sought interdict against the defenders disposing of the property at the price agreed until the creditor satisfied the court it had complied with its statutory duty. Interim interdict was granted at first instance. Sheriff Principal MacLeod[67] allowed an appeal stating: "Section 25 may impose certain duties upon a creditor, but it confers no right upon a debtor to call upon the creditor to demonstrate that he has fulfilled these duties".[68] Interdict was held to be incompetent.[69] It has been noted that if interdict was competent in these circumstances, the creditor would be effectively prevented from exercising the right to sell, granted by the court, except with the consent of the debtor.[70] It is thought probable that a debtor may not reduce a sale on the basis of a failure to comply with section 25.[71]

The onus of proof in demonstrating a breach of section 25 by a creditor lies on the debtor[72] and he must support his case with appropriately relevant and specific pleadings.[73] As in civil cases generally, the onus rests on the balance of probabilities though it has been described as "relatively high" compared to the average civil matter.[74] However, if the sale by the creditor is to a related company, the onus of proof may be transferred to the creditor to demonstrate that the best price was achieved.[75]

Employment of Professional Agents

8.12 A further issue under section 25 relates to the employment of professional agents by the heritable creditor. Delegation to a professional agent is a common exercise and will often be the appropriate course for a heritable creditor to follow.[76] In *Bisset*, the question before the court

---

is submitted, the case can no longer be said to be authority for a debtor to interdict a creditor from selling at under value standing the decisions in *Gupta, Associated Displays* and *Gordaviran*. See also Cusine, *op. cit.*, para. 8.30; Gordon, *Scottish Land Law* (2nd ed., 1999), paras. 20–57 and 20–187; and R. Rennie (ed.), *Scottish Conveyancing Statutes*, annotations by Cusine and Guthrie at para. A482.2. It remains competent in certain circumstances to interdict a sale where the heritable creditor is in breach of some other statutory provision such as s.126 of the Consumer Credit Act 1974 (c.39): see para. 2.5.

[66] 1988 S.C.L.R. 220; the case was followed by Sheriff Principal Nicholson in *Thomson v. Yorkshire Building Society*, 1994 S.C.L.R. 1014, discussed at para. 5.21.

[67] at Glasgow.

[68] p.222.

[69] A further ground of incompetency of the interdict was that missives had already been concluded constituting an enforceable contract of sale prior to the action being raised.

[70] Sheriff Principal Risk in *Gordaviran Ltd v. Clydesdale Bank plc*, 1993 S.C.L.R. 248 at p.251.

[71] Gretton and Reid, *op. cit.*, at para. 20–30.

[72] *Associated Displays*. The duty is not owed only to the debtor although in practice it is generally the debtor who will pursue an action. The action may therefore also be brought at the instance of another creditor dissatisfied with the efforts of the selling creditor.

[73] *Royal Bank of Scotland v. Johnston*, 1987 G.W.D. 1–5.

[74] Junor, "The Heritable Creditor's Right to Sell—The Arising Obligations?" 1997 S.L.G. 159.

[75] *Bisset*.

[76] *Dick v. Clydesdale Bank plc*, 1991 S.L.T. 678, p.681E.

was to what extent did such reliance by a creditor excuse it from its obligations in respect of price towards the debtor? This issue had been considered in *Dick* where Lord President Hope stated,

> "counsel for the defenders' submission was that it was a sufficient performance of the duty for the creditor to employ competent agents to market the subjects on his behalf and that he was entitled to rely on their experience and judgment as to how the best price for the subjects was to be achieved. The contention was that in the absence of criticism of the competence of the professional advisers who were employed in this case, and of any suggestion that there was any serious blunder on their part indicating a failure to sell at the best price, the pursuer's case was irrelevant ... There is no doubt that the defenders were entitled to employ professional advisers to market the subjects ... In the ordinary case the creditor may be regarded as having fulfilled the duties imposed upon him in regard to marketing of the subjects if he takes and acts upon appropriate professional advice",

but he continued in relation to the case in question

> "the extent of the defenders' personal responsibility in regard to the giving of instructions to their professional advisers ... cannot be answered sufficiently merely by pointing to the fact that professional advisers were employed".[77]

By contrast, Lord Cowie in that case dissented on this point stating

> "if the creditor ... employs competent agents to market [the security subjects], the creditor can only be said to have failed in his ... duties to obtain the best possible price for the subjects if the agents have to the knowledge of the creditor made a serious blunder resulting in a large diminution in the price realised".[78]

In *Bisset*, it was argued that the court's ruling in *Dick* was binding authority for the view that a heritable creditor was, in the absence of exceptional circumstances, to be taken as having fulfilled his duties if he took and acted upon professional advice. Lord Hamilton rejected this,[79] holding:

> "I prefer the approach ... that the duty remains throughout on the creditor to secure the statutory result ... it would be inappropriate

---

[77] p.681B–G. It is important to note that there was no criticism of the advisers in this case. It was the creditor's own acts which were at issue. Lord Mayfield agreed with the Lord President. However, the Lord President's comments here were described as *obiter* by Lord Hamilton in *Bisset*.

[78] p.682H–J; Lord Cowie placed reliance on Halsbury's *Laws of England* (4th ed.), Vol. 32, "Mortgage", para. 729, a passage he described as "entirely consistent with the principles of Scots law".

[79] *Dick* was distinguished on the basis that the observations in *Dick* on this subject were *obiter* and that *Dick* concerned a situation where the creditor's own acts and not those of a professional adviser were in issue.

in my judgment to exclude averments in this case from probation on the ground that the obligation of a heritable creditor in relation to the marketing and sale of the subjects are even in ordinary circumstances wholly discharged by his appointing reputedly competent professional advisers to carry through such tasks."[80]

It is submitted that the decision in *Bisset* is correct and that, even in the normal case, delegation to a professional adviser will not satisfy in itself the creditor's duty under section 25.[81]

Common Law Duties

8.13 In addition to the statutory duty under section 25, the heritable creditor owes a duty at common law to pay due regard to the interest of his debtor when he comes to sell the security subjects.[82] The creditor must take reasonable steps to obtain a full and fair market price for the subjects, even where the security is an *ex facie* absolute disposition.[83] In practice, claims under common law may amount to little if anything more than the creditor's statutory duties[84] and such claims may face the argument that they are for pure economic loss, with consequent difficulties.[85]

Consent of Other Secured Creditors to Sale

8.14 A prior security holder wishing to sell is free to do so without the consent of *pari passu* or postponed security holders but any proceeds after discharge of his own security must be distributed according to section 27 of the 1970 Act which will give the postponed security holder priority over other debts.[86] A postponed security holder may also sell[87]

---

[80] There is a very thorough review of the relevant authority by Lord Hamilton in this case. Particular reliance was placed by the Court on the decision of the High Court of Australia in *Commercial and General Acceptance v. Nixon* (1983) 152 C.L.R. 491, a case which had not been referred to in *Dick*. In that matter, Gibbs C.J. stated: "The duty to take reasonable care is one that the mortgagee is bound to perform, and he cannot escape liability for a breach of that duty by delegation to another".

[81] This is supported by the approach taken in *Davidson v. Clydesdale Bank plc*, 2002 G.W.D. 13–426, where the action brought against the creditor for the failure of their surveyors was not defended on the basis that the matter having been delegated, no right could lie against the creditor. But as both *Bisset* and *Davidson* are Outer House authority, the matter cannot yet be regarded as settled.

[82] *Dick v. Clydesdale Bank plc*, 1991 S.L.T. 678; *Rimmer v. Thomas Usher & Son Ltd*, 1967 S.L.T. 7; this case was brought following sale by a creditor under an *ex facie* absolute disposition but the case confirms that the principles stated apply also to sale by a creditor under a bond and disposition in security. See also *Aberdeen Trades Council v. Shipconstructors and Shipwrights Association*, 1949 S.C. (HL) 45 where Lord Normand (p.60), in consideration of the position of a creditor selling under an *ex facie* absolute disposition, quoted with approval Bell's *Principles* (10th ed.), s.912 to the effect that the creditor was obliged not to act "unfairly and without due regard to the interest of his debtors".

[83] *Rimmer* at p.9; Halliday, *Conveyancing Opinions*, p.314.

[84] *Dick v. Clydesdale Bank plc*, 1991 S.L.T. 678, p.680C–D; in *Davidson, supra* no. 81, the court noted that the common law duty averred did not extend as far as the statutory duty was breached, the common law duty was not considered further.

[85] Hood, "The Duties of a Standard Security Holder" 1994 J.L.S.S. 257.

[86] See para. 8.16.

[87] Though in practice sale is usually by the prior security holder.

but the recording of a disposition by a postponed security holder in implement of sale does not affect the rights of the holder of the prior security, to which the secured property remains subject.[88] However, the selling creditor has the same rights as the debtor to redeem the prior security.[89] The matter is more complicated when a *pari passu* creditor wishes to sell. The position is still regulated by the Heritable Securities (Scotland) Act 1894[90] which provides that in these circumstances, the *pari passu* creditor may attempt to obtain the consent of the other *pari passu* creditor(s), and if he cannot do so, he may apply to the sheriff[91] for warrant to sell the lands. The sheriff may order sale if he thinks it reasonable and expedient. The court may fix the price and other conditions of the sale. While that course is open, it appears that it is not mandatory and that the *pari passu* creditor may sell without court order.[92]

The Practical Effect of Sale

Where the creditor effects a sale of the security subjects and grants the purchaser a disposition of the subjects sold thereby, in implement of the sale, then, on that disposition being duly recorded, the subjects are disburdened of the standard security and of all other heritable securities and diligences ranking *pari passu* with, or postponed to the security.[93]

8.15

In this context, postponed securities and diligences include inhibitions. It has been held that the sole object of section 26(1) is to confer a disburdened title on the purchaser who buys from the heritable creditor and that the section does not operate to adjust the ranking rights of other creditors.[94] The provision does not have the effect of destroying or nullifying the rights of creditors under inhibitions registered after the standard security on the strength of which the subjects are sold.[95] In *Newcastle Building Society v. White*,[96] the creditor following default by its debtor and sundry procedure thereafter concluded missives to sell to a

---

[88] s.26(2); see also s.27(1)(b); a purchaser from a postponed security holder would be certain, of course, to insist on the clearance of prior securities.

[89] s.26(2); a similar right to redeem is provided for during the foreclosure process by s.28(6)(c); for a full discussion of the law on redemption, see para. 6.4.

[90] s.11.

[91] Jurisdiction is governed by s.29(1) of the 1970 Act which provides that, as with repossession actions in general, the relevant sheriff court is that with jurisdiction over any part of the security subjects, no matter their value.

[92] Halliday, *Conveyancing*, para. 54–41(2) relying on s.26(1) and para. 54–43 relying on s.27(2); but see Gordon, *op. cit.*, para. 20–185.

[93] s.26(1); an inhibition which is recorded before the security rights vests is not affected: *Cheltenham & Gloucester Building Society v. Mackin*, 1997 Civ.P.B. 17–9.

[94] *Sheriff Clerk of North Strathclyde v. Paterson*, unreported, June 11, 1984, per Sheriff Principal Caplan, the judgment being reported in full as part of the case report of *Halifax Building Society v. Smith*, 1985 S.L.T. (Sh.Ct) 25, p.31; the ranking rules for the application of sale proceeds are set out in s.27 for which see para. 8.16.

[95] *Halifax Building Society v. Smith, ibid*, per Sheriff Principal Caplan at p.28. While criticised in one respect (see para. 8.16), this decision was generally welcomed by Professor Gretton in "Inhibitions and Standard Securities" 1985 S.L.T. (News) 125 and the absence of reported case law on this aspect of s.26 since *Smith* suggests that the profession has adopted the reasoning therein as correct. The question of ranking has caused further problems under s.27 for which see para. 8.16.

[96] 1987 S.L.T. (Sh.Ct) 81.

third party in terms of which they were bound to exhibit a clear search in the personal register. The purchaser then discovered an outstanding inhibition (by another party) against the debtor, recorded after the creditor's standard security. The purchaser demanded that the creditor obtain a discharge of the inhibition and, when it refused, purported to rescind the contract. The creditor brought an action for implement of the missives and succeeded on appeal. Sheriff Principal Caplan[97] held that the offer by the heritable creditor to grant a disposition in favour of the defender was just as effective in releasing the subjects from the effect of the inhibition as the tender of a specific discharge by reason of the operation of section 26(1).[98]

Distribution of Sale Proceeds

8.16 Section 27 provides that when the creditor in a standard security receives the sale proceeds of the security subjects, he must hold them in trust and apply them in following order of priority—

(a) first, in payment of all expenses properly incurred by him in connection with the sale, or any attempted sale[99];
(b) secondly, in payment of the whole amount due under any prior security to which the sale is not made subject[1];
(c) thirdly, in payment of the whole amount due under the standard security, and in payment, in due proportion, of the whole amount due under a security, if any, ranking *pari passu* with his own security[2];
(d) fourthly, in payment of any amounts due under any securities with a ranking postponed to that of his own security, according to their ranking.[3]

Any residue must be paid to the person entitled to the security subjects at the time of sale.

A great deal of difficulty has arisen in relation to the interpretation of section 27(1)(d) and, in particular, as to what is covered by the word

---

[97] reversing the sheriff.
[98] in fact, by the time the appeal was heard, the heritable creditor had procured removal of the inhibition in the erroneous hope that this practical step would resolve the litigation. This may be attractive in certain circumstances, where the debt is small and an early practical resolution will favour the creditor. However, as was noted by the Sheriff Principal (p.84), the debt due under the inhibition may be substantial and the principle that such inhibitions as discussed in this case need not be formally discharged holds true whatever the value of the debt. It is fortunate that the case exists to provide an authoritative view on the operation of s.26 in these circumstances but the matter appears to have been a catalogue of errors on both sides—the defender clearly received the wrong advice as to the interpretation of s.26 and the pursuers, who failed to appeal an interlocutor allowing proof at that time, and only re-opened the interlocutor at appeal after the proof, were found liable for the whole expenses of the proof.
[99] s.27(1)(a); for a consideration of this provision, see *Bass Brewers Ltd v. Humberclyde Finance Group Ltd*, 1996 G.W.D. 19–1076.
[1] s.27(1)(b); if a real burden created by statute in favour of a local authority is to have any preference to heritable securities, that must be expressly indicated in the relevant statute: *Sowman v. City of Glasgow DC.*, 1983 S.L.T. 132.
[2] s.27(1)(c), provided that any such other security has been duly recorded.
[3] s.27(1)(d).

"securities". It appears that the word includes real burdens in favour of a public authority[4] but most of the controversy has centered on whether its meaning extends to inhibitions. In *Halifax Building Society v. Smith*,[5] Sheriff Principal Caplan, finding that the word "securities" should be "construed in a sense most appropriate to a general question of ranking",[6] held that the word does indeed cover inhibitions which can therefore[7] confer an effective preference on the inhibitor for the free proceeds of sale. However, this approach has been criticised by Professor Gretton (both before and after that decision) who has pointed out that inhibition is prohibitory in nature and has said that an inhibitor who wishes to recover from the sale proceeds must take the further steps of adjudication (before the sale) or arrestment (after the sale) if he is to secure any preference.[8] This position is also favoured by the Scottish Law Commission[9] who have recommended that the law be clarified such that an inhibitor may only rank on the proceeds of sale along with other diligence creditors if he has attached the property by the proposed new diligence of land attachment[10] or has arrested in the hands of the heritable creditor.[11]

The matter remains unclear. It would be difficult to criticise practitioners who follow the former view given the existing decision in *Smith* which has been followed,[12] but the law is simply too uncertain to say that that should be taken as the correct legal position.[13] Nonetheless, to avoid

---

[4] *Sowman, supra* no. 1, p.135.

[5] 1985 S.L.T. (Sh.Ct) 25.

[6] p.29.

[7] Without any other diligence.

[8] Gretton, "Inhibitions and Standard Securities" 1985 S.L.T. (News) 25; interestingly, as a result of earlier comment by Professor Gretton on the subject, Sheriff Principal Caplan was able to consider his views in *Smith* and rejected the argument indicating that if arrestment was to govern ranking, the inhibition would become "a valueless ornament". Gordon also favours the view that arrestment is required: *op. cit.*, para. 20–69.

[9] Discussion Paper on Diligence Against Land (Discussion Paper No. 107), October 1998, para. 3.163.

[10] See para. 9.3.2.

[11] Discussion Paper on Diligence Against Land, para. 3.164 comprising proposal No. 30; the Commission indicated that if it was eventually decided by the courts that an inhibitor should rank without other diligence, the law should changed such that his ranking is postponed to creditors who have used other diligence: para. 3.165.

[12] By Sheriff Shiach in *Abbey National Building Society v. Barclays Bank plc*, 1990 S.C.L.R. 639.

[13] See also Halliday, "Ranking of Heritable Creditors" 1981 J.L.S.S. 26, p.27 where Professor Halliday stated "It is submitted that it is clear that 'security' in section 27 must be construed in the more general sense as meaning any legal right of security however created". Professor Halliday also analysed the 1970 Act there and its use of the word "security" other than in what he called the "narrowly particularised sense" of "standard security" adopted by Professor Gretton. This article was in response to Professor Gretton's "Ranking of Heritable Creditors" 1980 J.L.S.S. 275. Professor Halliday's views were responded to and rejected by Professor Gretton in "Ranking of Heritable Creditors, a reply to a reply" 1981 J.L.S.S. 280. The issue is further considered by Professor Gretton in "Inhibitions and Conveyancing Practice" 1985 J.L.S.S. 392 and in his book *The Law of Inhibition and Adjudication* (2nd ed., 1996), pp.141–150; the conflicting authority on this issue is considered further by Cusine, *Standard Securities*, para. 8–34, where he also supports the view taken by Professor Gretton that inhibitions are not securities within the meaning of s.27(1). See also Love, Meston and Cusine "Ranking of Inhibitors", 1977 JLSS 424 and the articles cited at no. 8.

so far as possible a failed claim, a creditor wishing to create a preference on sale proceeds would be well advised to adopt the diligence of arrestment, given the relatively modest cost of that procedure and the certainty its use will bring.[14] Assuming the inhibition does create a preference,[15] it should be noted that it does not rank above all debts. Rather, debts contracted prior to the inhibition rank *pari passu* with it on a proper consideration of section 27 but debts contracted thereafter are deferred to a ranking lower than those.[16]

The rules on distribution of funds by a creditor selling under a bond and disposition in security are more complicated but the same basic rules apply.[17] There are no special rules which apply to distribution of sale proceeds by a creditor selling under an *ex facie* absolute disposition.[18]

It must not be forgotten, of course, that standard securities may secure non-monetary obligations.[19] There is no case law to provide guidance on the manner in which sale proceeds should be distributed where the creditor has sold as a result of a non-monetary default by the debtor. It appears likely that a creditor may retain sums as damages to compensate him for the default in question.[20]

Surplus Proceeds

8.17 In the normal case, surplus proceeds resulting from sale of the subjects by the creditor should be paid to the debtor in accordance with section 27. Where for any reason the creditor cannot obtain a discharge for a payment he would be obliged to make under these provisions, he may consign the sum due in the sheriff court for the person appearing to have the best right to the funds.[21]

Where the creditor has sold in the situation where a trustee in sequestration has been appointed to the estate of the debtor, a first ranking creditor should deduct the sums necessary to discharge his security and then pay the free proceeds of sale to the trustee, no matter what other creditors there may be. In *Alliance & Leicester Building Society v. Hecht*,[22] the pursuers sold certain property as heritable creditors under a standard security. Three other creditors (one of whom was a party to this action) had inhibited the debtor before the sale. By the time of the sale the debtor had been sequestrated, the first defender being the debtor's trustee. The heritable creditor raised an action of multiplepoinding as to the proper disposal of the free proceeds of sale.

---

[14] For an example of the effective use of arrestment in these circumstances, see *Lord Advocate v. Bank of India*, 1991 G.W.D. 13–823.
[15] With or without an arrestment.
[16] *Smith*, p.30, followed in *Abbey National, supra*.
[17] See Gordon, *op. cit.*, para. 20–65.
[18] Gordon, *op. cit.*, para. 20–101.
[19] See para. 1.2.
[20] Paisley, *Land Law* (2000), para. 11–19; Gretton, "The Concept of a Security" in *A Scots Conveyancing Miscellany* (D.J. Cusine ed., 1987), 126 at p.129 where this view is acknowledged to be speculative.
[21] s.27(2); this includes the debtor where his whereabouts are unknown; for practical considerations of the manner in which consignation should be effected, see Halliday, *Conveyancing*, para. 54–54.
[22] 1991 S.C.L.R. 562.

The trustee and inhibiting creditor defended and claimed that the action was incompetent. Sheriff Henry[23] agreed, dismissing the action and confirming: "I consider that the defenders' argument is correct to the effect that the correct procedure to be followed, where there is already a sequestration depending, would be to pay the residue of the fund to the trustee in bankruptcy."

Difficulties may also arise where the subjects are jointly owned by a housing association and a debtor of the creditor under a shared ownership agreement.[23a] In a repossession, the creditor may agree a course of action with the housing association and that the costs of recovery and sale of the subjects will be borne equally between them or in specified proportions. Given the complexities which may arise in such cases, the most prudent course for a creditor selling in such circumstances is to remit a percentage share of the gross sale proceeds to the housing association equivalent to its percentage share of the proprietorial interest in the subjects. Having done so, the housing association's interest in the sale proceeds is exhausted and the matter becomes simply one of accounting for the outlays incurred. This approach also allows a straightforward determination to be made of whether there are surplus proceeds due to the debtor in respect of his proprietorial share in the subjects, standing that the residue requires to be paid to the person entitled to the security subjects at the time of sale.[23b]

Notwithstanding the decision in *Alliance & Leicester*, if there is doubt generally as to the proper application of free proceeds, an action of multiplepoinding is the prudent course for a heritable creditor. This is the only way to ensure that the balance is not disposed of incorrectly and, therefore, of ensuring that a claim against the creditor for wrongful disposal of net free proceeds is avoided.[24] It will be apparent from the conflicting views on the interpretation of section 27 of the 1970 Act that there is plenty of room for doubt as to the destination of free proceeds and it is perhaps surprising that there have not been more reported instances of multiplepoinding actions on this provision. This route also has the attraction to the holder of the fund of forcing the hand of a creditor who has inhibited but exercised no other diligence as such a creditor cannot enter the action and may elect to exercise further diligence to allow him to enter the process, which, in turn, may resolve doubts as to the proper application of the proceeds.[24a]

If surplus proceeds are due to two or more parties, between whom there is conflict, a high degree of care requires to be taken in the distribution of the proceeds. In the case of joint debtors, in the absence of specific agreement from all debtors, the proceeds should be distributed equally.[25] Difficulties may also arise where one of the joint

---

[23] at Glasgow.

[23a] For a statutory definition of shared ownership agreement, albeit in a landlord and tenant context, see s.83(3) of the Housing (Scotland) Act 2001 (asp 10).

[23b] s.27(1) of the 1970 Act.

[24] This route also has the attraction that the expenses of the multiplepoinding action should be paid from the fund *in medio*.

[24a] See Gretton "Inhibitions, Securities, Reductions and Multiple Poindings", 1982 JLSS 13 and 68.

[25] *Dawson v. R. Gordon Marshall & Co*, 1996 G.W.D. 21–1243.

debtors has died. In such circumstances, the creditor may not use life policy proceeds due only to the deceased's estate to discharge the debt due by both debtors in terms of the security without exposing himself to a claim for recompense.[26] Matters are also complicated where an action of reduction has been raised by a trustee in sequestration to set aside a sale by the debtor. The free proceeds of sale should be placed on deposit receipt until the outcome of the action is known.[27]

Shortfall

8.18 Even if there is no residue left, the heritable creditor still has an obligation to account to the debtor for the overall distribution of funds.[28] If the sale funds are insufficient to discharge the sum due under the security, the debtor is not absolved of the outstanding sums. Rather, the heritable creditor becomes effectively an unsecured creditor for the balance known colloquially as a shortfall debt and may take any of the remedies open to unsecured creditors generally.[29] Summary diligence will often be competent to the heritable creditor based on the personal obligation and a warrant for execution in the standard security.

Protection of Purchasers

8.19 Purchasers who buy from heritable creditors have long been protected provided certain conditions are met. Those were set out for bonds and dispositions in security in section 41 of the Conveyancing (Scotland) Act 1924.[30] The 1970 Act[31] applies these provisions to standard securities. Section 41 of the 1924 Act provides:

> "(2) Where a disposition of land is duly recorded ... and that disposition bears to be granted in the exercise of a power of sale contained in a [security] deed ..., and the exercise of that power was *ex facie* regular, the title of a bona fide purchaser of the land for value shall not be challengeable on the ground that the debt had ceased to exist, unless that fact ... was known to the purchaser prior to the payment of the price, or on the ground of any irregularity relating to the sale or in any preliminary procedure thereto".[32]

Bona fide,[33] while not in itself an exact term, is more straightforward than *ex facie* regular.[34] On regularity, it is both appropriate and a matter

---

[26] *Christie's Executrix v. Armstrong*, 1996 S.L.T. 948.
[27] See Junor, *infra* no. 34, p.73.
[28] *Lord Advocate v. Bank of India*, 1991 G.W.D. 13–823.
[29] See Wilson, *The Scottish Law of Debt*, (2nd ed., 1991).
[30] as amended.
[31] s.32.
[32] It is specially provided by s.177(2) of the Consumer Credit Act 1974 that that Act does not affect the operation of s.41 of the 1924 Act (or its application to standard securities by s.32 of the 1970 Act).
[33] In good faith.
[34] Even if a trustee in sequestration has been appointed to the estate of the debtor, and challenges a disposition in favour of a third party purchaser from the debtor, the purchaser should be protected as the deed will have been granted in fulfillment of prior obligations. As such, the purchaser will be in good faith and so protected: Junor, "Sale of Security Subjects: Applying the Free Proceeds" 2000 S.L.P.Q. 72.

of common practice that a purchaser will seek to be assured that the heritable creditor has properly advertised the subjects and obtained the best price which can reasonably be obtained[35] but it is not thought necessary for a purchaser to satisfy himself that the calling-up notice or notice of default[36] have been properly served or that a decree for exercise of the power of sale has been properly obtained.[37] There is certainly no requirement to revert to the court for further permission to sell once a section 24 decree has been granted.[38] If of course there are circumstances which cast doubt on the validity of the manner in which the heritable creditor has come to sell, then these might be such that the purchaser would be in bad faith by failing to enquire further.[39]

---

[35] In practice this is done by obtaining certificates of advertisement which specify the nature of the advertisement which was carried out by the heritable creditor.

[36] The calling-up notice is much more likely.

[37] Cusine, *op. cit.*, para. 8–35; but a copy of the notice or decree will require to be obtained and, in the case of notices, there should be available some evidence of service. For an example of problems arising from evidence of service, rather than service itself, see C. Waelde (ed.), *Professor McDonald's Conveyancing Opinions* (1998), p.169 *et seq*; if a decree has been obtained in terms of s.24, it does not matter that a notice of default which preceded the court action had a fatal error, as the notice is not required as a preliminary step: see Halliday, *Conveyancing Opinions*, p.318.

[38] *United Dominions Trust Ltd, Noters*, 1977 S.L.T. (Notes) 56 where Lord Kincraig found that the sheriff court decree granting warrant to sell excluded the operation of s.227 in the Companies Act 1948 to have a disposition approved by the Court where the company was in liquidation (that provision is now to be found in s.127 of the Insolvency Act 1986 (c.45)).

[39] Halliday, *Conveyancing*, para. 48–35.

CHAPTER 9

FUTURE DEVELOPMENTS IN REPOSSESSION LAW

Amendments to The Mortgage Rights (Scotland) Act 2001[1]

9.1 It is too early to predict with any certainty how the courts will interpret the provisions of the 2001 Act. However, the very lack of certainty which already exists in relation to the method of service of certain notices may well mean that amending legislation will be required, particularly if the matter is interpreted in different ways by different sheriffs.[2]

One option which had appealed to creditors before the 2001 Act was passed was a standards based approach where the court would have had to consider precise guidelines, such as whether the loan was in its first year and whether more than one loan repayment had been made.[3] There seems little prospect of this approach now finding its way into legislation standing the wide discretion permitted to sheriffs under the 2001 Act.

9.2 Mortgage to Rent

Background

9.2.1 In July 2000, the Scottish Executive issued a draft consultation paper entitled *Mortgage to Rent Scheme*.[4] The essence of the scheme would be to provide government funding to allow the transfer of loans in arrears, held with secured creditors, into tenancy agreements, held with housing associations. The funding would be used to keep rental down and to pay repair costs. The scheme also envisages the provision of financial assistance to housing associations to assist their purchase of the security subjects from the debtor where there are arrears on the secured loan.[5] Outwith the provision of government funding, the scheme would work by the housing association charging rent to cover the cost of the capital required to purchase the property and pay for any repair costs.

---

[1] (asp 11), hereafter "the 2001 Act".
[2] Similar problems were experienced for 20 years after the introduction of the Conveyancing and Feudal Reform (Scotland) Act 1970 (c.35) in relation to the correct court procedure for certain repossession actions: see para. 2.2.11. It is to be hoped that any similar inconsistency which results from the 2001 Act may be cured more quickly by the additional legislative time now available in the Scottish Parliament.
[3] One source of concern for creditors is that in cases of mortgage fraud, where the initial payment may be made but no more, they will experience delay in recovering the subjects when they are at their most exposed. The 2001 Act offers no special protection where fraud is suspected of having been committed.
[4] The draft consultation paper is available from the Scottish Executive. The scheme is also known colloquially as "Mortgage Rescue".
[5] The purchase price under the scheme would be 100 per cent of the valuation (as determined by an independent valuation) less the repair costs necessary to the subjects: Draft Consultation Paper, s.4, para. 4. Any outstanding balance above the purchase price would require to be negotiated between the creditor and the debtor.

The purpose of such a scheme is stated be "to provide help to those households in mortgage difficulties by offering the flexibility to change the tenure of their home, from ownership to a tenancy in the social rented sector".[6] The benefits to debtors are said to be that they and their family may remain in their own homes; that homelessness or the prospect of living in unsuitable accommodation are avoided; that disruption to family life is reduced; and that the family is able to remain within an existing social support network.[7] The Executive also hopes creditors will benefit by the introduction of a further option for dealing with problem accounts and claims that losses may be reduced by the avoidance of auction sales.[8] There would also be benefits for local authorities including, it is said, savings to the public purse.[9]

The scheme is already under way, in different formats, in certain areas throughout Scotland[10] though it appears that a very low number of debtors have been assisted to date. The purpose of the consultation is to extend the scheme nationwide.

Operation of the National Scheme

It is essential to stress that, no matter what specific rules may be finally established, the Scottish Executive has made it quite clear that the scheme will be voluntary and that creditors will not be forced to take part against their wishes. As a result, there will be no statute enacted or even statutory instrument made to set out the terms of the scheme. Rather, a guidance paper will be issued once the detailed rules have been finalised.[11]

9.2.2

It is envisaged that a national coordinator[12] will be appointed to deal with overseeing the precise conditions[13] and general operation of the scheme and to monitor participation among lenders, the training of housing associations and the expenditure and results.[14]

---

[6] *ibid., para. 1.*
[7] *ibid.*, s.2, para. 11.
[8] *ibid.*, s.2, para. 12.
[9] *ibid.*, s.2, para. 13. The direct benefits to local authorities are the prevention of homelessness; avoidance of the need to process applications for housing and schooling; and reducing the burden on health authorities by cutting the number of rough sleepers or those who live in low quality accommodation. There are detailed calculations in the consultation paper (Annex B) on the savings to the community, compared with the cost of repossession, but these have been criticised by, *inter alia*, the CML who have asserted that some of the figures (for example court costs) included by the Executive in their calculations as a cost to the public are truly borne by others (largely the creditors or debtors).
[10] Including in West Lothian, North Lanarkshire and Clackmannanshire. The scheme was originally introduced in the early 1990s following a recognition by creditors and government that an alternative approach was required to deal with arrears during the last recession. A similar scheme is being introduced in Wales but it is believed there is no similar system in England.
[11] The provision of funding (see para. 9.2.4) will be through Communities Scotland which, in implementing the scheme, will effectively be making a grant to housing associations, for which it already has extensive powers.
[12] Hereafter referred to as "the NCO"; the post has already been advertised.
[13] Including the literature that will require to be produced to promulgate the scheme, how the scheme will affect housing associations and lenders in practice and many more of the precise operational details: Draft Consultation Paper, s.3, para. 2.
[14] It is recognised by the Scottish Executive that the first few years of the scheme will be something of a trial period following which the scheme may be subject to alteration or, if it is successful, there may be a move to permitting more flexible tenure of property generally.

Following an initial assessment of the eligibility of accounts in arrears, the creditor would take the decision of whether to refer the case to the NCO.[15] The NCO would undertake a more detailed assessment but, notwithstanding his involvement, the final decision of whether the scheme would be offered to the debtor would remain that of the creditor. If the lender chose not to proceed, it is said that that would be the end of the matter. On the other hand, if the creditor wished to proceed, the final details would be negotiated with the housing association and the debtor. The consultation paper suggested that the timescale from referral to the NCO to agreement on the final details should take a maximum of 22 working days.[16]

The CML has expressed concern about this timescale, particularly having regard to the administrative complexity of the scheme. In addition to an increase in creditors' costs, which would be added to the debtor's account, the delay over consideration of eligibility may cause arrears to mount further than would otherwise have been the case.

Eligibility[17]

9.2.3 Debtors would be ineligible for mortgage to rent where:

- The property is not the debtor's sole or main residence;
- The value of the property is greater than the national average in Scotland[18];
- The debtor has a second loan(s) for purposes other than for improvement or repair[19]; or
- The equity in the property exceeds £10,000.

Generally, creditors who have already tried out the scheme on a local basis regard it only as an option where the debtor is committed to resolving the difficulties. It is not used at present as a means for debtors to defer inevitable repossession.

Funding

9.2.4 The Scottish Executive has committed £9 million to the scheme over the next three years. The two methods of funding which the government would provide under the scheme are a rental subsidy and a payment towards repair costs. The subsidy would bring the rent down to the equivalent rent for similar properties in the locality, subject to a maximum contribution by the government of £25,000. The repairs payment, which would seek to improve housing quality in the private sector, would be offered subject to a maximum contribution of £6,000.[20]

---

[15] Draft Consultation Paper, s.3, para. 4; the CML have suggested that a protocol to standardise procedures before referral to the NCO should be drawn up.

[16] Draft Consultation Paper, s.3, para. 7.

[17] These provisions are set out in Draft Consultation Paper, s.4, para. 2.

[18] Although the figure for the national average is not provided, the paper indicates it would not be economical to include properties with a value above £70,000. The national average is believed to be around £69,000 as at the date of publication.

[19] Including a holiday or wedding; but there may be cases where it is difficult or impossible to establish with any degree of certainty the purpose for which the second loan was taken out and that could cause further dispute between creditors and debtors as to when the scheme should operate.

[20] Draft Consultation Paper, s.4, para. 7.

Problems

The CML have expressed concern that the scheme has been introduced **9.2.5** without sufficient consultation. Some of the largest mortgage lenders in the United Kingdom have declined to become involved due to the possible difficulty in release of information to the NCO having regard to data protection legislation.[21] Further outstanding issues include an appeals procedure for debtors refused mortgage to rent and whether there is a conflict of interest for creditors who assist debtors in this way.

A pressing concern with the scheme for creditors is how it will interact with the 2001 Act. As discussed above, the creditor has the key decision making role in the process. However, what if the creditor, at the initial sift stage, decides that the debtor is ineligible? Will the debtor, refused under the *Mortgage to Rent Scheme*, be able to rely on this fact in a mortgage rights application? Will he be able to say that the creditor's failure to operate the scheme in his case is a failure by the creditor (no matter what else it has done) to help him fulfil the obligations in default?[22]

This possibility may cause difficulties for creditors who decline to participate in the scheme at all. The Scottish Executive have said that they expect courts to recognise the voluntary nature of the mortgage to rent scheme when considering applications under the 2001 Act. Nonetheless, creditors have expressed concern as to whether debtors will be able to use such a consideration of the 2001 Act by a sheriff to mount what would effectively be an appeal against the creditor's decision on application of the mortgage to rent scheme. As noted above, there is currently no mechanism for resolving disputes between the creditor and debtor as to whether the debtor is indeed eligible for assistance under the mortgage to rent scheme. If courts do grant section 2 orders under the 2001 Act, on the basis that the creditor, in declining to operate the scheme in a particular case has not done all it could, the scheme will not be truly voluntary in nature. Rather, it may become virtually compulsory as a matter of practice. This is a source of particular concern when the scheme is not regulated by statutory provisions.

A further potential problem may arise from funding envisaged by the Scottish Executive. If funding is running low or has run out in a particular year, sheriffs may be asked to grant a section 2 order under the 2001 Act suspending the creditor's exercise of rights until the next year's *Mortgage to Rent Scheme* funding becomes available. The debtor could argue that such future funding means there is a reasonable period within which he will be able to fulfil his obligations.[23]

The potential conflict which could arise between the *Mortgage to Rent Scheme* and the 2001 Act is of particular concern to creditors as the former will only apply where there are low levels of equity in the property.

---

[21] Whereas if the requirement to co-operate was made mandatory by statute, that difficulty would be overcome: see para. 4.2.27.

[22] A consideration under s.2(2)(c) of the 2001 Act.

[23] s.2(2)(b) of the 2001 Act.

Conclusion

9.2.6 When the consultation paper was issued, it indicated that implementation was planned for Autumn 2001 for an initial three year period. The scheme is already well behind schedule, not least because of the lack of consultation at an earlier stage and the lukewarm reaction from the lending industry.[24] Nonetheless, the existence of the scheme on a local level and the determination of the Scottish Executive to see this through makes it likely that the scheme will be pushed through during the summer of 2002 and that mortgage to rent, like mortgage rights, will be a reality.

9.3 Changes to the Law of Diligence

Report on Diligence

9.3.1 In May 2001, the Scottish Law Commission issued its *Report on Diligence*.[25] Several new methods of enforcement were proposed including land attachments and attachments, both of which may have implications for secured creditors considering repossession. The Commission has also recommended the abolition of adjudication for debt.[26] The Scottish Executive has indicated that it is minded to implement the Commission's recommendations.[26a]

Land Attachment

9.3.2 The new diligence of land attachment would allow initially unsecured creditors to convert their debt into one which would give them the right to apply for warrant to sell subjects owned by the debtor.

It is proposed that following expiry of a charge,[27] an unpaid creditor would be entitled register a notice of land attachment in the property registers. Fourteen days after registration of the notice, the creditor would acquire a subordinate real right in security for payment of the debt. For those first 14 days, the notice will have the same effect as an inhibition restricted to the land in question. After six months, the creditor would apply to the court for authority to sell the land to pay or reduce the debt. If sale was impossible, the creditor could apply for decree of foreclosure.[28]

The diligence might be made available against a debtor's principal house[29] and there would be no limit, high or low, on the size of debt

---

[24] The CML complained that proposed introduction at that time did not allow sufficient opportunity for consultation on and review of the scheme.

[25] Scot Law Com. No. 183. The full text is available at http://*www.scotlawcom.gov.uk/*.

[26] *Report on Diligence*, para. 2.14.

[26a] *Enforcement of Civil Obligations in Scotland—A Consultation Paper*, April 2002, para. 5.293. The full text of the paper is available at *www.scotland.gsi.gov.uk/consultations/justice/ CivOb-00.asp*.

[27] Land attachment would not be competent on the dependence of the action: *Report on Diligence*, para. 3–39.

[28] *Report on Diligence*, para. 3.32.

[29] But the Commission has declined to make a recommendation on whether the principal dwellinghouse of the debtor could be sold: *Report on Diligence*, para. 3.32; see also para. 3.109 for the proposed definition of "principal dwellinghouse". The Scottish Executive favours the view that sale of the principal dwellinghouse should be permitted subject to appropriate debtor protection: *Enforcement of Civil Obligations in Scotland—A Consultation Paper*, April 2002, para. 5.290.

which could give rise to a notice of land attachment. Authority to sell the land could only be granted by the court if the debt was £1,500 or more at the time of the application to sell. Further, to justify the granting of authority to sell, the net sale proceeds would require to meet at least the expenses of the diligence and to allow the debt to be reduced by the lower of £500 or 10 per cent of the debt.[30] Authority to sell could be granted even where the property is jointly owned with another party although the court might take this into account in deciding whether to grant an application by the creditor.

When the application to sell is made, the court would grant an order requiring any prior security holder to disclose the amount outstanding and make an order appointing a surveyor to report on the open market value of the land. In considering whether to grant warrant of sale, the court would be directed to refuse the application for warrant if it was reasonable to do so in all the circumstances. In assessing what is reasonable, the sheriff would require to have regard to the nature of the debt and the reasons for its being incurred; the debtor's ability to pay the debt within an extended period; any action taken by the creditor to assist the debtor to fulfil his obligations; the ability of those living at the property to obtain reasonable alternative accommodation; and the personal circumstances of any such occupiers.[31]

If authority to sell is granted, a "suitably independent solicitor" would be appointed by the court to market and sell the attached land.[32] On sale, the proceeds would be applied as follows[33]:

(i) The creditor's sale expenses;
(ii) The sums due to prior security holders (so far as possible from sale proceeds);
(iii) The amount due to the attaching creditor and any creditors ranking *pari passu* ; and
(iv) The sums due to secured creditors (including creditors who have exercised diligence) postponed to the attaching creditor.

Attachment

A further diligence would also be available to the creditor in the form of an attachment which is proposed as the replacement for adjudication.[34] Such a diligence would be capable of attaching all property which is capable of being transferred, including moveable property.[35] As with land attachments, an attachment order would give the creditor a right over the attached property in security of payment of the debt, interest and expenses.[36] The creditor would then have the right to apply for a satisfaction order which would seek to satisfy the creditor's debt out of the attached property.[37] The satisfaction order referred to could be for

9.3.3

---

[30] *Report on Diligence*, para. 3.99.
[31] *ibid.*, para. 3.124.
[32] *ibid.*, para. 3.150.
[33] *ibid.*, para. 3.164.
[34] *ibid.*, para. 4.6.
[35] *ibid.*, para. 4.14.
[36] *ibid.*, para. 4.68.
[37] *ibid.*, para. 4.82.

various remedies including sale of the property and payment of the net free proceeds to the creditor or an order vesting the attached property in the creditor at a price fixed by the court. The proceeds of the diligence would be ascribed to the expenses of the diligence, interest on the sum due under the decree and then any other sum due on the decree (including the debt itself) in that order.[38]

Practical Effects

9.3.4 It is clear that the use of these new diligences recommended by the Scottish Law Commission could have the effect of bringing the field on unsecured debt recovery closer to that of repossessions, with a creditor acquiring rights in security which may allow him to sell the security subjects. The direct effect for heritable creditors, however, is less obvious but still tangible. First, secured creditors will have less control over the security subjects, in that they may be sold by a previously unsecured creditor in circumstances the originally secured creditor would not have wished. Secondly, those heritable creditors working at high loan to value ratios and tight profit margins will be alarmed by the recommendations that the expenses of the sale will be a first charge on the sale proceeds. Creditors in this field tend to have strict control over the level of sale costs they are prepared to pay but the same may not be said of the unsecured creditor who has obtained a warrant to sell based on one of the proposed new diligences.

9.4 Regulation of Repossessions by the Financial Services Authority[39]

Background

9.4.1 In June 2001, the FSA issued *Consultation Paper 98: The Draft Mortgage Sourcebook, Including Policy Statement on CP70*, which has come to be known as *CP98*,[40] the purpose of which was to set out detailed policy proposals for mortgage regulation. The paper included a draft mortgage sourcebook, being the rules and guidance the FSA proposed to make to put their policy into effect. In relation to arrears and repossessions, new rules were proposed in relation to arrears policy and procedures, the provision of information to customers in arrears and the fair treatment of customers in payment difficulties.[41]

Policy Considerations

9.4.2 The draft rules in this area[42] proposed, first, that a creditor should take reasonable steps to ensure that its policy and procedures include using reasonable efforts to reach agreement with a debtor to repay arrears[43]

---

[38] *Report on Diligence*, para. 4.98.
[39] Hereafter "the FSA".
[40] The full text is available at http://www.fsa.gov.uk/pubs/cp/98/index.html.
[41] For discussion of the policy underlying the draft rules in this area, see *CP98*, Chap. 15, pp.88 *et seq.*
[42] Which are all contained in *CP98* Mortgage Sourcebook in Annex B at Chap. 12, thereof pp.302 *et seq.*
[43] Defined as two or more missed payments.

having regard to the desirability of agreeing an alternative to repossession; adopting a reasonable approach to the time over which arrears should be repaid; and repossessing only where all other reasonable attempts to resolve the position have failed.[44] In determining a reasonable repayment period, the FSA said expressly that it expects creditors to follow the principle established in *Cheltenham and Gloucester Building Society v. Norgan*,[45] namely that consideration of repayment over the remaining part of the original term of the advance would be appropriate.[46]

Provision of Information

9.4.3 On provision of information to the debtor, the FSA proposed that within five working days, a creditor must give the debtor a list of the due payments that have been missed; the total of the arrears; a note of charges incurred and likely to be incurred; information of the consequences of failure to deal with the arrears, including repossession; and confirmation that the creditor is willing to discuss proposals with the debtor.[47] Before a repossession action is commenced, the draft rules provided that a creditor must provide an update of the information above; ensure that the debtor is informed of the need to register with the local authority with a view to avoiding homelessness; and state the action which the creditor intends to take regarding repossession.[48]

Fair treatment of Debtors

9.4.4 The FSA's proposals on fair treatment of debtors include regular provision of information; prompt response to any communication from the debtor; and the avoidance of pressure being placed on the debtor by excessive telephone calls or correspondence, or contact at an unsocial hour.[49]

Finally, where repossession does take place, the creditor would require to market the property for sale as soon as possible and obtain the best price that might reasonably be paid taking account of mortgage conditions and the continuing increase in arrears.[50]

Current Position

9.4.5 At the time of publication of *CP98*, it was not intended that the FSA would regulate mortgage advice as opposed to other aspects of mortgage business. This approach was criticised and on December 12, 2001, a decision was taken that mortgage advice would indeed be included within the ambit of FSA regulation. As a result, *CP98* was withdrawn. However, a further Consultation Paper is due to be issued by the FSA in summer 2002 and it is believed that the provisions on proposed

---

[44] *CP98* Mortgage Sourcebook, para. 12.3.2.
[45] [1996] 1 All E.R. 449; see para. 4.3.1.
[46] *CP98* Mortgage Sourcebook, para. 12.3.4.
[47] *ibid.*, para. 12.4.1.
[48] *ibid.*, para. 12.4.3.
[49] *ibid.*, para. 12.5.
[50] *ibid.*, para. 12.6.1.

regulation of arrears and possessions will be more or less identical to those set out above. The delay does mean however that the new rules are unlikely to be in place before April 2004. It is thought that the rules will not apply to postponed security holders, to current account loans or to securities granted before the regulations come into force.

While the rules will not apply for some time and, even then, will exclude from their provisions certain secured loans, there are several issues of importance which may conflict with the current Scottish legal position. The draft proposals set out above suggest at least that Scottish courts may be directed to make section 2 orders to the effect that repayment of arrears should be over the whole remaining term of the loan[51]; and that the creditor who has repossessed may no longer be entitled to sell at a time of his own choosing.[52]

Other Developments

9.5 There are likely to be changes affecting heritable creditors in the law on consumer credit which have been considered above.[53] The Scottish Executive is also considering pre-eviction procedure and the responsibility of creditors in respect of moveables following repossession.[54]

---

[51] For the current legal position, see para. 4.2.11.
[52] For the current legal position, see para. 8.10.
[53] See para. 2.5.
[54] See paras 5.22 and 7.3.

APPENDIX 1

MORTGAGE RIGHTS (SCOTLAND) ACT 2001

(2001 asp 11)

CONTENTS

	Section
Application to suspend enforcement of standard security	1
Disposal of application	2
Registration of order under section 2	3
Notices to debtors, proprietors and occupiers	4
Crown application	5
Interpretation	6
Commencement and short title	7

Schedule

Notices to debtors, proprietors and occupiers	
—Amendments to Schedule 6 to the 1970 Act	Part I
—Forms relating to proceedings under section 5 of the 1894 Act	Part II

The Bill for this Act of the Scottish Parliament was passed by the Parliament on 20th June 2001 and received Royal Assent on 25th July 2001

An Act of the Scottish Parliament to provide for the suspension in certain circumstances of enforcement rights of a creditor in a standard security over property used for residential purposes and the continuation of proceedings relating to those rights; to make provision for notifying tenants and other occupiers of enforcement action by a creditor in a standard security; and for connected purposes.

Application to suspend enforcement of standard security

1.—(1) This section applies where a creditor in a standard security over an interest in land used to any extent for residential purposes has—

(a) served—

(i) a calling-up notice under section 19 (calling-up of standard security), or

(ii) a notice of default under section 21 (notice of default),

(b) made an application to the court under section 24 (application to court for remedies on default) of that Act, or

(c) commenced proceedings under section 5 (power to eject proprietor in personal occupancy) of the Heritable Securities (Scotland) Act 1894 (c.44) (in this Act referred to as "the 1894 Act").

10.1

(2) The following persons may apply to the court for an order under section 2 of this Act—

(a) the debtor in the standard security or the proprietor of the security subjects (where the proprietor is not the debtor), if the security subjects (in whole or in part) are that person's sole or main residence,

(b) the non-entitled spouse of the debtor or the proprietor, where the security subjects (in whole or in part) are a matrimonial home and the sole or main residence of the non-entitled spouse,

(c) a person living together with the debtor or the proprietor as husband or wife or in a relationship which has the characteristics of the relationship between husband and wife except that the persons are of the same sex, if the security subjects (in whole or in part) are that person's sole or main residence,

(d) a person who has lived together with the debtor or the proprietor as mentioned in paragraph (c), if—

   (i) the security subjects (in whole or in part) are the sole or main residence of that person but not of the debtor or, as the case may be, the proprietor,
   (ii) that person lived together with the debtor or the proprietor as mentioned in that paragraph throughout the period of 6 months ending with the date on which the security subjects ceased to be the sole or main residence of the debtor or the proprietor, and
   (iii) the security subjects (in whole or in part) are the sole or main residence of a child under the age of 16 years who is a child of that person and of the debtor or the proprietor.

(3) In paragraph (d)(iii) of subsection (2), "child" includes a stepchild and any person brought up or treated by the person mentioned in that paragraph and the debtor or the proprietor as their child.

(4) An application under subsection (2) must be made—

(a) in the case mentioned in subsection (1)(a)(i), before the expiry of the period of notice in relation to the calling-up notice,

(b) in the case mentioned in subsection (1)(a)(ii), not later than one month after the expiry of the period of notice specified in the notice of default,

(c) in a case mentioned in subsection (1)(b) or (c), before the conclusion of the proceedings.

(5) The period of one month mentioned in subsection (4)(b) may be dispensed with or shortened by the person on whom the notice of default has been served, but only with the consent in writing of-

(a) any other person on whom the notice of default has been served,

Appendix 1 175

- (b) if the standard security is over a matrimonial home, the spouse of each person on whom the notice of default has been served, and
- (c) any person entitled to make an application under subsection (2) by virtue of paragraph (c) or (d) of that subsection.

(6) An application under subsection (2) in a case mentioned in subsection (1)(a) must be made by summary application.

(7) Any rights which the creditor has, or acquires, by virtue of the enactments mentioned in subsection (1)(a) to (c) may not be exercised—

- (a) at any time when an application under subsection (2) is competent,
- (b) at any time when such an application has been made but has not been determined.

(8) In a case mentioned in subsection (1)(a)—

- (a) section 19 (calling-up of standard security) of the 1970 Act has effect as if—
  - (i) in subsection (10), the words "effectively dispensed with or" and "dispense with or" were omitted,
  - (ii) after subsection (10) there were inserted—

  "(10A) Subsection (10) above does not permit the period of notice mentioned in the calling-up notice to be shortened to a period of less than one month.

  (10B) The period of notice mentioned in the calling-up notice may be shortened under subsection (10) above only with the consent in writing (in addition to any consent required by that subsection) of—
  - (a) any person entitled to make an application under subsection (2) of section 1 (application to suspend enforcement of standard security) of the Mortgage Rights (Scotland) Act 2001 (asp 11) by virtue of paragraph (c) or (d) of that subsection, and
  - (b) where the debtor in the standard security is not the proprietor—
    - (i) the debtor, and
    - (ii) if the standard security is over a matrimonial home (within the definition referred to in that subsection), the debtor's spouse.",
- (b) section 21 (notice of default) of that Act has effect as if subsection (3) of that section were omitted, and
- (c) Form C in Schedule 6 (procedures as to calling-up and default) to that Act has effect as if the words "dispensed with (or" were omitted.

Disposal of application

2.—(1) On an application under section 1(2) the court may— 10.2

(a) suspend the exercise of the rights which the creditor has, or may acquire, by virtue of the enactments mentioned in subsection (1)(a) to (c) of that section—

   (i) to such extent,
   (ii) for such period, and
   (iii) subject to such conditions,

   as the court thinks fit,

(b) if the application is made in proceedings under section 24 of the 1970 Act or section 5 of the 1894 Act, continue those proceedings to such date as the court thinks fit.

(2) The court may make an order under this section only where it considers it reasonable in all the circumstances to do so; and the court, in considering whether to make such an order and what its terms should be, is to have regard in particular to—

(a) the nature of and reasons for the default,

(b) the applicant's ability to fulfil within a reasonable period the obligations under the standard security in respect of which the debtor is in default,

(c) any action taken by the creditor to assist the debtor to fulfil those obligations, and

(d) the ability of the applicant and any other person residing at the security subjects to secure reasonable alternative accommodation.

(3) If, while an order under this section is in force, the obligations under the standard security in respect of which the debtor is in default are fulfilled, the standard security has effect as if the default had not occurred.

(4) In relation to an application under section 1(2) in the case mentioned in subsection (1)(a)(i) of that section, the preceding provisions of this section have effect with the following modifications—

(a) the power to specify a period in pursuance of subsection (1)(a) includes, without prejudice to the generality of that provision, power to specify the period which expires on the calling-up notice ceasing to have effect by virtue of section 19(11) of the 1970 Act,

(b) subsection (2)(a) is to be read as referring to the circumstances giving rise to the service of the calling-up notice,

(c) subsection (2)(b) is to be read as referring to the ability of the applicant to comply with the notice within a reasonable period,

(d) subsection (2)(c) is to be read as referring to any action taken by the creditor to assist the debtor to fulfil the debtor's obligations under the standard security, and

(e) subsection (3) does not apply.

(5) The court may, if requested to do so by the creditor or the applicant—

(a) vary or revoke an order made under subsection (1)(a),

(b) further continue proceedings continued under subsection (1)(b).

(6) Section 1 and this section are without prejudice to any rights which a debtor, proprietor or non-entitled spouse may have under any other enactment or rule of law.

(7) In section 1 and this section—

"applicant" means the person who makes an application under section 1(2),
"court" means the sheriff court,
"matrimonial home" and "non-entitled spouse" are to be construed in accordance with the Matrimonial Homes (Family Protection) (Scotland) Act 1981 (c.59).

Registration of order under section 2

3.—(1) Where the court makes an order under section 2 the clerk of court must, as soon as possible, send to the Keeper of the Register of Inhibitions and Adjudications, for recording in that Register—

(a) a certified copy of the order, and

(b) a notice complying with subsection (2).

(2) A notice referred to in subsection (1)(b)—

(a) must be in such form, and

(b) must contain such particulars of the order, the proceedings in which it was made and the standard security,

as may be prescribed by the Scottish Ministers by order made by statutory instrument.

(3) A statutory instrument containing an order under subsection (2) is subject to annulment in pursuance of a resolution of the Scottish Parliament.

10.3

Notices to debtors, proprietors and occupiers

4.—(1) After section 19 of the 1970 Act there is inserted—

"19A Notice to occupier of calling-up
(1) Where a creditor in a standard security over an interest in land used to any extent for residential purposes serves a calling-up

notice, he shall serve a notice in conformity with Form BB (notice to occupier) of Schedule 6 to this Act together with a copy of the calling-up notice.

(2) Notices under subsection (1) above shall be sent by recorded delivery letter addressed to "The Occupier" at the security subjects.

(3) If a creditor fails to comply with subsections (1) and (2) above, the calling-up notice shall be of no effect."

(2) In section 21 (notice of default) of that Act, after subsection (2) there is inserted—

"(2A) Section 19A of this Act applies where the creditor serves a notice of default as it applies where he serves a calling-up notice."

(3) In section 24 (application by creditor to court for remedies on default) of that Act, after subsection (2) there is inserted—

"(3) Where the creditor applies to the court under subsection (1) above, he shall, if the standard security is over an interest in land used to any extent for residential purposes—

> (a) serve on the debtor and (where the proprietor is not the debtor) on the proprietor a notice in conformity with Form E of Schedule 6 to this Act, and
> (b) serve on the occupier of the security subjects a notice in conformity with Form F of that Schedule.

(4) Notices under subsection (3) above shall be sent by recorded delivery letter addressed—

> (a) in the case of a notice under subsection (3)(a), to the debtor or, as the case may be, the proprietor at his last known address,
> (b) in the case of a notice under subsection (3)(b), to "The Occupier" at the security subjects."

(4) Where a creditor in a standard security over an interest in land used to any extent for residential purposes commences proceedings under section 5 (power to eject proprietor in personal occupancy) of the 1894 Act, the creditor must—

> (a) serve on the proprietor a notice in conformity with Form 1 in Part 2 of the schedule to this Act, and
> (b) serve on the occupier of the security subjects a notice in conformity with Form 2 in that Part of that schedule.

(5) Notices under subsection (4) must be sent by recorded delivery letter addressed—

> (a) in the case of a notice under subsection (4)(a), to the proprietor at the proprietor's last known address,
> (b) in the case of a notice under subsection (4)(b), to "The Occupier" at the security subjects.

(6) The schedule to this Act, Part 1 of which amends Schedule 6 to the 1970 Act (forms to be used in relation to calling-up and default) and Part 2 of which sets out the Forms referred to in subsection (4), has effect.

(7) The Scottish Ministers may, by order made by statutory instrument, amend—

> (a) the Notes inserted in Forms A and B in Schedule 6 to the 1970 Act by Part 1 of the schedule to this Act,
>
> (b) Forms BB, E and F in Schedule 6 to the 1970 Act,
>
> (c) the Forms set out in Part 2 of the schedule to this Act.

(8) A statutory instrument containing an order under subsection (7) is subject to annulment in pursuance of a resolution of the Scottish Parliament.

Crown application

5. This Act binds the Crown.

Interpretation

6. Except so far as the context otherwise requires, expressions used in this Act and in Part II of the 1970 Act have the same meanings in this Act as they have in that Part.

Commencement and short title

7.—(1) The preceding provisions of this Act come into force on such day as the Scottish Ministers may by order made by statutory instrument appoint.

(2) An order under subsection (1) may include such transitional and transitory provisions and savings as the Scottish Ministers think expedient.

(3) This Act may be cited as the Mortgage Rights (Scotland) Act 2001.

SCHEDULE
(introduced by section 4)

NOTICES TO DEBTORS, PROPRIETORS AND OCCUPIERS

PART 1

AMENDMENTS TO SCHEDULE 6 TO THE 1970 ACT

1. Schedule 6 to the 1970 Act (forms to be used in connection with calling-up of, or default under, standard security) is amended as follows.

2. In Form A (notice of calling-up of standard security) there is inserted, at the end of the notice—

> "**NOTE**: The Mortgage Rights (Scotland) Act 2001 gives you the right in certain circumstances to apply to the court to suspend the rights of C.D.

You have two months (which may be shortened only with your consent) to make an application. The court will have regard in particular to the circumstances giving rise to the service of this notice, your ability to comply with this notice, any action taken by C.D. to assist the debtor in the standard security to fulfil the obligations under it and the ability of you and anyone else residing at the property to find reasonable alternative accommodation. If you wish to make such an application, you should consult a solicitor. You may be eligible for legal aid depending on your circumstances, and you can get information about legal aid from a solicitor. You may also be able to get advice, including advice about how to manage debt, from any Citizens Advice Bureau or from other advice agencies."

10.12 3. In Form B (notice of default under standard security) there is inserted, at the end of the notice—

"**NOTE**: The Mortgage Rights (Scotland) Act 2001 gives you the right in certain circumstances to apply to the court to suspend the rights of C.D. You have two months (which may be shortened only with your consent) to make an application. The court will have regard in particular to the nature of and reasons for the default, your ability to fulfil the obligations under the standard security, any action taken by C.D. to assist the debtor in the standard security to fulfil those obligations and the ability of you and anyone else residing at the property to find reasonable alternative accommodation. If you wish to make such an application, you should consult a solicitor. You may be eligible for legal aid depending on your circumstances, and you can get information about legal aid from a solicitor. You may also be able to get advice, including advice about how to manage debt, from any Citizens Advice Bureau or from other advice agencies."

10.13 4. After Form B there is inserted—

"FORM BB

NOTICE TO OCCUPIER

To the Occupier (*address*)

A Notice of Calling-up of a standard security/Default under a standard security (*delete as appropriate*) has been served by C.D. on A.B. in relation to (*address of subjects*). A copy of the notice is attached.

If you are a tenant of A.B., in certain circumstances C.D. cannot take possession of the property without a court order. You should obtain legal advice about your rights as a tenant. You may be eligible for legal aid depending on your circumstances, and you can get information about legal aid from a solicitor. You may also be able to get advice from any Citizens Advice Bureau or from other advice agencies.

If you are the spouse or partner of A.B., the Mortgage Rights (Scotland) Act 2001 gives you the right in certain circumstances to apply to the court to suspend the rights of C.D. You have two months (which may be shortened only with your consent) to make an application. The court will have regard in particular to—

(*for a Notice of Calling-up*) the circumstances giving rise to the service of the Notice of Calling-up, your ability to comply with the notice, any action taken by C.D. to assist the debtor in the standard security to fulfil the obligations under it and the ability of you and anyone else residing at the property to find reasonable alternative accommodation.

(*for a notice of default*) the nature of and reasons for the default, your ability to fulfil the obligations under the standard security, any action taken

Appendix 1

by C.D. to assist the debtor in the standard security to fulfil those obligations and the ability of you and anyone else residing at the property to find reasonable alternative accommodation.
(*delete as appropriate*)
If you wish to make such an application, you should consult a solicitor. You may be eligible for legal aid depending on your circumstances, and you can get information about legal aid from a solicitor. You may also be able to get advice, including advice about how to manage debt, from any Citizens Advice Bureau or from other advice agencies.

Dated
(*Signature of C.D., or signature and designation of C.D.'s agent followed by the words Agent of C.D.*)"

5. After Form D there is inserted— **10.14**

"FORM E

To A.B. (*address*)
C.D. (*designation*), the creditor in a standard security by you (or by E.F.) in favour of C.D. (*or* of G.H. to which C.D. now has right) recorded in the Register for (*or, as the case may be*, registered in the Land Register for Scotland) on (*date*) has applied to the court under section 24 of the Conveyancing and Feudal Reform (Scotland) Act 1970 for warrant to exercise in relation to (*address of security subjects*) remedies to which he is entitled on the following default—
(*specify in detail the default in respect of which the application is made*)
A copy of the application is attached.

Dated
(*Signature of C.D., or signature and designation of C.D.'s agent followed by the words* Agent of C.D.)

NOTE: The Mortgage Rights (Scotland) Act 2001 gives you the right in certain circumstances to apply to the court for suspension of the rights of C.D. The court will have regard in particular to the nature of and reasons for the default, your ability to fulfil the obligations under the standard security, any action taken by C.D. to assist the debtor in the standard security to fulfil those obligations and the ability of you and anyone else residing at the property to find reasonable alternative accommodation. If you wish to make such an application, you should consult a solicitor. You may be eligible for legal aid depending on your circumstances, and you can get information about legal aid from a solicitor. You may also be able to get advice, including advice about how to manage debt, from any Citizens Advice Bureau or from other advice agencies.

FORM F

To the Occupier (*address*)
C.D. (*designation*) has applied to the court under section 24 of the Conveyancing and Feudal Reform (Scotland) Act 1970 for warrant to exercise in relation to (*address of security subjects*) remedies to which he is entitled on the default of A.B. (*designation*) in the performance of his obligations under a standard security over (*address of subjects*). A copy of the application is attached.
If you are a tenant of A.B. (or, if A.B. is not the proprietor of the subjects, of E.F. (being the proprietor)), in certain circumstances C.D. cannot take

possession of the property without a court order. You should obtain legal advice about your rights as a tenant. You may be eligible for legal aid depending on your circumstances, and you can get information about legal aid from a solicitor. You may also be able to get advice from any Citizens Advice Bureau or from other advice agencies. If you are the spouse or partner of A.B., the Mortgage Rights (Scotland) Act 2001 gives you the right in certain circumstances to apply to the court to suspend the rights of C.D. The court will have regard in particular to the nature of and reasons for the default, your ability to fulfil the obligations under the standard security, any action taken by C.D. to assist the debtor in the standard security to fulfil those obligations and the ability of you and anyone else residing at the property to find reasonable alternative accommodation. If you wish to make such an application, you should consult a solicitor. You may be eligible for legal aid depending on your circumstances, and you can get information about legal aid from a solicitor. You may also be able to get advice, including advice about how to manage debt, from any Citizens Advice Bureau or from other advice agencies.

Dated
(*Signature of C.D., or signature and designation of C.D.'s agent followed by the words* Agent of C.D.)"

10.15

PART 2

FORMS RELATING TO PROCEEDINGS UNDER SECTION 5 OF THE 1894 ACT

FORM 1

10.16 To A.B. (*address*)
C.D. (*designation*), the creditor in a standard security by you (*or* by E.F.) in favour of C.D. (*or* of G.H. to which C.D. now has right) recorded in the Register for (or, as the case may be, registered in the Land Register for Scotland) on (*date*) has commenced proceedings against you under section 5 of the Heritable Securities (Scotland) Act 1894 to eject you from (*address of security subjects*). A copy of the initial writ is attached.

Dated
(*Signature of C.D., or signature and designation of C.D.'s agent followed by the words* Agent of C.D.)

NOTE: The Mortgage Rights (Scotland) Act 2001 gives you the right in certain circumstances to apply to the court for suspension of the rights of C.D. The court will have regard in particular to the nature of and reasons for the default, your ability to fulfil the obligations under the standard security, any action taken by C.D. to assist the debtor in the standard security to fulfil those obligations and the ability of you and anyone else residing at the property to find reasonable alternative accommodation. If you wish to make such an application, you should consult a solicitor. You may be eligible for legal aid depending on your circumstances, and you can get information about legal aid from a solicitor. You may also be able to get advice, including advice about how to manage debt, from any Citizens Advice Bureau or from other advice agencies.

FORM 2

10.17 To the Occupier (*address*)
C.D. (*designation*) has commenced proceedings under section 5 of the Heritable Securities (Scotland) Act 1894 to eject A.B. from (*address of security subjects*). A copy of the initial writ is attached.

Appendix 1

If you are a tenant of A.B., in certain circumstances C.D. cannot take possession of the property without a court order. You should obtain legal advice about your rights as a tenant. You may be eligible for legal aid depending on your circumstances, and you can get information about legal aid from a solicitor. You may also be able to get advice from any Citizens Advice Bureau or from other advice agencies.

If you are the spouse or partner of A.B., the Mortgage Rights (Scotland) Act 2001 gives you the right in certain circumstances to apply to the court to suspend the rights of C.D. The court will have regard in particular to the nature of and reasons for the default, your ability to fulfil the obligations under the standard security, any action taken by C.D. to assist the debtor in the standard security to fulfil those obligations and the ability of you and anyone else residing at the property to find reasonable alternative accommodation. If you wish to make such an application, you should consult a solicitor. You may be eligible for legal aid depending on your circumstances, and you can get information about legal aid from a solicitor. You may also be able to get advice, including advice about how to manage debt, from any Citizens Advice Bureau or from other advice agencies.

Dated
(*Signature of C.D., or signature and designation of C.D.'s agent followed by the words* Agent of C.D.)

APPENDIX 2

SCOTTISH STATUTORY INSTRUMENTS MADE UNDER OR IN RELATION TO THE MORTGAGE RIGHTS (SCOTLAND) ACT 2001

11.1 The Mortgage Rights (Scotland) Act 2001 (Commencement and Transitional Provision) Order 2001

(S.S.I. 2001 No. 418 (C. 18))

Made   *8th November 2001*

Citation and interpretation

1.—(1) This Order may be cited as the Mortgage Rights (Scotland) Act 2001 (Commencement and Transitional Provision) Order 2001.
(2) In this Order "the Act" means the Mortgage Rights (Scotland) Act 2001.

Appointed day

2. The day appointed for the coming into force of the Act is 3rd December 2001.

Transitional provision

3. The Act shall not apply in a case where—

(a) a notice as mentioned in section 1(1)(a) of the Act is served;

(b) the application as mentioned in sub-paragraph (b) of that subsection is made; or

(c) the proceedings as mentioned in sub-paragraph (c) of that subsection are commenced;
before 3rd December 2001.

EXPLANATORY NOTE

(This note is not part of the Order)

This Order appoints 3rd December 2001 as the day on which the Mortgage Rights (Scotland) Act 2001 ("the Act") will come into force (article 2).

Article 3 makes transitional provision in respect of notices, applications and proceedings referred to in section 1(1) of the Act that have been served, made or commenced prior to 3rd December 2001. The Act will not apply in those circumstances.

Appendix 2 185

The Mortgage Rights (Scotland) Act 2001   **11.2**
(Prescribed Notice) Order 2001

(S.S.I. 2001 No. 419)

Made	*8th November 2001*
Laid before the Scottish Parliament	*12th November 2001*
Coming into force	*3rd December 2001*

Citation and commencement

1. This Order may be cited as the Mortgage Rights (Scotland) Act 2001 (Prescribed Notice) Order 2001 and shall come into force on 3rd December 2001.

Prescribed notice

2. The form of the notice contained in the Schedule to this Order, and the particulars contained in that notice, are hereby prescribed for the purposes of section 3(2) of the Mortgage Rights (Scotland) Act 2001.

SCHEDULE

Article 2

NOTICE

SHERIFF COURT, (*insert place of sheriff court*)

Date of order, (*insert date*)
A.B. (*insert designation and address*), **PURSUER(S)**

against

C.D. (*insert designation and address*), **DEFENDER(S)**

The Sheriff of (*insert name of sheriffdom*) at (*insert place of sheriff court*) has made an order, (*insert date*) under section 2 of the Mortgage Rights (Scotland) Act 2001—

    (*to suspend*) suspending for a period of (*insert period of suspension*) from (*give date on which suspension begins*) the exercise of the rights which the said C.D has or may acquire by virtue of the Conveyancing and Feudal Reform (Scotland) Act 1970 or the Heritable Securities (Scotland) Act 1894
    (*to continue*) continuing proceedings under section 24 of the Conveyancing and Feudal Reform (Scotland) Act 1970 / section 5 of the Heritable Securities (Scotland) Act 1894 until (*insert date to which proceedings are continued*)
    (*to vary*) varying the order (*insert details of previous order*) as follows (*insert details of variation*)
    (*to revoke*) revoking the order (*insert details of previous order*)
(*delete as appropriate*)
in respect of Security Subjects (*enter address*) as referred to in Standard Security granted by (*insert name of Granter(s)*) in favour of (*insert name of Grantee(s)*),

(*insert date of recording, specifying the Division of the General Register of Sasines, or the date of registration in the Land Register, as the case may be*),

a copy of which Order is annexed.

(*insert name*)

Sheriff Clerk Depute

EXPLANATORY NOTE

(This note is not part of the Order)

This Order prescribes the notice that is to be sent to the Keeper of the Register of Inhibitions and Adjudications where an order is made by the court under section 2 of the Mortgage Rights (Scotland) Act 2001. The Schedule to this Order sets out the notice that is to be sent.

11.3 Act of Sederunt (Amendment of Ordinary Cause Rules and Summary Applications, Statutory Applications and Appeals etc. Rules) (Applications under the Mortgage Rights (Scotland) Act 2001) 2002

(S.S.I. 2002 No. 7)

Made	10th January 2002
Coming into force	17th January 2002

Citation, commencement and interpretation

1.—(1) This Act of Sederunt may be cited as the Act of Sederunt (Amendment of Ordinary Cause Rules and Summary Applications, Statutory Applications and Appeals etc. Rules) (Applications under the Mortgage Rights (Scotland) Act 2001) 2002 and shall come into force on 17th January 2002.

(2) This Act of Sederunt shall be inserted in the Books of Sederunt.

(3) In this Act of Sederunt—

"the Ordinary Cause Rules" means the First Schedule to the Sheriff Courts (Scotland) Act 1907[2] and a rule referred to by number in paragraph 2 of this Act of Sederunt means the rule so numbered in the Ordinary Cause Rules; and

"the Summary Applications Rules" means the Act of Sederunt (Summary Applications, Statutory Applications and Appeals etc. Rules) 1999 and a rule referred to by number in paragraph 3 of this Act of Sederunt means the rule so numbered in the Summary Applications Rules.

Amendment of the Ordinary Cause Rules

2.—(1) The Ordinary Cause Rules shall be amended in accordance with the following paragraphs.

(2) In rule 3.2 (actions relating to heritable property) insert at the end—

"(3) In an action falling within section 1(1)(b) or (c) of the Mortgage Rights (Scotland) Act 2001, the initial writ shall include averments about those persons who appear to the pursuer to be entitled to apply for an order under section 2 of that Act and such persons shall, so far as known to the pursuer, be called as defenders for their interest.".

(3) In rule 3.3 (warrants of citation)—

  (a) after paragraph (1)(c) insert—

    "(d) an action to which rule 3.2(3) applies,"; and

  (b) insert at the end—

    "(4) In an action to which rule 3.2(3) applies, the warrant of citation shall be in Form O2A.".

(4) In rule 5.2 (form of citation and certificate)—

  (a) at the end of paragraph (1)(b) omit "or";

  (b) at the end of paragraph (1)(c) insert "or";

  (c) after paragraph (1)(c) insert-

    "(d) an action to which rule 3.2(3) applies,"; and

  (d) after paragraph (2) insert—

    "(2A) In an action to which rule 3.2(3) applies, citation shall be in Form O5A which shall be attached to a copy of the initial writ and warrant of citation and shall have appended to it a notice of intention to defend in Form O7.".

(5) After rule 34.11 (service on unnamed occupiers), insert—

"Applications under the Mortgage Rights (Scotland) Act 2001
34.12.—(1) In an action to which rule 3.2(3) applies, an application under either of the following provisions of the Mortgage Rights (Scotland) Act 2001 shall be made by minute in the action:—

    (a) section 1(2) (application to the court for an order under section 2);

    (b) section 2(5) (application to vary or revoke an order or to further continue proceedings).

(2) Any such minute may be lodged by a person who is entitled to make an application even although that person has not been called as a defender and such a person may appear or be represented at any hearing to determine the application.".

(6) In Appendix 1 (forms)—

(a) after Form O2 insert Form O2A;

(b) after Form O5 insert Form O5A; and
(c) for Form O6 substitute Form O6,
set out in Schedule 1 to this Act of Sederunt.

Amendment of the Summary Applications Rules

3.—(1) The Summary Applications Rules shall be amended in accordance with the following paragraphs.
 (2) In rule 2.7 (warrants, forms and certificate of citation)—

(a) in paragraph (4)(a), for "paragraph (5)" substitute "paragraphs (5) and (7A)(a)";
(b) in paragraph (4)(b), for "paragraph (7)" substitute "paragraphs (7) and (7A)(b),"; and
(c) after paragraph (7) insert—

"(7A) In a summary application falling within section 1(1)(b) or (c) of the Mortgage Rights (Scotland) Act 2001—

(a) the warrant of citation shall be in Form 6A; and
(b) citation shall be in Form 6B which shall be attached to a copy of the initial writ and warrant of citation.".

 (3) After rule 2.22 (applications for time to pay directions), insert—

"Applications under the Mortgage Rights (Scotland) Act 2001
2.22A—(1) This rule applies to a summary application to which rule 2.7(7A) applies.
 (2) Subject to paragraph (3), an application under either of the following provisions of the Mortgage Rights (Scotland) Act 2001 shall be made by minute in the summary application—

(a) section 1(2) (application to the court for an order under section 2);
(b) section 2(5) (application to vary or revoke an order or to further continue proceedings).

 (3) A defender may apply orally for an order under section 2 when the summary application first calls in court or as the sheriff otherwise directs.
 (4) A minute under paragraph (2) may be lodged by a person who is entitled to make an application even although that person has not been called as a defender and such a person may appear or be represented at any hearing to determine the application made in the minute.
 (5) Except where the sheriff otherwise directs, any such minute shall be lodged in accordance with, and regulated by, Chapter 14 of the Ordinary Cause Rules.".

 (4) In Schedule 1 (forms)—

(a) after Form 6 insert Forms 6A and 6B; and

Appendix 2

(b) for Form 7 substitute Form 7,
set out in Schedule 2 to this Act of Sederunt.

SCHEDULE 1

Paragraph 2(6)

Rule 3.3(4)

FORM O2A
Form of warrant in an action to which rule 3.2(3) applies

(*Insert place and date*) Grants warrant to cite the defender (*insert name and address*) by serving a copy of the writ and warrant and Form O7 on a period of notice of (*insert period of notice*) days and ordains him [*or* her] if he [*or* she]—

(a) intends to defend the action or make any claim, to lodge a notice of intention to defend with the sheriff clerk at (*insert place of sheriff court*) within the said period of notice after such service [and grants warrant to arrest on the dependence]; or

(b) intends to apply for an order under section 2 of the Mortgage Rights (Scotland) Act 2001, to lodge a minute applying for an order under that section before the conclusion of the proceedings.

[Meantime grants interim interdict *or otherwise as the case may be.*]

Rule 5.2(2A)

FORM O5A
Form of citation in an action to which rule 3.2(3) applies

CITATION

SHERIFFDOM OF (*insert name of Sheriffdom*)

AT (*insert place of Sheriff Court*)
[A.B.], (*insert designation and address*) Pursuer against [C.D.], (*insert designation and address*),

Defender

Court Ref No:

(*Insert place and date*). You [C.D.], are hereby served with this copy writ and warrant, with Form O7 (notice of intention to defend).

Form O7 is served on you for your use should you wish to intimate an intention to defend this action.

IF YOU WISH TO DEFEND THIS ACTION you should consult a solicitor with a view to lodging a notice of intention to defend (Form O7). The notice of intention to defend, together with the court fee of £ (*insert amount*), must be lodged with the Sheriff Clerk at the above address within 21 days (*or insert the appropriate period of notice*) of (*insert the date on which service was executed NB Rule 5.3(2) relating to postal service*).

A copy of any notice of intention to defend should be sent to the Solicitor for the pursuer at the same time as your notice of intention to defend is lodged with the Sheriff Clerk.

IF YOU WISH TO MAKE AN APPLICATION FOR AN ORDER UNDER SECTION 2 OF THE MORTGAGE RIGHTS (SCOTLAND) ACT 2001 you should consult a solicitor with a view to lodging a minute applying for an order under that section. The minute, together with the court fee of £ *(insert amount)*, must be lodged with the Sheriff Clerk at the above address before the conclusion of the proceedings.

IF YOU ARE UNCERTAIN AS TO WHAT ACTION TO TAKE you should consult a solicitor. You may be eligible for legal aid depending on your income, and you can get information about legal aid from a solicitor. You may also obtain advice from any Citizens' Advice Bureau, or other advice agency.

PLEASE NOTE THAT IF YOU DO NOTHING IN ANSWER TO THIS DOCUMENT the court may regard you as admitting the claim made against you and the pursuer may obtain decree against you in your absence.

Signed

[P.Q.], sheriff officer,

or [X.Y.] *(add designation and business address)*

Solicitor for the Applicant

Rule 5.2(3)

FORM O6
Form of certificate of citation
CERTIFICATE OF CITATION

(Insert place and date) I, hereby certify that upon the day of I duly cited [C.D.], Defender, to answer to the foregoing writ. This I did by *(state method of service; if by officer and not by post, add*: in presence of [L.M.], *(insert designation)*, witness hereto with me subscribing; *and where service executed by post state whether by registered post or the first class recorded delivery service)*.

(In actions in which a time to pay direction may be applied for, state whether Form O2 and Form O3 were sent in accordance with rule 3.3).

(In actions to which rule 3.2(3) applies, state whether Form O2A was sent in accordance with rule 3.3).

Signed

[P.Q.], Sheriff officer

[L.M.], witness

or [X.Y.]. *(add designation and business address)*

Solicitor for the pursuer

SCHEDULE 2

Paragraph 3(4)

Rule 2.7(7A)(a)

FORM 6A
Form of warrant of citation in an application to which rule 2.7(7A) applies

(*Insert place and date*). Grants warrant to cite the defender (*insert name and address*) by serving a copy of the writ and warrant together with Form 6B [on a period of notice of (*insert period of notice*) days] and ordains him [*or* her] if he [*or* she]—

  (a) intends to defend the action or make any claim to answer within the Sheriff Court House (*insert place and address of sheriff court*) [in Room No , *or in chambers, or otherwise, as the case may be*] on the day of at o'clock noon] [*or otherwise, as the case may be*]; or

  (b) intends to apply for an order under section 2 of the Mortgage Rights (Scotland) Act 2001 to be present or represented at that diet.

Rule 2.7(7A)(b)

FORM 6B
Form of citation in an application to which rule 2.7(7A) applies

SHERIFFDOM OF (*insert name of sheriffdom*)

AT (*insert place of sheriff court*)

[A.B.], (*insert designation and address*) Pursuer

against

[C.D.], (*insert designation and address*) Defender

Court ref. no:

(Insert place and date). You [C.D.], are hereby served with this copy writ and warrant, and you are required to answer it.

IF YOU WISH TO MAKE AN APPLICATION FOR AN ORDER UNDER SECTION 2 OF THE MORTGAGE RIGHTS (SCOTLAND) ACT 2001 you should be present or represented at the diet on (*insert date and time*) within (*insert name and address of sheriff court*)

IF YOU ARE UNCERTAIN AS TO WHAT ACTION TO TAKE you should consult a solicitor. You may be eligible for legal aid depending on your income, and you can get information about legal aid from a solicitor. You may also obtain advice from any Citizens' Advice Bureau, or other advice agency.

PLEASE NOTE THAT IF YOU DO NOTHING IN ANSWER TO THIS DOCUMENT the court may regard you as admitting the claim made against you and the pursuer may obtain decree against you in your absence.

Signed

[P.Q.], sheriff officer,

or [X.Y.] (*add designation and business address*)

Solicitor for the Applicant

Rule 2.7(8)

FORM 7
Form of certificate of citation
CERTIFICATE OF CITATION

(Insert place and date) I, hereby certify that upon the day of I duly cited [C.D.], Defender, to answer the foregoing writ. I did this by (*state method of service; [if by officer and not by post, add*: in the presence of [L.M.], (*insert designation*), witness hereto with me subscribing;] *and where service executed by post state whether by registered post or the first class recorded delivery service*).

(*In actions in which a time to pay direction may be applied for, state whether Form 4 and Form 5 were sent in accordance with rule 2.7(5) and (6).*)

(*In actions in which an order under section 2 of the Mortgage Rights (Scotland) Act 2001 may be applied for, state whether Form 6B was sent in accordance with rule 2.7(7A)(b).*)

Signed

[P.Q.], sheriff officer

[L.M.], witness

or [X.Y.] (*add designation and business address*)

Solicitor for the Pursuer

EXPLANATORY NOTE

(*This note is not part of the Act of Sederunt*)

This Act of Sederunt amends the Ordinary Cause Rules and the Summary Applications Rules so as to regulate proceedings in which an order under section 2 of the Mortgage Rights (Scotland) Act 2001 ("the 2001 Act") may be applied for by a defender (being applications under section 24 of the Conveyancing and Feudal Reform (Scotland) Act 1970 and proceedings under section 5 of the Heritable Securities (Scotland) Act 1894).

Appendix 2

The Ordinary Cause Rules are amended as follows—

(a) Rule 3.2 is amended by inserting a new provision requiring the initial writ in a relevant action to include averments about those persons who appear to the pursuer to be entitled to apply for such an order and requiring such persons so far as known to the pursuer to be called as defenders for their interest (paragraph 2(2).

(b) Rule 3.3 is amended so that the warrant of citation in a relevant action is in a particular form (form O2A) (paragraph 2(3)).

(c) Rule 5.2 is amended so that the form of citation in a relevant action is in a particular form (form O5A) (paragraph 2(4)).

(d) A new rule 34.12 is inserted to provide a procedure to be followed when a person wishes to apply for an order under section 2 of the 2001 Act (paragraph 2(5)).

(e) Paragraph 2(6) inserts the new forms O2A and O5A. It also substitutes the form of certificate of citation in an action (form O6) with a new form that includes a reference to the sending of a form O2A.

The Summary Applications Rules are amended as follows:-

(a) Rule 2.7 is amended so that the warrant and form of citation in a relevant action are in particular forms (forms 6A and 6B) (paragraph 3(2)).

(b) A new rule 22.2A is inserted so as to provide a procedure to be followed when a person wishes to apply for an order under section 2 of the 2001 Act (paragraph 3(3)).

(c) Paragraph 3(4) inserts the new forms 6A and 6B. It also substitutes the form of certificate of citation in an application (form 7) with a new form that includes a reference to the sending of a form 6B.

APPENDIX 3

11.4 Style Minute under Rule 34.12(1) of the Ordinary Cause Rules for the making of an application for a Section 2 Order under the 2001 Act

SHERIFFDOM OF [****] AT [****]
MINUTE
For
[MINUTER NAME]
[MINUTER ADDRESS]
Minuter[1]

In the cause
[CREDITOR NAME]
[CREDITOR ADDRESS]
Pursuer and Respondent

Against
[DEFENDER NAME]
[DEFENDER ADDRESS]
Defender

The Minuter craves the Court:

1. To continue this action made and proceeding under Section 24 of the Conveyancing & Feudal Reform (Scotland) Act 1970, for a period of six months, or until such date as the Court thinks fit, subject to such conditions as the Court may consider appropriate, all in terms of terms of the Mortgage Rights (Scotland) Act 2001 section 2(1)(b)

OR

1. To suspend the exercise by the Pursuer of its rights, or rights which it may acquire, by sisting the action for a period of six months or until such date as the court thinks fit.}

2. To find the Pursuer and Respondent liable in expenses in the event of their opposition hereto.

STATEMENT OF FACTS

1. This action is for repossession of the subjects known as and forming [SECURITY ADDRESS]. The action founds on Section 24 of the Conveyancing and Feudal Reform (Scotland) Act 1970

---

[1] Or defender and minuter; references hereafter to Minuter may be adapted to Defender and Minuter with appropriate modifications to the text.

and as such is an application to the court in accordance with section 1(1)(b) of the 2001 Act. On or about [DATE OF SECURITY], [DEBTOR NAME] ("the debtor") granted a standard security over the subjects in favour of the Pursuer. The Pursuer now seek to enforce rights in terms of the standard security. The security subjects are the Minuter's sole or main residence. This Court accordingly has jurisdiction. The Minuter is the [DETAIL RELATIONSHIP] of the debtor and as such is entitled to make this application in terms of section 1(2) of the 2001 Act.

2. In terms of the loan by the Pursuer to the debtor, secured by the standard security, the debtor is obliged to make payments of [DETAIL PAYMENTS]. The debtor has failed to comply with said obligation. The current level of arrears is [SPECIFY ARREARS]. The debtor's failure to make payment has arisen because [REASON FOR ARREARS]. The debtor is making efforts to allow him to repay the arrears within a reasonable period. In particular, he is [SPECIFY EFFORTS, for example, looking for new employment]. The Minuter is unable to clear the arrears at present but is prepared to make a payment of [DETAIL PAYMENT] each month towards the arrears. Such payments would clear the arrears within a reasonable period.

3. The debtor received several communications from the Pursuer prior to the raising of this action. However, the Pursuer failed to offer the debtor [SPECIFY OMISSION, for example no debt counselling]. The Pursuer has not offered the debtor the opportunity to capitalise his arrears to allow them to be repaid over the remaining term of the loan.

4. The security subjects are at present the home of the Minuter and [SPECIFY OTHERS]. The Minuter has applied for alternative accommodation from the local authority. The local authority is unable to provide any accommodation which would preclude the need for the children to change school. In the circumstances, the Minuter and her children living at the subjects are unable to secure reasonable alternative accommodation.

PLEA IN LAW

1. The Minuter being prepared to make payments towards the arrears and being unable to secure reasonable alternative accommodation, the exercise by the Pursuer of its rights in relation to the security subjects should be suspended/the proceedings should be continued to such date as the court thinks fit.

IN RESPECT WHEREOF

APPENDIX 4

THE CONVEYANCING & FEUDAL REFORM (SCOTLAND) ACT 1970 PART II

PART II

THE STANDARD SECURITY

The standard security

12.1   9.—(1) The provisions of this Part of this Act shall have effect for the purpose of enabling a new form of heritable security to be created to be known as a standard security.
    [2] (2) It shall be competent to grant and record in the Register of Sasines a standard security over land or real right in land to be expressed in conformity with one of the forms prescribed in Schedule 2 to this Act.
    [2] (2A) It shall not be competent to grant a standard security over a conservation burden (within the meaning of Part 4 of the Abolition of Feudal Tenure etc. (Scotland) Act 2000 (asp 500)).
    (3) A grant of any right over land or a real right in land for the purpose of securing any debt by way of a heritable security shall only be capable of being effected at law if it is embodied in a standard security.
    (4) Where for the purpose last-mentioned any deed which is not in the form of a standard security contains a disposition or assignation of land or a real right in land, it shall to that extent be void and unenforceable, and where that deed has been duly recorded the creditor in the purported security may be required, by any person having an interest, to grant any deed which may be appropriate to clear the Register of Sasines of that security.
    (5) A standard security may be used for any other purpose for which a heritable security may be used if any of the said forms is appropriate to that purpose, and for the purpose of any enactment affecting heritable securities a standard security, if so used, or if used as is required by this Act instead of a heritable security as defined therein, shall be a heritable security for the purposes of that enactment.
    (6) *Act of the Parliament of Scotland 1696, c. 5.* The Bankruptcy Act 1696, in so far as it renders a heritable security of no effect in relation to a debt contracted after the recording of that security, and any rule of law which requires that a real burden for money may only be created in respect of a sum specified in the deed of creation, shall not apply in relation to a standard security.
    (7) [*Repealed by the Tenants' Rights, etc. (Scotland) Act 1980 (c. 52), Sched. 5.*]
    [2] (8) For the purposes of this Part of this Act—

  [1] (a) "heritable security" (except in subsection (5) of this section if the context otherwise requires) means any security capable of

being constituted over any land or real right in land by disposition or assignation of that interest in security of any debt and of being recorded in the Register of Sasines;

(b) "interest in land" "real right in land" has the same meaning as it has for the purposes of sections 1 and 2 of this Act;

(c) "debt" means any obligation due, or which will or may become due, to repay or pay money, including any such obligation arising from a transaction or part of a transaction in the course of any trade, business or profession, and any obligation to pay an annuity or *ad factum praestandum*, but does not include an obligation to pay any rent or other periodical sum payable in respect of land, and "creditor" and "debtor", in relation to a standard security, shall be construed accordingly.

AMENDMENT
1. Applied by the Aviation Security Act 1982 (c. 36), Sched. 1, para. 11.
2. Amended by the Abolition of Feudal Tenure (Scotland) Act 2000 (asp.5), Sched 12, part 1 (effective June 9, 2000).

Import of forms of, and certain clauses in, standard security

10.—(1) The import of the clause relating to the personal obligation contained in Form A of Schedule 2 to this Act expressed in any standard security shall, unless specially qualified, be as follows—

(a) where the security is for a fixed amount advanced or payable at, or prior to, the delivery of the deed, the clause undertaking to make payment to the creditor shall import an acknowledgment of receipt by the debtor of the principal sum advanced or an acknowledgment by the debtor of liability to pay that sum and a personal obligation undertaken by the debtor to repay or pay to the creditor on demand in writing, at any time after the date of delivery of the standard security the said sum, with interest at the rate stated payable on the dates specified, together with all expenses for which the debtor is liable by virtue of the deed or of this Part of this Act;

(b) where the security is for a fluctuating amount, whether subject to a maximum amount or not and whether advanced or due partly before and partly after delivery of the deed or whether to be advanced or to become due wholly after such delivery, the clause undertaking to make payment to the creditor shall import a personal obligation by the debtor to repay or pay to the creditor on demand in writing the amount, not being greater than the maximum amount, if any, specified in the deed, advanced or due and outstanding at the time of demand, with interest on each advance from the date when it was made until repayment thereof, or on each sum payable from the date on which it became due until payment thereof, and at the rate stated payable on the dates specified, together with all expenses for which the debtor is liable by virtue of the deed or of this Part of this Act.

12.2

[1] (2) The clause of warrandice in the forms of standard security contained in Schedule 2 to this Act expressed in any standard security shall, unless specially qualified, import absolute warrandice as regards the land or real right in land over which the security is granted and the title deeds thereof, and warrandice from fact and deed as regards the rents thereof.

(3) The clause relating to 'consent to registration for execution' contained in Form A of Schedule 2 to this Act, expressed in any standard security shall, unless specially qualified, import a consent to registration in the Books of Council and Session, or, as the case may be, in the books of the appropriate sheriff court, for execution.

(4) The forms of standard security contained in Schedule 2 to this Act shall, unless specially qualified, import an assignation to the creditor of the title deeds, including searches, and all conveyances not duly recorded, affecting the security subjects or any part thereof, with power to the creditor in the event of a sale under the powers conferred by the security, but subject to the rights of any person holding prior rights to possession of those title deeds, to deliver them, so far as in the creditor's possession, to the purchaser, and to assign to the purchaser any right he may possess to have the title deeds made forthcoming.

AMENDMENT
1. Amended by the Abolition of Feudal Tenure (Scotland) Act 2000 (asp.5), Sched 12, part 1 (effective June 9, 2000).

Effect of recorded standard security, and incorporation of standard conditions

12.3   11.—[2] (1) Where a standard security is duly recorded, it shall operate to vest in the grantee a real right in security for the performance of the contract to which the security relates.

(2) Subject to the provisions of this Part of this Act, the conditions set out in Schedule 3 to this Act, either as so set out or with such variations as have been agreed by the parties in the exercise of the powers conferred by the said Part (which conditions are hereinafter in this Act referred to as "the standard conditions"), shall regulate every standard security.

[1] (3) Subject to the provisions of this Part of this Act, the creditor and debtor in a standard security may vary any of the standard conditions, other than standard condition 11 (procedure on redemption) and the provisions of Schedule 3 to this Act relating to the powers of sale and foreclosure and to the exercise of those powers, but no condition capable of being varied shall be varied in a manner inconsistent with any condition which may not be varied by virtue of this subsection.

(4) In this Part of this Act—

  (a) any reference to a variation of the standard conditions shall include a reference to the inclusion of an additional condition and to the exclusion of a standard condition;

  (b) any purported variation of a standard condition which contravenes the provisions of subsection (3) of this section shall be void and unenforceable.

AMENDMENT
1. As amended by the Redemption of Standard Securities (Scotland) Act 1971 (c. 45), s.1.
2. Amended by the Abolition of Feudal Tenure (Scotland) Act 2000 (asp.5), Sched 12, part 1 (effective June 9, 2000).

Standard security may be granted by person uninfeft

[1,2] **12.**—(1) Notwithstanding any rule of law, a standard security may be granted over land or a real right in land by a person but whose title thereto has not been completed by being duly recorded, if in the deed expressing that security the grantor deduces his title to that land or real right from the person who appears in the Register of Sasines as having the last recorded title thereto.

(2) A deduction of title in a deed for the purposes of the foregoing subsection shall be expressed in the form prescribed by Note 2 or 3 of Schedule 2 to the Act, and on such a deed being recorded as aforesaid the title of the grantee shall, for the purposes of the rights and obligations between the grantor and the grantee thereof, and those deriving right from them, but for no other purpose, in all respects be of the same effect as if the title of the grantor of the deed to the land or real right in land to which he has deduced title therein had been duly completed; and any references to a proprietor or to a person having the last recorded title shall in this Part of this Act be construed accordingly.

(3) There may be specified for the purposes of any deduction of title in pursuance of any provision of this Part of this Act any writing which it is competent to specify as a title, midcouple, or link in title for the purposes of section 5 of the Conveyancing (Scotland) Act 1924 (deduction of title).

AMENDMENT
1. Excluded by the Land Registration (Scotland) Act 1979 (c. 33), s.15(3).
2. Amended by the Abolition of Feudal Tenure (Scotland) Act 2000 (asp.5), Sched 12, part 1 (effective June 9, 2000).

Ranking of standard securities

[1] **13.**—(1) Where the creditor in a standard security recorded has received notice of the creation of a subsequent security over the same land or real right in land or over any part thereof, or of the subsequent assignation or conveyance of that land or real right, in the whole or in part, being a security, assignation or conveyance of that land or real right, in whole or in part, being a security, assignation or conveyance so recorded, the preference in ranking of the security of that creditor shall be restricted to security for his present advances and future advances which he may be required to make under the contract to which the security relates and interest present or future due thereon (including any such interest which has accrued or may accrue) and for any expenses or outlays (including interest thereon) which may be, or may have been, reasonably incurred in the exercise of any power conferred on any creditor by the deed expressing the existing security.

(2) For the purposes of the foregoing subsection—

(a) a creditor in an existing standard security duly recorded shall not be held to have had any notice referred to in that subsection, by reason only of the subsequent recording of the relevant deed in the Register of Sasines;

(b) any assignation, conveyance or vesting in favour of or in any other person of the interest of the debtor in the security subjects or in any part thereof resulting from any judicial decree, or otherwise by operation of law, shall constitute sufficient notice thereof to the creditor.

(3) Nothing in the foregoing provisions of this section shall affect—

(a) any preference in ranking enjoyed by the Crown; and

(b) any powers of the creditor and debtor in any heritable security to regulate the preference to be enjoyed by creditors in such manner as they may think fit.

AMENDMENT
1. Amended by the Abolition of Feudal Tenure (Scotland) Act 2000 (asp.5), Sched 12, part 1 (effective June 9, 2000).

Assignation of standard security

12.6 **14.**—(1) Any standard security duly recorded may be transferred, in whole or in part, by the creditor by an assignation in conformity with Form A or B of Schedule 4 to this Act, and upon such an assignation being duly recorded, the security, or, as the case may be, part thereof, shall be vested in the assignee as effectually as if the security or the part had been granted in his favour.

(2) An assignation of a standard security shall, except so far as otherwise therein stated, be deemed to convey to the grantee all rights competent to the grantor to the writs, and shall have the effect *inter alia* of vesting in the assignee—

(a) the full benefit of all corroborative or substitutional obligations for the debt, or any part thereof, whether those obligations are contained in any deed or arise by operation of law or otherwise.

(b) the right to recover payment from the debtor of all expenses properly incurred by the creditor in connection with the security, and

(c) the entitlement to the benefit of any notices served and of all procedure instituted by the creditor in respect of the security to the effect that the grantee may proceed as if he had originally served or instituted such notices or procedure.

Restriction of standard security

12.7 **15.**—[1] (1) The security constituted by any standard security duly recorded may be restricted, as regards any part of the land or real right in land burdened by the security, by a deed of restriction in conformity with Form C of Schedule 4 to this Act, and, upon that deed being duly recorded, the security shall be restricted to the land or real right contained in the standard security other than the part of that land or real right disburdened by the deed; and the land or real right thereby disburdened shall be released from the security wholly or to the extent specified in the deed.

(2) A partial discharge and deed of restriction of a standard security, which has been duly recorded, may be combined in one deed, which shall be in conformity with Form D of the said Schedule 4.

AMENDMENT
1. Amended by the Abolition of Feudal Tenure (Scotland) Act 2000 (asp.5), Sched 12, part 1 (effective June 9, 2000).

Variation of standard security

[1] **16.**—(1) Any alteration in the provisions (including any standard condition) of a standard security duly recorded, other than an alteration which may appropriately be effected by an assignation, discharge or restriction of that standard security, or an alteration which involves an addition to, or an extention of, the land or real right in land mentioned therein, may be effected by a variation endorsed on the standard security in conformity with Form E of Schedule 4 to this Act, or by a variation contained in a separate deed in a form appropriate for that purpose, duly recorded in either case.

(2) Where a standard security has been duly recorded, but the personal obligation or any other provision (including any standard condition) relating to the security has been created or specified in a deed which has not been so recorded, nothing contained in this section shall prevent any alteration in that personal obligation or provision, other than an alteration which may be appropriately effected by an assignation, discharge or restriction of the standard security, or an alteration which involves an addition to, or an extension of, the land or real right in land mentioned therein, by a variation contained in any form of deed appropriate for that purpose, and such a variation shall not require to be recorded in the Register of Sasines.

(3) [*Repealed by the Finance Act 1971 (c. 68), Sched. 14, Pt VI.*]

(4) Any variation effected in accordance with this section shall not prejudice any other security or right over the same land or real right in land, or over any part thereof, effectively constituted before the variation is recorded, or where the variation is effected by an unrecorded deed, before that deed is executed, as the case may be.

AMENDMENT
1. Amended by the Abolition of Feudal Tenure (Scotland) Act 2000 (asp.5), Sched 12, part 1 (effective June 9, 2000).

Discharge of standard security

17. A standard security duly recorded may be discharged, and the land or real right in land burdened by that security may be disburdened thereof, in whole or in part, by a discharge in conformity with Form F of Schedule 4 to this Act, duly recorded.

Redemption of standard security

[1] **18.**—(1) Subject to the provisions of subsection (1A) of this section the debtor in a standard security or, where the debtor is not the proprietor, the proprietor of the security subjects shall be entitled to

redeem the security on giving two months' notice of his intention so to do and in conformity with the terms of standard condition 11 and the appropriate Forms of Schedule 5 to this Act.

[2] (1A) Without prejudice to section 11 of the Land Tenure Reform (Scotland) Act 1974, the provisions of the foregoing subsection shall be subject to any agreement to the contrary, but any right to redeem the security shall be exercisable in conformity with the terms and Forms referred to in that subsection.

[3] (2) Where owing to the death or absence of the creditor, or to any other cause, the debtor in a standard security or, as the case may be, the proprietor of the security subjects (being in either case a person entitled to redeem the security) is unable to obtain a discharge under the foregoing provisions of this section, he may—

> (a) where the security was granted in respect of any obligation to repay or pay money, consign in any bank in Scotland, incorporated by or under Act of Parliament or by Royal Charter, the whole amount due to the creditor on redemption, other than any unascertained expenses of the creditor, for the person appearing to have the best right thereto, and
>
> (b) other case, apply to the court for declarator that the whole obligations under the contract to which the security relates have been performed.

[4] (3) On consignation, or on the court granting declarator as aforesaid, a certificate to that effect may be expede by a solicitor in the appropriate form prescribed by Form D of Schedule 5 to this Act, which on being duly recorded shall disburden the land or real right in land, to which the standard security relates, of that security.

(4) For the purposes of this section, "whole amount due" means the debt to which the security relates, so far as outstanding, and any other sums due thereunder by way of interest or otherwise.

AMENDMENTS
1. As amended by the Redemption of Standard Securities (Scotland) Act 1971 (c. 45), s.1.
2. Added by the Redemption of Standard Securities (Scotland) Act 1971 (c. 45), s.1, and as amended by the Land Tenure Reform (Scotland) Act 1974 (c. 38), s.11(6).
3. As amended by the Redemption of Standard Securities (Scotland) Act 1971 (c. 45), s.1.
4. Amended by the Abolition of Feudal Tenure (Scotland) Act 2000 (asp.5), Sched 12, part 1 (effective June 9, 2000).

Calling-up of standard security

12.10   19.—(1) Where a creditor in a standard security intends to require discharge of the debt thereby secured and, failing that discharge, to exercise any power conferred by the security to sell any subjects of the security or any other power which he may appropriately exercise on the default of the debtor within the meaning of standard condition 9(1)(a), he shall serve a notice calling-up the security in conformity with Form A of Schedule 6 to this Act (hereinafter in this Act referred to as a "calling-up notice"), in accordance with the following provisions of this section.

[2] (2) Subject to the following provisions of this section, a calling-up notice shall be served on the person having the last recorded title to the security subjects and appearing on the record as the proprietor, and should the proprietor of those subjects, or any part thereof, be dead then on his representative or the person entitled to the subjects in terms of the last recorded title thereto, notwithstanding any alteration of the succession not appearing in the Register of Sasines.

[2] (3) Where the person having the last recorded title to the security subjects was an incorporated company which has been removed from the Register of Companies, or a person deceased who has left no representatives, a calling-up notice shall be served on the Lord Advocate and, where the estates of the person having the last recorded title have been sequestrated under the Bankruptcy (Scotland) Act 1913, the notice shall be served on the trustee in the sequestration (unless such trustee has been discharged) as well as on the bankrupt.

(4) If the proprietor be a body of trustees, it shall be sufficient if the notice is served on a majority of the trustees infeft in the security subjects.

(5) It shall be an obligation on the creditor to serve a copy of the calling-up notice on any other person against whom he wishes to preserve any right of recourse in respect of the debt.

(6) For the purposes of the foregoing provisions of this section, the service of a calling-up notice may be made by delivery to the person on whom it is desired to be served or the notice may be sent by registered post or by the recorded delivery service to him at his last known address, or, in the case of the Lord Advocate, at the Crown Office, Edinburgh, and an acknowledgment, signed by the persons on whom service has been made, in conformity with Form C of Schedule 6 to this Act, or, as the case may be, a certificate in conformity with Form D of that Schedule, accompanied by the postal receipt shall be sufficient evidence of the service of that notice; and if the address of the person on whom the notice is desired to be served is not known, or if it is not known whether that person is still alive, or if the packet containing a calling-up notice is returned to the creditor with an intimation that it could not be delivered, that notice shall be sent to the Extractor of the Court of Session, and shall be equivalent to the service of a calling-up notice on the person on whom it is desired to be served.

(7) For the purposes of the last foregoing subsection, an acknowledgment of receipt by the said Extractor on a copy of a calling-up notice shall be sufficient evidence of the receipt by him of that notice.

(8) A calling-up notice served by post shall be held to have been served on the next day after the day of posting.

(9) Where a creditor in a standard security has indicated in a calling-up notice that any sum and any interest thereon due under the contract may be subject to adjustment in amount, he shall, if the person on whom notice has been served so requests, furnish the debtor with a statement of the amount as finally determined within a period of one month from the date of service of the calling-up notice, and a failure by the creditor to comply with the provisons of this subsection shall cause the calling-up notice to be of no effect.

[1] (10) The period of notice mentioned in the calling-up notice may be effectively dispensed with or shortened by the person on whom it is served, with the consent of the creditors, if any, holding securities *pari passu* with, or postponed to, the security held by the creditor serving the calling-up notice, by a minute written or endorsed upon the said notice, or a copy thereof, in conformity with Form C of Schedule 6 to this Act.

Provided that, without prejudice to the foregoing generality, if the standard security is over a matrimonial home as defined in section 22 of the Matrimonial Homes (Family Protection) (Scotland) Act 1981, the spouse on whom the calling-up notice has been served may not dispense with or shorten the said period without the consent in writing of the other spouse.

(11) A calling-up notice shall cease to have effect for the purpose of a sale in the exercise of any power conferred by the security on the expiration of a period of five years, which period shall run—

(a) in the case where the subjects of the security, or any part thereof, have not been offered for or exposed to sale, from the date of the notice.

(b) case where there has been such an offer or exposure, from the date of the last offer or exposure.

Amendment
1. As amended by the Matrimonial Homes (Family Protection) (Scotland) Act 1981 (c. 59), s.20.
2. Amended by the Abolition of Feudal Tenure (Scotland) Act 2000 (asp.5), Sched 12, part 1 (effective June 9, 2000).

Exercise of rights of creditor on default of debtor in complying with a calling-up notice

12.11   20.—(1) Where the debtor in a standard security is in default within the meaning of standard 9(1)(a), the creditor may exercise such of his rights under the security as he may consider appropriate, and any such right shall be in addition to and not in derogation from any other remedy arising from the contract to which the security relates or from any right conferred by any enactment or by any rule of law on the creditor in a heritable security.

(2) Where the debtor is in default as aforesaid, the creditor shall have the right to sell the security subjects, or any part thereof, in accordance with the provisions of this Part of this Act.

(3) A creditor in a standard security who is in lawful possession of the security subjects may let the security subjects, or any part thereof, for any period not exceeding seven years, or may make application to the court for warrant to let those subjects, or any part thereof, for a period exceeding seven years, and the application shall state the proposed tenant, and the duration and conditions of the proposed lease, and shall be served on the proprietor of the subjects and on any other heritable creditor having interest as such a creditor in the subjects.

(4) The court, on such an application as aforesaid and after such inquiry and such further intimation of the application as it may think fit, may grant the application as submitted, or subject to such variation as it

may consider reasonable in all the circumstances of the case, or may refuse the application.

(5) There shall be deemed to be assigned to a creditor who is in lawful possession of the security subjects all rights and obligations of the proprietor relating to—

(a) leases, or any permission or right of occupancy, granted in respect of those subjects or any part thereof, and

(b) the management and maintenance of the subjects and the effecting of any reconstruction, alteration or improvement reasonably required for the purpose of maintaining the market value of the subjects.

21.—(1) Where the debtor in a standard security is in default within the meaning of standard condition 9(1)(b), and the default is remediable, the creditor may, without prejudice to any other powers he may have by virtue of this Act or otherwise, proceed in accordance with the provisions of this section to call on the debtor and on the proprietor, where he is not the debtor, to purge the default. **12.12**

(2) For the aforesaid purpose the creditor may serve on the debtor and, as the case may be, on the proprietor a notice in conformity with Form B of Schedule 6 to this Act (hereinafter in this Act referred to as a "notice of default") which shall be served in the like manner and with the like requirements as to proof of service as a calling-up notice.

(3) For the purpose of dispensing with, or shortening, the period of notice mentioned in a notice of default, section 19(10) of this Act shall apply as it applies in relation to a calling-up notice.

(4) Notwithstanding the failure to comply with any requirement contained in the notice, a notice of default shall cease to be authority for the exercise of the rights mentioned in section 23(2) of this Act on the expiration of a period of five years from the date of the notice.

Objections to notice of default

22.—(1) Where a person on whom a notice of default has been served considers himself aggrieved by any requirement of that notice he may, within a period of fourteen days of the service of the notice, object to the notice by way of application to the court; and the applicant shall, not later than the lodging of that application, serve a copy of his application on the creditor, and on any other party on whom the notice has been served by the creditor. **12.13**

(2) On any such application the court, after hearing the parties and making such inquiry as it may think fit, may order the notice appealed against to be set aside, in whole or in part, or otherwise to be varied, or to be upheld.

(3) The respondent in any such application may make a counter-application craving for any of the remedies conferred on him by this Act or by any other enactment relating to heritable securities, and the court may grant any such remedy as aforesaid as it may think proper.

(4) For the purposes of such a counter-application as aforesaid, a certificate which conforms with the requirements of Schedule 7 to this Act may be lodged in court by the creditor, and that certificate shall be

prima facie evidence of the facts directed by the said Schedule to be contained therein.

Rights and duties of parties after service of notice of default to which objection is not taken, or where the notice is not set aside

12.14   23.—(1) Where a person does not object to a notice of default in accordance with the provisions of the last foregoing section, or where he has so objected and the notice has been upheld or varied under that section, it shall be his duty to comply with any requirement, due to be performed or fulfilled by him, contained in the notice or, as the case may be, in the notice as so varied.

(2) Subject to the provisions of section 21(4) of this Act, where a person fails to comply as aforesaid, the creditor, subject to the next following subsection, may proceed to exercise such of his rights on default under standard condition 10(2), (6) and (7) as he may consider appropriate.

[1] (3) At any time after the expiry of the period stated in a notice of default, or in a notice varied as aforesaid, but before the conclusion of any enforceable contract to sell the security subjects, or any part thereof, by virtue of the last foregoing subsection, the debtor or proprietor (being in either case a person entitled to redeem the security) may, subject to any agreement to the contrary, redeem the security without the necessity of observance of any requirement as to notice.

AMENDMENT
1. As amended by the Redemption of Standard Securities (Scotland) Act 1971 (c. 45), s.1.

Application by creditor to court for remedies on default

12.15   24.—(1) Without prejudice to his proceeding by way of notice of default in respect of a default within the meaning of standard condition 9(1)(b), a creditor in a standard security, where the debtor is in default within the meaning of that standard condition or standard condition 9(1)(c), may apply to the court for warrant to exercise any of the remedies which he is entitled to exercise on a default within the meaning of standard condition 9(1)(a).

(2) For the purposes of such an application as aforesaid in respect of a default within the meaning of standard condition 9(1)(b), a certificate which conforms with the requirements of Schedule 7 to this Act may be lodged in court by the creditor, and that certificate shall be *prima facie* evidence of the facts directed by the said Schedule to be contained therein.

Exercise of power of sale

12.16   [1] 25. A creditor in a standard security having right to sell the security subjects may exercise that right either by private bargain or by exposure to sale, and in either event it shall be the duty of the creditor to advertise the sale and to take all reasonable steps to ensure that the price at which all or any of the subjects are sold is the best that can reasonably obtained.

AMENDMENT
1. Applied (*mod.*) by S.I. 1986 No. 843.

Disposition by creditor on sale

26.—(1) Where a creditor in a standard security has effected a sale of **12.17** the security subjects, or any part thereof, and grants to the purchaser or his nominee a disposition of the subjects sold thereby, which bears to be in implement of the sale, then, on that disposition being duly recorded, those subjects shall be disburdened of the standard security and of all other heritable securities and diligences ranking *pari passu* with, or postponed to, that security.

(2) Where on a sale as aforesaid the security subjects remain subject to a prior security, the recording of a disposition under the foregoing subsection shall not affect the rights of the creditor in that security, but the creditor who has effected the sale shall have the like right as the debtor to redeem the security.

Application of proceeds of sale

27.—(1) The money which is received by the creditor in a standard **12.18** security, arising from any sale by him of the security subjects, shall be held by him in trust to be applied by him in accordance with the following order of priority—

   (a) first, in payment of all expenses properly incurred by him in connection with the sale, or any attempted sale;

   (b) secondly, in payment of the whole amount due under any prior security to which the sale is not made subject;

   (c) thirdly, in payment of the whole amount due under the standard security, and in payment, in due proportion, of the whole amount due under a security, if any, ranking *pari passu* with his own secuity, which has been duly recorded;

   (d) fourthly, in payment of any amounts due under any securities with a ranking postponed to that of his own security, according to their ranking,

and any residue of the money so received shall be paid to the person entitled to the security subjects at the time of sale, or to any person authorised to give receipts for the proceeds of the sale thereof.

(2) Where owing to the death or absence of any other creditor, or to any other cause, a creditor is unable to obtain a receipt or discharge for any payment he is required to make under the provisions of the foregoing subsection, he may, without prejudice to his liability to account therefor, consign the amount due (so far as ascertainable) in the sheriff court for the person appearing to have the best right thereto; and where consignation is so made, the creditor shall lodge in court a statement of the amount consigned.

(3) A consignation made in pursuance of the last foregoing subsection shall operate as a discharge of the payment of the amount due, and a certificate under the hand of the sheriff clerk shall be sufficient evidence thereof.

AMENDMENT
1. Applied (*mod.*) by S.I. 1986 No. 843.

Foreclosure

12.19   [1] **28.**—(1) Where the creditor in a standard security has exposed the security subjects to sale at a price not exceeding the amount due under the security and under any security ranking prior to, or *pari passu* with, the security, and has failed to find a purchaser, or where, having so failed, he has succeeded in selling only a part of the subjects at a price which is less than the amount due as aforesaid, he may, on the expiration of a period of two months from the date of the first exposure to sale, apply to the court for a decree of foreclosure.

(2) In any application under the last foregoing subsection the creditor shall lodge a statement setting out the whole amount due under the security but, without prejudice to the right of the debtor or of the proprietor to challenge that statement, it shall be sufficient for the purposes of the application for the creditor to establish to the satisfaction of the court that the amount so stated is not less than the price at which the security subjects have been exposed to sale or sold, where part of the subjects has been sold as aforesaid.

(3) Any application under subsection (1) of this section shall be served on the debtor in the standard security, the proprietor of the security subjects (if he is a person other than the debtor) and the creditor in any other heritable security affecting the security subjects as disclosed by a search of the Register of Sasines for a period of twenty years immediately preceding the last date to which the appropriate Minute Book of the said Register has been completed at the time when the application is made or by an examination of the title sheet of the security subjects in the Land Register of Scotland.

(4) The court may order such intimation and inquiry as it thinks fit and may in its discretion allow the debtor or the proprietor of the security subjects a period not exceeding three months in which to pay the whole amount due under the security and, subject to any such allowance, may—

(a) appoint the security subjects or the unsold part thereof to be re-exposed to sale at a price to be fixed by the court, in which event the creditor in the security may bid and purchase at the sale, or

(b) grant a decree of foreclosure in conformity with the provisions of the next following subsection.

(5) A decree of foreclosure shall contain a declaration that, on the extract of the degree being duly recorded, any right to redeem the security has been extinguished and that the creditor has right to the security subjects or the unsold part thereof, described by means of a particular description or by reference to a description thereof as in Schedule D to the Conveyancing (Scotland) Act 1924 or in Schedule G to the Titles to Land Consolidation (Scotland) Act 1868, including a reference to any conditions or clauses affecting the subjects or the unsold part thereof or in accordance with section 15 of the Land

Registration (Scotland) Act 1979, at the price at which the said subjects were last exposed to sale under deduction of the price received for any part thereof sold, and shall also contain a warrant for recording the extract of the decree in the Register of Sasines.

(6) Upon an extract of the degree of foreclosure being duly recorded, the following provisions of this subsection shall have effect in relation to the security subjects to which the decree relates—

(a) any right to redeem the security shall be extinguished, and the creditor shall have right to, and be vested in, the subjects as if he had received an irredeemable disposition thereof duly recorded from the proprietor of the subjects at the date of the recording of the extract of the decree;

(b) the subjects shall be disburdened of the standard security and all securities and diligences postponed thereto:

(c) the creditor who has obtained the decree shall have the like right as the debtor to redeem any security prior to, or *pari passu* with, his own security.

(7) Notwithstanding the due recording of an extract of a decree of foreclosure, any personal obligation of the debtor under the standard security shall remain in full force and effect so far as not extinguished by the price at which the security subjects have been acquired and the price for which any part thereof has been sold.

(8) Where the security subjects or any part thereof have been acquired by a creditor in the security by virtue of a decree of foreclosure under the provisions of this section, the title thereto of the creditor shall not be challengeable on the ground of any irregularity in the proceedings for foreclosure or on calling-up or default which preceded it; but nothing in the provisions of this subsection shall affect the competency of any claim for damages in respect of such proceedings against the creditor.

AMENDMENT
1. As amended by the Redemption of Standard Securities (Scotland) Act 1971 (c. 45), s.1, and the Land Registration (Scotland) Act 1979 (c. 33), Sched. 2, para. 4. See the Building Societies Act 1986 (c. 53), s.11(10), (15).

Procedure

29.—(1) The court for the purposes of this Part of this Act, and for the operation of section 11 of the Heritable Securities (Scotland) Act 1894 (application by *pari passu* creditor to sell), in relation to a standard security shall be the sheriff having jurisdiction over any part of the security subjects, and the sheriff shall be deemed to have such jurisdiction whatever the value of the subjects. **12.20**

(2), (3) [*Repealed by S.I. 1990 No. 661*].

Interpretation of Part II

[1] **30.**—(1) In this Part of this Act, unless the context otherwise requires, the following expressions have the meanings hereby respectively assigned to them, that is to say— **12.21**

"creditor" and "debtor" shall include any successor in title, assignee or representative of a creditor or debtor;

"debt" and "creditor" and "debtor", in relation to a standard security, have the meanings assigned to them by section 9(8) of this Act;

"duly recorded" means recorded in the appropriate division of the General Register of Sasines;

"exposure to sale" means exposure to sale by public roup, and exposed or re-exposed to sale shall be construed accordingly;

"heritable security" has the meaning assigned to it by the said section 9(8);

"interest in land" "real right in land" has the meaning assigned to it by the said section 9(8);

"Register of Sasines" means the appropriate division of the General Register of Sasines;

"the standard condition" are the conditions (whether varied or not) referred to in section 11(2) of this Act;

"whole amount due" has the meaning assigned to it by section 18(4) of this Act.

(2) For the purpose of construing this Part of this Act in relation to the creation of a security over a registered lease and to any subsequent transactions connected with that security, the following expressions shall have the meanings hereby respectively assigned to them, that is to say—

"conveyance" or "disposition" means assignation;

"convey" or "dispone" means assign;

"proprietor" means lessee;

"security subjects" means a registered lease subject to a security.

AMENDMENT
1. Amended by the Abolition of Feudal Tenure (Scotland) Act 2000 (asp.5), Sched 12, part 1 (effective June 9, 2000).

Saving

12.22　31. Nothing in the provisions of this Part of this Act shall affect the validity of any heritable security within the meaning of this Part which has been duly recorded before the commencement of this Act, and any such security may be dealt with, and shall be as capable of being enforced, as if this Part had not been passed.

Application of enactments

12.23　32. The provisions of any enactment relating to a bond and disposition or assignation in security shall apply to a standard security, except in so far as such provisions are consistent with the provisions of this Part of this Act, but, without prejudice to the generality of that exception, the enactments specified in Schedule 8 to this Act shall not so apply.

AMENDMENT
1. As amended by the Redemption of Standard Securities (Scotland) Act 1971 (c. 45), s.1.

APPENDIX 5

SCHEDULES 3, 6 and 7 TO THE CONVEYANCING AND FEUDAL REFORM (SCOTLAND) ACT 1970 (AS AMENDED BY THE 2001 ACT)

Section 11   SCHEDULE 3

THE STANDARD CONDITIONS

Maintenance and repair

1. It shall be an obligation on the debtor—   **13.1**

   (a) to maintain the security subjects in good and sufficient repair to the reasonable satisfaction of the creditor;

   (b) to permit, after seven clear days notice in writing, the creditor or his agent to enter upon the security subjects at all reasonable times to examine the condition thereof;

   (c) to make all necessary repairs and make good all defects in pursuance of his obligation under head (a) of this conditon within such reasonable period as the creditor may require by notice in writing.

Completion of buildings, etc., and prohibition of alterations, etc.

2. It shall be an obligation on the debtor—   **13.2**

   (a) to complete, as soon as may be practicable, any unfinished buildings and works forming part of the security subjects to the reasonable satisfaction of the creditor;

   (b) not to demolish, alter or add to any buildings or works forming part of the security subjects, except in accordance with the terms of a prior written consent of the creditor and in compliance with any consent, licence or approval required by law;

   (c) to exhibit to the creditor at his request evidence of that consent, licence or approval.

Observance of conditions in title, payment of duties, charges, etc., and general compliance with requirements of law relating to security subjects

3. It shall be an obligation on the debtor—   **13.3**

   (a) to observe any condition or perform any obligation in respect of the security subjects lawfully binding on him in relation to the security subjects;

   (b) to make due and punctual payment of any ground burden, teind, stipend, or standard charge, and any rates, taxes and other public burdens, and any other payments exigible in respect of the security subjects;

   (c) to comply with any requirement imposed upon him in relation to the security subjects by virtue of any enactment.

Planning notices, etc.

13.4 4. It shall be an obligation on the debtor—

    (a) where he has received any notice or order, issued or made by virtue of the Town and Country Planning (Scotland) Acts 1947 to 1969 or any amendment thereof, or any proposal so made for the making or issuing of any such notice or order, or any other notice or document affecting or likely to affect the security subjects, to give to the creditor, within fourteen days of the receipt of that notice, order or proposal, full particulars thereof;

    (b) to take, as soon as practicable, all reasonable or necessary steps to comply with such a notice or order or, as the case may be, duly to object thereto;

    (c) in the event of the creditor so requiring, to object or to join with the creditor in objecting to any such notice or order or in making representations against any proposal therefor.

Insurance

13.5 5. It shall be an obligation on the debtor—

    (a) to insure the security subjects or, at the option of the creditor, to permit the creditor to insure the security subjects in the names of the creditor and the debtor to the extent of the market value thereof against the risk of fire and such other risks as the creditor may reasonably require;

    (b) to deposit any policy of insurance effected by the debtor for the aforesaid purpose with the creditor;

    (c) to pay any premium due in respect of any such policy and, where the creditor so requests, to exhibit a receipt therefor not later than the fourteenth day after the renewal date of the policy;

    (d) to intimate to the creditor, within fourteen days of the occurrence, any occurrence which may give rise to a claim under the policy and to authorise the creditor to negotiate the settlement of the claim;

    (e) without prejudice to any obligation to the contrary enforceable against him, to comply with any reasonable requirement of the creditor as to the application of any sum received in respect of such a claim;

    (f) to refrain from any act or omission which would invalidate the policy.

Restriction on letting

13.6 6. It shall be an obligation on the debtor not to let, or agree to let, the security subjects, or any part thereof, without the prior consent in writing of the creditor, and "to let" in this condition includes to sub-let.

General power of creditor to perform obligations, etc., on failure of debtor and power to charge debtor

13.7 7.—(1) The creditor shall be entitled to perform any obligation imposed by the standard conditions on the debtor, which the debtor has failed to perform.

(2) Where it is necessary for the performance of any obligation as aforesaid, the creditor may, after giving seven clear days notice in writing to the debtor, enter upon the security subjects at all reasonable times.

(3) All expenses and charges (including any interest thereon), reasonably incurred by the creditor in the exercise of a right conferred by this condition, shall be recoverable from the debtor and shall be deemed to be secured by the security subjects under the standard security, and the rate of any such interest shall be the rate in force at the relevant time in respect of advances secured by the security, or, where no such rate is prescribed, shall be the bank rate in force at the relevant time.

Calling-up

8. The creditor shall be entitled, subject to the terms of the security and to any requirement of law, to call-up a standard security in the manner prescribed by section 19 of this Act. **13.8**

Default

9.—(1) The debtor shall be held to be in default in any of the following circumstances, that is to say— **13.9**

- (a) where a calling-up notice in respect of the security has been served and has not been complied with;
- (b) where there has been a failure to comply with any other requirement arising out of the security;
- (c) where the proprietor of the security subjects has become insolvent.

[1] (2) For the purposes of this condition, the proprietor shall be taken to be insolvent if—

- (a) he has become notour bankrupt, or he has executed a trust deed for behoof of, or has made a composition contract or arrangement with, his creditors;
- [2] (b) he has died and a judicial factor has been appointed under section 11A of the Judicial Factors (Scotland) Act 1889 to divide his insolvent estate among his creditors, or his estate falls to be administered in accordance with an order under section 421 of the Insolvency Act 1986;
- (c) where the proprietor is a company, a winding-up order has been made with respect to it, or a resolution for voluntary winding-up (other than a members' voluntary winding-up) has been passed with respect to it, or a receiver or manager of its undertaking has been duly appointed, or possession has been taken, by or on behalf of the holders of any debentures secured by a floating charge, of any property of the company comprised in or subject to the charge.

AMENDMENTS
1. Applied by the Sex Discrimination Act 1975 (c. 65), Sched. 3, para. 3(5)(b), the Race Relations Act 1976 (c. 74), Sched. 1, para. 3(5)(b) and the National Heritage Act 1980 (c. 17), Sched. 1, para. 3(4)(b).
2. As amended by the Bankruptcy (Scotland) Act 1985 (c. 66), Sched. 7, para. 8, the Insolvency Act 1985 (c. 65), Sched. 8, para. 18 and the Insolvency Act 1986 (c. 45), Sched. 14.

Rights of creditor on default

10.—(1) Where the debtor is in default, the creditor may, without prejudice to his exercising any other remedy arising from the contract to which the standard security relates, exercise, in accordance with the provisions of Part II of this Act **13.10**

and of any other enactment applying to standard securities, such of the remedies specified in the following sub-paragraphs of this standard condition as he may consider appropriate.

(2) He may proceed to sell the security subjects or any part thereof.

(3) He may enter into possession of the security subjects and may receive or recover the rents of those subjects or any part thereof.

(4) Where he has entered into possession as aforesaid, he may let the security subjects or any part thereof.

(5) Where he has entered into possession as aforesaid there shall be transferred to him all the rights of the debtor in relation to the granting of leases or rights of occupancy over the security subjects and to the management and maintenance of those subjects.

(6) He may effect all such repairs and may make good such defects as are necessary to maintain the security subjects in good and sufficient repair, and may effect such reconstruction, alteration and improvement on the subjects as would be expected of a prudent proprietor to maintain the market value of the subjects, and for the aforesaid purposes may enter on the subjects at all reasonable times.

(7) He may apply to the court for a decree of foreclosure.

Exercise of right of redemption

13.11   [1] 11.—(1) The debtor shall be entitled to exercise his right (if any) to redeem the security on giving notice of his intention so to do, being a notice in writing (hereinafter referred to as a "notice of redemption").

(2) Nothing in the provisions of this Act shall preclude a creditor from waiving the necessity for a notice of redemption, or from agreeing to a period of notice of less than that to which he is entitled.

(3)(a) A notice of redemption may be delivered to the creditor or sent by registered post or recorded delivery to him at his last known address, and an acknowledgment signed by the creditor or his agent or a certificate of postage by the person giving the notice accompanied by the postal receipt shall be sufficient evidence of such notice having been given.

(b) If the address of the creditor is not known, or if the packet containing the notice of redemption is returned to the sender with intimation that it could not be delivered, a notice of redemption may be sent to the Extractor of the Court of Session and an acknowledgment of receipt by him shall be sufficient evidence of such notice having been given.

(c) A notice of redemption sent by post shall be held to have been given on the day next after the day of posting.

(4) When a notice of redemption states that a specified amount will be repaid, and it is subsequently ascertained that the whole amount due to be repaid is more or less than the amount specified in the notice, the notice shall nevertheless be effective as a notice of repayment of the amount due as subsequently ascertained.

(5) Where the debtor has exercised a right to redeem, and has made payment of the whole amount due, or has performed the whole obligations of the debtor under the contract to which the security relates, the creditor shall grant a discharge in the terms prescribed in section 17 of this Act.

13.12   12. The debtor shall be personally liable to the creditor for the whole expenses of the preparation and execution of the standard security and any variation, restriction and discharge thereof and, where any of those deeds are recorded, the recording thereof, and all expenses reasonably incurred by the creditor in calling-up the security and realising or attempting to realise the security subjects, or any part thereof, and exercising any other powers conferred upon him by the security.

Interpretation

13.13 In this Schedule, where the debtor is not the proprietor of the security subjects, "debtor" means "proprietor", except

(a) in standard conditions 9(1), 10(1) and 12, and

(b) in standard condition 11, where "debtor" includes the proprietor.

Sections 19 and 21   SCHEDULE 6

PROCEDURES AS TO CALLING-UP AND DEFAULT

FORM A

NOTICE OF CALLING-UP OF STANDARD SECURITY

13.14 To A.B. (*address*)
TAKE NOTICE that C.D. (*designation*) requires payment of the principle sum of £   with interest thereon at the rate of   per centum per annum from the   day of   (*adding of necessary*, subject to such adjustment of the principal sum and the amount of interest as may subsequently be determined) secured by a standard security by you (*or* by E.F.) in favour of the said C.D. (*or* of G.H. to which the said C.D. has now right) recorded in the Register for   on   ; And that failing full payment of the said sum and interest thereon (*adding if necessary*, subject to any adjustment as aforesaid), and expenses within two months after the date of service of this demand, the subjects of the security may be sold.
Dated this   day of   .
(*To be signed by the creditor, or by his agent, who will add his designation and the words* Agent of the said C.D.)
In the case of a standard security for a non-monetary obligation this Form shall be adapted accordingly.

NOTE: The Mortgage Rights (Scotland) Act 2001 gives you the right in certain circumstances to apply to the court to suspend the rights of C.D. You have two months (which may be shortened only with your consent) to make an application. The court will have regard in particular to the circumstances giving rise to the service of this notice, your ability to comply with this notice, any action taken by C.D. to assist the debtor in the standard security to fulfil the obligations under it and the ability of you and anyone else residing at the property to find reasonable alternative accommodation. If you wish to make such an application, you should consult a solicitor. You may be eligible for legal aid depending on your circumstances, and you can get information about legal aid from a solicitor. You may also be able to get advice, including advice about how to manage debt, from any Citizens Advice Bureau or from other advice agencies.

FORM B

NOTICE OF DEFAULT UNDER STANDARD SECURITY

13.15 To A.B. (*address*)
TAKE NOTICE that C.D. (*designation*), the creditor in a standard security by you (*or* by E.F.) in favour of the said C.D. (*or* of G.H. to which the said C.D. has now right) recorded in the Register for   on   requires

fulfilment of the obligation(s) specified in the Schedule hereto in respect of which there is default; And that failing such fulfilment within one month after the date of service of this notice, the powers competent to the said C.D. on default may be exercised.

Dated this   day of   .
(*To be signed by the creditor, or by his agent, who will add his designation and the words* Agent of the said C.D.)

Schedule of Obligation(s) in respect of which there is default.

To (*specify in detail the obligation(s) in respect of which there is default*).

NOTE: The Mortgage Rights (Scotland) Act 2001 gives you the right in certain circumstances to apply to the court to suspend the rights of C.D. You have two months (which may be shortened only with your consent) to make an application. The court will have regard in particular to the nature of and reasons for the default, your ability to fulfil the obligations under the standard security, any action taken by C.D. to assist the debtor in the standard security to fulfil those obligations and the ability of you and anyone else residing at the property to find reasonable alternative accommodation. If you wish to make such an application, you should consult a solicitor. You may be eligible for legal aid depending on your circumstances, and you can get information about legal aid from a solicitor. You may also be able to get advice, including advice about how to manage debt, from any Citizens Advice Bureau or from other advice agencies.

FORM BB

NOTICE TO OCCUPIER

13.15/1 To the Occupier (*address*)

A Notice of Calling-up of a standard security/Default under a standard security (*delete as appropriate*) has been served by C.D. on A.B. in relation to (*address of subjects*). A copy of the notice is attached.

If you are a tenant of A.B., in certain circumstances C.D. cannot take possession of the property without a court order. You should obtain legal advice about your rights as a tenant. You may be eligible for legal aid depending on your circumstances, and you can get information about legal aid from a solicitor. You may also be able to get advice from any Citizens Advice Bureau or from other advice agencies.

If you are the spouse or partner of A.B., the Mortgage Rights (Scotland) Act 2001 gives you the right in certain circumstances to apply to the court to suspend the rights of C.D. You have two months (which may be shortened only with your consent) to make an application. The court will have regard in particular to—

(*for a Notice of Calling-up*) the circumstances giving rise to the service of the Notice of Calling-up, your ability to comply with the notice, any action taken by C.D. to assist the debtor in the standard security to fulfil the obligations under it and the ability of you and anyone else residing at the property to find reasonable alternative accommodation.

(*for a notice of default*) the nature of and reasons for the default, your ability to fulfil the obligations under the standard security, any action taken by C.D. to assist the debtor in the standard security to fulfil those obligations and the ability of you and anyone else residing at the property to find reasonable alternative accommodation.

(*delete as appropriate*)

If you wish to make such an application, you should consult a solicitor. You may be eligible for legal aid depending on your circumstances and you can get information about legal aid from a solicitor. You may also be able to get advice,

including advice about how to manage debt, from any Citizens Advice Bureau or from other advice agencies.
Dated
(*signature of C.D., or signature and designation of C.D.'s agent followed by the words* Agent of C.D.)

Form C

I, A.B., above named, hereby acknowledge receipt of the foregoing Notice of **13.16** (Calling-up), (Default) of which the foregoing is a copy of the notice *adding where appropriate* "and I agree to the period of notice being dispensed with (*or* shortened to   )."
 Dated this   day of   .
(*To be signed by the person on whom notice is served, or by his agent, who will add his designation and the words* Agent of the said A.B.).

Form D

Notice of (Calling-up) (Default), of which the foregoing is a copy, was posted (*or* **13.17** *otherwise, as the case may be*) to A.B. above named on the
day of   .
(*To be signed by the creditor, or by his agent, who will add his designation and the words* Agent of the said C.D. *and if posted the postal receipt to be attached.*)

Form E

To A.B. (*address*) **13.18**
C.D. (*designation*), the creditor in a standard security by you (or by E.F.) in favour of C.D. (*or* of G.H. to which C.D. now has right) recorded in the Register for (*or, as the case may be*, registered in the Land Register for Scotland) on (*date*) has applied to the court under section 24 of the Conveyancing and Feudal Reform (Scotland) Act 1970 for warrant to exercise in relation to (*address of security subjects*) remedies to which he is entitled on the following default—
(*specify in detail in respect of which the application is made*)
A copy of the application is attached.

Dated
(*Signature of C.D., or signature and designation of C.D.'s agent followed by the words* Agent of C.D.)

NOTE: The Mortgage Rights (Scotland) Act 2001 gives you the right in certain circumstances to apply to the court for suspension of the rights of C.D. The court will have regard in particular to the nature of and reasons for the default, your ability to fulfil the obligations under the standard security, any action taken by C.D. to assist the debtor in the standard security to fulfil those obligations and the ability of you and anyone else residing at the property to find reasonable alternative accommodation. If you wish to make such an application, you should consult a solicitor. You may be eligible for legal aid depending on your circumstances, and you can get information about legal aid from a solicitor. You may also be able to get advice, including advice about how to manage debt, from any Citizens Advice Bureau or from other advice agencies.

Form F

13.19 To the Occupier (*address*)

C.D. (*designation*) has applied to the court under section 24 of the Conveyancing and Feudal Reform (Scotland) Act 1970 for warrant to exercise in relation to (*address of security subjects*) remedies to which he is entitled on the default of A.B. (*designation*) in the performance of his obligations under a standard security over (*address of subjects*). A copy of the application is attached.

If you are a tenant of A.B. (or, if A.B. is not the proprietor of the subjects, of E.F. (being the proprietor)), in certain circumstances C.D. cannot take possession of the property without a court order. You should obtain legal advice about your rights as a tenant. You may be eligible for legal aid depending on your circumstances, and you can get information about legal aid from a solicitor. You may be able to get advice from any Citizens Advice Bureau or from other advice agencies.

If you are the spouse or partner of A.B., the Mortgage Rights (Scotland) Act 2001 gives you the right in certain circumstances to apply to the court to suspend the rights of C.D. The court will have regard in particular to the nature of and reasons for the default, your ability to fulfil the obligations under the standard security, any action taken by C.D. to assist the debtor in the standard security to fulfil those obligations and the ability of you and anyone else residing at the property to find reasonable alternative accommodation. If you wish to make such an application, you should consult a solicitor. You may be eligible for legal aid from a solicitor. You may also be able to get advice, including advice about how to manage debt, from any Citizens Advice Bureau or from other advice agencies.

Dated

(*Signature of C.D., or signature and designation of C.D.'s agent followed by the words* Agent of C.D.)

Sections 22 and 24   SCHEDULE 7

Contents of Certificate Stating a Default

13.20 1. A certificate which is lodged in court by the creditor for the purposes of section 22 or 24 of this Act shall contain the information required by the following provisions of this Schedule.

13.21 2. A certificate shall state—

- (i) the name and address of the creditor and shall specify the standard security in respect of which the default is alleged to have occurred by reference to the original creditor and debtor therein and to the particulars of its registration;

- (ii) the nature of the default with full details thereof.

13.22 3. The certificate shall be signed by the creditor or his solicitor, and a certificate which does not comply with the foregoing requirements of this Schedule shall not be received in evidence for the purposes of the said section 22 or 24.

APPENDIX 6

GUIDELINES IDENTIFIED BY LORD NICHOLLS IN *ROYAL BANK OF SCOTLAND PLC v. ETRIDGE (NO.2)* [2001] 3 W.L.R. 1021

For solicitors advising a surety. 14.1

"64. I turn to consider the scope of the responsibilities of a solicitor who is advising the wife. In identifying what are the solicitor's responsibilities the starting point must always be the solicitor's retainer. What has he been retained to do? As a general proposition, the scope of a solicitor's duties is dictated by the terms, whether express or implied, of his retainer. In the type of case now under consideration the relevant retainer stems from the bank's concern to receive confirmation from the solicitor that, in short, the solicitor has brought home to the wife the risks involved in the proposed transaction. As a first step the solicitor will need to explain to the wife the purpose for which he has become involved at all. He should explain that, should it ever become necessary, the bank will rely upon his involvement to counter any suggestion that the wife was overborne by her husband or that she did not properly understand the implications of the transaction. The solicitor will need to obtain confirmation from the wife that she wishes him to act for her in the matter and to advise her on the legal and practical implications of the proposed transaction.

65. When an instruction to this effect is forthcoming, the content of the advice required from a solicitor before giving the confirmation sought by the bank will, inevitably, depend upon the circumstances of the case. Typically, the advice a solicitor can be expected to give should cover the following matters as the core minimum. (1) He will need to explain the nature of the documents and the practical consequences these will have for the wife if she signs them. She could lose her home if her husband's business does not prosper. Her home may be her only substantial asset, as well as the family's home. She could be made bankrupt. (2) He will need to point out the seriousness of the risks involved. The wife should be told the purpose of the proposed new facility, the amount and principal terms of the new facility, and that the bank might increase the amount of the facility, or change its terms, or grant a new facility, without reference to her. She should be told the amount of her liability under her guarantee. The solicitor should discuss the wife's financial means, including her understanding of the value of the property being charged. The solicitor should discuss whether the wife or her husband has any other assets out of which repayment could be made if the husband's business should fail. These matters are relevant to the seriousness of the risks involved. (3) The solicitor

will need to state clearly that the wife has a choice. The decision is hers and hers alone. Explanation of the choice facing the wife will call for some discussion of the present financial position, including the amount of the husband's present indebtedness, and the amount of his current overdraft facility. (4) The solicitor should check whether the wife wishes to proceed. She should be asked whether she is content that the solicitor should write to the bank confirming he has explained to her the nature of the documents and the practical implications they may have for her, or whether, for instance, she would prefer him to negotiate with the bank on the terms of the transaction. Matters for negotiation could include the sequence in which the various securities will be called upon or a specific or lower limit to her liabilities. The solicitor should not give any confirmation to the bank without the wife's authority.

66. The solicitor's discussion with the wife should take place at a face-to-face meeting, in the absence of the husband. It goes without saying that the solicitor's explanations should be couched in suitably non-technical language. It also goes without saying that the solicitor's task is an important one. It is not a formality.

67. The solicitor should obtain from the bank any information he needs. If the bank fails for any reason to provide information requested by the solicitor, the solicitor should decline to provide the confirmation sought by the bank.

68. As already noted, the advice which a solicitor can be expected to give must depend on the particular facts of the case. But I have set out this 'core minimum' in some detail, because the quality of the legal advice is the most disturbing feature of some of the present appeals. The perfunctory nature of the advice may well be largely due to a failure by some solicitors to understand what is required in these cases."

For creditors looking for protection from the advice provided by a solicitor to the surety.

14.2 "79. I now return to the steps a bank should take when it has been put on inquiry and for its protection is looking to the fact that the wife has been advised independently by a solicitor.

(1) One of the unsatisfactory features in some of the cases is the late stage at which the wife first became involved in the transaction. In practice she had no opportunity to express a view on the identity of the solicitor who advised her. She did not even know that the purpose for which the solicitor was giving her advice was to enable him to send, on her behalf, the protective confirmation sought by the bank. Usually the solicitor acted for both husband and wife.

Since the bank is looking for its protection to legal advice given to the wife by a solicitor who, in this respect, is acting solely for her, I consider the bank should take steps to check *directly with the wife* the name of the solicitor she wishes to act for her. To this end, in future the bank should communicate directly with the wife, informing her that for its own protection it will require written confirmation from a solicitor, acting for her, to the effect that the solicitor has fully explained to her the nature of the documents and the practical implications they will have for her. She should be told that the purpose of this requirement is that thereafter she should not be able to dispute she is legally bound by the documents once she has signed them. She should be asked to nominate a solicitor whom she is willing to instruct to advise her, separately from her husband, and act for her in giving the necessary confirmation to the bank. She should be told that, if she wishes, the solicitor may be the same solicitor as is acting for her husband in the transaction. If a solicitor is already acting for the husband and the wife, she should be asked whether she would prefer that a different solicitor should act for her regarding the bank's requirement for confirmation from a solicitor.

The bank should not proceed with the transaction until it has received an appropriate response directly from the wife.

(2) Representatives of the bank are likely to have a much better picture of the husband's financial affairs than the solicitor. If the bank is not willing to undertake the task of explanation itself, the bank must provide the solicitor with the financial information he needs for this purpose. Accordingly it should become routine practice for banks, if relying on confirmation from a solicitor for their protection, to send to the solicitor the necessary financial information. What is required must depend on the facts of the case. Ordinarily this will include information on the purpose for which the proposed new facility has been requested, the current amount of the husband's indebtedness, the amount of his current overdraft facility, and the amount and terms of any new facility. If the bank's request for security arose from a written application by the husband for a facility, a copy of the application should be sent to the solicitor. The bank will, of course, need first to obtain the consent of its customer to this circulation of confidential information. If this consent is not forthcoming the transaction will not be able to proceed.

(3) Exceptionally there may be a case where the bank believes or suspects that the wife has been misled by her husband or is not entering into the transaction of her own free will. If such a case occurs the bank must inform the wife's solicitors of the facts giving rise to its belief or suspicion.

(4) The bank should in every case obtain from the wife's solicitor a written confirmation to the effect mentioned above.

80. These steps will be applicable to future transactions. In respect of past transactions, the bank will ordinarily be regarded as having discharged its obligations if a solicitor who was acting for the wife in the transaction gave the bank confirmation to the effect that he had brought home to the wife the risks she was running by standing as surety."

INDEX

Abandoned properties
calling-up notice, and, 2.7.1
Absolute disposition, *ex facie*
and see **Pre-existing securities**
background, 1.2
generally, 1.6
initial stages of enforcement, 3.1–3.5
Accuracy of notices
calling-up notice, and, 2.2.5
notice of default, and, 2.3.6
Action of reduction
applicability of doctrine, 5.11
cautioner's legal advice, 5.7
creditor's duty of good faith, 5.4
grounds, 5.2
introduction, 5.1
origin of doctrine, 5.3
policy issues, 5.10
presumption of undue influence, 5.8–5.9
proof of undue influence, 5.5
reliance on undue influence, 5.6
summary, 5.12
Advertising sale
generally, 8.9
introduction, 8.8
statutory basis, 12.16
Affidavits
sale, and, 8.6
Agents, employment of
sale, and, 8.12
Alterations
recovery of subjects, and, 7.5.3
Applicants
suspension order, and, 4.2.7
Application for suspension order
applicants, 4.2.7
considerations
applicant's ability to fulfil obligations, 4.2.14
creditor's assistance to debtor, 4.2.15
guidance, 4.2.19
introduction, 4.2.11–4.2.12
nature of and reasons for default, 4.2.13
reasonable alternative accommodation, 4.2.16
statutory basis, 10.2
disposal of applications
considerations, 4.2.13–4.2.16
introduction, 4.2.11–4.2.12
statutory basis, 10.2
generally, 4.2.8
proper court, 4.2.10

Application for suspension order—*cont.*
statutory basis, 10.1–10.2
time limits, 4.2.9
Arrangements for payment of arrears
generally, 6.6.3
Attachment
diligence, and, 9.3.3

Benefit, debtors on
generally, 6.6.1
Best price on sale
generally, 8.10
statutory basis, 12.16
Bond and disposition in security
and see **Pre-existing securities**
background, 1.2
generally, 1.6
initial stages of enforcement, 3.1–3.5
Bond of cash credit and disposition in security
and see **Pre-existing securities**
background, 1.2
generally, 1.6
initial stages of enforcement, 3.1–3.5

Calling-up notice
accuracy, 2.2.5
advantages, 2.2.13
challenge, 2.2.6
consumer credit cases, and, 2.5
content
accuracy, 2.2.5
generally, 2.2.1
prescribed form, 13.14
court action, and
defence, 2.2.12
generally, 2.2.10
procedure, 2.2.11
disadvantages, 2.2.13
ejection, and
defence, 2.2.12
generally, 2.2.10
procedure, 2.2.11
expenses, and, 2.2.8
failure to comply, 2.2.4
form, 13.14
introduction, 2.2
recovery of subjects, and, 7.1
restriction of period, 2.2.3
service
acknowledgment of receipt, 13.17
certificate of service, 13.16
generally, 2.2.2

Calling-up notice—*cont.*
statutory basis, 12.10
summary, 2.2.14
suspension, 2.2.7
suspension of creditor's rights, and
suspension order, and
   generally, 4.2.6
   introduction, 2.2.9
voluntary surrender, and, 2.7.1
Catholic and secondary securities
recovery of subjects, and, 7.6.2.1
Challenge to notices
calling-up notice, and, 2.2.6
consumer credit cases, and, 2.5
Challenges to validity of security
action of reduction
   applicability of doctrine, 5.11
   cautioner's legal advice, 5.7
   creditor's duty of good faith, 5.4
   grounds, 5.2
   introduction, 5.1
   origin of doctrine, 5.3
   policy issues, 5.10
   presumption of undue influence, 5.8–5.9
   proof of undue influence, 5.5
   reliance on undue influence, 5.6
   summary, 5.12
expenses
   amount recoverable, 5.18
   introduction, 5.17
   'reasonably incurred', 5.19
   suspension orders, and, 5.20
human rights, and
   application of ECHR, 5.14
   conclusion, 5.16
   introduction, 5.13
   remedies for breach, 5.15
introduction, 5.1
Conditions
and see **Standard conditions**
introduction, 1.5
statutory basis, 13.1–13.13
Consent of other creditors
sale, and, 8.14
Consumer credit cases
generally, 2.5
Contaminated land
recovery of subjects, and, 7.7.4
Contractual provisions
recovery of subjects, and, 7.6.2.3
Conveyancing & Feudal Reform (Scotland) Act 1970
amendments to, 10.4, 10.9–10.14
application of enactments, 12.23
definitions, 12.21
general provisions, 12.1–12.20
interpretation, 12.21
saving, 12.22
schedules, 13.1–13.19

Court action
calling-up notice, and
   defence, 2.2.12
   generally, 2.2.10
   procedure, 2.2.11
notice of default, and, 2.3.11
Creditor's powers on recovery of subjects
alterations, 7.5.3
foreclosure, 7.5.4
improvements, 7.5.3
introduction, 7.5
leases, 7.5.2
rent collection, 7.5.1
repairs, 7.5.3
Crown, application to
Mortgage Rights (Scotland) Act 2001, 10.5

Decree of repossession
generally, 5.21
Default, notice of
accuracy, 2.3.6
advantages, 2.3.12
challenge, 2.3.7
consumer credit cases, and, 2.5
content
   accuracy, 2.3.6
   generally, 2.3.2
   prescribed form, 13.15
court action, and, 2.3.11
disadvantages, 2.3.12
expenses, and, 2.3.9
failure to comply, 2.3.5
form, 13.15
introduction, 2.3
nature of default, 2.3.1
objection, 2.3.7
restriction of period, 2.3.4
service
   acknowledgment of receipt, 13.17
   certificate of service, 13.16
   generally, 2.3.3
statutory basis, 12.11–12.14
summary, 2.3.13
suspension, 2.3.8
suspension of creditor's rights, and
   generally, 4.2.6
   introduction, 2.3.10
voluntary surrender, and, 2.7.1
Defences
s.24 actions, and, 2.4.5
Determination of court action
action of reduction
   applicability of doctrine, 5.11
   cautioner's legal advice, 5.7
   creditor's duty of good faith, 5.4
   grounds, 5.2
   introduction, 5.1
   origin of doctrine, 5.3
   policy issues, 5.10
   presumption of undue influence, 5.8–5.9

Determination of court action—*cont.*
  action of reduction—*cont.*
    proof of undue influence, 5.5
    reliance on undue influence, 5.6
    summary, 5.12
  challenges to validity of security
    and see **Challenges to validity of security**
    action of reduction, 5.2–5.12
    expenses, 5.17–5.20
    human rights, and, 5.13–5.16
    introduction, 5.1
  decree of repossession, 5.21
  eviction, 5.22
  exception, 5.1
  expenses
    amount recoverable, 5.18
    introduction, 5.17
    'reasonably incurred', 5.19
    suspension orders, and, 5.20
  failure of creditor to comply with duty of good faith, 5.1
  human rights, and
    application of ECHR, 5.14
    conclusion, 5.16
    introduction, 5.13
    remedies for breach, 5.15
  introduction, 4.1
  Mortgage Rights (Scotland) Act 2001, under
    and see **Suspension of creditor's rights**
    applicants, 4.2.7
    application procedure, 4.2.8–4.2.19
    background, 4.2.2–4.2.3
    cost, 4.2.35
    creditor's steps, 4.2.6
    Crown, and, 4.2.33
    effects, 4.2.34–4.2.37
    guidance, 4.3–4.3.3
    introduction, 4.2.1
    outline of provisions, 4.2.4
    procedural considerations, 4.2.5
    registration, 4.2.20
    service of notices, 4.2.22–4.2.32
  non-enforcement of terms of security, 5.1
  ope exceptionis, 5.1
  setting aside security
    applicability of doctrine, 5.11
    cautioner's legal advice, 5.7
    creditor's duty of good faith, 5.4
    grounds, 5.2
    introduction, 5.1
    origin of doctrine, 5.3
    policy issues, 5.10
    presumption of undue influence, 5.8–5.9
    proof of undue influence, 5.5
    reliance on undue influence, 5.6
    summary, 5.12

Diligence, law of
  attachment, 9.3.3
  introduction, 9.3.1
  land attachment, 9.3.2
  practical effects, 9.3.4
Disposition
  sale, and, 8.7
Distribution of proceeds of sale
  generally, 8.16
  shortfall, and, 8.18
  statutory basis, 12.18
  surplus, and, 8.17

Ejection
  calling-up notice, and defence, 2.2.12
  generally, 2.2.10
  procedure, 2.2.11
  pre-existing securities, and, 3.5
Entering into possession
  creditor's powers
    alterations, 7.5.3
    foreclosure, 7.5.4
    improvements, 7.5.3
    introduction, 7.5
    leases, 7.5.2
    rent collection, 7.5.1
    repairs, 7.5.3
  generally, 7.4
  multiple creditors, 7.4.1
Eviction
  generally, 5.22
***Ex facie* absolute disposition**
  and see **Pre-existing securities**
  background, 1.2
  generally, 1.6
  initial stages of enforcement, 3.1–3.5
Expenses
  calling-up notice, and, 2.2.8
  court action, and
    amount recoverable, 5.18
    introduction, 5.17
    'reasonably incurred', 5.19
    suspension orders, and, 5.20
  notice of default, and, 2.3.9
  s.24 actions, and, 2.4.3

Failure of creditor to comply with duty of good faith
  generally, 5.1
Failure to comply
  calling-up notice, and, 2.2.4
  notice of default, and, 2.3.5
Fair treatment of debtors
  regulation by FSA, and, 9.4.4
Foreclosure
  generally, 7.5.4
  statutory basis, 12.19
Forms
  calling-up notice, and, 13.14
  notice of default, and, 13.15

Framework of repossession
  form of security, 1.2
  introduction, 1.1
  other remedies, 1.3
  standard conditions, 1.5
  standard security, 1.4
FSA, regulation by
  background, 9.4.1
  current position, 9.4.5
  fair treatment of debtors, 9.4.4
  information provision, 9.4.3
  policy considerations, 9.4.2
Future developments in the law
  diligence, of
    attachment, 9.3.3
    introduction, 9.3.1
    land attachment, 9.3.2
    practical effects, 9.3.4
  mortgage to rent scheme
    background, 9.2.1
    conclusion, 9.2.6
    eligibility, 9.2.3
    funding, 9.2.4
    operation, 9.2.2
    problems, 9.2.5
  other matters, 9.5
  regulation by FSA
    background, 9.4.1
    current position, 9.4.5
    fair treatment of debtors, 9.4.4
    information provision, 9.4.3
    policy considerations, 9.4.2
  service of notices, 9.1

Heritable Securities (Scotland) Act 1894
  general provision, 3.5
Human rights
  application of ECHR, 5.14
  conclusion, 5.16
  introduction, 5.13
  remedies for breach, 5.15

Improvements
  recovery of subjects, and, 7.5.3
Initial stages of enforcement
  pre-existing securities
    bond and disposition in security, 3.3
    ejection, and, 3.5
    ex facie absolute disposition, 3.4
    introduction, 3.1
    preliminary steps, 3.2
  standard securities
    calling-up notice, 2.2–2.2.14
    considerations for choice of action, 2.7–2.7.2
    consumer credit cases, 2.5
    introduction, 2.1
    notice of default, 2.3–2.3.13
    other steps, 2.6
    s.24 actions, 2.4–2.4.6
    warrant to exercise remedies, 2.4–2.4.6

Insolvent debtors
  generally, 6.3
Insolvent proprietor
  s.24 actions, and, 2.7.2

Leases
  recovery of subjects, and, 7.5.2
Liabilities of creditors on recovery of subjects
  avoidance of, 7.8
  contamination, 7.7.4
  introduction, 7.7
  miscellaneous, 7.7.5
  occupation, and, 7.7.3
  ownership, and, 7.7.2
  timing of, 7.7.1

Media interest
  generally, 6.6.2
Missives
  sale, and
    content, 8.4
    format, 8.3
Mortgage Rights (Scotland) Act 2001
  and see **Suspension of creditor's rights**
  application to Crown, 10.5
  citation, 10.7
  commencement
    generally, 10.7
    Order, 11.1
  general provisions, 10.1–10.4
  interpretation, 10.6
  Orders
    commencement, 11.1
    prescribed notice, 11.2
  schedule, 10.8–10.17
  transitional provision, 11.1
Mortgage to rent scheme
  background, 9.2.1
  conclusion, 9.2.6
  eligibility, 9.2.3
  funding, 9.2.4
  operation, 9.2.2
  problems, 9.2.5
  suspension order, and, 4.2.19
Movables
  recovery of subjects, and, 7.3

Nicholls **guidelines**
  and see **Action of reduction**
  creditors' protection, 14.2
  solicitor advising surety, 14.1
Non-enforcement of terms of security
  generally, 5.1
Notice of default
  accuracy, 2.3.6
  advantages, 2.3.12
  challenge, 2.3.7
  consumer credit cases, and, 2.5

Notice of default—*cont.*
content
  accuracy, 2.3.6
  generally, 2.3.2
  prescribed form, 13.15
court action, and
  introduction, 2.3.11, 2.4
disadvantages, 2.3.12
expenses, and, 2.3.9
failure to comply, 2.3.5
form, 13.15
introduction, 2.3
nature of default, 2.3.1
objection
  generally, 2.3.7
  statutory basis, 12.13
recovery of subjects, and, 7.1
restriction of period, 2.3.4
service
  acknowledgment of receipt, 13.17
  certificate of service, 13.16
  generally, 2.3.3
statutory basis, 12.11–12.14
summary, 2.3.13
suspension, 2.3.8
suspension of creditor's rights, and
  generally, 4.2.6
  introduction, 2.3.10
voluntary surrender, and, 2.7.1
Notices
suspension order, and
  generally, 4.2.21
  service of notices, 4.2.22–4.2.32

Objection to notices
calling-up notice, and, 2.2.6
consumer credit cases, and, 2.5
notice of default, and
  generally, 2.3.7
  statutory basis, 12.13
Occupation
recovery of subjects, and, 7.7.3
Ope exceptionis
generally, 5.1
Ordinary Cause Rules
amendment, 11.3
style minute, 11.4
Ownership
recovery of subjects, and, 7.7.2

Pre-existing securities
background, 1.2
generally, 1.6
initial stages of enforcement
  bond and disposition in security, 3.3
  ejection, and, 3.5
  ex facie absolute disposition, 3.4
  introduction, 3.1
  preliminary steps, 3.2
recovery of subjects, and, 7.1

Pre-existing securities—*cont.*
suspension of creditor's rights, and
  generally, 4.2.6
  introduction, 3.5
Pre-1970 Act securities
and see **Pre-existing securities**
background, 1.2
Prescribed notice
generally, 10.3
Order, 11.2
Proof of default (s.24 actions)
certificate, 13.18–13.20
generally, 2.4.1
Proper court
suspension order, and, 4.2.10
Purchaser protection
sale, and, 8.19

Recovering the subjects
alterations, 7.5.3
calling-up notice, and, 7.1
catholic and secondary securities, and, 7.6.2.1
contaminated land, and, 7.7.4
contractual provisions, and, 7.6.2.3
creditor's powers
  alterations, 7.5.3
  foreclosure, 7.5.4
  improvements, 7.5.3
  introduction, 7.5
  leases, 7.5.2
  rent collection, 7.5.1
  repairs, 7.5.3
entering into possession, and
  creditor's powers, 7.5–7.5.4
  generally, 7.4
  multiple creditors, 7.4.1
exercise of rights
  generally, 7.1
  statutory basis, 12.11
foreclosure
  generally, 7.5.4
  statutory basis, 12.19
improvements, 7.5.3
introduction, 7.1
leases, 7.5.2
liabilities of creditor's
  avoidance of, 7.8
  contamination, 7.7.4
  introduction, 7.7
  miscellaneous, 7.7.5
  occupation, and, 7.7.3
  ownership, and, 7.7.2
  timing of, 7.7.1
movables, and, 7.3
notice of default, and, 7.1
occupation, and, 7.7.3
ownership, and, 7.7.2
practical issues, 7.2
pre-existing securities, and, 7.1
rent collection, 7.5.1

Index

Recovering the subjects—*cont.*
  repairs, 7.5.3
  restrictions on exercise of rights
    catholic and secondary securities, 7.6.2.1
    contractual provisions, 7.6.2.3
    generally, 7.6.1
    introduction, 7.6
    security over a security, 7.6.2.2
  s.24 actions, and, 7.1
  sale
    advertising, 8.8–8.9
    affidavits, 8.6
    best price, 8.10
    common law duty, 8.13
    consent of other creditors, 8.14
    content of missives, 8.4
    disposition, 8.7
    distribution of proceeds, 8.16–8.18
    effect, 8.15
    employment of agents, 8.12
    format of missives, 8.3
    general issues, 8.2
    power, 8.1
    purchaser protection, 8.19
    remedies of debtor, 8.11
    searches, 8.5
    statutory basis, 12.16–12.18
  statutory basis
    foreclosure, 12.19
    generally, 12.11
    sale of security, 12.16–12.18

Redemption before possession
  generally, 6.4

Reduction of security
  applicability of doctrine, 5.11
  cautioner's legal advice, 5.7
  creditor's duty of good faith, 5.4
  grounds, 5.2
  introduction, 5.1
  origin of doctrine, 5.3
  policy issues, 5.10
  presumption of undue influence, 5.8–5.9
  proof of undue influence, 5.5
  reliance on undue influence, 5.6
  summary, 5.12

Registration of suspension order
  court rules, 11.3
  generally, 4.2.20
  prescribed notice, 11.2
  statutory basis, 10.3
  style minute, 11.4

Regulation by FSA
  background, 9.4.1
  current position, 9.4.5
  fair treatment of debtors, 9.4.4
  information provision, 9.4.3
  policy considerations, 9.4.2

Rent, collection of
  recovery of subjects, and, 7.5.1

Repairs
  recovery of subjects, and, 7.5.3

Restriction of period of notice
  calling-up notice, and, 2.2.3
  notice of default, and, 2.3.4

s.24 actions
  advantages, 2.4.6
  consumer credit cases, and, 2.5
  defence, 2.4.5
  disadvantages, 2.4.6
  expenses, and, 2.4.3
  insolvent proprietor, and, 2.7.2
  introduction, 2.4
  notice of default, and, 2.4
  procedure, 2.4.2
  proof of default
    certificate, 13.18–13.20
    generally, 2.4.1
  recovery of subjects, and, 7.1
  statutory basis, 12.15–12.19
  suspension of creditor's rights, and
    generally, 4.2.6
    introduction, 2.4.4

Sale of repossessed property
  advertising
    generally, 8.9
    introduction, 8.8
    statutory basis, 12.16
  affidavits, 8.6
  best price
    generally, 8.10
    statutory basis, 12.16
  common law duty, 8.13
  consent of other creditors, 8.14
  disposition, 8.7
  distribution of proceeds
    generally, 8.16
    shortfall, and, 8.18
    statutory basis, 12.18
    surplus, and, 8.17
  effect, 8.15
  employment of agents, 8.12
  general issues, 8.2
  missives
    content, 8.4
    format, 8.3
  power, 8.1
  purchaser protection, 8.19
  remedies of debtor, 8.11
  searches, 8.5
  statutory basis
    dispositions by creditor, 12.17
    distribution of proceeds, 12.18
    exercise of power, 12.16

Searches
  sale, and, 8.5

Security over a security
  recovery of subjects, and, 7.6.2.2

Service
  calling-up notice, and
    acknowledgment of receipt, 13.17
    certificate of service, 13.16
    generally, 2.2.2

Index

Service—*cont.*
  notice of default, and
    acknowledgment of receipt, 13.17
    certificate of service, 13.16
    generally, 2.3.3
Service of notices (suspension orders)
  future developments, 9.1
  introduction, 4.2.21
  method
    conclusion, 4.2.28
    court documents, 4.2.25
    forms adjusted by 2001 Act, 4.2.25
    forms introduced by 2001 Act, 4.2.26
Service of notices (suspension orders)—*cont.*
  method—*cont.*
    importance of observance of rules, 4.2.29
    introduction, 4.2.24
    practical issues, 4.2.27
  place, 4.2.31
  practical issues, 4.2.27
  proof, 4.2.32
  recipients, 4.2.30
  relevant notices, 4.2.22
  servers, 4.2.30
  time of, 4.2.23
Setting aside security
  applicability of doctrine, 5.11
  cautioner's legal advice, 5.7
  creditor's duty of good faith, 5.4
  grounds, 5.2
  introduction, 5.1
  origin of doctrine, 5.3
  policy issues, 5.10
  presumption of undue influence, 5.8–5.9
  proof of undue influence, 5.5
  reliance on undue influence, 5.6
  summary, 5.12
Spouse of debtors
  generally, 6.5.1–6.5.2
  introduction, 6.5
Standard conditions
  introduction, 1.5
  statutory basis
    generally, 12.3
    schedule, 13.1–13.13
Standard security
  background, 1.2
  calling-up
    generally, 2.2–2.2.14
    statutory basis, 12.10
  conditions
    introduction, 1.1
    statutory basis, 13.1–13.13
  considerations for choice of action
    insolvent proprietor, 2.7.2
    introduction, 2.7
    voluntary surrender, 2.7.1

Standard security—*cont.*
  default
    generally, 2.3–2.3.13
    statutory basis, 12.11–12.14, 13.14–13.20
  generally, 1.4
  initial stages of enforcement
    calling-up notice, 2.2–2.2.14
    considerations for choice of action, 2.7–2.7.2
    consumer credit cases, 2.5
    introduction, 2.1
    notice of default, 2.3–2.3.13
    other steps, 2.6
    s.24 actions, 2.4–2.4.6
    warrant to exercise remedies, 2.4–2.4.6
  notice of default
    generally, 2.3–2.3.13
    statutory basis, 12.11–12.14, 13.14–13.20
  s.24 actions
    generally, 2.4–2.4.6
    statutory basis, 12.15–12.19
  statutory basis
    assignation, 12.6
    calling-up, 12.10
    conditions, 13.1–13.13
    default, 12.11–12.14, 13.14–13.20
    discharge, 12.9
    effect of recording, 12.3
    foreclosure, 12.19
    generally, 12.1
    grant by person uninfelt, 12.4
    import of clauses, 12.2
    incorporation of conditions, 12.3
    ranking, 12.5
    redemption, 12.9
    restriction, 12.7
    s.24 actions, 12.15
    sale of security, 12.16–12.18
    suspension of enforcement, 10.1–10.3
    variation, 12.8
  suspension of enforcement
    statutory basis, 10.1–10.3
  warrant to exercise remedies
    generally, 2.4–2.4.6
    statutory basis, 12.15–12.19
Suspension of creditor's rights
  applicants, 4.2.7
  applications
    applicants, 4.2.7
    disposal, 4.2.11–4.2.16
    generally, 4.2.8
    proper court, 4.2.10
    statutory basis, 10.1–10.2
    time limits, 4.2.9
  background
    generally, 4.2.2
    political climate, 4.2.3

Suspension of creditor's rights—*cont.*
  calling-up notice, and
    generally, 4.2.6
    introduction, 2.2.9
  clearing default, and, 4.2.18
  considerations
    applicant's ability to fulfil obligations, 4.2.14
    creditor's assistance to debtor, 4.2.15
    guidance, 4.2.19
    introduction, 4.2.11–4.2.12
    nature of and reasons for default, 4.2.13
    reasonable alternative accommodation, 4.2.16
    statutory basis, 10.2
  cost, 4.2.35
  creditor's steps, 4.2.6
  Crown, and, 4.2.33
  debtors on benefits, and, 6.6.1
  disposal of applications
    considerations, 4.2.13–4.2.16
    introduction, 4.2.11–4.2.12
    statutory basis, 10.2
  effects
    cost, 4.2.35
    delay, 4.2.36
    introduction, 4.2.34
    lending industry reaction, 4.2.37
    time, 4.2.36
  expenses, and, 5.20
  guidance (English)
    'for such period', 4.3.2
    introduction, 4.3
    subject to such conditions, 4.3.3
    'within a reasonable period', 4.3.1
  insolvent debtors, and, 6.3
  introduction, 4.2.1
  method of service of notices
    conclusion, 4.2.28
    court documents, 4.2.25
    forms adjusted by 2001 Act, 4.2.25
    forms introduced by 2001 Act, 4.2.26
    importance of observance of rules, 4.2.29
    introduction, 4.2.24
    practical issues, 4.2.27
  mortgage to rent scheme, and, 4.2.19
  notice of default, and
    generally, 4.2.6
    introduction, 2.3.10
  notices
    generally, 4.2.21
    service of notices, 4.2.22–4.2.32
  pre-existing securities, and
    generally, 4.2.6
    introduction, 3.5
  procedure
    application, 4.2.8–4.2.19
    considerations, 4.2.5
    outline, 4.2.4
    registration, 4.2.20
    service of notices, 4.2.22–4.2.32

Suspension of creditor's rights—*cont.*
  procedure—*cont.*
    statutory basis, 10.1–10.3
  proper court, 4.2.10
  registration of order
    court rules, 11.3
    generally, 4.2.20
    prescribed notice, 11.2
    statutory basis, 10.3
    style minute, 11.4
  revocation of order
    registration, and, 4.2.20
  s.24 notices, and
    generally, 4.2.6
    introduction, 2.4.4
  service of notices
    introduction, 4.2.21
    method, 4.2.24–4.2.29
    place, 4.2.31
    practical issues, 4.2.27
    proof, 4.2.32
    recipients, 4.2.30
    relevant notices, 4.2.22
    servers, 4.2.30
    time of, 4.2.23
  spouses, and, 6.5
  tenants of debtors, and, 6.2
  terms of order, 4.2.17
  time limits, 4.2.9
Suspension of notices
  calling-up notice, and, 2.2.7
  notice of default, and, 2.3.8
Tenants of debtors
  generally, 6.2

Terms of order
  suspension order, and, 4.2.17
Time limits
  suspension order, and, 4.2.9

Undue influence
  and see **Reduction of security**
  applicability of doctrine, 5.11
  cautioner's legal advice, 5.7
  creditor's duty of good faith, 5.4
  grounds, 5.2
  introduction, 5.1
  origin of doctrine, 5.3
  policy issues, 5.10
  presumption, 5.8–5.9
  proof, 5.5
  reliance, 5.6
  summary, 5.12

Voluntary surrender
  calling-up notices, and, 2.7.1

Warrant to exercise remedies
  and see **s.24 actions**
  generally, 2.4–2.4.6
  statutory basis, 12.15–12.19